THE LIFE & LETTERS OF PETER ILICH TCHAIKOVSKY

The Life & Letters of PETER ILICH TCHAIKOVSKY

By Modeste Tchaikovsky

Edited from the Russian,
with an introduction, by
ROSA NEWMARCH

In two volumes
VOLUME TWO

VIENNA HOUSE
New York

This Vienna House edition,
first published in 1973,
is an unabridged republication of
the work originally published by
John Lane The Bodley Head, London, in 1906.

International Standard Book Number: 0-8443-0032-2
(Volume I)
International Standard Book Number: 0-8443-0033-0
(Volume II)
International Standard Book Number: 0-8443-0034-9
(Set of Volumes I & II)
Library of Congress Catalog Card Number: 73-86365

Printed in the United States of America

XI

1880–1881

To N. F. von Meck.

"KAMENKA, *September 4th* (16*th*), 1880.

"I am doing nothing whatever, only wandering through the forests and fields all day long. I want to take a change from my own work, with its eternal proof-correcting, and to play as much as possible of other people's music; so I have begun to study Mozart's *Zauberflöte*. Never was so senselessly stupid a subject set to such captivating music. How thankful I am that the circumstances of my musical career have not changed by a hair's breadth the charm Mozart exercises for me! You would not believe, dear friend, what wonderful feelings come over me when I give myself up to his music. It is something quite different from the stressful delight awakened in me by Beethoven, Schumann, or Chopin. . . . My contemporaries were imbued with the spirit of modern music from their childhood, and came to know Mozart in later years, after they had made acquaintance with Chopin, who reflects so clearly the Byronic despair and disillusionment. Fortunately, fate decreed that I should grow up in an unmusical family, so that in childhood I was not nourished on the poisonous food of the post-Beethoven music. The same kind fate brought me early in life in contact with Mozart, and thus opened up to me unsuspected horizons. These early impressions can never be effaced. Do you know that when I play Mozart, I feel brighter and younger, almost a youth again? But enough. I know that we do not agree in our appreciation of Mozart, and that my dithyramb does not interest you in the least."

To N. F. von Meck.

"KAMENKA, *September 9th (21st)*, 1880.

"How fleeting were my hopes of a prolonged rest Scarcely had I begun to enjoy a few days' leisure than an indefinable mood of boredom, even a sense of not being in health, came over me. To-day I began to occupy my mind with projects for a new symphony, and immediately I felt well and cheerful. It appears as though I could not spend a couple of days in idleness, unless I am travelling. I dread lest I should become a composer of Anton Rubinstein's type, who considers it his bounden duty to present a new work to the public every day in the week. In this way he has dissipated his great creative talent, and has only small change to offer instead of the sterling gold which he could have given us had he written in moderation. Lately I have been seeking some kind of occupation that would take me completely away from music for a time, and would seriously interest me. Alas, I have not discovered it! There is no guide to the history of music in Russian, and it would be a good thing if I could occupy myself with a book of this kind; I often think of it. But then I should have to give up composing for at least two years, and that would be too much. To start upon a translation—that is not very interesting work. Write a monograph upon some artist? So much has already been written about the great musicians of Western Europe. For Glinka, Dargomijsky, and Serov I cannot feel any enthusiasm, for, highly as I value their works, I cannot admire them as men. I have told you what I think of Glinka. Dargomijsky was even less cultured. As to Serov, he was a clever man of encyclopedic learning, but I knew him personally, and could not admire his moral character. As far as I understood him, he was not good-hearted, and that is sufficient reason why I do not care to devote my leisure to him. It would have been a delight to write the biography of Mozart, but it is impossible to do so after Otto Jahn, who devoted his life to the task.

"So there is no other occupation open to me but composition. I am planning a symphony or a string quartet. I do not know which I shall decide upon."

To N. F. von Meck.

" KAMENKA, *September* 12*th* (24*th*), 1880.

" I venture to approach you, dear friend, with the following request. An employé in a counting-house, here in
Kamenka, has a son who is remarkably gifted for painting.
It seemed to me cruel not to give him the means of studying, so I sent him to Moscow and asked Anatol to take
him to the School of Painting and Sculpture. All this was
arranged, and then it turned out that the boy's mainten-
ance would cost far more than I expected. And so I
thought I would ask you whether in your house there was
any corner in which this lad might live? Not, of course,
without some kind of supervision. He would only need a
tiny room with a bed, a cupboard, and a table where he
could sleep and work. Perhaps your servants would look
after him, and give him a little advice? The boy is of
irreproachable character : industrious, good, obedient, clean
in his person—in short, exemplary. I would undertake
his meals.[1] . . .
" I have also unearthed a musical talent here, in the
daughter of the local priest, and have been successful in
placing her at the Conservatoire."

To N. F. von Meck.

" KAMENKA, *September* 19*th* (*October* 1*st*), 1880.

"Yesterday I received an official intimation from the
Imperial Opera to the effect that my opera has been
accepted and will be produced in January. The libretto
has been passed by the censor with one or two exceptions :
the *Archbishop* must be called the *Wanderer* (?); ' every
allusion to the Cross must be omitted, and no cross may
be seen upon the stage.' There is nothing for it but to
submit."

---

[1] Unfortunately the boy did not turn out an artist of the first rank. But
his education was not wasted, for he is now drawing-master in a public school
in South Russia.

To N. F. von Meck.

"Kamenka, *September* 28*th* (*October* 10*th*), 1880.

"Nicholas Rubinstein has requested me to write an in portant work for chorus and orchestra, to be produced the Moscow Exhibition. Nothing is more unpleasant me than the manufacturing of music for such occasion . . . But I have not courage to refuse. . . ."

To N. F. von Meck.

"Kamenka, *October* 10*th* (22*nd*), 1880.

"You can imagine, dear friend, that recently my Mus has been very benevolent, when I tell you that I hav written two long works very rapidly: a Festival Overtur for the Exhibition and a Serenade in four movements fc string orchestra. The overture[1] will be very noisy. wrote it without much warmth of enthusiasm; therefore has no great artistic value. The Serenade, on the contrar I wrote from an inward impulse; I felt it, and venture t hope that this work is not without artistic qualities."

To N. F. von Meck.

"Kamenka, *October* 14*th* (26*th*), 1880.

". . . How glad I am that my opera pleases you! am delighted you find no 'Russianisms' in it, for I dreade this and had striven in this work to be as objective a possible."

To N. F. von Meck.

"Kamenka, *October* 14*th* (26*th*), 1880.

"Of course I am no judge of my own works, but I ca truthfully say that—with very few exceptions—they hav all been *felt* and *lived* by me, and have come straight fron my heart. It is the greatest happiness to know that ther is another kindred soul in the world who has such a tru

---

[1] The overture entitled *The Year 1812*, op. 49, for the consecration o the Cathedral of the Saviour, Moscow. It was one of the three commission suggested by N. Rubinstein, referred to in the previous letter.

and delicate appreciation of my music. The thought that she will discern all that I have felt, while writing this or that work, invariably warms and inspires me. There are few such souls; among those who surround me I can only point to my brothers. Modeste is very near to me in mind and sentiment. Among professional musicians I have met with the least congenial sympathy. . . .

"You ask why I have never written a trio. Forgive me, dear friend, I would do anything to give you pleasure —but this is beyond me! My acoustic apparatus is so ordered that I simply cannot endure the combination of pianoforte with violin or violoncello. To my mind the *timbre* of these instruments will not blend, and I assure you it is a torture to me to have to listen to a trio or sonata of any kind for piano and strings. I cannot explain this physiological peculiarity; I simply state it as a fact. Piano and orchestra—that is quite another matter. Here again there is no blending of tone; the piano by its elastic tone differs from all other instruments in *timbre;* but we are now dealing with two equal opponents: the orchestra, with its power and inexhaustible variety of colour, opposed by the small, unimposing, but high-mettled pianoforte, which often comes off victorious in the hands of a gifted executant. Much poetry is contained in this conflict, and endless seductive combinations for the composer. On the other hand, how unnatural is the union of three such individualities as the pianoforte, the violin and the violoncello! Each loses something of its value. The warm and singing tone of the violin and the 'cello sounds limited beside that *king* of instruments, the pianoforte; while the latter strives in vain to prove that it can sing like its rivals. I consider the piano should only be employed under these conditions: (1) As a solo instrument; (2) opposed to the orchestra; (3) for accompaniment, as the background to a picture. But a trio implies equality and relationship, and do these exist between stringed solo instruments and the piano? They do *not;* and this is the reason why there is always something artificial about a pianoforte trio, each of the three instruments being continually called upon to express what the composer imposes upon it, rather than what lies within its characteristic utterance; while the musician meets with perpetual difficulties in the distribution of the voices and grouping of the parts. I do full justice to the inspired art with which Beethoven, Schumann, and Mendelssohn have conquered these difficulties. I know there exist many trios containing music of admirable quality; but personally I do not care for the trio as a form, therefore I shall never produce anything sincerely inspired through the medium of this combination of sounds. I know, dear friend, that we disagree on this point, and that you, on the contrary, are fond of a trio; but in spite of all the similarity between our artistic temperaments, we remain two separate individualities; therefore it is not surprising that we should not agree in every particular."

During the autumn of 1880 Tchaikovsky suffered greatly from neuralgic headaches. He remained at Kamenka until early in November, when he returned to Moscow for a short time, in order to correct proofs and settle other business matters. Towards the end of the month he wrote to Nadejda von Meck from St. Petersburg :—

"*November 27th (December 9th)*, 1880.

"The directors of the Moscow Musical Society are greatly interested in my Liturgy (St. John Chrysostom). One of their number, named Alexeiev, gave a good fee to have it studied by one of the best choirs. This resulted in a performance of the work in the concert-room of the Moscow Conservatoire. The choir sang wonderfully well, and it was altogether one of the happiest moments in my musical career. It was decided to give the Liturgy at an extra concert of the Musical Society. On the same evening my Serenade for strings was played, in order to give me an agreeable surprise. For the moment I regard it as my best work. . . .

"Have I told you already that *Eugene Oniegin* is to be splendidly mounted at the Opera in Moscow? I am very pleased, because it will decide the important question whether the work will become part of the repertory or not, that is to say, whether it will keep its place on the stage. As I never intended it for this purpose, I did nothing on my own initiative to get it produced."

While in St. Petersburg, Tchaikovsky undertook to make some changes in his new opera, *The Maid of Orleans*. This was in order that the part of Joan of Arc herself might be taken by Madame Kamensky, a mezzo-soprano of unusual range and quality.

To N. F. von Meck.

"Moscow, *December 14th (26th)*, 1880.

"One newspaper blames me for having dedicated my opera, *The Maid of Orleans*, to Napravnik, and considers it an unworthy action on my part to win his good graces in this way. Napravnik—one of the few thoroughly honest musicians in Petersburg—will be very much upset. They also find fault with me because my opera is not on sale.

"All this is very galling and vexatious, but I do not let it trouble me much.

"I have sworn to myself to avoid Moscow and Petersburg in future."

To N. F. von Meck.

"Moscow, *December 17th (29th)*, 1880.

"I have been very much upset the last few days. Last year I received a letter from a young man, unknown to me, of the name of Tkachenko, containing the curious proposal that I should take him as my servant and give him music lessons in return. The letter was so clever and original, and showed such a real love of music, that it affected me very sympathetically. A correspondence between us followed, from which I learnt that he was already twenty-three, and had no musical knowledge. I wrote frankly to him that at his age it was too late to begin to study music. After this, I heard no more of him for nine months. The day before yesterday I received another letter from him, returning all my previous correspondence, in order that it might not fall into strange hands after his death. He took leave of me and said he had resolved to commit suicide. The letter was evidently written in a moment of great despair, and touched me profoundly. I saw from the postmark that it was written from Voronezh, and decided to telegraph to someone there, asking them to seek Tkachenko with the help of the police and tell him —if it were not already too late—he might expect a letter from me. Fortunately, Anatol had a friend at Voronezh, to whom we telegraphed at once. Last night I heard from him that Tkachenko had been discovered *in time*. He was in a terrible condition.

"I immediately sent him some money and invited him to come to Moscow. How it will end I do not know, but I am glad to have saved him from self-destruction."

At this time Tchaikovsky's valet, Alexis, was compelled to fulfil his military service, and master and servant were equally affected at the moment of separation.

On December 6th (18th) the *Italian Capriccio* was performed for the first time under the conductorship of Nicholas Rubinstein. Its success was incontestable, although criticism varied greatly as to its merits, and the least favourable described it as being marred by "coarse and cheap" effects. In St. Petersburg, where it was given a few weeks later by Napravnik, it met with scant appreciation ; Cui pronounced it to be "no work of art, but a valuable gift to the programmes of open-air concerts."

The performance of the Liturgy took place in Moscow on December 18th (30th). Thanks to the stir which had been made by the confiscation of Tchaikovsky's first sacred work, the concert was unusually crowded. At the close the composer was frequently recalled. Nevertheless, there was considerable difference of opinion as to the success of the work.

Tchaikovsky was not much affected by the views of the professional critics; but he was deeply hurt by a letter emanating from the venerable Ambrose, vicar of Moscow, which appeared in the *Rouss*. This letter complained that the Liturgy was the most sacred possession of the people, and should only be heard in church; that to use the service as a libretto was a profanation of the holy words. It concluded by congratulating the orthodox that the text had at least been treated by a worthy musician, but what would happen if some day a " Rosenthal" or a " Rosenbluhm" should lay hands upon it? Inevitably then " our most sacred words would be mocked at and hissed."

Fatigued by the excitement of these weeks, Tchaikovsky returned to Kamenka to spend Christmas in the restful quiet of the country.

The first performance of *Eugene Oniegin* at the Opera House in Moscow took place on January 11th (23rd), 1881. The scenery was not new and left much to be desired. The singers, with the exception of Madame Kroutikov, who took the part of Madame Larina, and Bartsal, who appeared as the Frenchman Triquet, were lacking in experience. The costumes, however, were perfectly true to history. The performance evoked much applause, but more for the composer than for the opera itself. The great public allowed the best situations in the work to pass unnoticed, but the opera found an echo in the hearts of the minority, so that gradually the work gained the appreciation of the crowd and won a lasting success.

To N. F. von Meck.

" Moscow, *January 12th (24th)*, 1881.

" Yesterday was the first night of *Eugene Oniegin.* I was oppressed by varied emotions, both at the rehearsals and on the night itself. At first the public was very reserved; by degrees, however, the applause grew and at the last all went well. The performance and mounting of the opera were satisfactory. . . .

" Tkachenko (the young man who wanted to commit suicide) has arrived. I have seen him. On the whole he made a sympathetic impression upon me. His sufferings are the outcome of the internal conflict which exists between his aspirations and stern reality. He is intelligent and cultivated, yet in order to earn his bread he has had to be a railway guard. He is very anxious to become a musician. He is nervous, and morbidly modest, and seems to be broken in spirit. Poverty and solitude have made him misanthropical. His views are rather strange, but he is by no means stupid. I am sorry for him and have agreed to look after him. I have decided that he shall go to the Conservatoire, and then it will be seen whether he can take up music, or some other career. It will not be difficult to make a useful and contented man of him."

To N. F. von Meck.

"Moscow, *January* 19*th* (31*st*), 1881.

"Dear, kind friend, it has come to this: I take up my pen to write to you unwillingly, because I feel the immediate need to pour out all the suffering and bitterness which is heaped up in me. You will wonder how a man who is successful in his work can still complain and rail at fate? But my successes are not so important as they seem; besides they do not compensate me for the intolerable sufferings I undergo when I mix in the society of my fellow-creatures; when I have to be constantly posing before them; when I cannot live as I wish, and as I am accustomed to do, but am tossed to and fro like a ball in the round of city life. . . .

"*Eugene Oniegin* does not progress. The prima donna is seriously ill, so that the opera cannot be performed again for some time. . . . The criticisms upon it are peculiar. Some critics find the 'couplets' for Triquet the best thing in the work and think Tatiana's part dry and colourless. Others think I have no inspiration, but great cleverness. The Petersburg papers write in chorus to rend my *Italian Capriccio*, declaring it to be vulgar; and Cui prophesies that *The Maid of Orleans* will turn out a commonplace affair."

To N. F. von Meck.

"PETERSBURG, *January* 27*th* (*February* 8*th*), 1881.

"I will tell you something about Tkachenko. He is an extraordinary being! I had looked after him in every respect, and he began his studies with great zeal. The day before I left Moscow he came to 'talk to me on serious business,' and the longer he talked, the more convinced I became that he is mentally and morally deranged. He has taken it into his head that *I am not keeping him for his own sake*, but in order *to acquire the reputation of a benefactor*. He added that he was not disposed to be the *victim* of my desire for popularity, and absolutely refused to recognise me as his benefactor, so I was not to reckon upon his gratitude.

"I replied coldly, and advised him to devote himself to his work, without troubling himself as to my motives for assisting him. I assured him I was quite indifferent as to his gratitude, that I was just leaving the town, and begged him not to waste his thoughts on me, but to fix them exclusively upon his work.

"I have entrusted him to the supervision of Albrecht, the Inspector of the Conservatoire.

"Have you heard of Nicholas Rubinstein's illness? His condition is serious, but in spite of it he goes about and does his work. The doctors insist upon his going away and taking rest; but he declares he could not live without the work he is used to. . . ."

On January 21st (February 2nd) Tchaikovsky's Second Symphony was given in its revised form at the Musical Society in St. Petersburg, and, according to the newspapers, met with a great success. Not a single critic, however, observed the changes in the work, nor that the first movement was entirely new.

To N. F. von Meck.

" PETERSBURG, *February* 1*st* (13*th*), 1881.

". . . The mounting of *The Maid of Orleans* will be very beggarly. The Direction, which has spent 10,000 (roubles) upon a new ballet, refuses to sacrifice a kopeck for the opera."

To the same.

" PETERSBURG, *February* 7*th* (19*th*), 1881.

" The opera has been postponed until February 13th. I shall set off the very next day. The plan of my journey is : Vienna, Venice, Rome. The rehearsals are in progress. Most of the artists show great sympathy for my music, of which I am very proud. But the officials are doing all in their power to spoil the success of the opera. A certain Loukashevich is trying by every kind of intrigue to prevent Madame Kamensky from taking the part of Joan of Arc. When at yesterday's rehearsal—for scenic and vocal reasons—I transferred a melody from Joan's part to that of Agnes Sorel, he declared *I had no right to do such a thing without permission.* Sometimes I feel inclined to withdraw the score and leave the theatre."

The production of *The Maid of Orleans* at the Maryinsky Theatre left a very unpleasant memory in Tchaikovsky's mind. The intrigues between the prima donnas, the hostile attitude of the Direction, his dissatisfaction with some of the singers—all embittered the composer in the highest degree. His artistic vanity was exceedingly sensitive, even when his best friends told him " the plain truth." He submitted to the criticisms of Napravnik, and followed his advice regarding many details, because he was convinced of this musician's goodwill and great experience. If he got through this trying time fairly well, it was thanks to the fact that he himself, as well as the artists who were taking part in the work, did not doubt that the opera would eventually have a great success.

On the day following the performance, Tchaikovsky wrote :—

"The success of the opera was certain, even after the first act . . . the second scene of the third act was least applauded, but the fourth act was very well received. Altogether I was recalled twenty-four times. Kamenskaya was admirable; she even acted well, which she seldom does. Prianichnikov was the best among the other singers."

Tchaikovsky started for Italy under this favourable impression, and first became aware through a telegram from Petersburg in the *Neue Freie Presse* that, in spite of an ovation from the public, *The Maid of Orleans* was "poor in inspiration, wearisome, and monotonous." This was his first intimation of the attacks upon the opera which were made by the Press, and which caused the opera to be hastily withdrawn from the repertory of the Maryinsky Theatre.

Cui, as usual, led the chorus of unfavourable opinion, but all the other critics were more or less in agreement with his views.

XII

Impatient for the sunshine, Tchaikovsky broke his journey at Florence, whence he wrote to Nadejda von Meck on February 19th (March 3rd), 1881 :—

"What light! What sunshine! What a delight to sit at the open window with a bunch of violets before me, and to drink in the fresh air! I am full of sensations. I feel so well, and yet so sad—I could weep. Yet I know not why. Only music can express these feelings."

To N. F. von Meck.

"ROME, *February 22nd* (*March 6th*), 1881.

"I have just been lunching with the Grand Dukes Serge and Paul Alexandrovich. The invitation came early this morning, and I had to go out in search of a dress-coat. It was no easy matter to procure one, for, being Sunday, nearly all the shops were closed. It was with difficulty that I arrived at the Villa Sciarra in proper time. The Grand Duke Constantine introduced me to his cousins, who showed me much kindness and attention. All three are very sympathetic; but you can imagine, with my misanthropical shyness, how trying I find such meetings with strangers, especially with men of that aristocratic world. On Tuesday there is a dinner at Countess Brobinsky's, and I have also been invited to a soirée by Countess Sollogoub. I did not expect to have to lead this kind of life in Rome. I shall have to leave, for no doubt other invitations await me which I cannot refuse. Lest I should offend somebody, I am weak enough invariably to accept. I have not strength of mind to decline all such engagements."

To Modeste Tchaikovsky.

"ROME, *February 26th (March 10th)*, 1881.

"I can just imagine how you are making fun of my worldliness! I cannot understand where I get strength to endure this senseless existence! Naturally, I am annoyed, and my visit to Rome is spoilt—but I have not altogether lost heart, and find occasional opportunities of enjoying the place. O society! What can be more appalling, duller, more intolerable? Yesterday I was dreadfully bored at Countess X.'s, but so heroically did I conceal my feelings that my hostess in bidding me good-bye said: 'I cannot understand why you have not come to me before. I am sure that after to-night you will repent not having made my acquaintance sooner.' This is word for word! She really pities me! May the devil take them all!"

To Modeste Tchaikovsky.

"NAPLES, *March 3rd (15th)*, 1881.

"Yesterday I was about to write to you when Prince Stcherbatiov came to tell me of the Emperor's death,[1] which was a great shock to me. At such moments it is

---

[1] Alexander II., who was assassinated on the bank of the Catharine Canal.

very miserable to be abroad. I long to be in Russia, nearer to the source of information, and to take part in the demonstrations accorded to the new Tsar . . . in short, to be living in touch with one's own people. It seems so strange after receiving such news to hear them chattering at table d'hôte about the beauties of Sorrento, etc.

"The Grand Dukes wanted to take me with them to Athens and Jerusalem, which they intended to visit a few days hence. But this has fallen through, for all three are on their way to Petersburg by now."

To Modeste Tchaikovsky.

"*March* 13*th* (25*th*), 1881.

"DEAR MODI,—In Nice I heard by telegram from Jurgenson that Nicholai Grigorievich (Rubinstein) was very ill. Then two telegrams followed from the Grand Hotel (1) that his state was hopeless, (2) that he had already passed away. I left Nice at once. Mentally, I endured the torments of the damned during my journey. I must confess, to my shame, I suffered less from the sense of my irreparable loss, than from the horror of seeing in Paris—in the Grand Hotel too—the body of poor Rubinstein. I was afraid I should not be able to bear the shock, although I exerted all my will-power to conquer this shameful cowardice. My fears were in vain. The body had been taken to the Russian church at six o'clock this morning. At the Hotel I found only Madame Tretiakov,[1] who never left Nicholas Rubinstein during the last six days of his life. She gave me all details."[2]

To N. F. von Meck.

"PARIS, *March* 16*th* (28*th*), 1881.

"You regret having written me the letter in which you gave expression to your anger against those who have embittered your life. But I never for an instant believed

---

[1] Wife of S. Tretiakov, the wealthy art patron, afterwards chief burgomaster of Moscow.

[2] These details, in the form of a long letter, were communicated by Tchaikovsky to the *Moscow Viedomosti.*

2 D

that you could really *hate* and *never forgive*, whatever might happen. It is possible to be a Christian in life and deed without clinging closely to dogma, and I am sure that un-Christian feelings could only dwell in you for a brief moment, as an involuntary protest against human wickedness. Such really good people as you do not know what *hate* means in the true sense of the word. What can be more aimless and unprofitable than hate? According to Christ's words, our enemies only injure us from *ignorance*. O, if only men could only be Christians in truth as well as in form! If only everyone was penetrated by the simple truths of Christian morality! That can never be, for then eternal and *perfect* happiness would reign on earth; and we are imperfect creations, who only understand goodness and happiness as the opposites of evil. We are, as it were, specially created to be eternally reverting to evil, to perpetually seek the ideal, to aspire to everlasting truth—and never to reach the goal. At least we should be indulgent to those who, in their blindness, are attracted to evil by some inborn instinct. Are they to be blamed because they exist only to bring the chosen people into stronger relief? No, we can only say with Christ, 'Lord, forgive them, they know not what they do.' I feel I am expressing *vague* thoughts *vaguely*—thoughts which are wandering through my mind, because a man who was good and dear to me has just vanished from this earth. But if I think and speak vaguely, I *feel* it all clearly enough. My brain is obscured to-day. How could it be otherwise in face of those enigmas—*Death, the aim and meaning of life, its finality or immortality?* Therefore the light of *faith* penetrates my soul more and more. Yes, dear friend, I feel myself increasingly drawn towards this, the one and only shield against every calamity. I am learning to love God, as formerly I did not know how to do. Now and then doubts come back to me; I still strive at times to conceive the inconceivable with my feeble intellect; but the voice of divine truth speaks louder within me. I sometimes find an indescribable joy in bowing before the Inscrutable, Omniscient God. I often pray to Him with tears in my eyes (where He is, what He is, I know not; but I know He exists), and implore Him to grant me love and peace, to pardon and enlighten me; and it is sweet to say to Him, 'Lord, Thy will be done,' because I know His will is *holy*. Let me also tell you that I see clearly the finger of God in my own life, showing me the way and upholding me in all danger. Why it has been God's will to shield me I cannot say. I wish to be *humble*, and not to regard myself as one of the elect, for God loves all His creatures equally. I only know He really cares for me, and I shed tears of gratitude for His eternal goodness. That is not enough. I want to accustom myself to the thought that all trials are good in the end. I want to love God always, not only when He sends me good, but when He proves me; for somewhere there must exist that kingdom of eternal happiness, which we seek so vainly upon earth. The time will come when all the questionings of our intellects will be answered, and we shall know why God sends us these trials. I want to believe that there is another life. When this desire becomes a fact, I shall be happy, in so far as happiness is possible in this world.

"To-day I attended the funeral service in the church, and afterwards I accompanied the remains to the Gare du Nord, and saw that the leaden coffin was packed in a wooden case and placed in a luggage van. It was painful and horrible to think that our poor Nicholai Grigorievich should return thus to Moscow. Yes, it was intensely painful. But faith has now taken root in me, and I took comfort from the thought that it was God's *inscrutable* and *holy* will."

To Modeste Tchaikovsky.

"PARIS, *March* 17*th* (29*th*), 1881.

"Modi, we shall soon meet again, so I will say nothing now about the last sad days. My present trip has been altogether unfortunate and calculated to weaken my love of going abroad. Once more I am face to face with changes which will affect my whole future life. First, the death of Nicholas Rubinstein, which is of great importance to me, and, secondly, the fact that Nadejda von Meck is on the verge of bankruptcy. I heard this talked about in Moscow, and begged her to tell me the truth. From her reply I see it is actually so. She writes that the sum I receive from her is nothing as compared to the millions that have been lost, and that she wishes to continue to pay it as before, but begs me not to mention it to anyone. But you see that this allowance is no longer a certainty, and therefore sooner or later I must return to my teaching. All this is far from cheerful."

To Nadejda von Meck.

" KAMENKA, *April* 29*th* (*May* 11*th*), 1881.

" I only stayed a few days in Moscow, where I was forced to collect all my strength in order to decline most emphatically the directorship of the Conservatoire. I arrived here to-day."

To P. Jurgenson.

" KAMENKA, *May* 7*th* (19*th*), 1881.

"As my sister is ill and has gone away with her husband, I am playing the part of the head of the family and spend most of my time with the children. This would be a nuisance if I did not care for them as though they were my own. . . . I have no inclination to compose. I wish you would commission something. Is there really nothing you want? Some external impulse might perhaps reawaken my suspended activity. Perhaps I am getting old and all my songs are sung."

To Nadejda von Meck.

" KAMENKA, *May* 8*th* (20*th*), 1881.

" I think I have now found a temporary occupation. In my present religious frame of mind it will do me good to dip into Russian church music. At present I am studying the ' rites,' that is to say, the root of our church tunes, and I want to try to harmonise them.

" Every day I pray that God may preserve and uphold you for the sake of so many people."

To P. Jurgenson.

"KAMENKA, *May 9th (21st)*, 1881.

" I beg you to send me the following :—

"(1) I want to write a Vesper service and require the words in full. If there is a book on sale, a kind of 'short guide to the Liturgy for laymen,' please send it to me.

"(2) I have begun to study the rites and ceremonials of the Church, but to acquire sufficient information on the subject I need Razoumovsky's *History of Church Music.* I send thanks in anticipation."

Tchaikovsky describes his condition at this time as " grey, without inspiration or joy," but " physically sound." He often felt that the spring of inspiration had run dry, but consoled himself with the remembrance that he had passed through other periods " equally devoid of creative impulse."

To E. Napravnik.

"KAMENKA, *June 17th (29th)*, 1881.

"Last winter, at N. Rubinstein's request, I wrote a Festival Overture for the concerts of the Exhibition, entitled *The Year 1812.* Could you possibly manage to have this played? If you like I will send the score for you to see. It is not of any great value, and I shall not be at all surprised or hurt if you consider the style of the music unsuitable to a symphony concert."

To Modeste Tchaikovsky.

"KAMENKA, *June 21st (July 3rd)*, 1881.

"My Vesper music compels me to look into many service books, with and without music. If you only knew how difficult it is to understand it all! Every service contains some chants that may be modified and others that may not. The latter—such as *Khvalitey* and *Velikoe slavoslovie* —do not present any great difficulties; but those that change—such as the canonical verses to *Gospodi vozzvakh* —are a science in themselves, for which a lifetime of study would hardly suffice. I should like at least to succeed in one Canon, the one relating to the Virgin. Imagine that, in spite of all assistance, I can arrive neither at the words nor the music. I went to ask our priest to explain it to me, but he assured me that he himself did not know anything about it and went through the routine of his office without referring to the Typikon. I am swallowed up in this sea of Graduals, Hymns, Canticles, Tropaires, Exapostelaires, etc., etc. I asked our priest how his assistant managed, and how he knew how, when, and where, to sing or read (for the Church prescribes to the smallest detail on what days, with what voice, and how many times things have to be read). He replied: ' I do not know ; before every service he has to look out something for himself.' If the initiated do not know, what can a poor sinner like myself expect?"

To P. Jurgenson.

"KAMENKA, *June* 21*st* (*July* 3*rd*), 1881.

" I have received Bortniansky's works and looked them through. To edit them would be a somewhat finicking and wearisome task, because the greater number of his compositions are dull and worthless. Why do you want to issue a 'Complete Edition'? Let me advise you to give up this plan and only bring out a 'Selection from the works of Bortniansky.' . . . 'Complete Edition'? An imposing word, but out of place in connection with a man of no great talent, who has written a mass of rubbish, and only about a dozen good things. I am doubtful whether I should lend my name to such a publication . . . on the other hand I am a musician, and live by my work; consequently there is nothing derogatory in my editing this rubbish for the sake of what I can earn. My pride, however, suffers from it. Think it over and send me a reply."

To N. F. von Meck.

"KAMENKA, *July* 3*rd* (15*th*), 1881.

" I am very glad, my dear, you like my songs and duets. I will take this opportunity of telling you which of these vocal compositions I care for most. Among the duets

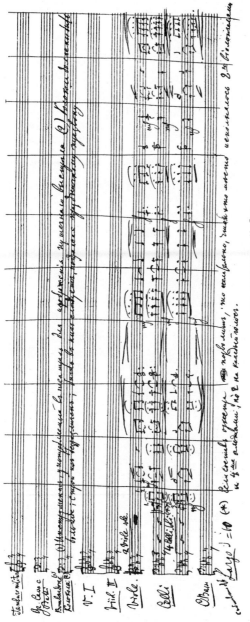

OPENING BARS FROM THE OVERTURE "1812"

From the MS. in the possession of P. Jurgenson, Moscow

I prefer 'Thränen' ('Tears'), and among the songs: (1) the one to Tolstoi's words, (2) the verses of Mickievicz, and (3) 'War ich nicht der Halm.' The 'Schottische Ballade' is also one of my favourites, but I am convinced it will never be so popular as I fancied it would. It should not be so much sung, as declaimed, but with the most impassioned feeling.

To P. Jurgenson.

"KAMENKA, *July* 31*st* (*August* 12*th*), 1881.

"I am working intensely hard at Bortniansky to get this dreadful work done as soon as possible. His works as a rule are quite antipathetic to me. I shall finish the job, for I always complete anything I have begun. But some day I shall actually burst with rage. . . ."

To N. F. von Meck.

"KAMENKA, *August* 24*th* (*September* 5*th*), 1881.

"I wish with all my heart you could hear my Serenade properly performed. It loses so much on the piano, and I think the middle movements—played by the violins—would win your sympathy. As regards the first and last movements you are right. They are merely a play of sounds, and do not touch the heart. The first movement is my homage to Mozart; it is intended to be an imitation of his style, and I should be delighted if I thought I had in any way approached my model. Do not laugh, dear, at my zeal in standing up for my latest creation. Perhaps my paternal feelings are so warm because it is the youngest child of my fancy. . . .

"As regards Balakirev's songs, I am quite of your opinion. They are actually little masterpieces, and I am passionately fond of some of them. There was a time when I could not listen to 'Selim's Song' without tears in my eyes, and now I rank 'The Song of the Golden Fish' very highly."

To S. I. Taneiev.

"*August 25th (September 6th)*, 1881.

"I am almost certain my Vespers will not please you. I see nothing in them which would win your approval. Do you know, Sergei Ivanovich, I believe I shall never write anything good again, I am no longer in a condition to compose. What form should I choose?—none of them appeal to me. Always the same indispensable *remplissage*, the same routine, the same revolting methods, the same conventions and shams. If I were young, this aversion from composition might be explained by the fact that I was gathering my forces, and would suddenly strike out some new path of my own making. But, alas! the years are beginning to tell. To write in a naïve way, as the bird sings, is no longer possible, and I lack energy to invent something new. I do not tell you this because I hope for your encouraging denial, but simply as a fact. I do not regret it. I have worked much in my time, in a desultory way, and now I am tired. It is time to rest. . . .

"Do not speak to me of coming back to the Conservatoire; at present this is impossible. I cannot answer for the future. You, on the contrary, seem made to carry on Rubinstein's work."

XIII

1881–1882

In one of his letters to Nadejda von Meck, written in 1876, Tchaikovsky says: "I no longer compose anything—a sure indication of an agitated mind."

From November, 1880, until September, 1881, Tchaikovsky wrote nothing—from which we may conclude that during this time he again underwent a period of spiritual and mental disturbance.

It is not surprising that during the time he spent in Moscow and Petersburg (November to February) he should not have written a note. We know that town life—to which was added at this time the anxieties attendant upon the production of two operas—stifled all his inclination for composing. His visit to Rome, with its many social obligations, was also unfavourable to creative work.

That Tchaikovsky continued to be silent even after his return to Kamenka cannot, however, be attributed to unsuitable surroundings or external hindrances. It points rather to a restless and unhappy frame of mind.

There were numerous reasons to account for this condition.

In the first place he was touched to the quick by the loss of Nicholas Rubinstein. In spite of their many differences he had loved him with all his heart, and valued him as "one of the greatest virtuosi of his day." He had also grown to regard him as one of the chief props of his artistic life. Nicholas Rubinstein was always the first, and best, interpreter of his works for pianoforte and orchestra. Whenever Tchaikovsky wrote a symphonic work, he already heard it in imagination as it would sound in the concert-room in Moscow, and knew beforehand that under Rubinstein's direction he would experience no disappointment. The great artist had the gift of discovering in Tchaikovsky's works beauties of which the composer himself was hardly conscious. There was the sonata, for instance, which Tchaikovsky "did not recognise" when he heard it played by N. Rubinstein. And now this sure and subtle interpreter of all his new works was gone for ever.

Apart from personal relations, Rubinstein's intimate connection with the Conservatoire had its influence upon Tchaikovsky. Although the latter had resigned his position there, he had not ceased to take an interest in the musical life of Moscow. After his friend's death Tchaikovsky was aware that everyone was waiting for him to decide whether he would take over Rubinstein's work. To accept this duty meant to abandon his career as a composer. There was no mental conflict, because he never hesitated for a moment in deciding that nothing in the world would make him give up his creative work. At the same time he felt so keenly the helpless position of the Conservatoire that he could not avoid some self-reproach; and thus the calm so needful for composition was constantly disturbed.

Another reason for his sadness was of a more intimate character. After many years of unclouded happiness, a time of severe trial had come to the numerous Davidov family, which was not without its influence upon Tchaikovsky. Kamenka, formerly his refuge from all the tempests of life, was no longer so peaceful a harbour, because his ever-increasing attachment to his sister's family made him more sensible of their joys and sorrows. At this time the shadows prevailed, for Alexandra Ilinichna was confined to bed by a long and painful illness, which eventually ended in her death.

Finally, Tchaikovsky suffered much at this time from the loss of his faithful servant Alexis Safronov, who had been in his service from 1873 to 1880, when he was called upon to serve his time in the army.

Tchaikovsky spent most of September, 1881, in Moscow, in the society of his brother Anatol. This visit was comparatively agreeable to him, because the greater part of Moscow society had not yet returned from their summer holidays, and he felt free.

He left Moscow on October 1st (13th).

To P. Jurgenson.

"KAMENKA, *October 8th (20th)*, 1881.

" I inhabit the large house where my sister's family used to live, but at present there are no other human beings but myself and the woman who looks after me. I have laid myself out to complete the arrangements of Bortniansky's works for double chorus in a month. Good Lord, how I loathe Bortniansky! Not himself, poor wretch, but his wishy-washy music! Yet if I had not undertaken this work I should find myself in a bad way financially. Were I to tell you how much money I got through in Moscow, without knowing why or wherefore, you would be horrified and give me a good scolding. . . ."

To P. Jurgenson.

" KAMENKA, *October* 11*th* (23*rd*), 1881.

" DEAR FRIEND,—I know you will laugh at me when you read this letter. . . . There is a young man here of eighteen or nineteen who is very clever and capable, but dislikes his present occupation because his domestic circumstances are miserable, and he longs for a wider sphere and experience of life. He has the reputation of being honest and industrious, and knows something of the book-trade. . . . Could you make him useful in your publishing house, or in the country? Dear friend, do look after him! What can I do for him? This is 'my fate' over again. In any case I shall not abandon him, for I am sure he would come to grief here.

" Laugh if you like, but have compassion and answer me." [1]

To Nadejda von Meck.

" KIEV, *November* 9*th* (21*st*), 1881.

" Because I am deeply interested in Church music just now, I go to the churches here very frequently, especially to the 'Lavra.' [2] On Sunday the bishop celebrated services in the monasteries of Michael and the Brotherhood. The singing in these churches is celebrated, but I thought it very poor, and pretentious, with a repertory of commonplace concert pieces. It is quite different in the 'Lavra,' where they sing in their own old style, following the traditions of a thousand years, without notes and without any attempts at concert-music. Nevertheless it is an

---

[1] P. Jurgenson took this young man into his business, where he remained some time. Like Tkachenko, he was nervous and peculiar, and gave Tchaikovsky much trouble and anxiety.

[2] Monasteries of the first rank.

original and grand style of sacred singing. The public think the music of the 'Lavra' is bad, and are delighted with the sickly-sweet singing of other churches. This vexes and enrages me. It is difficult to be indifferent to the matter. My efforts to help our church music have been misunderstood. My Liturgy is forbidden. Two months ago the ecclesiastical authorities in Moscow refused to let it be sung at the memorial service for Nicholas Rubinstein. The Archbishop Ambrose pronounced it to be a *Catholic* service. . . . The authorities are pig-headed enough to keep every ray of light out of this sphere of darkness and ignorance.

"To-morrow I hope to leave for Rome, where I expect to meet my brother Modeste."

To N. F. von Meck.

"ROME, *November 26th (December 8th),* 1881.

"The day before yesterday I was at the concert in honour of Liszt's seventieth birthday. The programme consisted exclusively of his works. The performance was worse than mediocre. Liszt himself was present. It was touching to witness the ovation which the enthusiastic Italians accorded to the venerable genius, but Liszt's works leave me cold. They have more poetical intention than actual creative power, more colour than form—in short, in spite of being externally effective, they are lacking in the deeper qualities. Liszt is just the opposite of Schumann, whose vast creative force is not in harmony with his colourless style of expression. At this concert an Italian celebrity played; Sgambati is a very good pianist, but exceedingly cold."

To N. F. von Meck.

"ROME, *November 27th (December 9th),* 1881.

"I cannot take your advice to publish my opera with a French title-page. Such advances to foreign nations are repugnant to me. Do not let us go to them, let them rather come to us. If they want our operas then—not the title-page only, but the full text can be translated, as in

the case of the proposed performance at Prag
as an opera has not crossed the Russian fror
necessary—to my mind—that it should be t
the language of those who take no interest i

To N. F. von Meck.

"ROME, *December 4th* (16*th*), 1881.

"Yesterday I received sad news from Kamenka. In the neighbourhood lies a little wood, the goal of my daily walk. In the heart of the wood lives a forester with a large and lovable family. I never saw more beautiful children. I was particularly devoted to a little girl of four, who was very shy at first, but afterwards grew so friendly that she would caress me prettily, and chatter delightful nonsense, which was a great pleasure to me. Now my brother-in-law writes that this child and one of the others have died of diphtheria. The remaining children were removed to the village by his orders, but, he adds, 'I fear it is too late.' Poor Russia! Everything there is so depressing, and then this terrible scourge which carries off children by the thousand."

The violin concerto was the only one of Tchaikovsky's works which received its first performance outside Russia. This exceptional occurrence took place in Vienna. The originality and difficulty of this composition prevented Leopold Auer, to whom it was originally dedicated, from appreciating its true worth, and he declined to produce it in St. Petersburg.[1] Two years passed after its publication, and still no one ventured to play it in public. The first to recognise its importance, and to conquer its difficulties, was Adolf Brodsky. A pupil of Hellmesberger's, he held a post at the Moscow Conservatoire for a time, but relinquished it in the seventies in order to tour in Europe. For two years he considered the concerto without, as he himself says, being able to summon courage to learn it.

[1] Some years later Auer changed his opinion and became one of the most brilliant interpreters of this work.

inally, he threw himself into the work with fiery energy and resolved to try his luck with it in Vienna. Hans Richter expressed a wish to make acquaintance with the new concerto, and finally it was included in the programme of one of the Philharmonic Concerts, December 4th, 1881 According to the critics, and Brodsky's own account, there was a noisy demonstration at the close of the performance in which energetic applause mingled with equally forcible protest. The former sentiment prevailed, and Brodsky was recalled three times. From this it is evident that the ill-feeling was not directed against the executant, but against the work. The Press notices were very hostile. Out of ten criticisms, two only spoke quite sympathetically of the concerto. The rest, which emanated from the pens of the best-known musical critics, were extremely slashing. Hanslick, the author of the well-known book, *On the Beautiful in Music*, passed the following judgment upon this work :—

" Mozart's youthful work (the *Divertimento*) would have had a more favourable position had it been played after, instead of before, Tchaikovsky's Violin Concerto ; a drink of cold water is welcome to those who have just swallowed brandy. The violinist, A. Brodsky, was ill-advised to make his first appearance before the Viennese public with this work. The Russian composer, Tchaikovsky, certainly possesses no commonplace talent, but rather one which is forced, and which, labouring after genius, produces results which are tasteless and lacking in discrimination. Such examples as we have heard of his music (with the exception of the flowing and piquant Quartet in D) offer a curious combination of originality and crudeness, of happy ideas and wretched affectations. This is also the case as regards his latest long and pretentious Violin Concerto. For a time it proceeds in a regular fashion, it is musical and not without inspiration, then crudeness gains the upper hand and reigns to the end of the first movement. The violin is no longer played, but rent asunder, beaten black and blue. Whether it is actually possible to give lear effect to these hair-raising difficulties I do not know, but I am sure Herr Brodsky in trying to do so made us suffer martyrdom as well as himself. The Adagio, with its tender Slavonic sadness, calmed and charmed us once more, but it breaks off suddenly, only to be followed by a finale which plunges us into the brutal, deplorable merriment of a Russian holiday carousal. We see savages, vulgar faces, hear coarse oaths and smell fusel-oil. Friedrich Fischer, describing lascivious paintings, once said there were pictures 'one could see stink.' Tchaikovsky's Violin Concerto brings us face to face for the first time with the revolting idea: May there not also be musical compositions which we can hear stink?'"

Hanslick's criticism hurt Tchaikovsky's feelings very deeply. To his life's end he never forgot it, and knew it by heart, just as he remembered word for word one of Cui's criticisms dating from 1866. All the deeper and more intense therefore was his gratitude to Brodsky. This sentiment he expressed in a letter to the artist, and in the dedication of the Concerto he replaced Auer's name by that of Brodsky.

While Tchaikovsky was touched by Brodsky's courage in bringing forward the Concerto, he was unable to suppress his sense of injury at the attitude of his intimate friend Kotek, who weakly relinquished his original intention of introducing the work in St. Petersburg. Still more did he resent the conduct of Auer, who, he had reason to believe, not only declined to produce the Concerto himself, but advised Sauret not to play it in the Russian capital.

To N. F. von Meck. ROME, 1881.

"Do you know what I am writing just now? You will be very much astonished. Do you remember how you once advised me to compose a trio for pianoforte, violin, and violoncello, and my reply, in which I frankly told you that I disliked this combination? Suddenly, in spite of this antipathy, I made up my mind to experiment in this form, which so far I have never attempted. The beginning of the trio is finished. Whether I shall carry it through, whether it will sound well, I do not know, but I should like to bring it to a happy termination. I hope you will believe me, when I say that I have only reconciled myself to the combination of piano and strings in the hope of giving you pleasure by this work. I will not conceal from you that I have had to do some violence to my feelings before I could bring myself to express my musical ideas in a new and unaccustomed form. I wish to conquer all difficulties, however; and the thought of pleasing you impels me and encourages my efforts."

To N. F. von Meck.

"ROME, *December 22nd*, 1881 (*January 3rd*, 1882).

"Things are well with me in the fullest sense of the word. . . . If everything were well in Russia, and I received good news from home, it would be impossible to conceive a better mode of life. But unhappily it is not so. Our dear, but pitiable, country is passing through a dark hour. A vague sense of unrest and dissatisfaction prevails throughout the land; all seem to be walking at the edge of a volcanic crater, which may break forth at any moment. . . .

"According to my ideas, now or never is the time to turn to the people for counsel and support; to summon us all together and to let us consider in common such ways and means as may strengthen our hands. The Zemsky Sobor—this is what Russia needs. From us the Tsar could learn the truth of things; we could help him to suppress rebellion and make Russia a happy and united country. Perhaps I am a poor politician, and my remarks are very naïve and inconsequential, but whenever I think the matter over, I see no other issue, and cannot understand why the same thought does not occur to him, in whose hands our salvation lies. Katkov, who describes all parliamentary discussions as talkee-talkee, and hates the words *popular representation* and *constitution*, confuses the idea of the Zemsky Sabor, which was frequently summoned in old days when the Tsar stood in need of counsel, with the Parliaments and Chambers of Western Europe. A Zemsky Sobor is probably quite opposed to a constitution in the European sense; it is not so much a question of giving us at once a responsible Ministry, and the whole routine of English parliamentary procedure, as of revealing the true state of things, giving the Government the confidence of the people, and showing us some indication of where and how we are being led.

"I had no intention of turning a letter to you into a political dissertation. Forgive me, dear friend, if I have bored you with it. I only meant to tell you the Italian sun is beautiful, and I am enjoying the glory of the South; but I live the life of my country, and cannot be completely at rest here so long as things are not right with us. Nor is the news I receive from my family in Russia very cheerful just now."

To P. Jurgenson.

"ROME, *January 4th* (16*th*), 1882.

"This season I have no luck. *The Maid of Orleans* will not be given again; *Oniegin* ditto; Auer intrigues against the Violin Concerto; no one plays the Pianoforte Concerto (the second); in short, things are bad. But what makes me furious, and hurts and mortifies me most, is the fact that the Direction, which would not spend a penny upon *The Maid of Orleans*, has granted 30,000 roubles for the mounting of Rimksy-Korsakov's *Sniegourochka*. Is it not equally unpleasant to you to feel that 'our subject' has been taken from us, and that Lel will now sing new music to the old words? It is as though someone had forcibly torn away a piece of myself and offered it to the public in a new and brilliant setting. I could cry with mortification."

To N. F. von Meck.

"ROME, *January* 13*th* (25*th*), 1882.

"The trio is finished. . . . Now I can say with some conviction that the work is not bad. But I am afraid, having written all my life for the orchestra, and only taken

2 E

late in life to chamber music, I may have failed to adapt the instrumental combinations to my musical thoughts. In short, I fear I may have arranged music of a symphonic character as a trio, instead of writing directly for my instruments. I have tried to avoid this, but I am not sure whether I have been successful."

To N. F. von Meck.

"ROME, *January* 16*th* (28*th*), 1882.

"I have just read the pamphlet you sent me (*La Vérité aux nihilistes*) with great satisfaction, because it is written with warmth, and is full of sympathy for Russia and the Russians. I must observe that it is of no avail as an argument against Nihilism. The author speaks a language which the Nihilists cannot understand, since no moral persuasion could change a tiger into a lamb, or induce a New Zealand cannibal to love his neighbour in a true Christian spirit. A Nihilist, after reading the pamphlet, would probably say: 'Dear sir, we know already from innumerable newspapers, pamphlets, and books, all you tell us as to the uselessness of our murders and dynamite explosions. We are also aware that Louis XVI. was a good king, and Alexander II. a good Tsar, who emancipated the serfs. Nevertheless we shall remain assassins and dynamiters, because it is our vocation to murder and blow up, with the object of destroying the present order of things.'

"Have you read the last volume of Taine's work upon the Revolution? No one has so admirably characterised the unreasoning crowd of anarchists and extreme revolutionists as he has done. Much of what he says respecting the French in 1793, of the degraded band of anarchists who perpetrated the most unheard-of crimes before the eyes of the nation, which was paralysed with astonishment, applies equally to the Nihilists. . . . The attempt to convince the Nihilists is useless. They must be exterminated; there is no other remedy against this evil."

At the end of January Tchaikovsky sent the Trio to Moscow with a request that it might be tried by Taneiev,

Grjimali, and Fitzenhagen. His letter to Jurgenson concludes as follows :—

"The Trio is dedicated to Nicholas G. Rubinstein. It has a somewhat plaintive and funereal colouring. As it is dedicated to Rubinstein's memory it must appear in an *édition de luxe*. I beg Taneiev to keep fairly accurately to my metronome indications. I also wish him to be the first to bring out the Trio next season. . . ."

To P. Jurgenson.

"ROME, *February 5th* (17*th*), 1882.

"MY DEAR FRIEND,—Your letters always bring me joy, comfort, and support. God knows I am not lying! You are the one regular correspondent through whom I hear all that interests me in Moscow—and I still love Moscow with a strange, keen affection. I say 'strange,' because in spite of my love for it I cannot live there. To analyse this psychological problem would lead me too far afield."

To A. Tchaikovsky.

"ROME, *February 7th* (19*th*), 1882.

"Toly, my dearest, I have just received your letter with the details of your engagement. I am heartily glad you are happy, and I think I understand all you are feeling, although I never experienced it myself. There is a certain kind of yearning for tenderness and consolation that only a wife can satisfy. Sometimes I am overcome by an insane craving for the caress of a woman's touch. Sometimes I see a sympathetic woman in whose lap I could lay my head, whose hands I would gladly kiss. When you are quite calm again — after your marriage — read *Anna Karenina*, which I have read lately for the first time with an enthusiasm bordering on fanaticism (*sic*). What you are now feeling is there wonderfully expressed with reference to Levin's marriage."

To P. Jurgenson.

"NAPLES, *February* 11*th* (23*rd*), 1882.

"Are you not ashamed of trying to 'justify' yourself of the accusation brought against you by my protégé Klimenko? I know well enough that you cannot be unjust. I know, on the other hand, that Klimenko is a crazy fellow who loses his head over Nekrassov's poetry and vague echoes of Nihilism. Nevertheless he is not stupid, and it would be a pity to discharge him. I feel unless he can make himself an assured livelihood in Moscow he will do no good elsewhere. I beg you to be patient a little longer, in the hope he will come to himself, and see where his own interests lie."

To N. F. von Meck.

"NAPLES, *February* 13*th* (25*th*), 1882.

"What a blessing to feel oneself safe from visitors—to be far from the noise of large hotels and the bustle of the town! What an inexhaustible source of enjoyment to admire this incomparable view, which stretches in all its beauty before our windows! All Naples, Vesuvius, Castellammare, Sorrento, lie before us. At sunset yesterday it was so divinely beautiful that I shed tears of gratitude to God. . . . I feel I shall not do much work in Naples. It is clearly evident that this town has contributed nothing to art or learning. To create a book, a picture, or an opera, it is necessary to become self-concentrated and oblivious of the outer world. Would that be possible in Naples? . . .

"Even the sun has spots, therefore it is not surprising that our abode, about which I have been raving, should gradually reveal certain defects. I suffer from a shameful weakness: I am mortally afraid of mice. Imagine, dear friend, that even as I write to you, a whole army of mice are probably conducting their manœuvres across the floor overhead. If a solitary one of their hosts strays into my room, I am condemned to a night of sleeplessness and torture. May Heaven protect me!"

Shortly afterwards, the landlord of this mouse-infested residence—the Villa Postiglione—turned out "an impudent thief," and Tchaikovsky, with his brother Modeste, returned to an hotel in the town.

To N. F. von Meck.

"NAPLES, *March 7th* (19*th*), 1882.

"To-day I finished my Vespers. . . . It is very difficult to work in Naples. Not only do its beauties distract one, but there is also the nuisance of the organ grinders. These instruments are never silent for an instant, and sometimes drive me to desperation. Two or three are often being played at the same time; someone will also be singing, and the trumpets of the Bersaglieri in the neighbourhood go on unceasingly from 8 a.m. until midday.

"In my leisure hours I have been reading a very interesting book, published recently, upon Bellini. It is written by his friend, the octogenarian Florimo. I have always been fond of Bellini. As a child I often cried under the strong impression made upon me by his beautiful melodies, which are impregnated with a kind of melancholy. I have remained faithful to his music, in spite of its many faults: the weak endings of his concerted numbers, the tasteless accompaniments, the roughness and vulgarity of his recitatives. Florimo's book contains not only Bellini's life, but also his somewhat extensive correspondence. I began to read with great pleasure the biography of this composer, who for long years past had been surrounded in my imagination with an aureole of poetical feeling. I had always thought of Bellini as a childlike, naïve being, like Mozart. Alas! I was doomed to disillusion. Bellini, in spite of his talent, was a very commonplace man. He lived in an atmosphere of self-worship, and was enchanted with every bar of his own music. He could not tolerate the least contradiction, and suspected enemies, intrigues, and envy in all directions; although from beginning to end of his career success never left him for a single day. Judging from his letters, he loved no one, and, apart his own interests, nothing existed for him. It is strange that the author of the book does not seem to have observed that these letters show

Bellini in a most unfavourable light, otherwise he would surely not have published them. Another book which I am enjoying just now is Melnikov's *On the Hills*. What an astonishing insight into Russian life, and what a calm objective attitude the author assumes to the numerous characters he has drawn in this novel! Dissenters of various kinds (*Rasskolniki*), merchants, moujiks, aristocrats, monks and nuns—all seem actually living as one reads. Each character acts and speaks, not in accordance with the author's views and convictions, but just as they would do in real life. In our day it is rare to meet with a book so free from 'purpose.'

10 p.m.

". . . One thing spoils all my walks here—the beggars, who not only beg, but display their wounds and deformities, which have a most unpleasant and painful effect upon me. But to sit at the window at home, to gaze upon the sea and Mount Vesuvius in the early morning, or at sunset, is such heavenly enjoyment that one can forgive and forget all the drawbacks of Naples."

Tchaikovsky spent a few days at Sorrento before going to Florence, whence he returned to Moscow about the middle of April.

XIV

To M. Tchaikovsky.

"KAMENKA, *May 10th (22nd)*, 1882.

"Modi, I am writing at night with tears in my eyes. Do not be alarmed—nothing dreadful has happened. I have just finished *Bleak House*, and shed a few tears, first, because I pity Lady Dedlock, and find it hard to tear myself away from all these characters with whom I have been living for two months (I began the book when I left Florence), and secondly, from gratitude that so great a writer as Dickens ever lived. . . . I want to suggest to you a capital subject for a story. But I am tired, so I will leave it until to-morrow.

" *Subject for a Story.*

" The tale should be told in the form of a diary, or letters to a friend in England. Miss L. comes to Russia. Everything appears to her strange and ridiculous. The family into which she has fallen please her—especially the children —but she cannot understand why the whole foundation of family life lacks the discipline, the sense of Christian duty, and the good bringing-up which prevail in English homes. She respects this family, but regards them as belonging to a different race, and the gulf between herself and them seems to grow wider. She draws into herself and remains there. Weariness and oppression possess her. The sense of duty, and the need of working for her family, keep her from despair. She is religious, in the English way, and finds the Russian Church, with its ritual, absurd and repugnant. Some of the family and their relations with her must be described in detail.

" A new footman appears upon the scene. At first she does not notice him at all. One day, however, she becomes aware that he has looked at her in particular—and love steals into her heart. At first she does not understand what has come over her. Why does she sympathise with him when he is working—others have to work too? Why does she feel so ill at ease when he waits on her? Then the footman begins to make love to the laundrymaid. In her feeling of hatred for this girl she realises she is jealous, and discovers her love. She gives the man all the money she has saved to go on a journey for his health, etc. She begins to love everything Russian. . . . She changes her creed. The footman is dismissed for some fault. She struggles with herself—but finally goes with him. One fine day he says to her : ' Go to the devil and take your ugly face with you! What do you want from me?' I really do not know how it all ends. . . ."

To N. F. von Meck.

" KAMENKA, *May* 29*th* (*June* 10*th*), 1882.

". . . You ask me why I chose the subject of *Mazeppa*. About a year ago K. Davidov (Director of the Petersburg

Conservatoire) passed on this libretto to me. It is arranged by Bourenin from Poushkin's poem *Poltava*. At that time it did not please me much, and although I tried to set a few scenes to music, I could not get up much enthusiasm, so put it aside. For a whole year I sought in vain for some other book, because the desire to compose another opera increased steadily. Then one day I took up the libretto of *Mazeppa* once more, read Poushkin's poem again, was carried away by some of the scenes and verses—and set to work upon the scene between Maria and Mazeppa, which is taken without alteration from the original text. Although I have not experienced as yet any of the profound enjoyment I felt in composing *Eugene Oniegin*; although the work progresses slowly and I am not much drawn to the characters—I continue to work at it because I have started, and I believe I may be successful. As regards Charles XII. I must disappoint you, dear friend. He does not come into my opera, because he only played an unimportant part in the drama between Mazeppa, Maria, and Kochoubey.'

The first symphony concert in the hall of the Art and Industrial Exhibition took place on May 18th (30th), 1882, under the direction of Anton Rubinstein. On this occasion Taneiev played Tchaikovsky's Second Pianoforte Concerto for the first time in public. It was received with much applause, but it was difficult to determine whether this was intended for the composer, or the interpreter.

To N. F. von Meck.

"GRANKINO, *June 9th (21st)*, 1882.

" The quiet and freedom of this place delight me. This is true country life! The walks are very monotonous ; there is nothing but the endless, level Steppe. The garden is large, and will be beautiful, but at present it is new. In the evening the Steppe is wonderful, and the air so exquisitely pure ; I cannot complain. The post only comes once a week, and there are no newspapers. One lives here in complete isolation from the world, and that has a great fascination for me.   Sometimes I feel—to a certain extent —the sense of perfect contentment I used always to experience in Brailov and Simaki.   O God, how sad it is to think that those moments of inexpressible happiness will never return!"[1]

To N. F. von Meck.

"GRANKINO, *July 5th (17th),* 1882.

"The news about Skobeliev only reached us a week after the sad catastrophe.   It is long since any death has given me a greater shock than this.   In view of the lamentable lack of men of mark in Russia, what a loss is this personality, on whom so many hopes depended!"

To P. Jurgenson.

"KAMENKA, *July 26th (August 7th),* 1882.

"My sister has just returned from Carlsbad, having stopped at Prague on the way to hear my *Maid of Orleans*, or *Panna Orleanska*, as she is called there.   It appears the opera was given in the barrack-like summer theatre, and both the performance and staging were very poor."

This first appearance of one of Tchaikovsky's operas upon the stage of a West-European theatre passed almost unnoticed.   The work had a *succès d'estime* and soon disappeared from the repertory of the Prague opera house. The Press were polite to the well-known symphonist Tchaikovsky, and considered that as regarded opera he deserved respect, sympathy, and interest, although he was not entitled to be called a dramatic composer "by the grace of God."

The programme of the sixth symphony concert (August 8th (20th) 1882) of the Art and Industrial Exhibition was made up entirely from the works of Tchaikovsky, and included: (1) *The Tempest ;* (2) Songs from *Sniegourochka ;* (3) the Violin Concerto (with Brodsky as

---

[1] Nadejda von Meck had sold Brailov.

soloist); (4) the *Italian Capriccio*; (5) Songs; (6) the Overture "1812." The last-mentioned work was now heard for the first time, and the Violin Concerto—although it had already been played in Vienna, London, and New York—for the first time in Russia. The success of these works, although considerable, did not equal that which has since been accorded them. Among many laudatory criticisms, one was couched in an entirely opposite spirit. Krouglikov said that the three movements of the Violin Concerto were so "somnolent and wearisome that one felt no desire to analyse it in detail." The "1812" Overture seemed to him "much ado about nothing." Finally, he felt himself obliged to state the "lamentable fact" that Tchaikovsky was "played out."

To Modeste Tchaikovsky.

"MOSCOW, *August* 15*th* (27*th*), 1882.

"DEAR MODI,—I found your letter when I came home an hour ago; but I have only just read it, because my mental condition was such that I had to collect myself first. What produces this terrible state?—I do not understand it myself. . . . Everything has tended to make to-day go pleasantly, and yet I am so depressed, and have suffered so intensely, that I might envy any beggar in the street. It all lies in the fact that life is impossible for me, except in the country or abroad. Why this is so, God knows—but I am simply on the verge of insanity.

"This undefinable, horrible, torturing malady, which declares itself in the fact that I cannot live a day, or an hour, in either of the Russian capitals without suffering, will perhaps be explained to me in some better world. . . . I often think that all my discontent springs from my own egoism, because I cannot sacrifice myself for others, even those who are near and dear to me. Then comes the comforting thought that I should not be suffering martyrdom except that I regard it as a kind of duty to come here now and then, for the sake of the pleasure it gives others. The devil knows! I only know this: that unattractive as

Kamenka may be, I long for my corner there, as one longs for some inexpressible happiness. I hope to go there to-morrow."

To N. F. von Meck.

" KAMENKA, *August 23rd (September 4th)*, 1882.

" DEAR, INCOMPARABLE FRIEND,—How lovely it is here! How freely I breathe once more! How delighted I am to see my dear room again! How good to live once more as one pleases, not as others order! How pleasant to work undisturbed, to read, to play, to walk, to be oneself, without having to play a different part a thousand times a day! How insincere, how senseless, is social life!"

XV

1882–1883

To N. F. von Meck.

" KAMENKA, *September 14th (26th)*, 1882.

" Never has any important work given me such trouble as this opera (*Mazeppa*). Perhaps it is the decadence of my powers, or have I become more severe in self-judgment? When I remember how I used to work, without the least strain, and knowing no such moments of doubt and uncertainty, I seem to be a totally different man. Formerly I wrote as easily, and as much in obedience to the law of nature, as a fish swims in water or a bird flies. Now I am like a man who carries a precious, but heavy, burden, and who must bear it to the last at any cost. I, too, shall bear mine to the end, but sometimes I fear my strength is broken and I shall be forced to cry halt!"

To Modeste Tchaikovsky.

" KAMENKA, *September 20th (October 2nd)*, 1882.

" I am writing on a true autumnal day. Since yesterday a fine rain has been falling like dust, the wind howls, the green things have been frost-bitten since last week—yet I am not depressed. On the contrary, I enjoy it. It is only in this weather that I like Kamenka; when it is fine, I always long to be elsewhere.

"I have begun the instrumentation of the opera. The introduction, which depicts Mazeppa and the galloping horse, will sound very well! . . ."

To E. Napravnik.

"KAMENKA, *September 21st (October 3rd)*, 1882.

"Kamenskaya tells me that in case of the revival of *The Maid of Orleans* she would be glad to undertake the part again, if I would make the cuts, changes, and transpositions which you require. Apart from the fact that it is very desirable this opera should be repeated, and that I am prepared to make any sacrifice for this end, your *advice* alone is sufficient to make me undertake all that is necessary without hesitation. . . . Yet I must tell you frankly, nothing is more unpleasant than the changing of modulations, and the transposition of pieces which one is accustomed to think of in a particular tonality, and I should be *very glad* if the matter could be arranged without my personal concurrence. At the same time, I repeat that I am willing to do whatever you advise."

To P. Jurgenson.

"KAMENKA, *October 20th (November 1st)*, 1882.

"The copy of the Trio which you sent me gave me the greatest pleasure. I think no other work of mine has appeared in such an irreproachable edition. The title-page delighted me by its exemplary simplicity."

The Trio was given for the first time at one of the quartet evenings of the Musical Society in Moscow, October 18th (30th). Judging from the applause, the public was very much pleased with the work, but the critics were sparing in their praise.

In a letter to the composer Taneiev says :—

" I have studied your Trio for more than three weeks, and worked at it six hours a day. I ought long since to have written to you about this glorious work. I have never had greater pleasure in studying a new composition. The majority of the musicians here are enchanted with the Trio. It also pleased the public. Hubert has received a number of letters asking that it may be repeated."

To S. I. Taneiev.

" KAMENKA, *October 29th* (*November 10th*), 1882.

" My best thanks for your letter, dear Serge Ivanovich. Your approval of my Trio gives me very great pleasure. In my eyes you are a great authority, and my artistic vanity is as much flattered by your praise, as it is insensible to the opinions of the Press, for experience has taught me to regard them with philosophical indifference. . . .

" *Mazeppa* creeps along tortoise-fashion, although I work at it daily for several hours. I cannot understand why I am so changed in this respect. At first I feared it was the loss of power that comes with advancing years, but now I comfort myself with the thought that I have grown stricter in self-criticism and less self-confident. This is perhaps the reason why it now takes me three days to orchestrate a thing that I could formerly have finished in one."

To N. F. von Meck.

" KAMENKA, *November 3rd* (15*th*), 1882.

". . . I think—if God grants me a long life—I shall never again compose an opera. I do not say, with you and many others, that opera is an inferior form of musical art. On the contrary, uniting as it does so many elements which all serve the same end, it is perhaps the richest of musical forms. I think, however, that personally I am more inclined to symphonic music, at least I feel more free and independent when I have not to submit to the requirements and conditions of the stage."

To N. F. von Meck.

"KAMENKA, *November 10th (22nd)*, 1882.

"Napravnik sends me word that *The Maid of Orleans* will be remounted in Prague, and Jurgenson writes that he would like to go there with me. I, too, would like to see my opera performed abroad. Very probably we shall go direct to Prague next week, and afterwards I shall return with him to Moscow, where I must see my brother. . . ."

To N. F. von Meck.

"MOSCOW, *November 23rd (December 5th)*, 1882.

"I have made the acquaintance of Erdmannsdörfer, who has succeeded Nicholas Rubinstein as conductor of the Symphony Concerts. He is a very gifted man, and has taken the hearts of the musicians and the public by storm. The latter is so fickle : it received Erdmannsdörfer with such enthusiasm, one would think it valued him far more highly than Rubinstein, who never met with such warmth. Altogether Moscow is not only reconciled to the loss of Rubinstein, but seems determined to forget him.

"I am torn to pieces as usual, so that I already feel like a martyr, as I always do in Moscow or Petersburg. It has gone to such lengths that to-day I feel quite ill with this insane existence, and I am thinking of taking flight."

To N. F. von Meck.

"MOSCOW, *December 5th (17th)* 1882.

"To the many fatigues of the present time, one more has been added ; every day I have to sit for some hours to the painter Makovsky. The famous art collector, P. Tretiakov, commissioned him to paint my portrait, so that I could not very well refuse. You can fancy how wearisome it is to me to have to sit for hours, when I find even the minutes necessary for being photographed simply horrible. Nevertheless the portrait seems very successful.[1]

---

[1] This portrait was one of the least successful of Makovsky's efforts. A far better portrait of the composer was made some years later by Kouznietsov. See frontispiece.

I forget if I have already told you that at the last concert but one my Suite was given with great success. Erdmannsdörfer proved a good conductor, although I think the Moscow Press and public greatly overrate his capabilities. . . . My work is not yet finished, so I shall hardly be able to leave before next week."

Tchaikovsky left Moscow on December 28th (January 9th, 1883), travelling by Berlin to Paris, where he met his brother Modeste, who was to accompany him to Italy.

To N. F. von Meck.

" BERLIN, *December* 31*st*, 1882 (*January* 12*th*, 1883).

" I broke my journey to rest here. Yesterday *Tristan and Isolde* (which I had never seen) was being given at the Opera, so I decided to remain another day. The work does not give me any pleasure, although I am glad to have heard it, for it has done much to strengthen my previous views of Wagner, which—until I had seen all his works performed—I felt might not be well grounded. Briefly summed up, this is my opinion : in spite of his great creative gifts, in spite of his talents as a poet, and his extensive culture, Wagner's services to art—and to opera in particular—have only been of a negative kind. He has proved that the older forms of opera are lacking in all logical and æsthetic *raison d'être*. But if we may no longer write opera on the old lines, are we obliged to write as Wagner does? I reply, *Certainly not.* To compel people to listen for four hours at a stretch to an endless symphony which, however rich in orchestral colour, is wanting in clearness and directness of thought; to keep singers all these hours singing melodies which have no independent existence, but are merely notes that belong to this symphonic music (in spite of lying very high these notes are often lost in the thunder of the orchestra), this is certainly not the ideal at which contemporary musicians should aim. Wagner has transferred the centre of gravity from the stage to the orchestra, but this is an obvious absurdity, therefore his famous operatic reform——viewed apart from its negative results—amounts to nothing. As regards the dramatic interest of his operas, I find them very poor, often childishly naïve. But I have never been quite so bored as with *Tristan and Isolde*. It is an endless void, without movement, without life, which cannot hold the spectator, or awaken in him any true sympathy for the characters on the stage. It was evident that the audience—even though Germans—were bored, but they applauded loudly after each act. How can this be explained? Perhaps by a patriotic sympathy for the composer, who actually devoted his whole life to singing the praise of Germanism."

To A. Merkling.

"Paris, *January 10th (22nd)*, 1882.

"I have seen a few interesting theatrical performances, among others Sardou's *Fedora*, in which Sarah Bernhardt played with *arch-genius*, and would have made the most poignant impression upon me if the play—in which a clever but cold Frenchman censures our Russian customs —were not so full of lies. I have finally come to the conclusion that Sarah is really a woman of genius.[1] I also enjoyed Musset's play, *On ne badine pas avec l'amour*. After the theatre I go to a restaurant and drink punch (it is bitterly cold in Paris). . . ."

To N. F. von Meck.

"Paris, *January 11th (23rd)*, 1883.

"I have just come from the Opera Comique, where I heard *Le Nozze di Figaro*. I should go every time it was given. I know my worship of Mozart astonishes you, dear friend. I, too, am often surprised that a broken man, sound neither in mind nor spirit, like myself, should still be able to enjoy Mozart, while I do not succumb to the depth and force of Beethoven, to the glow and passion of Schumann, nor the brilliance of Meyerbeer, Berlioz, and Wagner. Mozart is not oppressive or agitating. He captivates, delights and comforts me. To hear his

[1] It is interesting to know that this opinion was in direct opposition to that of Tourgeniev, who made some harsh criticisms upon the celebrated French actress.—R. N.

music is to feel one has accomplished some good action. It is difficult to say precisely wherein this good influence lies, but undoubtedly it is beneficial ; the longer I live and the better I know him, the more I love his music.

"You ask why I never write anything for the harp. This instrument has a beautiful timbre, and adds greatly to the poetry of the orchestra. But it is not an independent instrument, because it has no *melodic* quality, and is only suitable for harmony. True, artists like Parish-Alvars have composed operatic fantasias for the harp, in which there are melodies ; but this is rather forced. Chords, arpeggios—these form the restricted sphere of the harp, consequently it is only useful for accompaniments."

Before Tchaikovsky left Moscow he had been approached by Alexeiev, the president of the local branch of the Russian Musical Society, with regard to the music to be given at the Coronation festivities, to take place in the spring of 1883. A chorus of 7,500 voices, selected from all the educational institutions in Moscow, was to greet the Emperor and Empress with the popular 'Slavsia,' from Glinka's opera, *A Life for the Tsar.* The arrangement of this chorus, with accompaniment for string orchestra, was confided to Tchaikovsky. In January he accomplished this somewhat uncongenial task, and sent it to Jurgenson with the following remarks :—

"There are only a few bars of 'original composition' in the work, besides the third verse of the text, so if—as you say—I am to receive a fee from the city of Moscow, my account stands as below :—

"For the simplification of sixteen bars of choral and instrumental music, to be repeated three times . 3 r.
"For the composition of eight connecting bars . . 4 r.
"For four additional lines to the third verse, at forty kopecks per line . . 1 r. 60 k.

Total . . 8 r. 60 k. (16/11½)

2 F

"This sum I present to the city of Moscow. Joking apart, it is absurd to speak of payment for such a work, and, to me, most unpleasant. These things should be done gratuitously, or not at all."

To N. F. von Meck.

"PARIS, *February 5th (17th)*, 1883.

"I have not read Daudet's *L'Evangéliste*, although I have the book. I cannot conquer a certain prejudice; it is not the author's fault, but all these sects, the Salvation Army—and all the rest of them—are antipathetic to me, and since in this volume Daudet (whom I like as much as you do) deals with a similar subject, I have no wish to read it.

"As regards French music, I will make the following remarks in justification of my views. I do not rave about the music of the new French school as a whole, nor about each individual composer, so much as I admire the influence of the novelty and freshness which are so clearly discernible in their music. What pleases me is their effort to be eclectic, their sense of proportion, their readiness to break with hard-and-fast routine, while keeping within the limits of musical grace. Here you do not find that ugliness in which some of our composers indulge, in the mistaken idea that *originality* consists in treading under foot all previous traditions of beauty. If we compare modern French music with what is being composed in Germany, we shall see that German music is in a state of decadence, and that apart from the eternal fluctuation between Mendelssohn and Schumann, or Liszt and Wagner, nothing is being done. In France, on the contrary, we hear much that is new and interesting, much that is fresh and forceful. Of course, Bizet stands head and shoulders above the rest, but there are also Massenet, Delibes, Guirand, Lalo, Godard, Saint-Saëns. All these are men of talent, who cannot be compared with the dry *routinier* style of contemporary Germans."

To P. Jurgenson.

"PARIS, *February 6th* (18*th*), 1883.

"DEAR FRIEND,—To-day I received a telegram from Bartsal,[1] asking if my Coronation Cantata is ready, and for what voices it is written. I am replying that I have never composed such a Cantata. Apparently it is some absurdity which does not demand serious attention, and yet I am really somewhat agitated. The matter stands as follows. Early in December I met an acquaintance whom I have regarded for many years as a commonplace fool. But this fool was suddenly put upon the Coronation Commission. One day, after lunch, he took me aside and inquired : 'I trust you are not a Nihilist?' I put on an air of surprise, and inquired why he had to ask such a question. 'Because I think it would be an excellent thing if you were to compose something suitable for the Coronation—something in a festival way—something patriotic—in short, write something. . . .' I replied that I should be very pleased to compose something, but I could not supply my own text, that would have to be commissioned from Maikov, or Polonsky, then I should be willing to write the music. Our conversation ended here. Afterwards I heard that this man was saying all over Petersburg that he had commissioned me to write a Cantata. I had forgotten the whole story until the telegram came this morning. I am afraid the story may now be grossly exaggerated, and the report be circulated that I refused to compose such a work. I give you leave to use all possible means to have the matter put in the true light, and so to exonerate me."

To N. F. von Meck.

"PARIS, *February 24th* (*March 8th*), 1883.

"*Henry VIII.*, by Saint-Saëns, was recently given at the Grand Opéra. I did not go, but, according to the papers, the work had no signal success. I am not surprised, for I know his other operas, *Samson et Dalila*,

---

[1] A. I. Bartsal, chief manager of the Imperial Opera, in Moscow.

Etienne Marcel, and *La Princesse Jaune*, and all three have strengthened my conviction, that Saint-Saëns will never write a great dramatic work. Next week I will hear the opera, and tell you what I think of it.

"In consequence of his death, Wagner is the hero of the hour with the Parisian public. At all three Sunday concerts (Pasdeloup, Colonne and Lamoureux) the programmes have been devoted to his works, with the greatest success. Curious people! It is necessary to die in order to attract their attention. In consequence of the death of Flotow, there was a vacancy in the *Académie des Beaux Arts*. Gounod put me forward as one of the five candidates, but I did not attain to this honour. The majority of votes went to the Belgian composer Limnander."

XVI

At this time two unexpected and arduous tasks fell to Tchaikovsky's lot. The city of Moscow commissioned him to write a march for a fête, to be given in honour of the Emperor in the Sokolniky Park, and the Coronation Committee sent him the libretto of a lengthy cantata, with a request that the music might be ready by the middle of April. These works he felt it his duty to undertake. For the march he declined any payment, for reasons which he revealed to Jurgenson, under strict pledges of secrecy. When, two years earlier, his financial situation had been so dark that he had undertaken the uncongenial task of editing the works of Bortniansky, he had, unknown to all his friends, applied for assistance to the Tsar. After the letter was written, he would gladly have destroyed it, but his servant had already taken it to the post. Some days later he received a donation of 3,000 roubles (£300). He resolved to take the first opportunity of giving some return for this gift, and the Coronation March was the outcome of this mingled feeling of shame and gratitude.

His projected journey to Italy was abandoned, and he decided to remain some weeks longer in Paris.

To P. Jurgenson.

"PARIS, *March 9th (21st)*, 1883.

"About the middle of August I received, in Moscow, the manuscript of the *Vespers*, with the Censor's corrections. You then requested me to carry out these corrections. I altered what was actually essential. As regards the rest, I sent you an explanation to be forwarded to the Censor. . . . What has become of it? Either you have lost it, or the Censor is so obstinate and dense that one can do nothing with him. The absurdity is that I have not *composed* music to the words of the Vesper Service, but taken it from a book published by the Synodal Press. I have only harmonised the melodies as they stood in this book. . . . In short, I have improved everything that was capable of improvement. I will not endure the caprices of a drivelling pedant. He can teach me nothing, and the Synodal book is more important than he is. I shall have to complain about him. There . . . he has put me out for a whole day!"

To P. Jurgenson.

"PARIS, *April 14th (26th)*, 1883.

"You reproach me because the pieces Rubinstein played belong to Bessel.[1] I am very sorry, but I must say in self-justification that had I had any suspicion twelve years ago that it would be the least deprivation to you *not* to possess anything of mine, I would on no account have been faithless to you. . . . In those days I had no idea that I could wound your feelings by going to Bessel. Now I would give anything to get the pieces back again. A curious man Anton Rubinstein! Why could he not pay some attention to these pieces ten years ago? Why did he never play a note of my music then? That would indeed have been a service! I am grateful to him, even now, but it is a very different matter."

[1] Six pianoforte pieces, Op. 21.

To Modeste Tchaikovsky.

"PARIS, *April* 14*th* (26*th*), 1883
"(*Thursday in Passion Week*).

"DEAR MODI,—I am writing in a café in the Avenue Wagram. This afternoon I felt a sudden desire to be—if not actually in our church — at least somewhere in its vicinity. I am so fond of the service for to-day. To hold the wax-taper and make little pellets of wax after each gospel; at first, to feel a little impatient for the service to come to an end, and afterwards to feel sorry it is over! But I arrived too late, only in time to meet the people coming out and hear them speak Russian."

To N. F. von Meck.

"PARIS, *May* 3*rd* (15*th*), 1883.

" Loewenson's article, with its flattering judgment of me, does not give me much pleasure. I do not like the repetition of that long-established opinion that I am not a *dramatic musician*, and that I *pander* to the public. What does it mean — to have dramatic capabilities? Apparently Herr Loewenson is a Wagnerian, and believes Wagner to be a great master in this sphere. I consider him just the reverse. Wagner has genius, but he certainly does not understand the art of writing for the stage with breadth and simplicity, keeping the orchestra within bounds, so that it does not reduce the singers to mere speaking *puppets*. As to his assertion that I aim at effects to catch the taste of the great public, I can plead not guilty with a clear conscience. I have always written, and always shall write, with feeling and sincerity, never troubling myself as to what the public would think of my work. At the moment of composing, when I am aglow with emotion, it flashes across my mind that all who will hear the music will experience some reflection of what I am feeling myself. Then I think of someone whose interest I value—like yourself, for instance—but I have never deliberately tried to lower myself to the vulgar requirements of the crowd. If opera attracts me from time to time, it signifies that I have as much capacity for this as for any other form. If I have had many failures in this branch of music, it only proves that I am a long way from perfection, and make the same mistakes in my operas as in my symphonic and chamber music, among which there are many unsuccessful compositions. If I live a few years longer, perhaps I may see my *Maid of Orleans* suitably interpreted, or my *Mazeppa* studied and staged as it should be ; and then possibly people may cease to say that I am incapable of writing a good opera. At the same time, I know how difficult it will be to conquer this prejudice against me as an operatic composer. This is carried to such lengths that Herr Loewenson, who knows nothing whatever of my new work, declares it will be a *useless sacrifice* to the Moloch of opera. . . ."

To N. F. von Meck.

"BERLIN, *May 12th (24th)*, 1883.

". . . A report has been circulated in many of the Paris papers that Rubinstein had refused to compose a Coronation Cantata because he was not in sympathy with the *central figure of the festivities*. As Rubinstein's children are being educated in Russia, and this might be prejudicial to his interests—for even the most baseless falsehood always leaves some trace behind it—I sent a brief *dementi* to the *Gaulois* the day I left Paris. I cannot say if it will be published.[1]

"To-day *Lohengrin* is being given. I consider it Wagner's best work, and shall probably go to the performance. To-morrow I leave for Petersburg."

In April, 1883, *Eugene Oniegin* was heard for the first time in St. Petersburg, when it was performed by the Amateur Dramatic and Musical Society in the hall of the Nobles' Club. It was coolly received, and the performance made so little impression that it was almost ignored by the Press. Soloviev, alone, wrote an article of some length in the St. Petersburg *Viedomosti*, in which he said :—

[1] The letter appeared on May 23rd (June 4th), 1883.

"Tchaikovsky's opera — apart from the libretto and stage effects—contains much that is musically attractive. Had the composer paid more attention to Poushkin's words and shown greater appreciation of their beauty; had he grasped the simplicity and naturalness of Poushkin's forms—the opera would have been successful. Having failed in these requirements, it is not surprising that the public received the work coldly. . . ."

Nevertheless the opera survived several performances. The lack of success—apart from the quality of the music, which never at any time aroused noisy demonstrations of applause—must be attributed to the performance, which was excellent for amateurs, but still left much to be desired from the artistic point of view.

To N. F. von Meck.

"PETERSBURG, *May 24th* (*June 5th*), 1883.

" I hear the Cantata was admirably sung and won the Emperor's approval."

To N. F. von Meck.

"PODOUSHKINO, *June 15th* (*27th*), 1883.

" In my youth I often felt indignant at the apparent injustice with which Providence dealt out happiness and misfortune to mankind. Gradually I have come to the conviction that from our limited, earthly point of view we cannot possibly comprehend the aims and ends towards which God guides us on our way through life. Our sufferings and deprivations are not sent blindly and fortuitously; they are needful for our good, and although the good may seem very far away, some day we shall realise this. Experience has taught me that suffering and bitterness are frequently for our good, even in this life. But after this life *perhaps* there is another, and—although my intellect cannot conceive what form it may take—my heart and my instinct, which revolt from death in the sense of complete annihilation, compel me to believe in it.

Perhaps we may then understand the things which now appear to us harsh and unjust. Meanwhile, we can only pray, and thank God when He sends us happiness, and submit when misfortune overtakes us, or those who are near and dear to us. I thank God who has given me this conviction. Without it life would be a grievous burden. Did I not know that you, the best of human beings, and above all deserving of happiness, were suffering so much, not through an insensate blow aimed by a blind destiny, but for some divine end which my limited reason cannot discern—then, indeed, there would remain for me in life nothing but despair and loathing. I have learnt not to murmur against God, but to pray to Him for all who are dear to me."

To Modeste Tchaikovsky.

"Podoushkino,[1] *July 3rd* (15*th*), 1883.

"My incapacity for measuring time correctly is really astonishing! I believed I should find leisure this summer for everything—for reading, correspondence, walks; and suddenly I realise that from morning to night I am tormented with the thought that I have not got through all there was to do. . . . Added to which, instead of resting from composition, I have taken it into my head to write a Suite. Inspiration will not come; every day I begin something and lose heart. Then, instead of waiting for inspiration, I begin to be afraid lest I am played out, with the result that I am thoroughly dissatisfied with myself. And yet the conditions of life are satisfactory: wonderful scenery and the society of those I love. . . ."

During this visit to Podoushkino, Tchaikovsky wrote to Jurgenson concerning their business relations. Actually, this connection remained unbroken to the end of the composer's life, but at this moment it suffered a temporary strain. Tchaikovsky acknowledged that his publisher had often been most generous in his payments, but as

[1] From Petersburg Tchaikovsky went on a visit to his brother Anatol, who had taken summer quarters at Podoushkino, near Moscow.

regards his new opera *Mazeppa* he felt aggrieved at the small remuneration proposed by Jurgenson. This work, he said, ought, logically speaking, to be worth ten times as much as ten songs, or ten indifferent pianoforte pieces. He valued it at 2,400 roubles (£240). On the other hand, he asked no fee for his Coronation Cantata.

To N. F. von Meck.

"PODOUSHKINO, *August* 10*th* (22*nd*), 1883.

"Yesterday a council was held by the Opera Direction to consider the staging of *Mazeppa*. Everyone connected with the Opera House was present. I was astonished at the zeal—I may say enthusiasm—which they showed for my opera. Formerly what trouble I had to get an opera accepted and performed! Now, without any advances on my part, Petersburg and Moscow contend for my work. I was told yesterday that the direction at St. Petersburg had sent the scenic artist Bocharov to Little Russia, in order to study on the spot the moonlight effect in the last act of *Mazeppa*. I cannot understand the reason of such attentions on the part of the theatrical world—there must be some secret cause for it, and I can only surmise that the Emperor himself must have expressed a wish that my opera should be given as well as possible in both capitals.[1]

"The corrections are now complete, and I am sending you the first printed copy. Dear friend, now I must take a little rest from composition, and lie fallow for a time. But the *cacoethes scribendi* possesses me, and all my leisure hours are devoted to a Suite. I hope to finish it in a day or two, and set to work upon the instrumentation at Kamenka.

"My health is better. I have gone through such a terrible attack of nervous headache, I thought I must have died. I fell asleep so worn out, I had not even strength to undress. When I awoke I was well."

---

[1] This agreeable change in the attitude of the authorities towards Tchaikovsky was due to the influence of I. Vsievolojsky, who had recently been appointed Director of the Opera House.

XVII

1883–1884

To N. F. von Meck.

"VERBOVKA, *September* 10*th* (22*nd*), 1883.

"With regard to my opera, you have picked out at first sight the numbers I consider the best. The scene between Mazeppa and Maria will, thanks to Poushkin's magnificent verses, produce an effect even off the stage. It is a pity you will not be able to see a performance of *Mazeppa.* Allow me, dear friend, to point out other parts of the opera which can easily be studied from the pianoforte score: In Act I. (1), the duet between Maria and Andrew; (2), Mazeppa's *arioso.* Act II. (1), the prison scene; (2), Maria's scene with her mother. Act III., the last duet."

To M. Tchaikovsky.

"VERBOVKA, *September* 12*th* (24*th*), 1883.

". . . I bought Glazounov's Quartet in Kiev, and was pleasantly surprised. In spite of the imitations of Korsakov, in spite of the tiresome way he has of contenting himself with the endless repetition of an idea, instead of its development, in spite of the neglect of melody and the pursuit of all kinds of harmonic eccentricities—the composer has undeniable talent. The form is so perfect, it astonishes me, and I suppose his teacher helped him in this. I recommend you to buy the Quartet and play it for four hands. I have also Cui's opera, *The Prisoner of the Caucasus.* This is utterly insignificant, weak, and childishly naïve. It is most remarkable that a critic who has contended throughout his days against routine, should now, in the evening of his life, write a work so shamefully conventional."

To Modeste Tchaikovsky.

"VERBOVKA, *September 19th (October 1st),* 1883.

". . . On my arrival here I found a parcel from Tkat-chenko at Poltava. It contained all my letters to him. As on a former occasion, when he thought of committing suicide, he sent me back two of my letters, I understood at once that he wished by this means to intimate his immediate intention of putting an end to his existence. At first I was somewhat agitated ; then I calmed myself with the reflection that my Tkatchenko was certainly still in this world. In fact, to-day I received a letter from him asking for money, but without a word about my letters. His, as usual, is couched in a scornful tone. He is a man to be pitied, but not at all sympathetic." [1]

To M. Tchaikovsky.

"VERBOVKA, *September 26th (October 8th),* 1883.

" My Suite progresses slowly ; but it seems likely to be successful. I am almost sure the Scherzo (with the Har-monica) and the Andante ('Children's Dreams') will please. My enthusiasm for *Judith* has made way for a passion for *Carmen.* I have also been playing Rimsky-Korsakov's *Night in May*, not without some enjoyment."

To Frau von Meck.

"VERBOVKA, *September 28th (October 10th),* 1883.

" I will tell you frankly, dear friend, that, although I gladly hear some operas—and even compose them myself —your somewhat paradoxical view of the untenability of operatic music pleases me all the same. Leo Tolstoi says the same with regard to opera, and strongly advised me to give up the pursuit of theatrical success. In *Peace and War* he makes his heroine express great astonishment and dissatisfaction with the falseness and limitations of operatic action. Anyone who, like yourself, does not live in society and is not therefore trammelled by its conven-

---

[1] This was the end of all relations between Tchaikovsky and Tkatchenko.

tions, or who, like Tolstoi, has lived for years in a village and only been occupied with domestic events, literature, and educational questions, must naturally feel more intensely than others the complete falseness of Opera. I, too, when I am writing an opera feel so constrained and fettered that I often think I will never compose another. Nevertheless, we must acknowledge that many beautiful things of the first order belong to the sphere of dramatic music, and that the men who wrote them were directly inspired by the dramatic ideas. Were there no such thing as opera, there would be no *Don Juan*, no *Figaro*, no *Russlan and Lioudmilla.* Of course, from the point of view of the sane mind, it is senseless for people on the stage—which should reflect reality—to sing instead of speaking. People have got used to this absurdity, however, and when I hear the sextet in *Don Giovanni* I never think that what is taking place before me is subversive of the requirements of artistic truth. I simply enjoy the music, and admire the astonishing art of Mozart, who knew how to give each of the six voices its own special character, and has outlined each personality so sharply that, forgetful of the lack of *absolute truth*, I marvel at the depth of *conditional truth*, and my intellect is silenced.

"You tell me, dear friend, that in my *Eugene Oniegin* the musical pattern is more beautiful than the canvas on which it is worked. I must say, however, that if my music to *Eugene Oniegin* has the qualities of warmth and poetic feeling, it is because my own emotions were quickened by the beauty of the subject. I think it is altogether unjust to see nothing beautiful in Poushkin's poem but the versification. Tatiana is not merely a provincial ' Miss,' who falls in love with a dandy from the capital. She is a young and virginal being, untouched as yet by the realities of life, a creature of pure feminine beauty, a dreamy nature, ever seeking some vague ideal, and striving passionately to grasp it. So long as she finds nothing that resembles an ideal, she remains unsatisfied but tranquil. It needs only the appearance of a man who—at least externally—stands out from the commonplace surroundings in which she lives, and at once she imagines her ideal has come, and in her passion becomes oblivious of self.

Poushkin has portrayed the power of this virginal love with such genius that—even in my childhood—it touched me to the quick. If the fire of inspiration really burned within me when I composed the 'Letter Scene,' it was Poushkin who kindled it; and I frankly confess, without false modesty, that I should be proud and happy if my music reflected only a tenth part of the beauty contained in the poem. In the 'Duel Scene' I see something far more significant than you do. Is it not highly dramatic and touching that a youth so brilliant and gifted (as Lensky) should lose his life because he has come into fatal collision with a false code of mundane 'honour'? Could there be a more dramatic situation than that in which that 'lion' of town-life (Oniegin), partly from *sheer boredom*, partly from petty annoyance, but without purpose—led by a fatal chain of circumstances—shoots a young man to whom he is really attached? All this is very simple, very ordinary, if you like, but poetry and the drama do not exclude matters of simple, everyday life."

To N. F. von Meck.

"KAMENKA, *October 11th (23rd)*, 1883.

" My work is nearly finished. Consequently, so long as I have no fresh composition in view, I can quietly enjoy this glorious autumn weather.

" My Suite has five movements: (1) Jeux de sons, (2) Valse, (3) Scherzo burlesque, (4) Rêves d'enfants, (5) Danse baroque."

To N. F. von Meck.

" *October 25th (November 6th)*, 1883.

" Every time I finish a work I think rapturously of a season of complete idleness. But nothing ever comes of it; scarcely has the holiday begun, before I weary of idleness and plan a new work. This, in turn, takes such a hold on me that I immediately begin again to rush through it with unnecessary haste. It seems my lot to be always hurrying to finish something. I know this is equally bad for my nerves and my work, but I cannot control myself. I only rest when I am on a journey;

that is why travelling has such a beneficial effect on my health. Probably I shall never settle anywhere, but lead a nomadic existence to the end of my days. Just now I am composing an album of 'Children's Songs,' an idea I have long purposed carrying out. It is very pleasant work, and I think the little songs will have a great success."

To Frau von Meck.

"KAMENKA, *November 1st (13th)*, 1883.

"I should feel quite happy and contented here, were it not for the morbid, restless need of hurrying on my work, which tires me dreadfully, without being in the least necessary. . . .

"I had a fancy to renew my study of English. This would be harmless, were I content to devote my leisure hours quietly to the work. But no: here again, I am devoured by impatience to master enough English to read Dickens easily, and I devote so many hours a day to this occupation that, with the exception of breakfast, dinner, and the necessary walk, I literally spend every minute in hurrying madly to the end of something. This is certainly a disease. Happily, this feverish activity will soon come to an end, as my summons to the rehearsals in Moscow will shortly be due."

XVIII

Towards the end of November Tchaikovsky left Kamenka for Moscow, where, after a lapse of sixteen years, his First Symphony was given at a concert of the Musical Society. He was greatly annoyed to find that the preparations for *Mazeppa* were proceeding with exasperating slowness. "It is always the way with a State theatre," he wrote at this time to Nadejda von Meck. "Much promised, little performed." While at Moscow, he played his new Suite to some of the leading musicians, who highly approved of the work.

A few days later he went to meet Modeste in Petersburg. He left the dry cold of a beautiful Russian winter in Moscow, and found the more northern capital snowless, but windy, chilly, and "so dark in the morning that even near the window I can hardly see to write."

The journeys to and fro involved by the business connected with *Mazeppa*, and all the other difficulties he had to encounter in connection with it, were very irksome to Tchaikovsky. At this time he vowed never to write another opera, since it involved the sacrifice of so much time and freedom.

To N. F. von Meck.

"Moscow, *December* 11*th* (23*rd*), 1883.

"How can you think me capable of taking offence at anything you may say, especially with regard to my music? I cannot always agree with you, but to be offended because your views are not mine would be impossible. On the contrary, I am invariably touched by the warmth with which you speak of my compositions, and the originality and independence of your judgment pleased me from the first. For instance, I am glad that, in spite of my having composed six operas, when you compare Opera with Symphony or Chamber music, you do not hesitate to speak of it as a lower form of art. In my heart I have felt the same, and intend henceforth to renounce operatic music; although you must acknowledge opera possesses the advantage of touching the musical feeling of the *masses;* whereas symphony appeals only to a smaller, if more select, public. . . ."

Christmas and the New Year found Tchaikovsky still in Moscow, awaiting the rehearsals for *Mazeppa*. As usual, when circumstances detained him for any length of time in town, he suffered under the social gaieties which he had not the strength of will to decline. Laroche was staying in the same hotel as Tchaikovsky, and was in a hypochondriacal condition. "He needs a *nurse*," says Tchaikovsky in one of his letters, "and I have undertaken the part, having no work on hand just now. When I depart, he will relapse into the same apathetic state."

At last, on January 15th (27th), the rehearsals for the opera began, and with them a period of feverish excitement. The preparations for *Mazeppa* had been so long postponed that they now coincided with the staging of the work in Petersburg. Tchaikovsky declined the invitation to be present at the rehearsals there, feeling he could safely entrust his opera to the experienced supervision of Napravnik.

The first performance of *Mazeppa* in Moscow took place on February 3rd (15th), under the direction of H. Altani. The house was crowded and brilliant. The audience was favourably disposed towards the composer, and showed it by unanimous recalls for him and for the performers. Nevertheless, Tchaikovsky felt instinctively that the ovations were accorded to him personally, and to such of the singers who were favourites with the public, rather than to the opera itself. The ultimate fate of *Mazeppa*, which attracted a full house on several occasions, but only kept its place in the repertory for a couple of seasons, confirmed this impression. The failure may be attributed in some degree to the quality of the performance. Some of the singers had no voices, and those who were gifted in this respect lacked the necessary musical and histrionic training, so that not one number of the opera was rightly interpreted. Only the chorus was irreproachable. As regards the scenery and dresses, no opera had ever been so brilliantly staged. The Moscow critics were fairly indulgent to the opera and to its composer. To Nadejda von Meck, Tchaikovsky wrote: " The opera was successful in the sense that the singers and myself received ovations. . . . I cannot attempt to tell you what I went through that day. I was nearly crazed with excitement."

2 G

To E. Pavlovskaya.[1]

"Moscow, *February 4th* (16th), 1884.

"DEAR AND SUPERB EMILIE KARLOVNA,—I thank you heartily, incomparable Maria, for your indescribably beautiful performance of this part. God give you happiness and success. I shall never forget the deep impression made upon me by your splendid talent."

After informing a few friends of his intended journey— amongst them Erdmannsdörfer—Tchaikovsky left Moscow just at the moment when the public had gathered in the Concert Hall to hear his new Suite.

The Suite (No. 2 in C) had such a genuine and undisputed success under Erdmannsdörfer's excellent direction on February 4th (16th), that it had to be repeated by general request at the next symphony concert, a week later. The Press was unanimous in its enthusiasm, and even the severe Krouglikov was moved to lavish and unconditional praise.

The Petersburg performance of *Mazeppa*, under Napravnik, took place on February 7th (19th). The absence of the composer naturally lessened its immediate success, but the impression was essentially the same as in Moscow: the opera obtained a mere *succès d'estime*. As regards acting, the performance of the chief parts (Mazeppa and Maria) was far less effective than at its original production. On the other hand, the staging and costumes excelled in historical fidelity and brillancy even those of the Moscow performance. Comparing the reception of *Mazeppa* in the two capitals, we must award the palm to the Petersburg critics for the unanimity with which they "damned" the work.

---

[1] The singer who created the part of Maria in the Moscow performance of *Mazeppa*.

To N. F. von Meck.

"BERLIN, *February 7th* (19*th*), 1884.

"Early this morning I received a telegram from Modeste, who informs me that the performance of *Mazeppa* in Petersburg yesterday was a complete success, and that the Emperor remained to the end and was much pleased.[1] To morrow I continue my journey to Paris and from thence to Italy, where I might possibly join Kolya and Anna,[2] unless I should disturb their *tête-à-tête*. I dread being alone. . . ."

To M. Tchaikovsky.

"PARIS, *February* 18*th* (*March* 1*st*), 1884.

"Modi, I can well imagine how difficult it must have been for you to lie to me as to the '*grand succès*' of *Mazeppa* in Petersburg. But you did well to tell a lie, for the *truth* would have been too great a blow, had I not been prepared for it by various indications. Only yesterday did I learn the worst in a letter from Jurgenson, who not only had the cruelty to blurt out the plain truth, but also to reproach me for not having gone to Petersburg. It came as a thunderbolt upon me, and all day I suffered, as though some dreadful catastrophe had taken place. Of course, this is exaggeration, but at my age, when one has nothing more to hope in the future, a slight failure assumes the dimensions of a shameful fiasco. Were I different, could I have forced myself to go to Petersburg, no doubt I should have returned crowned with laurel wreaths. . . ."

To P. Jurgenson.

"PARIS, *February* 18*th* (*March* 1*st*), 1884.

"It is an old truth that no one can hurt so cruelly as a dear friend. Your reproach is very bitter. Do you not understand that I know better than anyone else how

---

[1] On account of Tchaikovsky's nervous condition the account of the success of *Mazeppa* was slightly overdrawn.

[2] Nicholas and Anna von Meck, *née* Davidov (Tchaikovsky's niece), who were on their wedding tour.

much I lose, and how greatly I injure my own success, by my unhappy temperament? As a card-sharper, who has cheated all his life, lifts his hand against the man who has made him realise what he is, so nothing makes me so angry as the phrase: 'You have only yourself to blame.' It is true in this case; but can I help being what I am? The comparative failure of *Mazeppa* in Petersburg, of which your letter informed me, has wounded me deeply—very deeply. I am in a mood of darkest despair."

To N. F. von Meck.

"PARIS, *February 27th* (*March 10th*), 1884.

"You have justly observed that the Parisians have become Wagnerites. But in their enthusiasm for Wagner, which is carried so far that they neglect even Berlioz—who, a few years ago, was the idol of the Paris public—there is something insincere, artificial, and without any real foundation. I cannot believe that *Tristan and Isolde*, which is so intolerably wearisome on the stage, could ever charm the Parisians. . . . It would not surprise me that such excellent operas as *Lohengrin, Tannhäuser*, and the *Flying Dutchman* should remain in the repertory. These, originating from a composer of the first rank, must sooner or later become of general interest. The operas of the later period, on the contrary, are false in principle; they renounce artistic simplicity and veracity, and can only live in Germany, where Wagner's name has become the watch-word of German patriotism. . . ."

To N. F. von Meck.

"PARIS, *February 29th* (*March 12th*), 1884.

". . . Napravnik writes that the Emperor was much astonished at my absence from the first performance of *Mazeppa*, and that he showed great interest in my music; he has also commanded a performance of *Eugene Oniegin*, his favourite opera. Napravnik thinks I must not fail to go to Petersburg to be presented to the Emperor. I feel if I neglect to do this I shall be worried by the thought that the Emperor might consider me ungrateful, and so I have decided to start at once. It is very hard, and I have to make a great effort to give up the chance of a holiday in the country and begin again with fresh excitements. But it has to be done."

XIX

The official command to appear before their Imperial Majesties was due to the fact that on February 23rd (March 6th), 1884, the order of St. Vladimir of the Fourth Class had been conferred upon Tchaikovsky. The presentation took place on March 7th (19th), at Gatchina. Tchaikovsky was so agitated beforehand that he had to take several strong doses of bromide in order to regain his self-possession. The last dose was actually swallowed on the threshold of the room where the Empress was awaiting him, in agony lest he should lose consciousness from sheer nervous breakdown.

To Anatol Tchaikovsky.

"PETERSBURG, *March 10th (22nd),* 1884.

"I will give you a brief account of what took place. Last Saturday I was taken with a severe chill. By morning I felt better, but I was terribly nervous at the idea of being presented to the Emperor and Empress. On Monday at ten o'clock I went to Gatchina. I had only permission to appear before His Majesty, but Prince Vladimir Obolensky had also arranged an audience with the Empress, who had frequently expressed a wish to see me. I was first presented to the Emperor and then to the Empress. Both were most friendly and kind. I think it is only necessary to look once into the Emperor's eyes, in order to remain for ever his most loyal adherent, for it is difficult to express in words all the charm and sympathy of his manner. She is also bewitching. Afterwards I had to visit the Grand Duke Constantine Nicholaevich, and yesterday I sat with him in the Imperial box during the whole of the rehearsal at the Conservatoire."

To N. F. von Meck.

"PETERSBURG, *March* 13*th* (25*th*), 1884.

"What a madman I am! How easily I am affected by the least shadow of ill-luck! Now I am ashamed of the depression which came over me in Paris, simply because I gathered from the newspapers that the performance of *Mazeppa* in Petersburg had not really had the success I anticipated! Now I see that in spite of the ill-feeling of many local musicians, in spite of the wretched performance, the opera really pleased, and there is no question of reproach, as I feared while I was so far away. There is no doubt that the critics, who unanimously strove to drag my poor opera through the mire, were not expressing the universal opinion, and that many people here are well disposed towards me. What pleases me most is the fact that the Emperor himself stands at the head of this friendly section. It turns out that I have no right to complain; on the contrary, I ought rather to thank God, who has shown me such favour.

"Have you seen Count Leo Tolstoi's *Confessions*, which were to have come out recently in the *Russkaya Myssl* ('Russian Thought'), but were withdrawn by order of the Censor? They have been privately circulated in manuscript, and I have just succeeded in reading them. They made a profound impression upon me, because I, too, know the torments of doubt and the tragic perplexity which Tolstoi has experienced and described so wonderfully in the *Confessions*. But *enlightenment* came to me earlier than Tolstoi; perhaps because my brain is more simply organised than his; and perhaps it has been due to the continual necessity of work that I have suffered less than Tolstoi. Every day, every hour, I thank God for having given me this faith in Him. What would have become of me, with my cowardice, my capacity for depression, and—at the least failure of courage—my desire for *non-existence*, unless I had been able to believe in God and submit to His will?"

About the end of the seventies Tchaikovsky kept an accurate diary. Ten years later he relaxed the habit, and only made entries in his day-book while abroad, or on important occasions. Two years before his death the composer burnt most of these volumes, including all those which covered the years between his journeys abroad in 1873 and April, 1884.

The following are a few entries from the later diaries:—

"*April 13th (25th)*, 1884.

". . . After tea I went to Leo's,[1] who soon went out, while I remained to strum and think of something new. I hit upon an idea for a pianoforte Concerto [afterwards the Fantasia for pianoforte, op. 56], but it is poor and not new. . . . Played Massenet's *Hérodiade*. . . read some of Otto Jahn's *Life of Mozart*."

On April 16th (28th) Tchaikovsky began his third orchestral Suite, and we can follow the evolution of this work, as noted from day to day in his diary.

"*April 16th (28th)*, 1884.

"In the forest and indoors I have been trying to lay the foundation of a new symphony . . . but I am not at all satisfied. . . . Walked in the garden and found the germ, not of a symphony, but of a future Suite."

"*April 17th (29th)*.

". . . Jotted down a few ideas."

"*April 19th (May 1st)*.

"Annoyed with my failures. Very dissatisfied because everything that comes into my head is so commonplace. Am I played out?"

April 24th (May 6th).

"I shall soon be forty-four. How much I have been through, and—without false modesty—how little I have accomplished! In my actual vocation I must say—hand on heart—I have achieved nothing perfect, nothing which can serve as a model. I am still seeking, vacillating.

---

[1] His brother-in-law, Leo Davidov.

And in other matters? I read nothing, I know nothing. . . . The period of quiet, undisturbed existence is over for me. There remain agitation, conflict, much that I, such as I am, find hard to endure. No, the time has come to live by *oneself* and in *one's own way !*"

"*April 26th (May 8th).*

"This morning I worked with all my powers at the Scherzo of the Suite. Shall work again after tea."

"*April 30th (May 12th),* 1884.

"Worked all day at the Valse (Suite), but without any conviction of success."

Extracts from a Letter to Anna Merkling.

"KAMENKA, *April 27th (May 9th),* 1884.

"Many thanks, dear Anna, for your thought of me on the 25th (May 7th). . . . Without bitterness, I receive congratulations upon the fact that I am a year older. I have no wish to die, and I desire to attain a ripe old age; but I would not willingly have my youth back and go through life again. Once is enough! The past, of which you speak with regret, I too regret it, for no one likes better to be lost in memories of old days, no one feels more keenly the emptiness and brevity of life—but I do not wish to be young again. . . . I cannot but feel that the sum total of good which I enjoy at present is far greater than that which stood to my credit in youth: therefore I do not in the least regret my forty-and-four years. Nor sixty, nor seventy, provided I am still sound mentally and physically! At the same time one ought not to fear death. In this respect I cannot boast. I am not sufficiently penetrated by religion to regard death as the beginning of a new life, nor am I sufficiently philosophical to be satisfied with the prospect of *annihilation.* I envy no one so much as the religious man. . . ."

Diary.

"*May 2nd (14th).*

"The Valse gives me infinite trouble. I am growing old. . . ."

"*May 6th* (18*th Sunday*).

"Went to church. I was very susceptible to religious impressions, and felt the tears in my eyes. The simple, healthy, religious spirit of the poorer classes always touches me profoundly. The worn-out old man, the little lad of four, who goes to the holy water of his own accord."

"*May 8th* (20*th*), 1884.

"Worked all morning. Not without fatigue, but my Andante progresses, and seems likely to turn out quite nice . . . finished the Andante. I am very pleased with it."

At this time Tchaikovsky resolved to take a small country house on his own account. "I want no land," he wrote to Nadejda von Meck, "only a little house, with a pretty garden, *not too new*. A *stream* is most desirable. The neighbourhood of a forest (which belonged to someone else) would be an attraction. The house must stand alone, not in a row of country villas, and, most important of all, be within easy reach of a station, so that I can get to Moscow at any time. I cannot afford more than two to three thousand roubles."

Diary.
"*May* 11*th* (23*rd*), 1884.

"The first movement of the Suite, which is labelled 'Contrasts,' and the theme ·

has grown so hateful since I tormented myself about it all day long that I resolved to set it aside and invent something else. After dinner I squeezed the unsuccessful movement out of my head. What does it mean? I now work with such difficulty! Am I really growing old?

"*May 12th (24th).*

"After tea I took up the hateful 'Contrasts' once more. Suddenly a new idea flashed across me, and the whole thing began to flow."

"*May 17th (29th).*

"Played Mozart, and enjoyed it immensely. An idea for a Suite from Mozart."

"*May 18th (30th).*

"I am working too strenuously, as though I were being driven. This haste is unhealthy, and will, perhaps, reflect upon the poor Suite. My work (upon the variations before the finale) has been very successful. . . ."

"*May 21st (June 2nd).*

"Worked well. Four variations completed."

"*May 23rd (June 4th).*

". . . . The Suite is finished."

To P. Jurgenson.

"GRANKINO, *June 20th (July 2nd),* 1884.

"I live here in a very pleasant way, a quiet, countrified existence, but I work hard. A work of greater genius than the new Suite never was!!! My opinion of the new-born composition is so optimistic; God knows what I shall think of it a year hence. At least it has cost me some pains."

To S. I. Taneiev.

"GRANKINO, *June 30th (July 12th),* 1884.

". . . . Although it was interesting to hear your opinion of my songs, I was rather angry with you for saying nothing whatever about your own work, plans, etc.

"Your criticisms of the songs—the end of the 'Legend,' and the abuse of the minor in the 'Lied vom Winter'— are very just. . . . I should like to say your praise was equally well deserved, but modesty forbids. So I will not say you are right, but that I am pleased with your commendations. . .

" At the present moment I am composing a third Suite. I wanted to write a Symphony, but it was not a success. However, the title is of no consequence. I have composed a big symphonic work in four movements: (1) Andante; (2) another Valse; (3) Scherzo; (4) Theme and Variations. It will be finished by the end of the summer, for I am working regularly and with zeal. Besides this, I am planning a concert-piece for pianoforte in two movements. It would be a fine thing if the work could be played during the coming season ! "

To N. F. von Meck.

" GRANKINO, *July 14th (26th),* 1884.

" I shall not set to work upon the pianoforte Concerto, of which I wrote to you, before autumn or early winter. Of course, it will be difficult ever again to find such an ideal interpreter as Nicholas Rubinstein, but there is a pianist whom I had in my mind when I thought of a second Concerto. This is a certain young man, called d'Albert, who was in Moscow last winter, and whom I heard several times in public and at private houses. To my mind he is a pianist of *genius,* the legitimate successor of Rubinstein. Taneiev—whom I value very highly as musician, teacher, and theorist—would also be a suitable interpreter, if he had just that *vein of virtuosity* wherein lies the secret of the magic spell which great interpreters exercise over the public."

To Modeste Tchaikovsky.

" SKABEIEVKA, *July 28th (August 9th),* 1884.

" The coachman will have told you our adventures. All went well as far as Kochenovka. There I had supper, and read *Sapho* by the mingled light of the moon and a lantern, keeping an anxious eye upon the lightning that was flashing all around. At 11.30 p.m. we resumed our journey. The storm came nearer and nearer, until it broke over our heads. Although the constant flashes were mild, and the rain wetted us through, my nerves were overstrained. I was convinced we should miss the train. . . . Fortunately it was late. Here we had an appalling storm. The sight of it at the hour of sunset, which still glowed here and there through the clouds, was so grand that, forgetful of my fears, I stood by the door to watch it. The rest of the journey was comfortable. I read *Sapho*, which I do not like."

To N. F. von Meck.

"SKABEIEVKA, *July 25th* (*August 6th*), 1884.

". . . You ask my opinion upon Daudet's *Sapho* . . . in spite of his great talent, this author has long since dropped out of favour with me. If Daudet had not dedicated the book to his sons in order to display the fact that it contained a lesson and a warning, I should say that he had described the sensuality and depravity of the hero and heroine very simply and picturesquely, with considerable sympathy. But in view of this dedication I feel indignant at the Pharisaism and false virtuousness of the author. In reality he wants to tickle the depraved taste of his public, and describes with cynical frankness the immorality of Parisian life, while pretending to deliver a sermon to his sons. He would have us believe him to be pursuing a moral aim, actuated by the noble aspiration of saving the young from evil ways. In reality his only aim was to produce a book which would please the immoral Parisian public, and to make money by it. One must own that he has attained his object. The book will have a great success, like Zola's *Pot-Bouille*, the novels of Guy de Maupassant, and similar works of the new French school. When we reflect upon the group of people, and their way of life, as depicted by the author, we come to the conclusion that under the cloak of verisimilitude and realism the novel is fundamentally false. Sapho is an impossible being; at least I never came across a similar combination of honourable feeling and baseness, of nobility and infamy. Yet the author always sympathises with his heroine, and although, judging from the dedication, she is intended to inspire his sons with horror and repulsion, she must really seem very attractive to them. On the other hand, the virtuous characters in the book could not appeal sympathetically either to Daudet's sons, or to anyone else; the tiresome Divonne, the hero's impossible sister, and the rest of them—all these people are quite artificial. Sapho is an overdrawn type of a Parisian cocotte, but there is something true to nature in her. The others are not alive. Most insipid of all is Irène. Any young man reading the book must realise why Sapho succeeded in supplanting her in the heart of her husband Jean. It is here that Daudet's hypocrisy is so evident, for while we ought to sympathise with Irène as greatly as we despise Sapho, in reality we involuntarily take the part of the depraved heroine. At the same time we cannot deny the great talent and mastery displayed in the book. Two or three dozen pages are wonderfully written."

XX

Early in September, 1884, Tchaikovsky went to stay at Plestcheievo, a country property which Nadejda von Meck had purchased after circumstances compelled her to sell Brailov. Here he led the kind of life which suited him best—reading, composing, and studying the works of other musicians, in undisturbed quiet and freedom from social duties.

To N. F. von Meck.

" PLESTCHEIEVO, *September 8th (20th)*, 1884.

" I have realised two intentions since I came here—the study of two works hitherto unknown to me—Moussorgsky's *Khovanstchina* and Wagner's *Parsifal*. In the first I discovered what I expected : pretensions to realism, original conceptions and methods, wretched technique, poverty of invention, occasionally clever episodes, amid an ocean of harmonic absurdities and affectations. . . . *Parsifal* leaves an entirely opposite impression. Here we are dealing with a great master, a genius, even if he has gone somewhat astray. His wealth of harmony is so luxuriant, so vast, that at length it becomes fatiguing, even to a specialist. What then must be the feelings of an ordinary mortal who has wrestled for three hours with this flow of complicated harmonic combinations? To my mind Wagner has killed his colossal creative genius with *theories*. Every preconceived theory chills his incontestable creative impulse. How could Wagner abandon himself to inspiration, while he believed he was grasping some particular theory of music-drama, or musical truth, and, for the sake of this, turned from all that, according to his predecessors, constituted the strength and beauty of music? If the singer may not *sing*, but—amid the deafening clamour of the orchestra—is expected to declaim a series of set and colourless phrases, to the accompaniment of a gorgeous, but disconnected and formless symphony, is that opera?

"What really astounds me, however, is the seriousness with which this philosophising German sets the most inane subjects to music. Who can be touched, for instance, by *Parsifal*, in which, instead of having to deal with men and women similar in temperament and feeling to ourselves, we find legendary beings, suitable perhaps for a ballet, but not for a music drama? I cannot understand how anyone can listen without laughter, or without being bored, to those endless monologues in which Parsifal, or Kundry, and the rest bewail their misfortunes. Can we sympathise with them? Can we love or hate them? Certainly not; we remain aloof from their passions, sentiments, triumphs, and misfortunes. But that which is unfamiliar to the human heart should never be the source of musical inspiration. . . ."

To N. F. von Meck.

"PLESTCHEIEVO, *October 3rd* (15*th*), 1884.

"This is my last evening here, and I feel both sadness and dread. After a month of complete solitude it is not easy to return to the vortex of Petersburg life. To-day I put all the bookshelves and music-cases in order. My conscience is clear as to all your belongings. But I must confess to one mishap: one night I wound the big clock in my bedroom with such energy that the weights fell off, and it now wants repairing. Dear and incomparable friend, accept my warmest thanks for your hospitality. I shall keep the most agreeable memories of Plestcheievo.

How often, when I am in Petersburg, will my thoughts stray back to this dear, quiet house! Thank you again and again."

To N. F. von Meck.

"PETERSBURG, *October* 12*th* (24*th*), 1884.

"DEAR FRIEND,—When a whole week passes without my finding time to write to you, you may conclude what a busy life I am leading. . . . The first night[1] of *Eugene Oniegin* is fixed for Friday, October 19th (31st)."

Thanks to Napravnik, this was by far the finest performance of *Eugene Oniegin* that had hitherto been seen. Never had this complicated score received so perfect an interpretation, both as a whole and as regards detail, because never before had a man so gifted, so capable and sympathetic, stood at the head of affairs. Yet even this first performance was by no means irreproachable. Since then, the St. Petersburg public has heard finer interpretations of the parts of Tatiana, Eugene, and others, and has seen more careful staging of the work. The soloists gave a thoughtful rendering of their parts, but nothing more. Not one of them can be said to have "created" his or her part, or left a traditional reading of it.

The success of the opera was great, but not phenomenal. There was no hissing, but between the acts, mingled with expressions of praise and appreciation, many criticisms and ironical remarks were audible.

These unfavourable views came to light in the Press. Cui thought the mere choice of the libretto of *Eugene Oniegin* proved that Tchaikovsky was lacking in "discriminating taste," and was not capable of self-criticism. The chief characteristic of the opera was its "wearisome monotony." Tchaikovsky, he considered, was too fond of airing his troubles in his music. Finally, he pronounced the work to be "still-born, absolutely valueless and weak."

Most of the other critics agreed with this view.

[1] At the Imperial Opera.

Tchaikovsky himself was "satisfied." He had not realised, any more than the critics, that the crowded theatre signified the first great success of a Russian opera since Glinka's *A Life for the Tsar*. In spite of the Press notices, it was not merely a success, but a triumph; a fact which became more and more evident. Dating from the second performance, *Eugene Oniegin* drew a long series of packed audiences, and has remained the favourite opera of the Russian public to this day.

This success did not merely mark an important event in the history of Russian opera, it proved the beginning of a new era in the life of Tchaikovsky himself. Henceforward his name, hitherto known and respected among musicians and a fairly wide circle of musical amateurs, was now recognised by the great public, and he acquired a popularity to which no Russian composer had ever yet attained in his own land. Together with his increase of fame, his material prospects improved. *Eugene Oniegin* transformed him from a needy into a prosperous man, and brought him that complete independence which was so necessary to his creative work.

It is instructive to observe that all this was the outcome of an opera which was never intended to appeal to the masses; but written only to satisfy the composer's enthusiasm for Poushkin's poem, without any hope—almost without any desire—of seeing it performed on a large stage.

In spite of its success, this performance of *Eugene Oniegin* was a great strain upon the composer's nerves. He felt bound to stay for the second performance, after which he left St. Petersburg for Davos, having in view a twofold object: to take a short rest, and to visit his friend Kotek, of whose condition he had just received disquieting intelligence. Tchaikovsky broke his journey in Berlin, where he saw Weber's *Oberon* at the Opera. Instead of being bored by this work, as he expected, he enjoyed it very much. "The music is often enchanting," he wrote to his brother, "but the subject is absurd, in the style of *Zauberflöte*. However, it is amusing, and I roared with laughter in one place, where at the sound of the magic horn the entire *corps de ballet* fall flat on the stage and writhe in convulsions. . . . I also went to Bilse's and heard the Andante from my own quartet. This everlasting Andante ; they want to hear no other work of mine !"

On November 12th (24th) he arrived at Davos. He expected to find a wilderness, in which neither cigarettes nor cigars were to be had, and the civilised aspect of the place, the luxurious hotels, the shops, and the theatre made upon him the fantastic impression of a dream. He had dreaded the meeting with Kotek, lest his friend should be changed beyond recognition by the ravages of consumption. He was agreeably surprised to find him looking comparatively well. But this was only a first impression ; he soon realised that Kotek's condition was serious. He remained a few days at Davos, rejoiced his friend's heart by his presence, had a confidential interview with the doctor, and left for Paris on November 17th (29th), after having provided liberally for the welfare of the invalid.

To P. Jurgenson.

"ZURICH, *November 18th (30th)*, 1884.

" . . . I have received a letter from Stassov urging me to present the following manuscripts to the Imperial Public Library :

(1) 'Romeo and Juliet,'
(2) 'The Tempest,'
(3) 'Francesca,'
(4) 'The String Quartet, No. 3,'

and any others I like to send. Of the above works you do not possess the first two ('The Tempest' was lost long ago !), but please send him the others. . . . Be so good as to reply personally, or simply to send such scores as you can spare."

2 H

To M. Tchaikovsky.

"Paris, *December 3rd* (15*th*), 1884.

" I can scarcely tell you, dear Modi, how wearisome the last few days have been—although I cannot say why. It proceeds chiefly from home-sickness, the desire for a place of my own ; and even the knowledge that I start for Russia to-morrow brings no satisfaction, *because I have no home anywhere.* Life abroad no longer pleases me. . . . I must have a *home*, be it in Kamenka, or in Moscow. I cannot go on living the life of a wandering star. . . . Where will my *home* be ? "

With the year 1884 closes the second period in Tchaikovsky's artistic career. To distinguish it from the " Moscow period," which was inseparably connected with his teaching at the Conservatoire, it might be described as the " Kamenka period." Not only because from 1878–84 Kamenka was his chief place of residence, but still more because the life there answered to the whole sum of his requirements, to all which characterised his spiritual condition during these years. After the terrible illness in 1877 he found in Kamenka, far more than in San Remo, Clarens, or France, all he needed for his recovery ; during these seven years, it was at Kamenka that he gathered force and recuperated for the life which was becoming infinitely more strenuous and many-sided.

Those who have been at death's door often speak of their return to health as the happiest time in their lives. Tchaikovsky could say the same of the first years of the Kamenka period. Happy in the friendship of Nadejda von Meck and surrounded by his sister's family, who loved him, and whom he loved, his whole life shows no gladder days than these.

But with a gradual return to a normal state of mind Tchaikovsky's relations to his environment underwent a change. As the years went on, Kamenka became too

narrow a circle for him; he felt the want of "social intercourse"; the sympathy of his relations ceased to be the
one thing indispensable; the conditions of the family life
palled, and sometimes he grumbled at them. By the
middle of the eighties, he was so much stronger that he
was possessed by a desire for complete independence and
liberty of action. He no longer dreaded either *absolute
solitude, or the society of those whose interests were identical
with his own.* By *absolute solitude* we do not mean that
solitary leisure which he enjoyed during his visits to
Brailov and Simaki, during which he was cared for, as
in a fairy tale, by the invisible hand of the truest of
friends, but rather that independence and freedom in every
detail of existence which constitutes the solitude of the
typical bachelor's life.

In 1878 Tchaikovsky's dread of this kind of solitary
existence, like his fear of social intercourse, was a symptom
of his terrible mental suffering. Now his desire for both
independence and society must be regarded as a sign of
complete recovery. Hence his increasing disposition in
his letters to grumble at Kamenka, and his final decision
to leave it. This resolve—like so many important decisions
in Tchaikovsky's life—was not the result of mature reflection. As usual, he allowed himself to be guided by
negative conclusions. . . . He knew well enough that he
must and would change his manner of life; he knew the
kind of life that would suit him for the time being—that
must be in the country; he observed with surprise his increasing need of social intercourse—but he had no definite
idea how he should reconcile these contradictory requirements and, on the very eve of his new departure in life, he
asks the question: "Where will my home be made?'

The answer to this question is contained in the following period of his life and work.

PART VI

I

STRONG and energetic, fearing neither conflict nor effort, the Tchaikovsky who entered upon this new phase of life in no way resembled the man we knew in 1878.

The duties connected with his public career no longer dismayed him; on the contrary, they proved rather attractive, now he had strength to cope with them. At the same time interests stirred within him such as could not have been satisfied in his former restricted existence. Thanks to the enormous success of *Eugene Oniegin*, his fame had now reached every class in educated Russia, and he was compelled to accept a certain rôle which—at least, in these first days of success—was not unpleasant to him. He was glad to pay attentions to others, to help everyone who came his way, because by this means he could show his gratitude to the public for the enthusiastic reception accorded to his work. He was no longer a misanthropist, rather he sought those to whom he was dear, not only as a man, but as a personage. Amongst these, his old and faithful friends in Moscow took the first place. These intimacies were now renewed, and every fresh meeting with Laroche, Kashkin, Jurgenson, Albrecht, Hubert, and Taneiev gave him the keenest delight. Although death had separated him from Nicholas Rubinstein, he showed his devotion to the memory of his friend by taking the deepest interest in his orphaned children.

In February, 1885, Tchaikovsky was unanimously elected Director of the Moscow branch of the Russian Musical Society.

As the most popular musician in Russia, he no longer avoided intercourse with his fellow-workers. He was ready with advice, assistance and direction, and regarded it as a duty to answer every question addressed to him. His correspondence with his "colleagues" would fill a book in itself.

He received letters not only from professional musicians, but from amateurs, male and female, students, enthusiastic girls, officers, and even occasionally from priests. To all these letters he replied with astonishing conscientiousness and strove, in so far as he could, to fulfil all their requests, which often led to touching, or sometimes grotesque, expressions of gratitude from the recipients of his favours.

As a composer Tchaikovsky no longer stood aloof, leaving the fate of his compositions to chance; nor did he regard it as *infra dig.* to make them known through the medium of influential people. After a convalescence which had lasted seven years, Tchaikovsky returned to all these activities with vigour and enjoyment, although after a time his courage flagged, and all his strength of will had to be requisitioned to enable him "to keep up this sort of existence." Enthusiasm waned, and there succeeded—in his own words—"a life-weariness, and at times an insane depression; something hopeless, despairing, and final—and (as in every Finale) a sense of triviality."

The new conditions of his life are reflected in his constantly increasing circle of acquaintances. In every town he visited he made new friends, who were drawn to him with whole-hearted affection. With many of them he entered into brisk correspondence. In some cases this was continued until his death; in other instances the exchange of letters ceased after a year or two, to make way for a fresh correspondence.

The most important and interesting of Tchaikovsky's correspondents during this time are: Julie Spajinsky, wife of the well-known dramatist (1885–1891); Emilie Pavlovskaya, the famous singer, with whom Tchaikovsky became acquainted during the rehearsal for *Mazeppa* in 1884, and continued to correspond until 1888; the Grand Duke Constantine Constantinovich·; the composer Ippolitov-Ivanov and his wife, the well-known singer, Zaroudna; Vladimir Napravnik, son of the conductor: the pianists Sapellnikov and Siloti. With Glazounov, Désirée Artôt, Brodsky, Hubert, his cousin Anna Merkling, and many others, there was an occasional exchange of letters.

The greater part of these communications, notwithstanding the intimate style and frankness of the writer's nature, bear signs of effort, and give the impression of having been written for duty's sake. Taken as a whole, they are not so important, or so interesting, as the letters to Nadejda von Meck, and to Tchaikovsky's own family, belonging to the Moscow period.

The same may be said of the majority of new acquaintances made during the later years of his life, of which no epistolary record remains. These were so numerous that it would be impossible to speak of them individually. They included such personalities as Liadov, Altani, Grieg, Sophie Menter, Emil Sauer, Louis Diemer, Colonne, Carl Halir. Besides these, he was in touch with a vast number of people belonging to the most varied strata of social life. Among them was Legoshin, valet to his friend Kondratiev. Tchaikovsky got to know this man by the death-bed of his master, and valued his purity of heart and integrity more and more as years went by. Another unprofessional friend was the celebrated Russian general, Dragomirov. While travelling to France by sea, he made the acquaintance of an extraordinarily gifted boy, the son of Professor Sklifasskovsy. The friendship was brief as it was touching, for the youth died a year later. Tchaikovsky was deeply affected by his loss, and dedicated to his memory the *Chant Elégiaque*, op. 72.

All these new friendships served to surround the composer with that atmosphere of affection and appreciation which was as indispensable to him as his daily bread. But none of them were as deep and lasting as the ties of old days, none so close and intimate ; nor did they contribute any new element to his inner life. . . .

One word as to the dearest of all his later affections. His sister, A. Davidov, had three sons. The second of these, Vladimir, had always been Tchaikovsky's favourite from childhood. Up to the age of eighteen, however, these pleasant relations between uncle and nephew had not assumed any deep significance. But as Vladimir Davidov grew up, Tchaikovsky gradually felt for him a sentiment which can only be compared to his love for the twins, Toly and Modi, in their youth. The difference of age was no hindrance to their relations. Tchaikovsky preferred the companionship of his nephew ; was always grieved to part with him ; confided to him his inmost thoughts, and finally made him his heir, commending to this young man all those whom he still desired to assist and cherish, even after his death.

II

To N. F. von Meck.

"MOSCOW, *January* 1st (13th), 1885.

"It is so long since I wrote, dear friend ! Two events have interrupted my correspondence with you : on Christmas Eve I received a telegram announcing the death of Kotek. Not only was I much upset by this intelligence, but the sad duty of breaking the news to his parents devolved upon me. . . . I have also had to make the difficult corrections in my new Suite myself. Hans von Bülow is shortly to conduct in Petersburg, and all must be ready four or five days hence. While I was away nothing was done here. I was furious, rated Jurgenson and the engravers, and worked till I was worn out; therefore I have had no time to lament for poor Kotek."

To N. F. von Meck.

"Moscow, *January 5th* (17*th*), 1885.

"All my thoughts are now directed towards taking up my abode in some village near Moscow. I am no longer satisfied with a nomadic existence, and am determined to have a *home of my own* somewhere. As I am sure I am not in a position to buy a country house, I have decided to rent one."

The first performance of the Third Suite, which took place at a symphony concert in Petersburg, on January 12th (24th), 1885, under Von Bülow's direction, was a veritable triumph for Tchaikovsky. Never before had any of his works been received with such unanimous enthusiasm. Doubtless this was partly owing to the accessible and attractive character of the music, but far more to the admirable way in which it was interpreted.

Hans von Bülow was a great pianist, yet in this sphere he had rivals who almost overshadowed his fame. As a conductor, however, he ranked, after Richard Wagner, as the first man of his day. In spite of his years he was as enthusiastic as a youth, highly strung, receptive, and a fine all-round musician. He knew how to bring out every detail in a work, and thus infused his own virtuoso-inspiration into each individual player. Under him—in spite of his mannerisms and ungraceful movements—the orchestra performed wonders, and threw new light upon the most hackneyed works (such as the overture to *Freischütz*), holding the attention of the audience from the opening phrase to the last chord.

Quick, restless, and continually under the influence of some inspiration, he was as extreme and pitiless in his dislikes as he was sentimental and enthusiastic in his sympathies. He could not merely like or dislike. He hated or adored.

After having been in turn a passionate partisan of the classical masters, of Wagner and of Brahms, he became in the seventies a great admirer of Russian music, and was devoted to Tchaikovsky's works. His devotion was then at its zenith, consequently he put into his interpretation of the Third Suite not merely his accustomed experience, but all the fire of his passing enthusiasm. I say " passing," because some ten years later this enthusiasm had somewhat cooled, and he had begun to rave over the works of Richard Strauss, who at that time had scarcely entered upon his career as a composer.

To N. F. von Meck.

" Moscow, *January* 18*th* (30*th*), 1885.

" DEAR, KIND FRIEND,—Forgive me my indolence, and for so seldom writing. To-day I returned from Petersburg, where I spent a week of feverish excitement. The first few days were taken up by the rehearsals for the concert at which my new Suite was to be performed. I had a secret presentiment that it would please the public. I experienced both pleasure and fear. But the reality far surpassed my expectations. I have never had such a triumph ; I could see that the greater part of the audience was touched and grateful. Such moments are the best in an artist's life. . . . On the 15th (27th) *Oniegin* was performed in the presence of the Emperor and Empress, and other members of the Tsar's family. The Emperor desired to see me. We had a long and friendly conversation, in the course of which he asked all about my life and musical work, and then took me to the Empress, who paid me the most touching attention. The following evening I returned to Moscow."

On January 16th (28th), the new Suite was given in Moscow, under Erdmannsdörfer. It met with considerable success, but not with such appreciation as in Petersburg. Erdmannsdörfer's interpretation was fine, but lacked the inspiration by means of which Hans von Bülow had electrified his audience. At this time Tchaikovsky was in search of an operatic subject. Just then, says his brother Modeste, " I was in Moscow, and remarked one day that certain scenes from Shpajinsky's play, *The Enchantress*, would make an effective opera without using the whole drama as a libretto." The following day Tchaikovsky wrote to the author, asking permission to use the play for musical setting. Shpajinsky replied that he would be pleased to co-operate with the composer.

When the time came for Tchaikovsky to find a residence in his native land, or to go abroad according to his usual custom, he was seized with an inexplicable fear of the journey, and sent his servant Alexis to take a furnished house, in the village of Maidanovo, near Klin. "The house," he wrote to Nadejda von Meck, "contains many beautifully furnished rooms, and has a fine view. Apparently it is a pleasant place to live in, but the number of rooms gives me some anxiety, because they must be heated in winter." Finally he decided to take it for a year, and should it prove beyond his means, to look out for something more suitable in the meanwhile.

The village of Maidanovo lies close to the town of Klin. The manor house stands upon a high bank, overlooking the river Sestra, and is surrounded by a large park. Once it belonged to an aristocratic Russian family, but had gradually fallen into decay. Nevertheless, it bore many traces of its former splendour : the remains of a rosary in front of the façade, arbours, lakes, little bridges, rare trees, an orangery and a marble vase, placed in a shady spot in the park. In 1885 this property was already spoilt by the numerous country houses built by rich owners in the immediate neighbourhood. But Tchaikovsky was so enamoured of the scenery of Great Russia that he was quite satisfied with a birch or pine wood, a marshy field, the dome of a village church and, in the far distance, the dark line of some great forest. The chief motive, however, for his choice of this neighbourhood, where he lived to the end of his days, was not so much the charm of scenery as its situation between the two capitals. Klin lies near Moscow, and is also easily accessible from Petersburg, so that Tchaikovsky was within convenient distance from either city; while at the same time he was beyond the reach of accidental visitors, who now frequently molested him.

The first glimpse of Maidanovo disappointed Tchaikovsky. All that seemed splendid and luxurious to his man Alexis appeared in his eyes tasteless and incongruous. Nevertheless, he felt it would be pleasant as a temporary residence. The view from the windows, the quiet and sense of being *at home*, delighted him. The cook was good and inexpensive. The only other servants he employed were a moujik and a washerwoman. "In spite of my disappointment," he writes to his brother, "I am contented, cheerful, and quiet. . . . I am now receiving the newspapers, which makes life pleasanter. I read a great deal, and am getting on with English, which I enjoy. I eat, walk, and sleep when—and as much as—I please—in fact I live."

III

To E. Pavlovskaya.

"Maidanovo, *February 20th* (*March 4th*), 1888.

"Dear Emilie Karlovna,—I rather long for news of you. Where are you now? I have settled down in a village. My health is not good . . . in Carnival week I suffered from the most peculiar nervous headaches. . . . As I felt sure my accursed and shattered nerves were to blame, and I only wanted rest, I hurried into the country. . . . My *Vakoula* will be quite a respectable opera, you can feel sure of that. I always see you as Oxana, and so you dwell in my company without suspecting it. I have made every possible alteration which could retrieve the work from its unmerited oblivion. I hope it will be quite ready by Easter. I intend to begin a new opera in spring, so I shall once more have an opportunity of spending all my time with my 'benefactress.'"[1]

In February Taneiev played the new Fantasia for pianoforte in Moscow. Its immediate success was very great, but probably the applause was as much for the favourite pianist as for the work itself, for neither in Moscow nor yet in Petersburg — where Taneiev played it a year later—did this composition take any lasting hold upon the public.

To N. F. von Meck.

"MAIDANOVO, *March 5th* (17*th*), 1885.

"DEAR FRIEND,—Your letter gave me food for reflection. You are quite right : property is a burden, and only he who owns nothing is quite free. But, on the other hand, one must have a *home*. If I could live in Moscow, I should rent a house there. But it is not sufficient to *rent* a place in the country if one wants to feel at home. Here in Maidanovo, for instance, I have already found it very unpleasant to have my landlady living close by. I cannot plant the flowers I like, nor cut down a tree that obstructs my view. I cannot prevent people from walking in front of my windows, because there are other houses let in the park. I think, with my reserved character and nature, it would be better to have a little house and garden of my own. . . .

"The Russian solitudes of which you speak do not frighten me. One can always take a great store of books and newspapers from town, and, moreover, I am very simple in my tastes.

"I do not at all agree with your idea that in our country

[1] Tchaikovsky addressed Emilie Pavlovskaya by this term in gratitude for her splendid interpretation of the heroine in *Mazeppa*.

it must always be *horrid, dark, marshy*, etc. Even as the Esquimaux, or the Samoyede, loves his icy northern land, I love our Russian scenery more than any other, and a Russian landscape in winter has an incomparable charm for me. This does not hinder me in the least from liking Switzerland or Italy, in a different way. To-day I find it particularly difficult to agree with you about the poverty of our Russian scenery: it is a bright, sunny day, and the snow glistens like millions of diamonds. A wide vista lies before my window. . . . No! it is beautiful here in this land of ours, and one breathes so easily under this boundless horizon.

"It seems to me you think too gloomily, too despairingly, of Russia. Undoubtedly there is much to be wished for here, and all kinds of deceit and disorder do still exist. But where will you find perfection? Can you point out any country in Europe where everyone is perfectly contented? There was a time when I was convinced that for the abolishment of autocracy and the introduction of law and order, political institutions, such as parliaments, chambers of deputies, etc., were indispensable, and that it was only necessary to introduce these reforms with great caution, then all would turn out well, and everyone would be quite happy. But now, although I have not yet gone over to the camp of the ultra-conservatives, I am very doubtful as to the actual utility of these reforms. When I observe what goes on in other countries, I see everywhere discontent, party conflict and hatred; everywhere—in a greater or less degree —the same disorder and tyranny prevails. Therefore I am driven to the conclusion that there is no ideal government, and, until the end of the world, men will have to endure in patience many disappointments with regard to these things. From time to time great men—benefactors of mankind—appear, who rule justly and care more for the common welfare than for their own. But these are very exceptional. Therefore I am firmly convinced that the welfare of the great majority is not dependent upon *principles* and *theories*, but upon those individuals who, by the accident of their birth, or for some other reason, stand at the head of affairs. In a word, mankind serves man, not a personified principle. Now arises the question: Have we a *man* upon whom we can stake our hopes? I answer, Yes, and this man is the Emperor. His personality fascinates me; but, apart from personal impressions, I am inclined to think that the Emperor is a good man. I am pleased with the caution with which he introduces the new and does away with the old order. It pleases me, too, that he does not seek popularity; and I take pleasure also in his blameless life, and in the fact that he is an honourable and good man. But perhaps my politics are only the *naïveté* of a man who stands aloof from everyday life and is unable to see beyond his own profession."

To E. K. Pavlovskaya.

"MAIDANOVO, *March* 14th (26th), 1885.

"I am now arranging the revised score of *Vakoula*, orchestrating the new numbers and correcting the old. I hope to have finished in a few weeks. The opera will be called *Cherevichek*,[1] to distinguish it from the numerous other *Vakoulas*: Soloviev's and Stchourovsky's for instance. The authorities have promised to produce the opera in Moscow; it will hardly be possible in Petersburg, as they have already accepted two new operas there.

"As to *The Captain's Daughter*,[2] if only I could find a clever librettist, capable of carrying out such a difficult task, I would begin the work with pleasure. Meanwhile I have made a note of *The Enchantress*, by Shpajinsky. The latter has already started upon the libretto. He will make many alterations and, if I am not mistaken, it will make a splendid background for the music. You will find it your most suitable rôle. If *Les Caprices d'Oxane* should be produced, you will continue to play the part of my 'benefactress,' for you give me incredibly more than I give you. But if, with God's help, I achieve *The Enchantress*, I hope I may become your benefactor in some degree. Here you shall have a fine opportunity to display your art."

---

[1] This means *The Little Shoes*, but the opera has since been republished as *Les Caprices d'Oxane.*   [2] A tale by Poushkin.

To N. F. von Meck.

"MAIDANOVO, *April 3rd (15th),* 1885.

"MY DEAREST FRIEND,—I am once more back in Maidanovo, after a week and a half of travelling hither and thither. I worked almost without a break through the whole week before Palm Sunday and the whole of Passion Week, in order to be ready for the Easter festival. By Saturday everything was finished, and (although not well) I arrived in Moscow in time for the early service. I did not pass my holidays very pleasantly, and at the end of Easter Week I went to Petersburg, where I had to see Polonsky, author of the libretto of *Vakoula,* about the printing of the opera in its new form. I stayed four days in Petersburg, and spent them with my relations in the usual running about, which I found as wearisome as it was fatiguing. On Monday I travelled to Moscow in order to attend the reception of the Grand Duke Constantine Nicholaevich, who was to be present at the performance of the opera at the Conservatoire. As a member of the Musical Committee, I could not avoid taking part in the official reception to the Grand Duke, which I found a great bore. The performance went very well. Many thanks for sending me the articles in the *Novoe Vremya.* I had already seen them, and was very pleased with their warmth of tone. I am never offended at frank criticism, for I am well aware of my faults, but I feel very bitterly the cold and inimical note which pervades Cui's criticisms. It is not very long since the Russian Press (principally the Petersburg organs) began to notice me in a friendly spirit. Ivanov, the author of the articles in the *Novoe Vremya,* had formerly no good opinion of me, and used to write in a cold and hostile manner, although in Moscow I taught him theory for three years, and did not in the least deserve his enmity, as everyone knows. I can never forget how deeply his criticism of *Vakoula* wounded me ten years ago."

To Rimsky-Korsakov.

" MAIDANOVO, *April 6th* (18*th*), 1885.

" DEAR NICHOLAS ANDREIEVICH,—Since I saw you last I have had so much to get through in a hurry that I could not spare time for a thorough revision of your primer. But now and again I cast a glance at it, and jotted down my remarks on some loose sheets. To-day, having finished my revision of the first chapter, I wanted to send you these notes, and read them through again. Then I hesitated: should I send them or not? All through my criticism of your book[1] ran a vein of irritation, a grudging spirit, even an unintentional suspicion of hostility towards you. I was afraid the mordant bitterness of my observations might hurt your feelings. Whence this virulence? I cannot say. I think my old hatred of teaching harmony crops up here; a hatred which partly springs from a consciousness that our present theories are untenable, while at the same time it is impossible to build up new ones; and partly from the peculiarity of my musical temperament, which lacks the power of imparting conscientious instruction. For ten years I taught harmony, and during that time I loathed my classes, my pupils, my text-book, and myself as teacher. The reading of your book reawakened my loathing, and it was this which stirred up all my acrimony and rancour. . . . Now I am going to lay a serious question before you, which you need not answer at once, only after due consideration and discussion with your wife.

" Dare I hope that you would accept the position of Director of the Moscow Conservatoire should it be offered you? I can promise you beforehand so to arrange matters that you would have sufficient time for composing, and be spared all the drudgery with which N. Rubinstein was overwhelmed. You would only have the supervision of the musical affairs.

" Your upright and ideally honourable character, your distinguished gifts, both as artist and as teacher, warrant my conviction that in you we should find a splendid

---

[1] A course of harmony.

Director. I should consider myself very fortunate could I realise this ideal.

"So far, I have not ventured to speak of it to anyone, and beg you to keep the matter quiet for the present.

"Think it over, dear friend, and send me your answer.[1] . . ."

To E. K. Pavlovskaya.

"MAIDANOVA, *April* 12*th* (24*th*), 1885.

"MY DEAR EMILIE KARLOVNA,—Your exceedingly malicious criticism of *The Enchantress* not only failed to annoy me, but awoke my gratitude, for I wanted to know your opinion. I had even thought of asking you if you would go to see the play itself and give me your impressions. My conception and vision of the type of Natasha differs entirely from yours. Of course, she is a licentious woman; but her spell does not consist merely in the fact that she can win people with her fine speeches. This spell might suffice to draw customers to her inn—but would it have power to change her sworn enemy, the Prince, into a lover? Deep hidden in the soul of this light woman lies a certain moral force and beauty which has never had any chance of development. *This power is love.* Natasha is a strong and womanly nature, who can only love once, and she is capable of sacrificing all and everything to her love. So long as her love has not yet ripened, Natasha dissipates her forces, so to speak, in current coin; it amuses her to make everyone fall in love with her with whom she comes in contact. She is merely a sympathetic, attractive, undisciplined woman; she knows she is captivating, and is quite contented. Lacking the enlightenment of religion and culture—for she is a friendless orphan—she has but one object in life—to live gaily. Then appears *the* man destined to touch the latent chords of her better nature, and she is transfigured. Life loses all worth for her, so long as she cannot reach her goal; her beauty, which, so far, had only possessed an instinctive and elementary power of attraction, now becomes a strong weapon in her hand, by which, in a single moment, she shatters the oppos-

---

[1] Rimsky-Korsakov courteously, but decidedly, declined the offer.

2 I

ing forces of the Prince—his hatred. Afterwards they surrender themselves to the mad passion which envelops them and leads to the inevitable catastrophe of their death; but this death leaves in the spectator a sense of peace and reconciliation. I speak of what is going to be in my opera; in the play everything is quite different. Shpajinsky quite understands my requirements, and will carry out my intentions in delineating the principal characters. He will soften down the hardness of Natasha's *manières d'être*, and will give prominence to the power of her moral beauty. *He and I—you* too, later, if only you will be reconciled to this rôle—will so arrange things that in the last act there shall not be a dry eye in the audience. This is my own conception of this part, and I am sure it *must* please you, and that you will not fail to play it splendidly. My enthusiasm for *The Enchantress* has not made me unfaithful to the desire, so deeply rooted in my soul, to illustrate in music those words of Goethe's: 'The eternal feminine draws us onward.' The fact that the womanly power and beauty of Natasha's character remain so long hidden under a cloak of licentiousness, only augments the dramatic interest. Why do you like the part of Traviata or of Carmen? Because power and beauty shine out of these two characters, although in a somewhat coarser form. I assure you, you will also learn to like *The Enchantress.*"

To M. Tchaikovsky.

"MAIDANOVO, *April 26th* (*May 8th*), 1885.

"The business connected with *Cherevichek* has ended very well. Vsievolojsky put an end to the irresolution of the so-called management and ordered the opera to be produced in the most sumptuous style. I was present at a committee at which he presided, when the mounting was discussed. They will send Valetz, the scene-painter, to Tsarskoe-Selo, so that he may faithfully reproduce some of the rooms in the palace. I am very pleased."

FRAGMENT FROM A LETTER IN WHICH TCHAIKOVSKY SKETCHES A THEME
FOR "THE ENCHANTRESS"

To P. Jurgenson.

"Maidanovo, *April 26th* (*May 8th*), 1885.

" The position of my budget is as follows : I possess (together with the Moscow royalty which I have not yet received) 6,000 roubles. From Petersburg and Moscow there must still be about 800 or 1,000 roubles to come in; the honorarium from the church music, 300 roubles ; the honorarium from the Moscow Musical Society, 300 roubles.

" Total : 6000 + 800 + 300 + 300 = 7,500 (*sic !*).

" Up to the present I have not received more than 3,000 roubles from you.

" Consequently the capital which you have in hand amounts to 4,500–5000 roubles. A nice little sum."

To N. F. von Meck.

"Moscow, *May 26th* (*June 7th*), 1885.

" . . . I am completely absorbed in the affairs of the Conservatoire, and have decided that the position of Director shall be offered to Taneiev. If I do not succeed in this, I shall retire from the Committee. Finally, I can tell you what, so far, I have said to no one here : I hate every public office more than ever. Oh, God! how many disappointments have I experienced and how many bitter truths I have learnt! No! next year I must get right away."

Tchaikovsky actually succeeded in getting Taneiev chosen as Director of the Conservatoire. Through him Hubert, who had long been absent from the Conservatoire, was once more reinstated as a teacher. To support Taneiev's authority Tchaikovsky determined to resume his place upon the teaching staff, and undertook the gratuitous class for composition. This only necessitated his attendance once a month to supervise the work of the few (two to three) students of which the class was composed.

To S. I. Taneiev.

" MAIDANOVO, *June 13th (25th)*, 1885.

"Alexeiev has told me that according to the rules of the Conservatoire it is not permissible for me to be both teacher and member of Committee. Of course, I will not go back on my word, and I leave it to you to decide which would be the most useful—to remain on the Committee, or undertake the somewhat honorary post of professor. I think it would be best to remain on the Committee, but just as you like. In any case I will do my duty conscientiously, on the condition that my freedom is not curtailed and that I may travel whenever I please. . . .

" So, my dear chief, my fate lies in your hands.

" After some hesitation I have made up my mind to compose *Manfred*, because I shall find no rest until I have redeemed my promise, so rashly given to Balakirev in the winter. I do not know how it will turn out, but meantime I am very discontented. No! it is a thousand times pleasanter to compose without any programme. When I write a programme symphony I always feel I am not paying in sterling coin, but in worthless paper money."

IV

Tchaikovsky began the composition of *Manfred* in June. The following letter from Balakirev, dated 1882, led him to choose this subject for a symphonic work.

M. Balakirev to P. Tchaikovsky.

" PETERSBURG, *October 28th (November 9th)*, 1882.

" Forgive me for having left your last letter so long unanswered. I wanted to write to you in perfect peace and quiet, but many things hindered me. You are more fortunate than we are, for you do not need to give lessons, and can devote your whole time to art. I first offered the subject about which I spoke to you to Berlioz, who declined my suggestion on account of age and ill-health.

Your *Francesca* gave me the idea that you were capable of treating this subject most brilliantly, provided you took great pains, subjected your work to stringent self-criticism, let your imagination fully ripen, and did not hurry. This fine subject—Byron's *Manfred*—is no use to me, for it does not harmonise with my intimate moods.

"Let me tell you first of all that your Symphony—like the Second Symphony of Berlioz—must have an *idée fixe* (the *Manfred* theme), which must be carried through all the movements. Now for the programme:—

"*First Movement*. Manfred wandering in the Alps. His life is ruined. Many burning questions remain unanswered; nothing is left to him but remembrance. The form of the ideal Astarte floats before his imagination; he calls to her in vain: the echo of the rocks alone repeats her name. Thoughts and memories burn in his brain and prey upon him; he implores the forgetfulness that none can give him (F♯ minor, second theme D major and F♯ minor).

"*Second Movement*. In complete contrast to the first. Programme: The customs of the Alpine hunters: patriarchal, full of simplicity and good humour. Adagio Pastorale (A major). Manfred drops into this simple life and stands out in strong contrast to it. Naturally at the beginning a little hunting theme must be introduced, but in doing this *you must take the greatest care not to descend to the commonplace*. For God's sake avoid copying the common German fanfares and hunting music.

"*Third Movement*. Scherzo fantastique (D major). Manfred sees an Alpine fairy in the rainbow above a waterfall.

"*Fourth Movement*. Finale (F♯ minor). A wild Allegro representing the caves of Ariman, whither Manfred has come to try and see Astarte once more. The appearance of Astarte's wraith will form the contrast to these infernal orgies (the same theme which was employed in the first movement in D major now reappears in D♭ major; in the former it dies away like a fleeting memory, and is immediately lost in Manfred's phase of suffering—but now it can be developed to its fullest extent). The music must be light, transparent as air, and ideally virginal. Then comes the repetition of Pandemonium, and finally the sunset and Manfred's death.

"Is it not a splendid programme? I am quite convinced that if you summon up all your powers it will be your *chef-d'œuvre*.

"The subject is not only very deep, but in accordance with contemporary feeling; for all the troubles of the modern man arise from the fact that he does not know how to preserve his ideals. They crumble away and leave nothing but bitterness in the soul. Hence all the sufferings of our times."

To N. F. von Meck.

"MAIDANOVO, *June* 13*th* (25*th*), 1885.

"DEAR FRIEND.—I can at last congratulate you on the beautiful weather. I should enjoy it twice as much if Maidanovo were more congenial to me. But alas! the lovely park, the beautiful views, and the splendid bath, are all alike spoiled by the *summer visitors*. I cannot take a step in the park without coming across some neighbour. It was beautiful in the winter, but I ought to have thought of the summer and the summer tourist.

"I am deep in the composition of a new symphonic work. Shpajinsky could not send me the first act of *The Enchantress* at the date agreed upon, so without losing any time, in April I set to work upon the sketches for a programme Symphony, upon the subject of Byron's *Manfred*. I am now so deep in the composition of this work that the opera will probably have to be laid aside for some time. The Symphony gives me great trouble. It is a very complicated and serious work. There are times when it seems to me it would be wise to cease from composing for a while; to travel and rest. But an unconquerable desire for work gains the upper hand and chains me to my desk and piano."

To E. K. Pavlovskya.

"MAIDANOVO, *July* 20*th* (*August* 1*st*), 1885.

". . . I have been playing through some numbers from *Harold*. A very interesting work and a clever one, well thought out and full of talent. But are you not surprised that Napravnik, who is so against Wagner, should have written a genuine Wagnerian opera? I was filled with astonishment."

To N. F. von Meck.

"MAIDANOVO, *August 3rd* (*15th*), 1885.

"The horizon has been shrouded for days in thick mist, caused, they say, by forest fires and smouldering peat-mosses. This mist gets thicker and thicker, and I begin to fear we shall be suffocated. It has a very depressing effect. In any case my mental condition has been very gloomy of late. The composition of the *Manfred* Symphony—a work highly tragic in character—is so difficult and complicated that at times I myself become a Manfred. All the same, I am consumed with the desire to finish it as soon as possible, and am straining every nerve: result—extreme exhaustion. This is the eternal *cercle vicieux* in which I am for ever turning without finding an issue. If I have no work, I worry and bore myself; when I have it, I work far beyond my strength."

To N. F. von Meck.

"MAIDANOVO, *August 31st* (*September 12th*), 1885.

". . . My fate, that is to say the question of my future home, is at last decided. After a long and unsuccessful search I have agreed to my landlady's proposal to remain at Maidanovo. I shall not stay in the uncomfortable and unsuitable house in which I have been living, but in one which she herself has occupied. This house stands somewhat apart from the others, and a large piece of the garden is to be fenced in and kept for my especial use; the house itself was thoroughly done up last summer. Although the neighbourhood is not what I could wish, yet, taking into consideration the proximity of a large town with station, shops, post, telegraph office, doctor and chemist—and also my dislike for searching further—I have decided to take this place for two years. It is pleasant and comfortable, and I think I shall feel happy there. I am now starting to furnish, and shall enter on my tenancy on September 15th. If during the next two years I feel comfortably settled, I shall not search any more, but remain there to the end of my days. It is indeed time that I had a settled home."

V

1885–1886

All the important epochs in Tchaikovsky's life were preceded by a transition period in which he tried, as it were, whether the proposed change would be feasible or not. From 1861–2, before he became a student at the Conservatoire, he was half-musician, half-official; in 1866, before he became a professor at the Conservatoire, and entirely a Muscovite, he was for eight months half-Petersburger and half-Muscovite; in 1877, before he gave up his professorship and started on what he called "the nomadic life" of the last seven years, he was half-professor and half-tourist; now, from February to September, 1885, he was rather a summer visitor than an inhabitant of the village of Maidanovo, but he had proved the firmness of his decision to remain there. It was only in the beginning of September that he became the true "hermit of Klin," who, alas, was often compelled to leave his hermitage. As he had now decided to settle down in a home of his own, he proceeded to make it comfortable. . . . With a schoolgirl's *naïveté* in all practical questions of life, Tchaikovsky could not do much himself towards furnishing his little home, and handed over the task to his servant Alexis. He himself only helped by purchasing the most unnecessary things (for example, he bought two horses, which he sold again with great difficulty, also an old English clock, which proved quite useless), or by furnishing his library with books and music. He was as pleased as a child, and was never tired of talking of "my cook," "my washerwoman," "my silver," "my tablecloths," and "my dog." He considered all these to be of the very best, and praised them to the skies. With the exception of some portraits and ikons, all the remainder of Tchaikovsky's movable property dates its existence from this time.

In comparison with the luxurious houses of other men in his position, painters, writers, and artists, Tchaikovsky's home was very modest. It contained only what was absolutely necessary. He did not possess beautiful or luxurious things, because his means were decidedly smaller than those of his colleagues in Western Europe, and also because he paid but little attention to outward appearances. If tables, cupboards, or curtains fulfilled their purpose fairly well, he was quite content. Workmanship and material were matters of indifference to him. He also troubled very little about "style" (he could not distinguish one style from another); even if a table was shaky, or the door of a cupboard refused to close, he took it all quite calmly. He would not surround himself with luxury, because his money belonged less to himself than to others, and because, even at the close of his life, when his income was 20,000 roubles a year, he remained free from all pretentious notions.

Little as Tchaikovsky troubled about buying furniture, he cared still less about the placing of it. He entrusted the matter entirely to the will of his servant, who, knowing and taking into consideration his little fancies and habits, arranged everything just as "his master liked it," without paying any heed to beauty or tastefulness. Tchaikovsky preferred that nothing should be altered in his surroundings; he found it most disagreeable to have to accustom himself to anything new, still more to miss any of his old friends. Henceforth a certain tradition which surrounded every piece of furniture was always considered, if possible, at each removal, so that wherever Tchaikovsky might be, the appearance of his room remained the same. The division of his time in Klin was never changed to the end of his life.

Tchaikovsky rose between seven and eight a.m. Took tea (generally without anything to eat) between eight and nine, and then read the Bible. After which he occupied himself with the study of the English language, or with reading such books as provided not only recreation, but instruction. In this way he read Otto Jahn's *Life of Mozart* in the original, the philosophical writings of Spinoza, Schopenhauer, and many others. He next took a walk for about three-quarters of an hour. If Tchaikovsky talked while taking his morning tea, or took his walk in company with a visitor, it signified that he did not intend to compose that day, but would be scoring, writing letters, or making corrections. During his life at Klin, when engaged on a new work, he could not endure company, not only in the morning, but also during the day. In earlier days in Moscow, abroad, or in Kamenka, he had to content himself with the solitude of his room during his hours of active work. The presence of his servant Alexis did not in any way disturb him. The latter, the sole witness of the creative process of the majority of his master's works, did not even appear to hear them, and only once unexpectedly gave expression to his enthusiasm for the Chorus of Maidens in the third scene of *Eugene Oniegin*, to the great astonishment and perturbation of his master. To his "perturbation," because he feared in future to be continually overheard and criticised. But this was fortunately the only flash of enlightenment which penetrated Safronov's musical darkness.

Manfred was the last work Tchaikovsky composed in anything but complete isolation, and this is probably the reason why the task proved so difficult, and cost him such moments of depression. The principal advantage of his new surroundings was the enjoyment of complete solitude during his hours of work.

We may mention that his reserve as to his compositions dates from this time. In the earlier days of his musical life Tchaikovsky had been very communicative about his work ; even before his compositions were finished he was ready to discuss them. In the evening he would ask the opinion of those with whom he lived upon what he had composed in the morning, and was always willing to let them hear his work. In course of time, however, the circle of those to whom he communicated the fruits of his inspiration became ever smaller, and when he played any of his compositions he begged his hearers to keep their opinions to themselves. From 1885 he ceased to show his works to anyone. The first to make acquaintance with them was the engraver at Jurgenson's publishing house.

Tchaikovsky never wasted time between 9.30 and 1 p.m., but busied himself in composing, orchestrating, making corrections, or writing letters. Before he began a pleasant task he always hastened to get rid of the unpleasant ones. On returning from a journey he invariably began with his correspondence, which, next to proof-correcting, he found the most unpleasant work. In the nineties his correspondence had attained such volume that Tchaikovsky was frequently engaged upon it from morning till night, and often answered thirty letters a day.

Tchaikovsky dined punctually at 1 p.m., and, thanks to his excellent appetite, always enjoyed any fare that was set before him, invariably sending a message of thanks to the cook by Safronov. As he was always very abstemious and plain in his meals, it often happened that his guests, instead of complimenting the cook, felt inclined to do just the contrary. Wet or fine, Tchaikovsky always went for a walk after dinner. He had read somewhere that, in order to keep in health, a man ought to walk for two hours daily. He observed this rule with as much conscientiousness and superstition as though some terrible catastrophe would follow should he return five minutes too soon. Solitude was as necessary to him during this walk as during his work. Not only a human being, but even a favourite dog was a bother.

Every witness of his delight in nature spoilt his enjoyment ; every expression of rapture destroyed the rapture itself, and in the very moment when he said to his companion, " How beautiful it is here ! " it ceased to be beautiful in his eyes.

Most of the time during these walks was spent in composition. He thought out the leading ideas, pondered over the construction of the work, and jotted down fundamental themes. In Klin there are carefully preserved many little exercise books, which he had used for this purpose. If in absence of mind Tchaikovsky had left his note-book at home, he noted down his passing thoughts on any scrap of paper, letter, envelope, or even bill, which he chanced to have with him. The next morning he looked over these notes, and worked them out at the piano. With the exception of two scenes in *Eugene Oniegin*, some piano pieces, and songs, he always worked out his sketches at the piano, so that he should not trust entirely to his indifferent memory. He always wrote out everything very exactly, and here and there indicated the instrumentation. In these sketches the greater part of a work was generally quite finished. When it came to the orchestration he only copied it out clearly, without essentially altering the first drafts. When he was not busy with music during his walks, he recited aloud or improvised dramatic scenes (almost always in French). Sometimes he occupied himself by observing insects. In the garden at Grankino was an ant-hill, to which he played the part of benefactor, providing it with insects from the steppe.

During the first year of his life at Maidanovo Tchaikovsky himself ruined the charm of these walks. Like every good-hearted summer visitor he had given tips lavishly to the village children. At first it was a pleasure, but afterwards turned into a veritable nuisance. The children waited for him at every corner, and when they noticed that he began to avoid them, they surprised him in the most unexpected places in the forest. This quest of pennies spread from the children to the young people of the village, nay, even to the men and women, so that at last he could hardly take a step without being waylaid by beggars. There was nothing left for Tchaikovsky but to keep within the precincts of his park.

About 4 p.m. Tchaikovsky went home to tea, read the papers if he was alone, but was very pleased to talk if he had visitors. At five he retired once more and worked till seven. Before supper, which was served at 8 p.m., Tchaikovsky always took another constitutional. This time he liked to have company, and generally went into the open fields to watch the sunset. In the autumn and winter he enjoyed playing the piano either alone, or arrangements for four hands if Laroche or Kashkin were there. After supper he sat with his guests till 11 p.m., playing cards or listening while one of them read aloud. Laroche was his favourite reader, not because he showed any particular talent that way, but because at every phrase his face expressed his enjoyment, especially if the author of the book happened to be Gogol or Flaubert. When there were no visitors, Tchaikovsky read a number of historical books dealing with the end of the eighteenth or beginning of the nineteenth century, or played patience—and was a little bored. At 11 p.m. he went to his room, wrote up his diary, and read for a short time. He never composed in the evening after the summer of 1866.

Unexpected guests were treated most inhospitably, but to invited guests he was amiability itself, and often gave himself the pleasure of gathering together his Moscow friends—Kashkin, Hubert, Albrecht, Jurgenson, and Taneiev. But those who stayed with him longest and most frequently were Laroche, Kashkin, and myself.

VI

In the beginning of the eighties Tchaikovsky's fame greatly increased in Europe and America, not only without any co-operation on his part, but even without his being aware of it. More and more frequently came news of the success of one or other of his works, and letters from various celebrated artists who had played his compositions, or wished to do so. The Committees of the Paris "Sebastian Bach Society" and the Association for the National Edition of Cherubini's works both elected him an honorary member. Nevertheless it surprised him greatly to learn that a Paris publisher (Félix Mackar) had proposed to P. Jurgenson to buy the right of bringing out his works in France. The sum which Jurgenson received was not indeed excessive, but it testified to the fact that Tchaikovsky's fame had matured and reached the point when it might bring him some material advantage. Incidentally it may be mentioned that P. Jurgenson, without any legal obligation, handed over to Tchaikovsky half the money he received from F. Mackar, so that the former became quite suddenly and unexpectedly a capitalist, although at the end of the year he was not a single kopek to the good. After F. Mackar had become the representative of Tchaikovsky's interests in Paris he pushed his works with great zeal. First of all he induced him to become a member of the Society of Composers and Publishers, the aim of which was to enforce a certain fee for every work by one of its members performed in public. The yearly sum which Tchaikovsky now began to draw from France can be taken as an authentic proof of the growth of his popularity in that country. This sum increased every year until 1893. After Tchaikovsky's death it suddenly decreased in a very marked manner. Elsewhere I will give some explanation of this curious fact.

PETER ILICH TCHAIKOVSKY

Mackar also started his gratuitous *Auditions* of Tchaikovsky's works. These *Auditions*, in spite of the free admission, were not very well patronised by the Paris public, who were satiated with music. But they produced one very important result. The best artists (Marsick, Diemer, and others) willingly took part in them, and henceforth Tchaikovsky's name appeared more often in the programmes of the Paris concerts.

To E. K. Pavlovskaya.

"MAIDANOVO, *September 9th (21st)*, 1885.

". . . *Manfred* is finished, and I have set to work upon the opera without losing an hour. . . . The first act (the only one in hand) is splendid: life and action in plenty. If nothing prevents me I hope to have the sketch ready by the spring: so that I may devote next year to the instrumentation and working out. The opera can then be produced in the season 1887–8. Dear E. K., do please say a good word on every possible occasion for *The Enchantress*."

To A. P. Merkling.

"MAIDANOVO, *September 13th (25th)*, 1885.

". . . Annie, first of all I am going to flatter you a little and then ask you to do something for me. After much searching and trouble I have rented a very pretty house here in Maidanovo. . . . I am now furnishing this house . . . now . . . some good people . . . have promised . . . if I am not mistaken . . . that is, how shall I express myself? . . . to sew . . . woollen *portières* . . . or curtains . . . that is, I would like to know . . . perhaps at once . . . if you would . . . I, in a word . . . oh! how ashamed I am . . . write please, how what . . . now, I hope, I have made myself understood. . . ."[1]

---

[1] Anna Petrovna kept her promise, and made the curtains which ornament the dining-room at Klin till this day.

To A. S. Arensky.

"MAIDANOVO, *September 25th (October 7th),* 1885.

"DEAR ANTON STEPANOVICH,—Pardon me if I force my advice upon you. I have heard that $5/4$ time appears twice in your new Suite. It seems to me that the mania for $5/4$ time threatens to become a habit with you. I like it well enough if it is indispensable to the musical idea, that is to say if the time signature and rhythmic accent respectively form no hindrance. For example, Glinka, in the chorus of the fourth act of *A Life for the Tsar*, clearly could not have written in anything else but $5/4$ time: here we find an actual $5/4$ rhythm that is a continual and uniform change from $2/4$ to $3/4$:

"It would be curious, and certainly 'an effort to be original,' to write a piece with a simple rhythm of $2/4$ or $3/4$ time in $5/4$ time. You will agree with me that it would have been very stupid of Glinka to have written his music thus:

"It would be the same to the ear whether $2/4$ or $3/4$: it would not be a mathematical blunder, but a very clumsy musical one.

"You have made just such a mistake in your otherwise beautiful *Basso ostinato.* I made the discovery yesterday that in this instance $5/4$ time was not at all necessary. You must own that a series of three bars of $5/4$ is mathematically equal to a similar series of $3/4$ time;[1] in music, on the contrary, the difference between them is quite as sharp as between $3/4$ and $6/8$.

[1] A series of five bars of $3/4$ is evidently meant.

" In my opinion, your *Basso ostinato* should in 3/4 or 6/4 time, but not in 5/4.

" I cannot imagine a more distinct five-bar rhythm in 3/4 time. What do you think ? "

To N. F. von Meck.

" MAIDANOVO, *September 27th (October 9th)*, 1885.

" The first act of *The Enchantress* lies finished before me, and I am growing more and more enthusiastic over the task in prospect.

" Dear friend, I like your arrogant views upon my opera. You are quite right to regard this insincere form of art with suspicion. But for a composer opera has some irresistible attraction; it alone offers him the means of getting into touch with the great public. My *Manfred* will be played once or twice, and then disappear; with the exception of a few people who attend symphony concerts, no one will hear it. Opera, on the contrary—and opera alone—brings us nearer to our fellows, inoculates the public with our music, and makes it the possession, not only of a small circle, but—under favourable circumstances—of the whole nation. I do not think this tendency is to be condemned; that is to say, Schumann, when he wrote *Genoveva*, and Beethoven, when he wrote *Fidelio*, were not actuated by ambition, but by a natural desire to increase the circle of their hearers and to penetrate as far as possible into the heart of humanity. Therefore we must not only pursue what is merely effective, but choose subjects of artistic worth which are both interesting and touching."

2 K

To M. Tchaikovsky.

"MAIDANOVO, *October 1st* (13*th*), 1885.

"What a wretch Zola is!! A few weeks ago I accidentally took up his *Germinal*, began to read it, got interested, and only finished it late at night. I was so upset that I had palpitations, and sleep was impossible. Next day I was quite ill, and now I can only think of the novel as of some fearful nightmare. . . ."

To P. Jurgenson.

"MAIDANOVO, *October 9th* (21*st*), 1885.

"DEAR FRIEND,—Hubert tells me you do not think it possible to publish *Manfred* this season. Is this true? The question is this, I cannot allow two opportunities to slip: (1) Bülow is conducting in Petersburg; (2) Erdmannsdörfer is conducting in Moscow—perhaps his last season—and, in spite of all, he is one of the few people on whom I can depend. On the other hand, I am not in a position to spend an incredible amount of trouble on a work which I regard as one of my very best, and then wait till it is played *some time*. As far as I am concerned, it is all the same to me whether it is played from written or printed notes—so long as it is done. I believe it might be ready by February. But if you think that this is quite impossible, then I propose that you decline *Manfred* altogether (this will not offend me at all, for I know you cannot do the impossible for the sake of my whims). Only understand that I cannot on any account wait till next season, and cost what it may, I will see *Manfred* produced. Do not take my caprice (if it is a caprice) amiss, and answer me at once."

To N. F. von Meck.

"MAIDANOVO, *October 11th* (23*rd*), 1885.

". . . As regards the lofty significance of symphony and chamber music in comparison with opera, let me only add that to refrain from writing operas is the work of a hero, and we have one such hero in our time—Brahms. Cui has justly remarked in one of his recent articles that Brahms, both as man and artist, has only followed the highest ideals—those which were worthy of respect and admiration. Unfortunately his creative gift is poor, and does not correspond to his great aspirations. Nevertheless he is a hero. This heroism does not exist in me, for the stage with all its glitter attracts me irresistibly."

VII

To N. F. von Meck.

"MAIDANOVO, *November* 19*th* (*December* 1*st*), 1885.

". . . I spent a week in Moscow, and was present at three concerts. The first, given by Siloti, who has just returned from abroad to serve his time in the army. He has made great progress. Then the Musical Society gave a concert and quartet-matinée, at which the celebrated Paris violinist, Marsick, played. All three concerts gave me great pleasure, as I have not heard any good music for so long. For a musician who writes as much as I do it is very necessary and refreshing to hear foreign music from time to time. Nothing inspires me more than listening to a great foreign work: immediately I want to write one equally beautiful.

"I have also been once or twice to the Conservatoire, and was very pleased to notice that Taneiev is just the Director we wanted under the circumstances. His work shows resolution, firmness, energy, and also capability. I hear nothing about *Les Caprices d'Oxane*, and begin to fear the work will not be produced this season."

The following letter was written after Ippolitov-Ivanov had communicated the success of *Mazeppa* in Tiflis.

To M. M. Ippolitov-Ivanov.[1]

"*December 6th* (18*th*), 1885.

". . . As to *Mazeppa*, accept my warmest thanks. My brother and his wife, who live in Tiflis, and had seen the opera in Moscow and Petersburg, tell me it went splendidly.

"For some time I have been longing to find a subject— not too dramatic—for an opera, and then to write a work suitable to the resources of the provincial stage. Should God grant me a long life, I hope to carry out this plan, and thus to obliterate the unpleasant recollections of the immeasurable trouble which the rehearsals of *Mazeppa* must have left with you. But the harder your task, the warmer my thanks."

To Modeste Tchaikovsky.

"MAIDANOVO, *December 9th* (21*st*), 1885.

"I am going to Moscow on December 14th (26th), principally to decide the fate of *Les Caprices d'Oxane*. I shall make heroic efforts to have my opera produced. I am advised to conduct it myself, and it is possible I may decide to do so. In any case, I shall spend the holidays in Petersburg. . . . I am working very hard at the corrections of *Manfred*. I am still convinced it is my best work. Meanwhile *The Enchantress* is laid aside, but the first act is quite finished. The libretto is splendid. In this I am lucky."

To N. F. von Meck.

"MAIDANOVO, *December 11th* (23*rd*), 1885.

". . . My Third Suite was played at the last concert. The public gave me an enthusiastic ovation. . . . Lately we have had such lovely moonlight nights, without a breath of wind. O God, how beautiful they are! The Russian winter has a particular charm for me, but that does not prevent me from planning a journey to Italy in

[1] The present Professor of Composition at the Moscow Conservatoire and Director of the Private Opera in Moscow.

the spring. I am thinking of going by sea from Naples to Constantinople, then to Batoum, and thence by train to Tiflis to visit my brother Anatol, who is already expecting me."

To S. I. Taneiev.

"MAIDANOVO, *December* 11*th* (23*rd*), 1885.

". . . Imagine! I am rejoicing at the thought of hearing Beethoven's First Symphony. I had no suspicion that I liked it so much. The reason is perhaps that it is so like my idol, Mozart. Remember that on October 27th, 1887, the centenary of *Don Juan* will be celebrated."

To P. Jurgenson.

"*December* 22*nd* (*January* 3*rd*), 1885.

". . . I have only just now been able to consider this question of *Manfred*, of Mackar, and the fee, and this is my decision: Even were *Manfred* a work of the greatest genius, it would still remain a symphony which, on account of its unusual intricacy and difficulty, would only be played once in ten years. This work cannot therefore bring any profit either to you or Mackar. On the other hand, I value it highly. How is the material value of such a work to be decided? I may be wrong, but it seems to me my best composition, and a few hundred roubles would not repay me for all the work and trouble I have put into it. If you were very rich, I would unhesitatingly demand a very large sum, on the grounds that you could recover your outlay on other things—but you are not at all rich. As for Mackar—to speak frankly—I am greatly touched by his cheerful self-sacrifice, for certainly he can have made very little out of my works in France. After having just received 20,000 francs from him, we must not show ourselves too grasping, especially as we know that there is not much to be made out of *Manfred*."

"In short, I have made up my mind to claim nothing from Mackar, or from you, and have already told him this. I tell you also, so that you should not demand the promised thousand francs from him. The demanding of payment for restoration of his copy—is your affair."

To N. F. von Meck.

"MAIDANOVO, *January* 13*th* (25*th*), 1886.

"DEAR FRIEND,— . . . This time I have not brought back any pleasant impressions with me from Petersburg. My operas—I do not know why—have not been given lately, and I feel this the more bitterly because, owing to the unusual success of *Oniegin*, it appears that the Direction has been urging that it should be given with greater frequency. The new symphony *Manfred* is completely ignored, for no preparations for its production are being made. In all this I do not recognise any enmity towards me personally, for in truth I have no enemies, but a kind of contempt which is a little wounding to my artistic vanity. Certainly this is an unfavourable year for me. They have decided not to give *Les Caprices d'Oxane* in Moscow this season, and I had been expecting it so impatiently!

"I have a piece of news for you to-day, which pleased me very much. I had observed that here in Maidanovo the village children are constantly idle and run about without any occupation, which induced me to consult with the local priest about the founding of a school. This has proved to be possible, so long as I assure them an annual sum. I have consented to do so, and the priest began to take the necessary steps about two months ago. The official permission to open a school has arrived and the instruction can begin this week. I am very glad."

To N. F. von Meck.

"MAIDANOVO, *January* 14*th* (26*th*), 1886.

". . . The priest came to see me to-day, and brought me an invitation to the opening of the school on the 19th. I am proud to have initiated this work. I hope some good will come of it. In spite of the greatest care and moderation, I suffer from dyspepsia. It is not serious, and I have no doubt a cure at Vichy will completely set me up."

To N. F. von Meck.

"Moscow, *February 4th* (16*th*), 1886.

"How difficult it is after receiving your money to say in the baldest way, 'Money received, many thanks!' If only you had an inkling of all the happiness I owe you, and the whole meaning of that 'independence and freedom' which are the result of my liberty. Life is an unbroken chain of little unpleasantnesses and collision with human egoism and pride, and only he can rise above these things who is free and independent. How often do I say to myself: *Well that it is so, but how if it were otherwise?*

"Just lately I had some very unpleasant frictions which only just fell short of open quarrels, but failed to upset me because I could appear to ignore the wrong inflicted upon me. Yes, in the last few years of my life there have been many occasions on which I have sincerely felt the debt of gratitude I owe to you. And yet I usually send you the receipt as if it were a matter of course. My gratitude has no limits, my dear."

To N. F. von Meck.

"Maidanovo, *February 6th* (18*th*), 1886.

". . . . To-day I returned from Moscow, where I have been attending Rubinstein's concerts once a week. Were it only a question of listening to that marvellous pianist, I should not have found the journeys at all tedious, in spite of my dislike of leaving home. But I had to go to all the dinners and suppers which were held in his honour, which I generally found intolerably wearisome and most injurious to my health. At the last concert Rubinstein played pieces by Henselt, Thalberg, Liszt, and others. There was very little artistic choice, but the performance was indeed astonishing."

To N. F. von Meck.

"Maidanovo, *February 14th* (26*th*), 1886.

". . . . The festival which the town of Moscow held in Rubinstein's honour was a great success. He was visibly touched by the energy and warmth with which the Muscovites expressed their affection for him. Indeed, everyone must recognise that Rubinstein is worthy of all such honour. He is not only a gifted artist, but also a most honourable and generous man."

Diary.

"MAIDANOVO, *February 22nd (March 8th),* 1886.

"What an unfathomable gulf lies between the Old and the New Testament! Read the psalms of David, and at first it is impossible to understand why they have taken such a high place from an artistic point of view; and, secondly, why they should stand beside the Gospels. David is altogether *of this* world. He divides the whole of humanity into two unequal portions: sinners (to which belong the greatest number) and the righteous, at whose head he places himself. In every psalm he calls down God's wrath upon the sinner and His praise upon the righteous; yet the reward and the punishment are both worldly. The sinners shall be undone, and the righteous shall enjoy all the good things of this earthly life. How little that agrees with Christ's teaching, who prayed for His enemies, and promised the good no earthly wealth, but rather the kingdom of heaven! What touching love and compassion for mankind lies in these words: 'Come unto Me, all ye that labour and are heavy laden'! In comparison with these simple words all the psalms of David are as nothing."

Diary.

"*February 28th (March 12th),* 1886.

". . . . At tea I read through Alexis Tolstoi's *St. John Chrysostom* and *The Sinner,* which reduced me to tears. While in this agitation of spirit, into which any strong artistic enjoyment throws me, I received a telegram from the Conservatoire: 'The Grand Duke is coming.' So all plans go to the devil! Despair, irresolution, and even terror at the prospect of the journey. Went in and fed my landlady's hungry dog. In the twilight I was overcome with insane depression. Played through my

Second Suite, and was glad to find it not so bad as I had imagined."

Diary.

"*March 1st (13th)*, 1886.

". . . . Played through *Nero*, and cannot sufficiently marvel at the audacious coolness of the composer. The very sight of the score makes me fume. However, I only play this abomination because the sense of my superiority —at least, as regards conscientiousness—strengthens my energy. I believe I compose badly, but when I come across such an atrocity, written in all earnestness, I feel a certain relief. I am ashamed to show so much anger over such a publication—but there is no need to disguise one's feelings in a diary."

To N. F. von Meck.

"MAIDANOVO, *March 13th (25th)*, 1886.

" DEAR FRIEND,—I have not written to you for a long time owing to a ten days' visit to Moscow. . . . I devoted two days to the rehearsal of *Manfred*, and attended the concert at which it was played. I am quite satisfied; I am sure it is my best symphonic work. The performance was excellent, but it seemed to me the public were un-intelligent and cold, although they gave me quite an ovation at the end. . . ."

The very short and sparse Press notices of *Manfred* add nothing essential to Tchaikovsky's words. They merely confirm the fact that the Symphony received an excellent rendering, but the author's high opinion of his work only held good as regards the first two movements; later on he came to reckon the other movements, the Pastorale, Ariman's Kingdom, and Manfred's Death, as being on a level with *The Oprichnik*, one of the least favoured of his works.

Although out of chronological order, I may mention here that on the occasion of a performance of this work in Petersburg (December, 1886) Cui gave it the most enthusiastic and unreserved praise. Everything pleased him, especially the Scherzo, and his criticism closed with these words: "We must be grateful to Tchaikovsky for having enriched the treasury of our national symphonic music."

VIII

To M. Tchaikovsky.

"TIFLIS, *April 1st (13th)*, 1886.

". . . I left Moscow on March 23rd (April 4th), and travelled direct to Taganrog to Hyppolite, whose guest I was for two days, so as to arrive in Vladikavkas on the 28th.

"Early on Sunday (30th) I started in a four-horse post-carriage, accompanied by a guard, whose sole duty is to look after the requirements and comforts of the travellers. I had not slept the preceding night on account of the horrible bed and the insects (when I think of the *best* hotel in Vladikavkas I feel quite sick), and thought therefore that the beauties of the Georgian Road would make but little impression on me. The road is, however, so grand, so astonishingly beautiful, that I never thought of sleeping the whole day long. The variety of impressions did not allow my interest to flag for a moment. At first the approach to the mountains was slow, although they appeared to be quite close to us, and yet we still drove on and on. Then the valley of the Terek became narrower, and we reached the wild and gloomy Darjal Gorge. Afterwards we ascended into the region of snow. Shortly before I started on my journey there had been an avalanche, and hundreds of miserable-looking natives were busy shovelling away the snow. At last we were driving higher and higher between great snow walls, and it was necessary to put on our furs. By six o'clock we were descending into the Aragva Valley, and spent the night in Mlety. I occupied the *imperial rooms*. After the dirt of the Vladikavkas hotel I found the clean rooms, good beds, and daintily-set table very delightful. I dined, took a little walk by moonlight in the gallery, and went to bed at nine o'clock. Next morning I started off again. Already we could feel the breath of the south in the air; the sides of the mountains were cultivated, and constantly there came in sight picturesque *aouli*[1] and all kinds of dwellings. The descent was made at a terrific pace, considering the curves of the road. Not far from Dushet such a wonderful view came in sight that I almost wept with delight. The further we descended, the more the influence of the south wind was felt. At last we reached Mtskhet (noted for the ruins of its castle and the celebrated cathedral), and at half-past five we reached Tiflis. Toly and his wife were not there; they had not expected me till later, and had gone to meet me at Mtskhet. They did not arrive till eight o'clock. Meanwhile I had had time to wash, dress, and see something of the town. It is delightful. The trees are not yet all green; the fruit trees are in full blossom; a mass of flowers in the gardens. It is as warm as in June—in a word, really spring—just as it was four years ago when we left Naples. The chief streets are very lively; splendid shops, and quite a European air. But when I came to the native quarters I found myself in entirely new surroundings. The streets mean and narrow, as in Venice; on both sides an endless row of small booths and all kinds of workshops, where the natives squat and work before the eyes of the passers-by. . . ."

To N. F. von Meck.

"TIFLIS, *April 6th* (18*th*), 1886.

"I begin to know Tiflis quite well already, and have seen the sights. I have been in the baths, built in Oriental style. Visited the celebrated churches, amongst others the Armenian church, where I was not only very much interested in the peculiarities of the service, but also in the singing; I also visited David's monastery on the hill, where Griboiedov[2] lies buried. One evening I went to a concert given by the Musical Society, where a very poor, thin orchestra played Beethoven's Third Symphony,

---

[1] Caucasian villages.
[2] The celebrated Russian dramatist.

Borodin's *Steppes*, and my Serenade for strings, to a public which was conspicuous by its absence. Many excellent musicians live in Tiflis; the most prominent are the talented composer Ippolitov-Ivanov and the pianist Eugene Korganov, an Armenian, and a former student of the Moscow Conservatoire. They show me every attention, and although I should much prefer to remain incognito, I am much touched by this proof of the love and sympathy of my fellow-workers. I had certainly not expected to find my music so widely known in Tiflis. My operas are played oftener here than anywhere else, and I am pleased that *Mazeppa* is such a great favourite."

Diary.

"TIFLIS, *April 11th* (*23rd*), 1886.

"While waiting for Korganov I busied myself with looking through his works. He came first, then Ippolitov-Ivanov. The poor Armenian (a very nice man and a good musician) was very grieved at my criticism. Then Ivanov played his things : very good."

To M. Tchaikovsky.

"TIFLIS, *April 23rd* (*May 5th*), 1886.

"MODI,—I only remain a few days longer in Tiflis. I could count this month the happiest in my life, if it were not for the visitors, and for my social existence. I do not think I have yet written to you of the honour paid me on the 19th. It was simply splendid. At eight o'clock, accompanied by Pani,[1] I entered the Director's box, which was decorated with flowers and foliage. The whole theatre rose, and amid great applause I was presented with a silver wreath and many others. A deputation from the Musical Society read an address. Then the concert began, which consisted entirely of my works. There were endless cheers ! I have never experienced anything like it before. After the concert, a subscription supper, with many toasts. A most exhausting evening, but a glorious remembrance."

[1] Anatol's wife.

This was the first great honour in Tchaikovsky's life, and made a most agreeable impression on him, as proving the recognition of his merit by the Russian nation. Tchaikovsky, in the depths of his heart, was well aware that fame would eventually come, and that he would be worthy of it. He did not realise, however, that what he had already created was as worthy of fame as what he should create in the future. He knew, indeed, that the popularity of his name had greatly increased in the last few years, but he was still far from suspecting the truth. The honour paid him in Tiflis revealed to him his real relation to the Russian public. This revelation was so pleasing to his artistic vanity that it overcame for a moment his characteristic timidity and his dislike of posing before the public.

IX

Just at this time Tchaikovsky had to travel to Paris on important family business. He wished also to take this opportunity of making acquaintance with his Paris publisher, Mackar. To avoid the fatigue of the wearisome railway journey, he thought of taking the steamer from Batoum to Italy, thence by train to France. But owing to cholera at Naples, the French steamer belonging to the Batoum-Marseilles line did not call at the Italian port. Tchaikovsky therefore gave up his idea of visiting Italy, and took a through ticket for Marseilles by one of the steamers of the " Packet Company."

To A. Tchaikovsky.

" STEAMSHIP 'ARMENIA,' *May 3rd* (15*th*), 1886.

" . . . I am feeling less home-sick to-day, and better able to enjoy the sea, the mountains, and the sun . . . but how stupid it is, that one can only be alone in one's cabin ! On deck, scarcely a quarter of an hour passes without

someone beginning a conversation. I know all the passengers already, but have not taken to anyone. The
captain talks to me about music, and enrages me by his
stupid opinions. A Frenchman, a doctor from Trebizond,
also sets up to be a lover of music, and thinks it his duty
—now he has discovered I am a musician—to talk to me
about this detestable art, which seems to possess the quality
of interesting everybody. . . ."

To A. Tchaikovsky.

" ARCHIPELAGO, *May 6th* (18*th*), 1886.

" The day before yesterday, about midday, we reached
the Bosphorus in the most glorious weather. It is wonderfully beautiful, and the further one goes the more beautiful
it becomes. About three o'clock we arrived at Constantinople. The motion was very great during the passage
into the harbour. About five o'clock we got into a boat,
and were rowed over to the town. The captain had made
up his mind to stay twenty-four hours in Constantinople,
so I thought I would spend the night at an hotel. The
next day I visited the places of interest. The cathedral
of St. Sophia delighted and astonished me. But, on the
whole, I do not much care for Constantinople, and the
famous Constantinople dogs simply make me feel sick.
By 5 p.m. we were once more on board, and started
immediately. New passengers had joined the ship. I preferred to remain in my own snug little cabin ; the whole
evening I watched the water and the moonlight, and
absorbed all the poetry of a sea journey. To-day is a
little rougher. Many are ill—even men. I am quite well,
and find a certain pleasure in the motion, and in watching
the foaming blue waves. No trace of fear. I am quite
accustomed to my surroundings, and have made friends
with everyone, especially a Turkish officer, who is travelling to Paris."

To M. Tchaikovsky.

" ' ARMENIA,' *May 8th* (20*th*), 1886.

" . . . To-day the sea is just like a mirror. So far we
have been very lucky, and it is impossible to imagine

nything more beautiful than such a journey. Of course here are some wearisome moments, especially when they egin to talk of music. The chief offender is an Englishman, who continually bothers me with questions as to whether I like this or that song by Tosti, Denza, etc. Also a French doctor, who has invented a new piano in which every sign for transposition ($\sharp$, $\flat$, $\times$, $\flat\flat$) has its own keynote. He talks incessantly of his awful invention, and gives me long pamphlets on the subject. We have already passed Sicily and the heel of the Italian boot. Etna is smoking a little, and to the left there is a horrible pillar of smoke and fire which excites us all very much. The captain cannot say for certain what it means, and seems somewhat disturbed by it. Consequently I, too, feel a little afraid."

To A. Tchaikovsky.

"'ARMENIA,' *May 9th* (21*st*), 1886.

"The pillar of smoke and fire about which I wrote yesterday proves to be a terrible eruption of Mount Etna, not at the top, but at the side. This eruption was distinctly visible at a distance of three hundred versts, and the nearer we came the more interesting was the sight. Alexis woke me at two in the morning, that I might see this unique spectacle. We were in the Straits of Messina; the sea, which had been quite calm all day, was now very rough; I cannot describe the beauties of the moonlight, the fire from Mount Etna, and the swelling waves. At 3 a.m. I went back to bed and at five the captain sent a sailor to wake me, so that I might see the town of Messina, the sunrise, and the eruption on the other side. Later we passed between the volcano Stromboli and a new little island giving forth smoke; at least, the captain, who knows these parts well, has never suspected a volcano here and thinks it may portend a serious eruption. To-day the weather is splendid and the sea much quieter."

Diary.

"PARIS, *May 21st (June 2nd)*, 1886.

"I decided to go and see Mackar. What I suffered, an
how excited I was, passes description. Ten times I trie
to go in, and always turned away again—even a large glas
of absinthe did not help me. At last I went. He wa
expecting me. I had pictured him a little man like Wuch.
He is astonishingly like Bessel. We talked a little (some
one near me was buying my works), and then I lef
Naturally I felt a weight off my heart."

To P. V. Tchaikovsky.[1]

"PARIS, *June 1st (13th)*, 1886.

" . . . Yesterday I had breakfast with old Madam Viar
dot. She is such a stately and interesting woman; I wa
quite enchanted. Although seventy, she only looks abou
forty. She is very lively, amiable, gay, and sociable
and knew how to make me feel at home from the ver
first moment."

Later Tchaikovsky wrote the following details to Na
dejda von Meck concerning his acquaintance with Madam
Viardot:—

" . . . Madame Viardot often speaks about Tourgeniev
and described to me how he and she wrote 'The Song o
Love Triumphant' together. Have I already told yo
that I was with her for two hours while we went throug
the *original score* of Mozart's *Don Juan*, which thirt
years ago her husband had picked up very cheaply an
quite by accident? I cannot tell you what I felt at th
sight of this musical relic. I felt as if I had shaken Mozar
by the hand and spoken to him! . . ."

To Modeste Tchaikovsky.

"*June 23rd (11th)*, 1886.

"Yesterday, at the invitation of Ambroise Thomas,
visited the Conservatoire during the examination of th

---

[1] Anatol's wife.

pianoforte class. He is a very nice, friendly old man. A certain Madame Bohomoletz, a rich lady (half Russian), gave a dinner in my honour, followed by a musical evening, at which my quartet was played (Marsick and Brandoukov) and my songs were sung. . . . Leo Délibes has visited me ; this touched me very deeply. Certainly it seems I am not as unknown in Paris as I thought. . . ."

I will add to this short and disjointed account that Tchaikovsky was received in a most friendly manner by Professor Marmontel, a warm admirer of his works, also by the composers Lalo, Lefèbre, Fauré, and others. The meeting with Colonne and Lamoureux is described by Tchaikovsky himself in a later letter :—

". . . I saw Colonne several times. He was very friendly, and expressed a wish to give a concert of my compositions. He asked me to send him some of my new scores to Aix-les-Bains, so that he could arrange a programme during the course of the summer. He continually lamented his *poverty* and the ' *terrible* Concurrence Lamoureux.' As to Lamoureux, he was amiability itself, and made me a thousand promises."

Tchaikovsky was thrown into close contact with many other artists, several of whom, like the well-known pianist Diemer, for instance, remained his devoted friends to the end.

X

To N. F. von Meck.

" MAIDANOVO, *June* 18*th* (30*th*), 1886.

" How glad I am to be at home once more ! How dear and cosy is my little house which, when I left, lay deep in snow, and is now surrounded by foliage and flowers ! The three months I spent abroad were lost time as regards work, but I feel I have gained in strength, and can now devote my whole time to it without exhausting myself."

2 L

Diary.   "*July 8th (20th)*, 1886.

" . . . Worked atrociously again. And yet people say I am a genius! Nonsense!"

To P. Jurgenson.

"MAIDANOVO, *July 19th (31st)*, 1886.

"DEAR FRIEND,—I completely understand the difficulties of your situation. One of my letters to you is wanted for publication. You possess hundreds of my letters, but not one suitable to the case. Very natural; our correspondence was either too business-like, or too intimate. How can I help you? I cannot commit forgery, even for the pleasure of appearing in Mme. La Mara's book ; [1] I cannot write a letter especially for her collection and take this lucky opportunity of displaying myself in the most favourable light as musician, thinker, and man. Such a sacrifice on the altar of European fame is repugnant to me, although, on the other hand, it would be false to say that Mme. La Mara's wish to place me among the prominent musicians of our time did not flatter me in the least. On the contrary, I am very deeply touched and pleased by the attention of the well-known authoress, and openly confess I should be very glad to be included in the company of Glinka, Dargomijsky, and Serov. If she were not in such a hurry, it would be better to send to one of my musical friends, such as Laroche, who could not fail to find among all my letters some with detailed effusions about my musical likes and dislikes ; in short, a letter in which I speak quite candidly as a musician. But there is no time, and Laroche is away. Is it not curious that it should be difficult to find a suitable letter from a man who has carried on—and still carries on—the widest correspondence, dealing not only with business matters, but with artistic work? I am continually exchanging letters with four brothers, a sister, several cousins, and many friends, besides a quantity of casual correspondence

---

The authoress of the well-known works, *Musikalische Studienköpfe* and *Musik Briefe aus fünf Jahrhunderten.* Tchaikovsky's letter appears in the second volume of the latter.

with people often unknown to me. The necessity of sacrificing so much of my time to letter-writing is such a burden to me that, from the bottom of my heart, I curse all the postal arrangements in the world. The post often causes me sad moments, but it also brings me the greatest joy. One person plays the chief part in the story of the last ten years of my life: she is my good genius; to her I owe all my prosperity and the power to devote myself to my beloved work. Yet I have never seen her, never heard her voice; all my intercourse with her is through the post. I can certainly say I flood the world with my correspondence, and yet I am not in a position to help you out of your difficulty.

"There is nothing to be done, but to send this letter itself to Mme. La Mara. If it does not represent me in the least as a musician, it will at any rate give the authoress a chance of satisfying her flattering wish to place me among the prominent musicians of the day."

Diary.

"*August 1st* (13*th*), 1886.

". . . Played *Manon* at home. It pleased me better than I expected. I spent moments of longing and loneliness."

"*August 2nd* (14*th*).

". . . Played *Manon*. To-day Massenet seems to cloy with sweetness."

"*August 4th* (16*th*).

". . . Played Massenet at home. How stale he has grown! The worst of it is, that in this staleness I trace a certain affinity to myself."

To N. F. von Meck.

"MAIDANOVO, *August 4th* (16*th*), 1886.

". . . I feel at my best when I am alone; when trees, flowers, and books take the place of human society. O God, how short life is! How much I have yet to accomplish before it is time to leave off! How many projects!

When I am quite well—as I am at present—I am seize with a feverish thirst for work, but the thought of th shortness of human life paralyses all my energy. It wa not always so. I used to believe I could, and must, carr out all my ideas to completion; therefore my impulse towards creative work were then more lasting and mor fruitful. In any case I hope to have the outline of th opera (*The Enchantress*) ready in a month's time, an then to begin the orchestration."

Diary.

"*August 6th* (18*th*), 1886.

" Played the conclusion of the sickly *Manon* an Lefèbre's inanities to the end."

"*August* 15*th* (27*th*).

". . . Worked a little before and after supper. Kouma' Arioso is finished. Read Loti's *Pêcheurs d'Islande*. No very pleased with it. The tone of the descriptions remin me of that . . . Zola and . . ."

"*August* 18*th* (30*th*).

" Walked in the garden. Worked and completel finished the rough sketches for the opera. Thank God !"

To M. Tchaikovsky.

" MAIDANOVA, *September*, 9*th* (21*st*), 1886.

". . . I have been all through Vietinghov-Scheel' opera. Good heavens! what a weak piece of work He is a child, and no mature artist. It is a shame suc a work should be given at the Imperial Opera. However in this way the Direction have done Rubinstein a grea service. His *Demon* appears a masterpiece in compariso with that little Scheel affair. To tell the truth, at presen the best operas in the world are composed by P. I. Tchai kovsky, and *The Enchantress* is the most beautiful of them all. A gem all round. At least so it appears to me a this moment. Probably it appears to Vietinghov tha his *Tamara* is far more beautiful; and God alone know which of us is right."

Diary.

"*September 20th (October 2nd),* 1886.

"Tolstoi never speaks with love and enthusiasm of any prophet of Truth (with the exception of Christ), but rather with contempt and hatred. We do not know how he regards Socrates, Shakespeare, or Gogol. We do not know if he cares for Michael Angelo and Raphael, Tourgeniev, George Sand, Dickens and Flaubert. Perhaps his sympathies and antipathies in the sphere of philosophy and art are known to his intimates, but this inspired talker has never openly let fall a word which could enlighten us as to his attitude towards those great spirits who are on an equality with him. For instance, he has told me that Beethoven had no talent (as compared with Mozart), but he has never expressed himself in writing either on music or any kindred subject. Truly I think this man inclines only before God or the people, before humanity as a whole. There is no individual before whom he would bow down. Suitaiev was not an individual in Tolstoi's eyes, but the people itself, the personified wisdom of the people. It would be interesting to know what this giant liked or disliked in literature.

"Probably after my death it will be of some interest to the world to hear of my musical predilections and prejudices, the more so that I have never expressed them by word of mouth.

"I will begin by degrees, and when touching upon contemporary musicians I shall also speak of their personalities.

"To begin with Beethoven, whom I praise unconditionally, and to whom I bend as to a god. But what is Beethoven to me? I bow down before the grandeur of some of his creations, but I do not love Beethoven. My relationship to him reminds me of that which I felt in my childhood to the God-Jehovah. I feel for him—for my sentiments are still unchanged—great veneration, but also fear. He has created the heaven and the earth, and although I fall down before him, I do not love him. Christ, on the contrary, calls forth exclusively the feeling of *love*. He is God, but also Man. He has suffered like ourselves. We pity Him and love in Him the ideal side of man's nature. If Beethoven holds an analogous place in my heart to the God Jehovah, I love Mozart as the musical Christ. I do not think this comparison is blasphemous. Mozart was as pure as an angel, and his music is full of divine beauty.

"While speaking of Beethoven I touch on Mozart. To my mind, Mozart is the culminating point of all beauty in the sphere of music. He alone can make me weep and tremble with delight at the consciousness of the approach of that which we call the ideal. Beethoven makes me tremble too, but rather from a sense of fear and yearning anguish. I do not understand how to analyse music, and cannot go into detail. . . . Still I must mention two facts. I love Beethoven's middle period, and sometimes his first; but I really hate his *last*, especially the latest quartets. They have only brilliancy, nothing more. The rest is chaos, over which floats, veiled in mist, the spirit of this musical Jehovah.

"I love everything in Mozart, for we love everything in the man to whom we are truly devoted. Above all, *Don Juan*, for through that work I have learnt to know what music is. Till then (my seventeenth year) I knew nothing except the enjoyable *semi-music* of the Italians. Although I love everything in Mozart, I will not assert that every one of his works, even the most insignificant, should be considered a masterpiece. I know quite well that no single example of his Sonatas is a great creation, and yet I like each one, because it is his, because he has breathed into it his sacred breath.

"As to the forerunner of both these artists, I like to play Bach, because it is interesting to play a good fugue; but I do not regard him, in common with many others, as a great genius. . Handel is only fourth-rate, he is not even interesting. I sympathise with Glück in spite of his poor creative gift. I also like some things of Haydn. These four great masters have been surpassed by Mozart. They are rays which are extinguished by Mozart's sun."

To the Grand Duke Constantine Constantinovich.

"*September,* 1886.

"YOUR IMPERIAL HIGHNESS,—Permit me to thank you cordially for your valued present and your sympathetic letter. Very highly do I esteem the attention of which you have thought me worthy.

"I only regret, your Highness, that while looking for poems for my songs which are to be dedicated to her Majesty, I had not as yet the pleasure of possessing that charming little book which, thanks to your flattering attention, is now in my hands. How many of your poems glow with that warm and sincere feeling which makes them suitable for musical setting! When I read your collection of verses I determined at once to select some for my next song-cycle, and to dedicate them, with your gracious permission, to your Highness. I should be much pleased if you would accept this dedication as the expression of my sincere devotion."

To N. F. von Meck.

"MAIDANOVO, *October 5th (17th),* 1886.

". . . What you say about *my conducting* is as balm to my wounded heart. The consciousness of my inability to conduct has been a torment and a martyrdom to me all my life. I think it is contemptible and shameful to have so little self-control that the mere thought of stepping into the conductor's desk makes me tremble with fright. This time too—although I have already promised to conduct myself—I feel when the time comes my courage will vanish and I shall refuse."

Diary.

"MAIDANOVO, *October 7th (19th),* 1886.

"Played Brahms. It irritates me that this self-conscious mediocrity should be recognised as a genius. In comparison with him, Raff was a giant, not to speak of Rubinstein, who was a much greater man. And Brahms is so chaotic, so dry and meaningless!"

XI

At the end of October Tchaikovsky went to Petersburg to be present at the first performance of Napravnik's opera *Harold*. But as the performance was constantly postponed, he finally returned to Maidanovo without waiting for it. Nevertheless, the journey was not without results for Vsievolojsky, Director of the Imperial Opera, commissioned Tchaikovsky for the first time to compose a ballet. Joukovsky's *Undine* was chosen as a subject.

Judging from all accounts, this visit to Petersburg must have convinced Tchaikovsky of his great popularity there. Not only did he meet with a very friendly reception from the composers, with Rimsky-Korsakov at their head, but he received from an anonymous well-wisher, through the medium of Stassov, a premium of 500 roubles, usually bestowed on the best musical novelty of the season, judged in this instance to be *Manfred*. He was also honoured by a brilliant gathering on the occasion of his election as honorary member of the St. Petersburg Chamber Music Society.

To Rimsky-Korsakov.

"*October* 30*th* (*November* 11*th*), 1886.

"DEAR NICHOLAS ANDREIEVICH,—I have a favour to ask. Arensky is now quite recovered, although I find him somewhat depressed and agitated. I like him so much and wish you would sometimes take an interest in him, for, as regards music, he venerates you more than anyone else. The best way of doing this would be to give one of his works at one of your next concerts. There, where all Russian composers find a place, should be a little room for Arensky, who, at any rate, is as good as the rest. But as you would not like to offend anyone, I propose that you should put one of Arensky's works in the programme of your fourth concert instead of my *Romeo* over-

ure. He needs stirring up ; and such an impulse given
y you would count for so much with him, because he
oves and respects you. Please think it over and grant my
ish. Thereby you will make your deeply devoted pupil
Arensky) very happy.

"In conclusion, I must add that your 'Spanish Capriccio'
s a *colossal masterpiece of instrumentation*, and you may
egard yourself as the greatest master of the present day."

To M. Tchaikovsky.

"Moscow, *November* 19*th* (*December* 1*st*), 1886.

". . . I arrived in Moscow early to-day. There has
lready been a rehearsal. I was ill again after my last
etter to you. This time I was so bad that I decided to
end for the doctor. It seemed to me that I was about to
ave a strange illness. Suddenly I received a telegram
aying that I must be at the rehearsal.[1] I answered that
he rehearsal was not to be thought of, for I could not
ravel. But at the end of half an hour I suddenly felt so
vell that—in spite of terrible disinclination—I went to
Moscow. Every trace of headache, which for ten days
ad so affected me, vanished. Is not this a curious patho-
ogical case ? "

To A. S. Arensky.

"*November* 24*th* (*December* 6*th*), 1886.

"DEAR FRIEND ANTON STEPANOVICH,—I only received your welcome letter yesterday ; I knew already from
Taneiev that you had composed *Marguerite Gautier* and
dedicated it to me. Thank you cordially for this dedication. The attention and honour you have shown me touch
me deeply. *Marguerite* lies beside me on the table, and—
in my free moments, which are not many—I cast a glance
at it here and there, with much interest and pleasure.
Please do not feel hurt that I did not write you my
impressions at once. At the first glance I found the work
very interesting, because you have entirely departed from
your accustomed style. *Marguerite* has so little resemblance to the Suite and the Symphony that one could

---

[1] Of *Cherevichek*, "The Little Shoes."

easily suppose it came from the pen of a different man. The elegance of form, harmony, and orchestration are the same, but the character of the theme and its working out are quite different. Naturally the question arises: Is it better than the Symphony and the Suite? At present I cannot answer."

Although somewhat anticipating my narrative, I will insert here an extract from a later letter of Tchaikovsky's, in which he gives Arensky his opinion of *Marguerite Gautier*.

To A. Arensky.

"MAIDANOVO, *April 2nd* (*14th*), 1887.

"DEAR ANTON STEPANOVICH,—I wrote to you in August that I would pronounce judgment on *Marguerite Gautier* as soon as I had heard the work and had leisure to study the score. I held it all the more my duty to wait because, although I value your talent very highly, I do not like your Fantasia. It is very easy to praise a man who is highly esteemed. But to say to him: 'Not beautiful; I do not like it,' without basing one's judgment on a full explanation, is very difficult. . . .

"I must state my opinion briefly. First the choice of subject. It was very painful and mortifying to me, and to all your friends, that you had chosen *La Dame aux Camelias* as the subject of your Fantasia. How can an educated musician—when there are Homer, Shakespeare, Gogol, Poushkin, Dante, Tolstoi, Lermontov, and others—feel any interest in the production of Dumas *fils*, which has for its theme the history of a demi-mondaine adventuress which, even if written with French cleverness, is in truth false, sentimental, and vulgar? Such a choice might be intelligible in Verdi, who employed subjects which could excite people's nerves at a period of artistic decadence; but it is quite incomprehensible in a young and gifted Russian musician, who has enjoyed a good education, and is, moreover, a pupil of Rimsky-Korsakov and a friend of S. Taneiev.

"Now for the music: (1) *The Orgies.*—If we are to realise in these orgies a supper after a ball at the house of a light woman, in which a crowd of people participate, eat mayonnaise with truffles, and afterwards dance the *cancan*, the music is not wanting *in realism*, fire, and brilliancy. It is, moreover, saturated with Liszt, as is the whole Fantasia. Its beauty—if one looks at it closely—is purely on the surface ; there are no enthralling passages. Such beauty is not *true* beauty, but only a forced imitation, which is rather a fault than a merit. We find this superficial beauty in Rossini, Donizetti, Bellini, Mendelssohn, Massenet, Liszt, and others. But they were also masters in their own way, though their chief characteristic was not the Ideal, after which we ought to strive. For neither Beethoven, nor Bach (who is wearisome, but still a genius), nor Glinka, nor Mozart, ever strove after this surface beauty, but rather the ideal, often veiled under a form which at first sight is unattractive.

"(2) *Pastorale in Bougival.*—Oh God ! If you could only understand how unpoetical and unpastoral this Bougival is, with its boats, its inns, and its *cancans !* This movement is as good as most conventional pastoral ballets that are composed by musicians of some talent.

"(3) *The Love Melody*

is altogether beautiful. It reminds me of Liszt. Not of any particular melody, but it is in his style, after the manner of his semi-Italian melodies, which are wanting in the plasticity and simplicity of the true Italian folk airs. Moreover, the continuation of your theme :

is not only beautiful, but wonderful; it captivates both the ear and the heart.

"No one can ever reproach you with regard to the technical part of your work, which deserves unqualified praise."

To Modeste Tchaikovsky.

"Moscow, *December* 4*th* (16*th*), 1886.

"MY DEAR MODI,—Something very important happened to-day. I conducted the first orchestral rehearsal in such style that all were astonished (unless it were mere flattery), for they had expected I should make a fool of myself. The nearer came the terrible day, the more unbearable was my nervousness. I was often on the point of giving up the idea of conducting. In the end I mastered myself, was enthusiastically received by the orchestra, found courage to make a little speech, and raised the bâton. Now I know I *can* conduct, I shall not be nervous at the performance."

To N. F. von Meck.

"Moscow, *January* 14*th* (26*th*), 1887.

"MY VERY DEAR FRIEND,—I have been enjoying your hospitality for a week.[1] I live in your house as if under the wing of Christ. Your servants are so careful of my welfare that I cannot praise them enough. I only regret that I can be so little at home. Daily rehearsals. I take a walk every morning, and by eleven o'clock I am waiting in the conductor's desk. The rehearsal is not over till four o'clock, and then I am so tired that when I return home I have to lie down for a while. Towards evening I feel better and take some food.

"The conducting gives me great anxiety and exhausts my whole nervous system. But I must say it also affords me great satisfaction. First of all, I am very glad to have conquered my innate, morbid shyness; secondly, it is a good thing for a composer to conduct his own work, instead of having constantly to interrupt the conductor to draw his attention to this, or that, mistake; thirdly, all my colleagues have shown me such genuine sympathy that I am quite touched by it, and very pleased. Do you know I feel much less agitation than when I sit at the rehearsal doing nothing. If all goes well, I believe that not only will my nerves be none the worse, but it will have a beneficial effect on them."

[1] Tchaikovsky was staying in N. F. von Meck's house at this time.

The first performance of *Les Caprices d'Oxane* took place at Moscow on January 19th (31st), 1887, and had a far-reaching influence on Tchaikovsky's future, because he then made his first successful attempt at conducting. The great interest which the production of a new opera always awakens was thereby doubled, and all the places were taken before the opening night. The singers did their work conscientiously; there was no fault to be found, but no one made a memorable "creation" of any part. The mounting and costumes were irreproachable.

The public greeted the composer-conductor with great enthusiasm. Gifts of all kinds showed plainly that it was Tchaikovsky himself who was honoured, not the new conductor and composer of *Les Caprices d'Oxane*. The opera was a success; four numbers had to be repeated *da capo*.

The Press criticisms on this occasion were all favourable, even the *Sovremenny Izvesty*, in which Krouglikov, as we know, generally criticised Tchaikovsky's works so severely. In short, the opera really had a brilliant success; far greater than that achieved by *Eugene Oniegin* in Petersburg. Neverthess this opera only remained in the repertory for two seasons.

But little can be said about that which interests us most—the impression made by Tchaikovsky's conducting. The severest judge and critic, Tchaikovsky himself, was satisfied. We know in what an objective spirit he criticised the success of his works, so we can safely believe him when he says he fulfilled his task satisfactorily. He describes this memorable evening as follows :—

To E. K. Pavlovskaya.

"Moscow, *January 20th* (*February 1st*), 1887.

"I did not expect to be very excited on the day of the performance, but when I awoke, quite early, I felt really ill, and could only think of the approaching ordeal as of a horrible nightmare. I cannot describe what mental agonies

I suffered during the course of the day. Consequently, at the appointed hour, I appeared half dead at the theatre. Altani accompanied me to the orchestra. Immediately the curtain went up and, amid great applause, I was presented with many wreaths from the chorus, orchestra, etc. While this took place, I somewhat recovered my composure, began the Overture well, and by the end felt quite master of myself. There was great applause after the Overture. The first Act went successfully, and afterwards I was presented with more wreaths, among them yours, for which many thanks. I was now quite calm, and conducted the rest of the opera with undivided attention. It is difficult to say if the work really pleased. The theatre was at least half-full of my friends. Time and future performances will show if the applause was for me personally (for the sake of past services), or for my work. Now the question is, how did I conduct? I feel some constraint in speaking about it. Everyone praised me; they said they had no idea I possessed such a gift for conducting. But is it true? Or is it only flattery? I shall conduct twice more, and after the third time I ought to know for certain how much truth there is in all this."

I have seldom seen Tchaikovsky in such a cheerful frame of mind as on that evening. We did not reach home till after five o'clock in the morning, and he immediately sank into a deep sleep. After so many days of anxiety and excitement he really needed rest! No one was more unprepared than he for the sad news which reached us next morning.

About seven o'clock I was aroused by a telegram which announced the death of our niece Tatiana, the eldest daughter of Alexandra Davidov. She had died quite suddenly at a masked ball in Petersburg. Not only was she a near relative, but also a highly gifted girl of great beauty. It required considerable resolution on my part to break the sad news to my brother when he awoke at eleven o'clock, happy and contented, and still under the pleasant impressions of the previous evening.

In spite of this heavy blow, Tchaikovsky did not alter his decision to conduct *Les Caprices d'Oxane* for two nights longer. The constant activity, and anxiety of a different nature, helped to assuage the violence of his grief.

XII

To N. F. von Meck.

"Maidanovo, *February 2nd* (14*th*), 1887.

"I have now been at home five days, yet there is no question of rest; on the contrary, I am working with such feverish haste at *The Enchantress* that I feel quite exhausted. I cannot live without work, but why do circumstances always compel me to be in a hurry, to have to overtax my strength? I see such an endless pile of work before me to which I am pledged that I dare not look into the future. How short life is! Now that I have probably reached that last step which means the full maturity of my talent, I look back involuntarily and, seeing so many years behind me, glance timidly at the path ahead and ask: Shall I succeed? Is it worth while? And yet it is only now that I begin to be able to compose without self-doubt, and to believe in my own powers and knowledge."

To N. F. von Meck.

"Maidanovo, *February 9th* (21*st*), 1887.

"I am already dreaming of a time when I shall give concerts abroad. But of what does one not dream? If only I were twenty years younger!!! One thing is certain: my nerves are much stronger, and things which formerly were not to be thought of are now quite possible. Undoubtedly I owe this to my free life, relieved from all anxiety of earning my daily bread. And who but you, dear friend, is the author of all the good things fate has brought me?

"The concert will take place in Petersburg on March 5th."

On February 23rd (March 7th) Tchaikovsky went to Petersburg to attend the rehearsals for the Philharmonic Concert, at which the St. Petersburg public was to make his acquaintance as a conductor, from which dated the commencement of a whole series of similar concerts which made his name known in Russia, Europe and America.

On February 28th (March 12th) the first rehearsal took place, and Tchaikovsky writes in his diary in his customary laconic style: "Excitement and dread." Henceforth, to the very end of his life, it was not the concert itself so much as the first rehearsal which alarmed him. By the second rehearsal he had usually recovered himself. Abroad, he found it particularly painful to stand up for the first time before an unknown orchestra.

All the important musical circles in Petersburg showed a lively interest in Tchaikovsky's début as a concert conductor. The three rehearsals attracted a number of the first musicians, who encouraged him by their warm words of sympathy. No début could have been made under more favourable conditions.

The concert itself, which took place on March 5th (17th), in the hall of the Nobles' Club, went off admirably. The programme consisted of: (1) Suite No. 2 (first performance in St. Petersburg), (2) Aria from the opera *The Enchantress*, (3) the "Mummers' Dance" from the same opera, (4) Andante and Valse from the Serenade for strings, (5) *Francesca da Rimini*, (6) Pianoforte solos, (7) Overture "*1812*."

The hall was full to overflowing, and the ovations endless. The Press criticisms of the music, as well as of Tchaikovsky's conducting, proved colourless and commonplace, but on the whole laudatory. Even Cui expressed some approbation for Tchaikovsky as a conductor, although he again found fault with him as a composer.

Tchaikovsky's diary contains the following brief account of the concert: "My concert. Complete success. Great enjoyment—but still, why this drop of gall in my honey-pot?"

In this question lie the germs of that weariness and suffering which had their growth in Tchaikovsky's soul simultaneously with his pursuit of fame, and reached their greatest intensity in the moment of the composer's greatest triumphs.

To N. F. von Meck.

"MAIDANOVO, *March 12th (24th),* 1887.

"The Empress has sent me her autograph picture in a beautiful frame.[1] This attention has touched me deeply, especially at a time when she and the Emperor have so many other things to think about."

Diary.

"Ippolitov-Ivanov and his wife came very late, about ten o'clock. I met them out walking. At first I felt annoyed to see them, and vexed at my work being interrupted ; but afterwards these good people (she is extremely sympathetic) made me forget everything, except that it is the greatest pleasure to be in the society of congenial friends. Ivanov played, and she sang beautiful fragments from his opera *Ruth* (the duet especially charmed me). They left at six. Worked before and after supper."

To Modeste Tchaikovsky.

"MAIDANOVO, *March 15th (27th),* 1887.

"*Ruth* pleases me more and more. I believe Ippolitov-Ivanov will come to the front, if only because he has something original about him, and this 'something' is also very attractive."

Diary.

"*March 16th (28th),* 1887.

"I will not conceal it : all the poetry of country life and solitude has vanished. I do not know why. *Nowhere do I feel so miserable as at home.* If I do not work, I torment

---

[1] In return for the dedication of the twelve songs.

myself, am afraid of the future, etc. Is solitude really necessary to me? When I am in town, country life seems a paradise; when I am here, I feel no delight whatever. To-day, in particular, I am quite out of tune."

"*March* 19*th* (31*st*).

"Have just read through my diary for the last two years. Good heavens! how could my imagination have been so deceived by the melancholy bareness of Maidanovo? How everything used to please me!"

"*March* 26*th* (*April* 7*th*).

"Read through Korsakov's 'Snow-Maiden,' and was astonished at his mastery. I envy him and ought to be ashamed of it."

"*March* 30*th* (*April* 11*th*).

"After supper I read the score of *A Life for the Tsar*. What a master! How did Glinka manage to do it? It is incomprehensible how such a colossal work could have been created by an amateur and—judging by his diary—a rather limited and trivial nature."

"*April* 16*th* (28*th*).

"Played through *The Power of the Evil One*.[1] An almost repulsive musical monstrosity; yet, at the same time, talent, intuition, and imagination."

To N. F. von Meck.

"MAIDANOVO, *April* 24*th* (*May* 6*th*), 1887.

"MY VERY DEAR FRIEND,—I wished to leave Maidanovo a month ago, and yet I am still here. My work (the orchestration of the opera) detains me. This work is not really difficult, but it takes time. I notice that the older I grow, the more trouble my orchestration gives me. I judge myself more severely, am more careful, more critical with regard to light and shade. In such a case the country is a real boon. Saint-Saëns has invited me to be present at both his concerts at Moscow, but I have courteously refused. Poor Saint-Saëns had to play to an

[1] Opera by Serov.

empty room. I knew it would be so, and that the poor Frenchman would take it deeply to heart, so I did not wish to be a witness of his disappointment. But also I did not want to interrupt my work."

Tchaikovsky stayed at Maidanovo to complete the instrumentation of the whole score of *The Enchantress*, and left on May 9th to visit his sick friend, Kondratiev, before starting on his journey to the Caucasus.

XIII

To N. F. von Meck.

"THE CASPIAN SEA, *May 28th (June 9th)*, 1887.

" I left Moscow on the 20th. At Nijni-Novogorod I had great trouble in securing a second-class ticket for the steamer, *Alexander II.* This steamer is considered the best, and is therefore always full. My quarters were very small and uncomfortable, but I enjoyed the journey down the Volga. It was almost high tide, and therefore the banks were so far away that one could almost imagine oneself at sea. Mother Volga is sublimely poetical. The right bank is hilly, and there are many beautiful bits of scenery, but in this respect the Volga cannot compare with the Rhine, nor even with the Danube and Rhône. Its beauty does not lie in its banks, but in its unbounded width and in the extraordinary volume of its waters, which roll down to the sea without any motion. We stopped at the towns on the way just long enough to get an idea of them. Samara and the little town of Volsk pleased me best, the latter having the most beautiful gardens I have ever seen. We reached Astrakhan on the fifth day. Here we boarded a little steamer, which brought us to the spot where the mouth of the Volga debouches into the open sea, where we embarked on a schooner, on board which we have been for the last two days. The Caspian Sea has been very treacherous. It was so stormy during the night that I was quite frightened. Every moment it seemed as if the trembling ship must break up beneath the force of the waves; so much so that I could not close an eye all night. But in spite of this I was not sea-sick. We reached Baku to-day. The storm has abated. I shall not be able to start for Tiflis until to-morrow morning, for we cannot catch the train to-day."

On the journey between Tsaritsin and Astrakhan, Tchaikovsky had a very droll experience. He had managed so cleverly that no one on board knew who he was. One day a little musical entertainment was got up, and Tchaikovsky offered to undertake the accompanying. It so happened that a lady amateur placed one of his own songs before him and explained to him the manner in which he was to accompany it. On his timidly objecting, the lady answered that she must know best, as Tchaikovsky himself had gone through the song in question with her music mistress. The same evening a passenger related how Tchaikovsky had been so delighted with the tenor Lody in the rôle of Orlik in *Mazeppa*[1] that after the performance "he fell on Lody's neck and wept tears of emotion."

To N. F. von Meck.

"TIFLIS, *May* 30*th* (*June* 11*th*), 1887.

"Baku, in the most unexpected fashion, has turned out to be an altogether beautiful place, well planned and well built, clean and very characteristic. The Oriental (especially the Persian) character is very prevalent, so that one could almost imagine oneself to be on the other side of the Caspian Sea. It has but one drawback: the complete lack of verdure. . . .

"On the day after my arrival I visited the neighbourhood of the naphtha wells, where some hundred boring-towers throw up a hundred thousand *pouds* of naphtha every minute. The picture is grand but gloomy. . . .

"The road between Baku and Tiflis runs through a stony, desolate country."

[1] Orlik's part is written for a bass, and Lody has a tenor voice.

The end of this journey was Borjom, where he intended to pass the whole summer in the family of his brother Anatol. He reached there on June 11th. He only learnt to appreciate by degrees the enchanting beauty of the neighbourhood. The horizon, shut in by lofty mountains, the sombre flora, their luxuriance, and the depth of the shadows, made an unpleasant impression upon him at first. Only after he had learnt to know the inexhaustible number and variety of the walks did he begin to like this country more and more. When, ten days later, his brother Modeste arrived at Borjom he was already full of enthusiasm and ready to initiate him into all the beauties of the place.

Tchaikovsky worked very little while at Borjom, only spending an hour a day at the instrumentation of the "Mozartiana" Suite.

At the commencement of July Tchaikovsky left Borjom in response to a telegram from his friend Kondratiev, who had been removed to Aix-la-Chapelle, in the hopes that the baths might prolong his life for a few months. Kondratiev's condition was so critical that Tchaikovsky could not do less than interrupt his own cure and join his friend as soon as possible.

To Modeste Tchaikovsky.

"AIX-LA-CHAPELLE, *July* 16*th* (28*th*), 1887.

"I do not dislike Aix—that is all I can say. What is really bad here is the atmosphere, saturated as it is with smells of cooking, cinnamon, and other spices. I think sorrowfully of the air in Borjom, but I try to dwell upon it as little as possible. However, I feel more cheerful here than I did on the journey. I see that my arrival has given much pleasure to Kondratiev and Legoshin, and that I shall be of use to them."

Diary.

" Aix, *July 22nd* (*August 3rd*), 1887.

" I sit at home full of remorse. The cause of my remorse is this : life is passing away and draws near to its end, and yet I have not fathomed it. Rather do I drive away those disquieting questions of our destiny when they intrude themselves upon me, and try to hide from them. Do I live truly ? Do I act rightly ? For example, I am now sitting here, and everyone admires my *sacrifice*. Now there is no question of sacrifice. I lead a life of ease, gormandise at the *table d'hôte*, do nothing, and spend my money on luxuries, while others want it for absolute necessities. Is not that the veriest egoism ? I do not act towards my neighbours as I ought."

To P. Jurgenson.

" Aix, *July 29th* (*August 10th*), 1887.

" DEAR FRIEND,—To-day I am sending you my Mozart Suite, registered. Three of the borrowed numbers in the Suite are pianoforte pieces (Nos. 1, 2, 4); one (No. 3) is the chorus ' Ave Verum.' Of course, I should be glad if the Suite could be played next season. That is all."

Tchaikovsky's " heroic act " of friendship consumed more than a month of his time. While paying full tribute to the generosity of his undertaking, we must confess that he failed to grasp the relation between wishing and doing. Tchaikovsky, filled with real and self-denying compassion for the sufferings of his neighbour, was wanting—as in all practical questions of life—in the necessary ability, self-control, and purpose. In the abstract, no one had more sympathy for his neighbour than he ; but in reality no one was less able to do much for him. Anyone who could ask the trivial question : " Where wadding, needles, and thread could be bought ? " would naturally lose his head at the bedside of a dying man. The consciousness of his helplessness and incapacity to lessen his friend's suffering

in the least, his irresolution in face of the slightest difficulty, rendered Tchaikovsky's useless visit to Aix all the
more painful. He suffered for the dying man and for
himself. The result was that he did "too much" for
friendship and "too little" for his sick friend ; at least, in
comparison to the extraordinary sacrifice of strength
which his generous action demanded. When, at the end
of August, the dying man's nephew came to relieve him,
Tchaikovsky fled from Aix, deeply grieved at parting from
his friend "for ever," humbled at his own mental condition,
and angry at his inability "to see the sad business through
to the end." Exhausted, and wrathful with himself, he
arrived at Maidanovo on August 30th (September 11th),
where the news of Kondratiev's death reached him a fortnight later.

Diary.

" *September* 21*st* (*October* 3*rd*), 1887.

"How short is life ! How much I have still to do, to
think, and to say ! We keep putting things off, and meanwhile death lurks round the corner. It is just a year since
I touched this book, and so much has changed since
then. How strange ! Just 365 days ago I was afraid
to confess that, in spite of the glow of sympathetic feeling which Christ awoke in me, I dared to doubt His
divinity. Since then my *religion* has become more clearly
defined, for during this time I have thought a great deal
about God, life, and death. In Aix especially I meditated
on the fatal questions : why, how, for what end ? I should
like to define my religion in detail, if only I might be
quite clear, once for all, as to my faith, and as to the
boundary which divides it from speculation. But life and
its vanities are passing, and I do not know whether I shall
succeed in expressing the *symbol* of that faith which has
arisen in me of late. It has very definite forms, but I do
not use them when I pray. I pray just as before ; as
I was taught. Moreover, God can hardly require to know
how and why we pray. God has no need of prayers.
But we have."

On October 20th (November 1st) *The Enchantress* was produced under the bâton of the composer, and the performance was altogether most brilliant and artistic.

On this first night Tchaikovsky does not appear to have observed that the opera was a failure. He thought, on the contrary, that it pleased the public. After the second performance (on October 23rd), which—notwithstanding that it went better than the first—still failed to move the audience to applause, he first felt doubts as to its success. The indifference of the public was clearly apparent after the third and fourth representations, when his appearance in the conductor's desk was received in chilling silence. It was only then that he realised that *The Enchantress* was a failure. On the fifth night the house was empty.

Tchaikovsky, as we shall see, ascribed this failure to the ill-will of the critics. After I had read through all the notices—says Modeste—it seemed to me that, in the present instance, my brother had done them too much honour. In none of the eleven criticisms did I trace that tone of contempt and malicious enjoyment with which his other operas had been received. No one called *The Enchantress* a "still-born nonentity," as Cui had said of *Eugene Oniegin;* no one attempted to count up the deliberate thefts in *The Enchantress*, as Galler had done with *Mazeppa*. The reason for the failure of *The Enchantress* must be sought elsewhere : possibly in the defective interpretation of both the chief parts ; but more probably in the qualities of the music, which still awaits its just evaluation at the hands of a competent critic.

To N. F. von Meck.

"Moscow, *November* 13*th* (25*th*), 1887.

"My dear Friend,—Please forgive me for so seldom writing. I am passing through a very stirring period of my life, and am always in such a state of agitation that it is impossible to speak to you from my heart as I should wish. After conducting my opera four times, I returned here, about five days ago, in a very melancholy frame of mind. In spite of the ovation I received on the opening night, my opera has not taken with the public, and practically met with no success. From the Press I have encountered such hatred and hostility that, even now, I cannot account for it. On no other opera have I expended so much labour and sacrifice; yet never before have I been so persecuted by the critics. I have given up the journey to Tiflis, for I shall scarcely have time to get sufficient rest in Maidanovo before I have to start on my concert tour abroad. I conduct first in Leipzig, and afterwards in Dresden, Hamburg, Copenhagen, Berlin, and Prague. In March I give my own concert in Paris, and from there I go to London, as I have received an invitation from the Philharmonic Society. In short, a whole crowd of new and strong impressions are awaiting me."

The Symphony Concert of the Russian Musical Society, November 14th (26th), was the first concert ever conducted by Tchaikovsky in Moscow. The programme consisted exclusively of his own works, including "Mozartiana" (first time), *Francesca da Rimini*, the Fantasia for pianoforte, op. 56 (Taneiev as soloist), and the Arioso from *The Enchantress*. On the following day the same programme was repeated by the Russian Musical Society at a popular concert. The "Mozartiana" Suite was a great success (the "Ave Verum" was encored), and the Press—in contradistinction to that of St. Petersburg—spoke with great warmth and cordiality of the composer and conductor.

To P. Jurgenson.

"*November 24th (December 6th)* 1887.

" In to-day's paper I accidentally saw that the eighth performance of *The Enchantress* was given before a half-empty house. It is an undoubted *fiasco*. This failure has wounded me in my inmost soul, for I never worked with greater ardour than at *The Enchantress*. Besides, I feel ashamed when I think of you, for you must have sustained a terrible loss. I know well enough that some day the opera will be reinstated, but when? Meanwhile it makes me very bitter. So far I have always maintained that the Press could not influence one's success or failure; but now I am inclined to think that it is only the united attack of these hounds of critics which has ruined my opera. The devil take them! Why this spite? Just now, for example, in to-day's number of the *Novosti*, see how they rail at our Musical Society and at me, because of this Popular Concert! Incomprehensible!"

Part VII

I

1888

WITH December, 1887, began a new and last period in the life of Tchaikovsky, during which he realised his wildest dreams of fame, and attained to such prosperity and universal honour as rarely fall to the lot of an artist during his lifetime. Distrustful and modest (from an excess of pride), he was now in a perpetual state of wonder and delight to find himself far more appreciated in Russia and abroad than he had ever hoped in the past. Physically neither better nor worse than in former years, possessing the unlimited affections of those whom he loved in return, —he was, to all appearance, an example of mortal happiness, yet in reality he was less happy than before.

Those menacing blows of fate—like the opening of Beethoven's Fifth Symphony—had sounded, although muffled and distant, even on the day of Tchaikovsky s first concert (March 5th); while that intangible and groundless sense of bitterness—that "touch of gall," as he himself calls it—was present even in that triumphant moment when he found himself master of the orchestra and all its tempestuous elements, as though prophetic of those sufferings which overshadowed the last years of his life. At the time he did not understand this vague warning; afterwards, when it came back to him, he realised it had been a friendly caution, not to continue the chase for fame; not to take up occupations that went against his nature, nor to spend his strength upon the attainment of things which would come of themselves; finally, to cling to his true vocation, lest disappointment should await him in the new path he had elected to follow. In February he wrote to Nadejda von Meck: "New and powerful impressions continually await me. Probably my fame will increase, but would it not be better to stay at home and work? God knows! I can say this: I regret the time when I was left in peace in the solitude of the country." And this regret grew keener, as his weariness grew more intolerable. The more he accustomed his temperament to unsuitable occupations, the further he advanced his reputation, the more complete was his disenchantment with the prize. Radiant and glittering as it had appeared from afar, seen closer, it proved insignificant and tarnished. Hence the profound disillusionment, "the insane depression," the something "hopeless and final" which make so dark a background to the picture of his brilliant success at home and abroad.

Tchaikovsky left Russia on December 15th (27th) and arrived in Berlin two days later. Here he was to meet Herr N—— who was acting as his concert agent during this tour. He had no sooner settled in his hotel than, picking up a newspaper, his eye fell upon a paragraph to the effect that: "To-day, December 29th, the Russian composer Tchaikovsky arrives in Berlin. To-morrow his numerous friends (?) and admirers (?) will meet to celebrate his arrival by a luncheon at the —— restaurant, at one o'clock. Punctual attendance is requested." "No words could describe my horror and indignation," wrote Tchaikovsky. "At that moment I could cheerfully have murdered Herr N——. I went out to breakfast at a café in the Passage, and afterwards to the Museum, walking in fear and trembling lest I should meet Herr N—— or some of my numerous *friends and admirers.*"

TCHAIKOVSKY IN 1888
(From a photograph by Reitlinger, Paris)

The following morning the dreaded interview with his agent took place. Tchaikovsky found him not altogether unsympathetic, but during the entire tour he realised that he was dealing with a very peculiar and eccentric man, whom he never really understood.

To Modeste Tchaikovsky.

" LEIPZIG, *December* 21*st*, 1887 (*January 2nd*, 1888).

" I have made acquaintance with Scharwenka and a number of other people. I also met Artôt.[1] Everyone was astonished to see me with N——, who follows me like my own shadow. At three o'clock I left for Leipzig, luckily without N—— for once, and was met by Brodsky, Siloti, and two of my admirers. I had supper with Brodsky. There was a Christmas-tree. His wife and sister-in-law are charming—really good Russian women. All the time the tears were in my eyes. Next day I took a walk (it was New Year's Day), and went back to dine with Siloti at Brodsky's. He was just trying a new trio by Brahms. The composer himself was at the piano. Brahms is a handsome man, rather short and stout.[2] He was very friendly to me. Then we sat down to table. Brahms enjoys a good drink. Grieg, fascinating and sympathetic, was there too.[3] In the evening I went to

---

[1] Their first meeting since 1869.

[2] In an account of his visit to Leipzig, which Tchaikovsky afterwards published as the *Diary of My Tour in 1888*, he characterises the German composer more fully : " Brahms is rather a short man, suggests a sort of amplitude, and possesses a very sympathetic appearance. His fine head—almost that of an old man—recalls the type of a handsome, benign, elderly Russian priest. His features are certainly not characteristic of German good looks, and I cannot conceive why some learned ethnographer (Brahms himself told me this after I had spoken of the impression his appearance made upon me) chose to reproduce his head on the first page of his books as being highly characteristic of German features. A certain softness of outline, pleasing curves, rather long and slightly grizzled hair, kind grey eyes, and a thick beard, freely sprinkled with white—all this recalled at once the type of pure-bred Great Russian so frequently met with among our clergy. Brahms's manner is very simple, free from vanity, his humour jovial, and the few hours spent in his society left me with a very agreeable recollection."

[3] In the same series of articles appeared the following sketch of Grieg : " There entered the room a very short, middle-aged man, exceedingly fragile

the Gewandhaus, when Joachim and Hausmann played the new Double Concerto of Brahms for violin and 'cello, and the composer himself conducted. I sat in the Directors' box, and made acquaintance with such numbers of people that I could not keep pace with them all. The Directors informed me that my rehearsal was fixed for the next day. What I suffered during the evening—in fact the whole time—cannot be described. If Brodsky and Siloti had not been there, I think I should have died. I spent a terrible night. The rehearsal took place early this morning. I was formally introduced to the orchestra by Carl Reinecke. I made a little speech in German. The rehearsal went well in the end. Brahms was there, and yesterday and to-day we have been a good deal together. We are ill at ease, because we do not really like each other, but he takes great pains to be kind to me. Grieg is charming. Dined with Siloti. Quartet concert at night. The new trio of Brahms. Home-sick. Very tired.

"You cannot imagine a finer room than at the Gewandhaus. It is the best concert-room I ever saw in my life."

To P. I. Jurgenson.

"LEIPZIG, *December 24th*, 1887 (*January 5th*, 1888).

"Yesterday the public rehearsal took place. I was very nervous, but my success was unusually flattering. . . . To-night, however, all may be reversed, for it is by no means certain that I shall not make a fool of myself. I have seen a good deal of Brahms. He is by no means a total abstainer, but he is very pleasant, and not so vain as I expected. But it is Grieg who has altogether won my heart. He is most taking and sympathetic, and his wife

in appearance, with shoulders of unequal height, fair hair brushed back from his forehead, and a very slight, almost boyish, beard and moustache. There was nothing very striking about the features of this man, whose exterior at once attracted my sympathy, for it would be impossible to call them handsome or regular ; but he had an uncommon charm, and blue eyes, not very large, but irresistibly fascinating, recalling the glance of a charming and candid child. I rejoiced in the depths of my heart when we were mutually introduced to each other, and it turned out that this personality, which was so inexplicably sympathetic to me, belonged to a musician whose warmly emotional music had long ago won my heart. It was Edvard Grieg."

equally so. Reinecke is very amiable. At the first rehearsal he introduced me to the band, and I made the following speech: 'Gentlemen, I cannot speak German, but I am proud to have to do with such a . . . such a . . . that is to say . . . I am proud . . . I cannot.' The band is splendid ; I could not have believed that our musicians—good as they are—were still so far behind a first-rate German orchestra."

"December 25th (January 6th).

" The concert has gone off well. The reception of the Suite was good, but not to be compared with that at the public rehearsal, when the audience consisted almost entirely of students and musicians. After the concert I went to a banquet arranged in my honour by Reinecke. He related much that was interesting about Schumann and, generally speaking, I felt very much at ease with him. Afterwards I had to go on to a fête given by the Russian students, and I did not get home until very late. Now I am just off to a Tchaikovsky Festival held by the Liszt-Verein. It begins at 11 a.m."

The Press notices upon Tchaikovsky's début in Leipzig as conductor and composer were numerous and lengthy. Keeping in view the importance of this occasion, and the influence it exercised on his future career, it has been thought well to give some extracts from the most interesting of these criticisms, which will be found in the Appendix.[1]

At the Tchaikovsky Festival given by the Liszt-Verein, his Quartet, op. 11, Trio, and some of his smaller compositions were included in the programme. The following day the composer returned to Berlin, where he arranged with the Directors of the Philharmonic Society to give a concert of his works on February 8th. He then left for Hamburg in the company of Adolf Brodsky, where the latter was to take part in a concert conducted by Hans von Bülow. As Tchaikovsky had the prospect of a few days' leisure,

[1] See Appendix C, p. 762.

he decided to spend them in Lübeck, whence he wrote to his brother Modeste on December 30th, 1887 (January 11th 1888) :—

"What joy! I do so enjoy finding myself in a strange town, in a capital hotel, with the prospect of five peaceful days before me! I arrived in Hamburg with Brodsky at 6 a.m. The rehearsal for Bülow's concert began at ten o'clock. Bülow was delighted to see me. He has altered and aged. He seems, too, calmer, more subdued, and softer in manner. . . . I went to the concert in the evening. Bülow conducted with inspiration, especially the 'Eroica.' I came on here to-day. It is very pleasant. What a blessing to be silent! To feel that no one will be coming, that I shall not be dragged out anywhere!"

To Modeste Tchaikovsky.

"*January* 1*st* (13*th*), 1888.

" . . . At last January (old style) has come. Now at any rate I can reckon four months to my return to Russia. I went to the theatre yesterday. Barnay was the star in *Othello.* He is sometimes astounding, quite a genius, but what an agonising play! Iago is too revolting—such beings do not exist."

On January 1st, 1888, a piece of good fortune fell to Tchaikovsky's lot. Thanks to the efforts of Vsievolojsky, Director of the Imperial Opera, the Emperor bestowed upon him a life pension of 3,000 roubles (£300) per annum.

To Modeste Tchaikovsky.

"HAMBURG, *January* 10*th* (22*nd*), 1888.

"On my appearance I was enthusiastically received by the orchestra, and their applause was supported by the public, which was not the case in Leipzig. I conducted without agitation, but towards the end I grew so tired I was afraid I could not hold out. Sapellnikov[1] played

---

[1] Pupil of Brassin and Madame Sophie Menter at the St. Petersburg Conservatoire, and, later on, an intimate friend of Tchaikovsky.

splendidly. After the concert there was a large party at the house of Bernuth, the Director of the Philharmonic. About a hundred guests were present, all in full-dress. After a long speech from Bernuth, I replied in German, which created a *furore*. Then we began to eat and drink. Yesterday was terrible; I cannot describe how I was torn to pieces, nor how exhausted I felt afterwards. In the evening there was a gala in my honour, at which my compositions were exclusively performed. The Press was very favourable.

" After the *soirée* followed a fearful night of it, in company with many musicians, critics, and amateurs, admirers of my music. I feel befogged. To-day I start for Berlin. Bülow is very amiable."

The programme of the concert at which Tchaikovsky made his first appearance in Hamburg was as follows: Tchaikovsky's Serenade for strings, Pianoforte Concerto in B♭ minor (Sapellnikov), the Theme and Variations from his Third Suite, and Haydn's " Oxford " Symphony.[1]

Between the Hamburg and Berlin concerts Tchaikovsky was anxious for a little repose, and decided to spend a few days at Magdeburg. On the one day spent in Berlin *en passant* he heard, for the first time, a work by Richard Strauss. " Bülow has taken him up just now," he wrote to his brother, " as formerly he took up Brahms and others. To my mind such an astounding lack of talent, united to such pretentiousness, never before existed."

Tchaikovsky now began to receive invitations from many musical centres to conduct his own works. Colonne had engaged him for two concerts in Paris on March 11th and 18th. Several other offers, including Weimar and the Dresden Philharmonic, had to be refused because the dates did not fit in with his plans.

On the advice of Bülow, Wolf, and other friends he decided to alter the programme of the forthcoming concert at Berlin, for which he had put down his *Francesa da Rimini*.

---

[1] For Press notices see Appendix C, p. 764.

2 N

"Perhaps they are right," he says in a letter to his brother "The taste of the German public is quite different to ours Now I understand why Brahms is idolised here, although my opinion of him has not changed. Had I known this sooner, perhaps I, too, might have learnt to compose in a different way. Remind me later to tell you about my acquaintance with the venerable Ave-Lallemant,[1] which touched me profoundly.

"Sapellnikov made quite a sensation in Hamburg. He really has a great talent. He is also a charming and good-hearted young man."

To V. Napravnik.

"MAGDEBURG, *January*, 12th (24th), 1888.

"The newspapers have published long articles about me. They 'slate' me a good deal, but pay me far more attention than our own Press. Their views are sometimes funny. A critic, speaking of the variations in the Third Suite, says that one describes a sitting of the Holy Synod and another a dynamite explosion."

---

[1] Chairman of the Committee of the Philharmonic Society. In the *Diary of My Tour* Tchaikovsky says: "This venerable old man of over eighty paid me great attention. . . . In spite of his age and his infirmity, he attended two rehearsals, the concert, and the party at Dr. Bernuth's. Herr Lallemant candidly confessed that many of my works which had been performed in Hamburg were not at all to his mind ; that he could not endure my noisy instrumentation and disliked my use of the instruments of percussion. For all that he thought I had in me the making of a really good German composer. Almost with tears in his eyes he besought me to leave Russia and settle permanently in Germany, where classical conventions and traditions of high culture could not fail to correct my faults, which were easily explicable by the fact of my having been born and educated in a country so un-enlightened and so far behind Germany. . . . I strove my best to overcome his prejudice against our national sentiments, of which, moreover, he was quite ignorant, or only knew them through the speeches of the Russophobist section. We parted good friends."

To Modeste Tchaikovsky.

"LEIPZIG, *January 20th (February 1st),* 1888.

". . . How shall I describe all I am experiencing just now? Continual home-sickness, some well-nigh intolerable hours, and a few very pleasant moments. I intended to spend a few quiet days here, instead of which I am whirled along in a stream of gaiety: dinners, visits, concerts, suppers, the theatre, etc. My sole comfort is the society of Siloti, Brodsky (I am quite in love with his wife and sister-in-law), and Grieg and his wife. But besides these, every day I make new and sympathetic acquaintances. I take Sapellnikov with me wherever I go, and have introduced him to many people in the musical world. Wherever he plays he creates a sensation. I am more and more convinced of his superb talent. . . . I went to a Quartet Concert, at which I heard a quartet by an exceedingly gifted Italian, Busoni. I quickly made friends with him. At an evening given by Brodsky I was charmed with a new sonata by Grieg. Grieg and his wife are so quaint, sympathetic, interesting, and original that I could not describe them in a letter. I regard Grieg as very highly gifted. To-day I dine with him at Brodsky's. To-night is the extra concert in aid of the funds for the Mendelssohn Memorial, and to-morrow the public rehearsal of the Gewandhaus Concert, at which Rubinstein's symphony will be given. Afterwards I am giving a dinner to my friends at a restaurant, and start for Berlin at five o'clock. How tired I am!"

"*January 23rd (February 4th).*

". . . to-day I got rid of N——. We parted in peace, but my purse was lighter by five hundred marks in consequence. I do not regret it in the least; I would have given a good deal more to see the last of this gentleman."

To Modeste Tchaikovsky.

"BERLIN, *January 23rd (February 4th).*

". . . I have made great progress in my conducting. . . . Wolf gave a large dinner-party at my desire, in order that all the great lights here might hear Sapellnikov. All the critics were there. Sapellnikov created a *furore*. For the last three weeks we have been inseparable. I have grown so fond of him, and he so attached and good to me—just as though he were a near relation. Since Kotek's days I have never cared for anyone so much. It is impossible to imagine anyone more sympathetic, gentle, kindly ; more delicate-minded and distinguished. On his return I beg you not only to be friendly to him, but to introduce him to all our relatives. I consider him—and I am not alone in my opinion—a future genius as regards the piano. Yesterday Bock had a party. Artôt was there. I was inexpressibly glad to see her again ; we made friends at once, without a word as to the past. Her husband, Padilla, embraced me heartily. To-morrow she gives a dinner. As an elderly woman she is just as fascinating as twenty years ago."

To N. F. von Meck.

"LEIPZIG, *January* 30*th* (*February* 11*th*), 1888.

"MY DEAR FRIEND,—My concert in Berlin was a great success.[1] I had a splendid orchestra to deal with and musicians who were in sympathy with me from the very first rehearsal. The programme was as follows :—

"(1) Overture, *Romeo and Juliet ;* (2) Pianoforte Concerto, played by Siloti ; (3) Introduction and Fugue from the First Suite ; (4) Andante from the First Quartet ; (5) Songs, sung by Fräulein Friede ; (6) Overture, "*1812.*"

"The public gave me a most enthusiastic reception. Of course, all this is very pleasant, but at the same time I feel so worn out I hardly know how I am to get through all that lies before me. . . . Can you recognise in this Russian musician, touring all over Europe, the man who, a few years ago, fled from life and society, and lived in solitude abroad, or in the country ?

"A real triumphal festival awaits me in Prague. The programme of my week's visit there is already arranged, and has been sent to me. It includes any number of ovations and receptions. The idea is to give my concert

---

[1] For Press notices see Appendix C, p. 767.

there a certain patriotic and anti-German character. This puts me in an awkward position, because I have been received in a very friendly way in Germany."

In spite of the applause of the public and the flattering notices in the Press, Tchaikovsky's visit made less impression in Berlin than in Leipzig and Hamburg. Whereas in the latter towns his concerts were the great events of the day, in the capital the début of a Russian composer passed comparatively unnoticed amid a thousand other interests. A brief entry in his diary on January 28th about "a bucket of cold water" seems to point to a certain disillusionment as to the character of his reception in Berlin. Possibly he had heard rumours that the concert-room had been liberally "papered," and in this way a certain amount of artificial enthusiasm spread through the audience.

In any case, it was Leipzig, rather than Berlin, that showed the greater interest in Tchaikovsky during this tour, and he was glad to return there for a few days before leaving Germany. "I have come back to Leipzig," he wrote to a relative on January 30th (February 11th), 1888, "as I had promised to be present at the concert given in my honour by the Liszt-Verein. The concert could not come off, so yesterday, at my request, Wagner's *Meistersinger* was performed at the theatre instead. I had never heard this opera. Early this morning I was awakened by the strains of the Russian hymn. An orchestra was serenading me. They played for nearly an hour under my windows, and the whole hotel ran out to see and hear."

The marvellous performance of *Meistersinger* under Nikisch, and the touching ovation in the form of a serenade, were the closing events of Tchaikovsky's first concert tour in Germany. In Bohemia and France far more brilliant receptions awaited him, but these were of quite a different nature.

II

On January 31st (February 12th) Tchaikovsky, accompanied by Siloti, arrived at the frontiers of Bohemia. The triumphal character of the reception which awaited him was soon made apparent by the extraordinary attentions of the railway officials. At one of the last stations before Prague, a deputation of members of various societies had assembled to welcome him. At Prague a representative of the " Russian Club" awaited him on the platform, having come expressly from Vienna to pay him this compliment. He presented Tchaikovsky with an address in Russian. This was followed by a speech in Czech, delivered by Dr. Strakaty, the representative of the " Umclecká Beseda,"[1] after which children presented him with flowers, and he was hailed with prolonged cries of " Slava!" (Hurrah!). The carriage which awaited him, and the suite of rooms at the Hotel de Saxe, were provided for him at the expense of the Artists' Club.

In the evening he was invited to hear Verdi's *Otello*, and a box was reserved for him at the Opera House. Rieger, "the leader of the Czech people," was the first to greet the guest, after which followed many of the most prominent men in Bohemia.

The following day Tchaikovsky received a visit from Dvořák, and the two composers quickly made friends with each other.

It is impossible to give in detail the programme drawn up for each day of the composer's visit to Prague. He made an almost royal progress to all the chief places of interest. On one occasion, entering the " Rathaus " while

---

[1] The Artists' Club.

ALEXANDER SILOTI

PETER ILICH TCHAIKOVSKY

a session was being held, the entire body of members rose to greet him. One evening he was serenaded by the famous Choral Union " Hlahol." He listened to the songs from his balcony, and afterwards came down to thank the singers in person. An offer, made in the course of his speech, to compose something expressly for the Society was received with loud cheering. On February 6th (18th) he was invited to the Students' Union and presented to the students. In his diary he speaks of this as " a very solemn and touching ceremony." Accompanied by cries of " Slava ! " and " Na Sdrava ! " he was next led off to the public rehearsal of the concert. The evening wound up with a brilliant *soirée* at the Town Club (Meschtschanska Beseda).

The first concert itself took place on February 7th (19th), in the " Rudolfinum." The programme consisted entirely of Tchaikovsky's music, and included : (1) Overture, *Romeo and Juliet;* (2) Concerto for Pianoforte (B♭ minor), played by Siloti ; (3) Elégie from the Third Suite ; (4) Violin Concerto, played by Halir ; (5), Overture, " *1812.*" Of all these works the last-named excited the greatest applause. Tchaikovsky sums up his impressions as follows : " Undoubtedly it was the most eventful day of my life. I have become so attached to these good Bohemians . . . and with good reason ! Heavens, what enthusiasm ! Such as I have never known, but in my own dear Russia ! "

Two days later, on February 9th (21st), the second concert was given in the *foyer* of the Opera House. This time the programme comprised : (1) Serenade for strings ; (2) Variations from the Third Suite ; (3) Pianoforte Solos (Siloti) ; (4) Overture, " *1812.*" The ovations were even more hearty, and the gifts more costly, than at the first concert. "An overwhelming success," says Tchaikovsky in his diary. " A moment of absolute bliss. But only one moment."

On the evening of February 10th (22nd), sped by farewell addresses, and smothered in flowers, the composer took leave of the festive city of Prague.

Although the chief object of Tchaikovsky's tour was to make his works more widely known in Europe, and to carry them beyond the confines of his native land, he combined with this aim—although in a lesser degree—the desire to see for himself the extent of his reputation and to reap some profit by it. Distrustful and modest as he was, he made no great demands in this respect, and even the appreciation he received in Germany quite surpassed his expectations. The honour done him in Prague far outstripped his wildest dreams. These ten days were the culminating point of Tchaikovsky's fame during his life-time. Allowing that nine-tenths of the ovations lavished on him were really intended for Russia, even then, he could not fail to be flattered that he was the chosen recipient of the sympathy of the Czechs for the Russians, since it proved that he was already famous as a composer. It was flatter-ing, too, to feel that he was honoured by a nation which could be regarded as one of the most musical in the world. It pleased him that Prague—the first place to recognise the genius of Mozart—should pay him honour, thus uniting his fate with that of the illustrious German. It touched Tchaikovsky deeply to feel that those who gave him one "moment of absolute happiness" were descendants of the same race which, long ago, had given a portion of joy to him who was his teacher and model, both as man and as musician. This strange coincidence was the most flattering event of his life—the highest honour to which he had ever ventured to aspire.

Simultaneously with this climax of his renown, came one of the bitterest experiences of his life. The Russian Press did not give a line to this triumph of a native com-poser in Prague. He felt this to be a profound injury, which surprised and mortified him the more, because all these triumphs in his life were regarded as important events even by the Czechs themselves. It was most painful to realise that Russia, for whom the greater part of these honours were intended, knew nothing whatever about them; that on account of the attitude of the Press towards him, personally, this warm sympathy, meant for his countrymen as a whole, would never be known to them, nor evoke any response.

Quite another kind of ovation awaited Tchaikovsky in Paris. Here, too, his success surpassed his expectations; but the sympathy of the French capital differed as widely in character from that which was shown him in Prague as the Czechs differ from the French in their musical tastes and their relations towards the Russians. There is no country in which music is better loved, or more widely understood, than in Bohemia. Nor is there any other nation which feels such appreciation for all that is Russian ; not merely as a matter of passing fashion, but on account of actual kinship between the Eastern and Western Slav. In Bohemia, therefore, both as a musician and a native of Russia, Tchaikovsky had been received with a warmth and sincerity hardly to be expected from France. It is true a little political feeling influenced his reception in Paris ; it was just the beginning of the Franco-Russian *rapprochement,* so that everything Russian was the fashion of the hour. Many French people, who were not in the least musical, regarded it as their duty to express some appreciation of Tchaikovsky—simply because he was a Russian. All this, like the French sympathy itself, had no solid foundation of national affinity, but merely sprang from an ephemeral political combination. The enthusiastic, explosive, but fleeting, craze of the French for all that was Russian showed itself in hats *à la* Kronstadt, in shouting the Russian national anthem simultaneously with the " Marseillaise," in ovations to the clown Durov, and in a "patronising" interest for our art and literature—as species of curiosities—rather than in the hearty relations of two countries drawn together by true affinity of aims and sympathies. Naturally the festivities of Kronstadt, Toulon, and Paris led to no real appreciation of Poushkin, Gogol, Ostrovsky, Glinka, Dargomijsky, or Serov, only, at the utmost, to a phase of fashion, thanks to which Tolstoi and Dostoievsky found a certain superficial vogue, without being understood in their fullest value. Tchaikovsky was also a modern, and this lent a kind of brilliance to his reception in Paris ; but it was purely external. . . . It may truly be said that all Prague welcomed the composer ; whereas in Paris only the musicians and amateurs, a few newspapers in favour of the Franco-Russian alliance, and that crowd which is always in pursuit of novelty, were interested in Tchaikovsky's visit.

Time has proved the respective value of these ovations. Although it is now fifteen years since Tchaikovsky visited Prague, his operas still hold their own in the repertory of the theatre, and his symphonic music is still as well known there and as much loved as in Russia. In Paris, on the contrary, not only are his works rarely given, either on the stage or in the concert-room, but his name— although it has gained in renown all over Europe—is not considered worthy of inclusion among those which adorn the programmes of the Conservatoire concerts. And yet those who are at the head of this institution are the same men who honoured him in 1888. Is not this a proof of that hidden but smouldering antipathy which the French really feel for the Russian spirit—that spirit which Tchaikovsky shares in common with his great predecessors in music, and with the representatives of all that Russia has produced of lofty and imperishable worth ?

Tchaikovsky arrived in Paris on February 12th (24th), and went almost straight from the station to the rehearsal of his Serenade for strings, which—conducted by the composer—was to be played by Colonne's orchestra at a *soirée* given by M. N. Benardaky.

N. Benardaky had married one of the three sisters Leibrock, operatic artists well known to the Russian public. He had a fine house in Paris, frequented by the *élite* of the artistic world. As a wealthy patron of art—and as a fellow-countryman—he inaugurated the festivities in Tchaikovsky's honour by this musical evening.

Over three hundred guests were present, and, besides his Serenade for strings, Tchaikovsky conducted the Andante from his Quartet and presided at the piano. The composer was grateful to his kindly host for the unexpected and—according to Parisian custom—absolutely indispensable *réclame* which this entertainment conferred upon him. To ensure the success of the evening, and in return for the service done him, Tchaikovsky felt himself obliged to run from rehearsal to rehearsal, from musician to musician. To appear as a conductor before this assemblage of amateurs—more distinguished for vanity than for love of art—and to earn their languid approval, seemed to him flattering and important. But when we reflect what far greater trouble and fatigue this entailed upon him than his appearance before the Gewandhaus audience—whose opinion was really of weight and value—we cannot but regret the waste of energy and the lowering of the artist's dignity. When we think of him, exhausted and out of humour, amid this crowd of fashionably attired strangers, who to-morrow would be "consecrating" the success of the latest chansonette singer, or the newest dance of a Loie Fuller—we cannot but rebel against fate, who took him from his rural quiet, from the surroundings to which he was attached, in which—sound in body and mind—it was his pleasure to plan some new composition in undisturbed solitude. Thank God, my brother comforted himself with the belief that it was necessary to suffer this martyrdom cheerfully, and that he did not live to realise that it was indeed useless, for nowhere did he make a greater sacrifice for popularity's sake with smaller results than in Paris.

Those musicians who had been absent during Tchaikovsky's visit to Paris in 1886 now made his acquaintance for the first time. All of them, including Gounod, Massenet, Thomé and others, received him with great cordiality and consideration. The sole exception was Reyer, the composer of *Salammbô*, whose indifference was the less hurtful to Tchaikovsky because he did not esteem him greatly as a musician. Of the *virtuosi* with whom he now became acquainted, Paderewski made the most impression upon him.

Among the brilliant Parisian gatherings held in Tchaikovsky's honour must be mentioned the memorable evening at Colonne's; the *soirée* given by the aristocratic amateur, Baroness Tresderne, at whose house in the Place Vendôme Wagner's Trilogy had been heard for the first time in Paris ("Marchionesses, duchesses—bored," is Tchaikovsky's laconic entry in his diary the day after this entertainment); the fête at the Russian Embassy; a reception at Madame Pauline Viardot's; and an entertainment arranged by the *Figaro*.

Tchaikovsky made two public appearances in the double capacity of composer and conductor; both these were at the Châtelet concerts. At the first, half the programme was devoted to his works, including the Serenade for strings, Fantasia for pianoforte (Louis Diemer), Songs (Madame Conneau), pieces for violoncello (Brandoukov), and Theme and Variations from the Third Suite.

On ascending to the conductor's desk he was received with a storm of applause, intended as much for his nationality as for his personality. Of his orchestral works, the Valse from the Serenade won most success, and had to be repeated in order to satisfy the audience.

The second concert, which took place a week later, consisted almost exclusively of Tchaikovsky's works. The

Variations from the Third Suite, the Elégie, and Valse from the Serenade, and the pieces for violoncello were repeated; to which were added the Violin Concerto (Marsick) and *Francesca da Rimini*. The applause was as vociferous as on the first occasion, although comparatively little of it fell to the lot of *Francesca*.

As long as they dealt with the private performances in the houses of Benardaky, Colonne, Madame Tresderne, or at the *Figaro*, the representatives of the Paris Press spoke with enthusiasm of the composer, of his works, and his nationality. After the public concerts, however, there was a sudden change of tone, and their fervour waned. It seemed they had most of them studied Cui's book, *La Musique en Russie*, to good purpose, for, without quoting their source of information, they discovered that Tchaikovsky "was not so Russian as people imagined," that he did not display "much audacity or a strong originality," wherein lay the chief charm of the great Slavs: Borodin, Cui, Rimsky-Korsakov, Liadov, etc.

The Western cosmopolitanism of Tchaikovsky's works was made a subject of reproach. "The German dominates and absorbs the Slav," says one critic, who had looked for "impressions exotiques" at the Châtelet—perhaps for something in the style of the music of Dahomey, which had created such a sensation at the Jardin d'Acclimatation.

The remaining critics, who had not read Cui's book, disapproved of the length of Tchaikovsky's works, and held up to him as models, Saint-Saëns and other modern French composers. His own sense of disappointment appears in a letter addressed to P. Jurgenson towards the end of his visit:—

"I have expended a great deal of money, and even more health and strength," he writes.[1] "In return I have

[1] In a later letter to Jurgenson he says: "One has to choose between never travelling, or coming home with empty pockets. I had hardly decided

gained some celebrity, but every hour I ask myself—Why? Is it worth while? And I come to the conclusion it is far better to live quietly without fame."

From Paris Tchaikovsky crossed to England.

"The journey to London was terrible," he wrote to Nadejda von Meck. "Our train was brought to a standstill in the open country in consequence of a snowstorm. On the steamer it was alarming, for the storm was so severe that every moment we dreaded some catastrophe."

Tchaikovsky only spent four days in London. No one welcomed him, no one paid him special attention, or worried him with invitations. Except for a complimentary dinner given to him by Berger, the Secretary of the Philharmonic Society, he spent his time alone, or in the society of the violinist Ondricek and his wife. Yet, in spite of appearances, his visit to London had brilliant results for his future reputation. Next to Russia and America his music at present is nowhere more popular than in England.

He conducted the Serenade for strings and the Variations from the Third Suite. "The success was great," he wrote, in the letter quoted above. "The Serenade pleased most, and I was recalled three times, which means a good deal from the reserved London public. The Variations were not so much liked, but all the same they elicited hearty applause."

The leading London papers mostly gave Tchaikovsky the credit of a signal success. The *Musical Times*

to throw up everything and fly home, when paid engagements were offered me on all sides; at Angers, with a fee of £40; the same at Geneva, in London (at the Crystal Palace) for a sum not stated; but I gave them all up. You are mistaken in your calculations as to the result of my journey. For London I received £25 instead of £20 (thanks to my great success, the Directors of the Philharmonic were moved to add an extra £5), and you omitted the £25 from Hamburg. My journey was certainly not a financial success; but I did not undertake it for the sake of the money."

only regretted that he had not chosen some more serious work for his début before the London public. "The Russian composer was received with signs of unanimous approbation," said the *Times*, while the *Daily Chronicle* felt convinced that Tchaikovsky must have been fully satisfied with the extraordinarily warm welcome accorded him by the Londoners.

"Thus ended the torments, fears, agitations, and—to speak the truth—the joys of my first concert tour abroad." In these words Tchaikovsky concludes his letter to N. F. von Meck, from which the above extracts have been quoted.

III

After a long journey—six nights in the train—Tchaikovsky reached Tiflis on March 26th (April 7th), 1888. Here he stayed with his brother Hyppolite, whom he had not seen for two years. About the end of April he travelled north to take possession of the country house at Frolovskoe, which had been prepared for him during his absence by his servant Alexis. He describes it as a highly picturesque spot, lying on a wooded hill on the way from Moscow to Klin. It was simpler and not so well furnished as Maidanovo. There was no park planted with lime trees, there were no marble vases; but its unpretentiousness was an added recommendation in Tchaikovsky's eyes. Here he could be alone, free from summer excursionists, to enjoy the little garden (with its charming pool and tiny islet) fringed by the forest, behind which the view opened out upon a distant stretch of country—upon that homely, unassuming landscape of Central Russia which Tchaikovsky preferred to all the sublimities of Switzerland, the Caucasus, and Italy. Had not the forest been gradually exterminated, he would never have quitted Frolovskoe, for although he only lived there for three years, he became greatly attached to the place. A month before his death, travelling from Klin to Moscow, he said, looking out at the churchyard of Frolovskoe: " I should like to be buried there."

To Modeste Tchaikovsky.

" KLIN, *May 15th (27th)*, 1888.

" I am in love with Frolovskoe. The neighbourhood is a paradise after Maidanovo. It is, indeed, so beautiful that when I go out for half an hour's walk in the morning, I feel compelled to extend it to two hours. . . . I have not yet begun to work, excepting at some corrections. To speak frankly, I feel as yet no impulse for creative work. What does this mean? Have I written myself out? No ideas, no inclination? Still I am hoping gradually to collect material for a symphony.

" To-day we were to have sown seeds and planted flowers in the beds in front of the house. I was looking forward to it with such pleasure, but the rain has hindered us. By the time you arrive all our seeds will be in."

To the Grand Duke Constantine Constantinovich.

" FROLOVSKOE, *May 30th (June 11th)*, 1888.

" YOUR HIGHNESS,—I am very glad you were not offended by my remarks, and thank you most heartily for your explanations in reference to them.[1] In matters of versification I am only an amateur, but have long wished to become thoroughly acquainted with the subject. So far, I have only reached the stage of inquiry. Many questions interest me to which no one seems able to give a clear and decided reply. For instance, when I read Joukovsky's translation of the *Odyssey*, or his *Undine*, or Gniedich's version of the *Iliad*, I suffer under the intolerable monotony of the Russian hexameter as compared with the Latin (I do not know the Greek), which has strength, beauty, and variety. I know that the fault lies in the fact that we do not use the spondee, but I cannot

---

[1] The Grand Duke Constantine had sent Tchaikovsky a volume of his verses.

TCHAIKOVSKY'S HOUSE AT FROLOVSKOE

understand why this should be. To my mind we ought to employ it. Another question that greatly occupies me is why, as compared with Russian poetry, German verse should be less severe in the matter of regular rhythm and metre. When I read Goethe I am astonished at his audacity as regards metrical feet, the cæsura, etc., which he carries so far that, to an unpractised ear, many of his verses scarcely seem like verse. At the same time, the ear is only taken by surprise—not offended. Were a Russian poet to do the same, one would be conscious of a certain lameness. Is it in consequence of the peculiar qualities of our language, or because tradition allows greater freedom to the Germans than to us? I do not know if I express myself correctly ; I only state that, as regards regularity, refinement, and euphony, much more is expected from the Russian than from the German poet. I should be glad to find some explanation of this. . . ."

To N. F. von Meck.

"FROLOVSKOE, *June 1st* (13*th*), 1888.

" . . . . Just now I am busy with flowers and flower-growing. I should like to have as many flowers as possible in my garden, but I have very little knowledge or experience. I am not lacking in zeal, and have indeed taken cold from pottering about in the damp. Now, thank goodness, it is warmer weather ; I am glad of it, for you, for myself, and for my dear flowers, for I have sown a quantity, and the cold nights made me anxious for them. . . . ."

To N. F. von Meck.

"FROLOVSKOE, *June 10th* (22*nd*), 1888.

" . . . . Now I shall work my hardest. I am dreadfully anxious to prove not only to others, but also to myself, that I am not yet *played out* as a composer. . . . Have I already told you that I intend to write a symphony? The beginning was difficult ; now, however, inspiration seems to have come. We shall see!"

2 O

To the Grand Duke Constantine Constantinovich.

"FROLOVSKOE, *June* 11*th* (*23rd*), 1888.

"YOUR IMPERIAL HIGHNESS,—I am the more glad to hear your favourable verdict upon my songs, because I was afraid you would think them weak. . . . I composed them at a time when my state of mind was anything but promising for good work. At the same time, I did not wish to postpone the setting of your words, as I had informed you long ago of my intention with regard to them. . . .

"I am not at all astonished that you should write beautiful verses without being an adept in the science of versification. Several of our poets—Plestcheiev for one—have told me the same. All the same, I think it would be better if some of our gifted Russian poets were more interested in the technique of their art. 'I am sick of four iambic feet,' said Poushkin, and I would add that sometimes his readers get weary of it too. To discover new metres and rare rhythmic combinations must be very interesting. Were I a poet, I should certainly try to write in varied rhythms like the Germans. . . ."

To N. F. von Meck.

"FROLOVSKOE, *June* 22*nd* (*July* 4*th*), 1888.

". . . . Lately I have been in frequent correspondence with the Grand Duke Constantine Constantinovich, who sent me his poem, 'St. Sebastian,' with the request that I would say what I thought of it. On the whole I liked it, but I criticised a few details very freely. He was pleased with this, but defended himself, and thus a brisk exchange of letters has taken place. He is not only gifted, but surprisingly modest, devoted to art, and ambitious to excel in it rather than in *the service*. He is also an excellent musician—in fact, a rare and sympathetic nature.

"It is well that the political horizon is clearer, and if it be true that the German Emperor is to visit Russia, we may say with some certainty that the horrors of war will not break out for many years to come. . . ."

Diary.

"*June 27th (July 9th)*, 1888.

",It seems to me letters are not perfectly sincere—I am judging by myself. No matter to whom I am writing, I am always conscious of the effect of my letter, not only upon the person to whom it is addressed, but upon any chance reader. Consequently I embroider. I often take pains to make the tone of a letter simple and sincere—at least to make it *appear* so. But apart from letters written at the moment when I am worked upon, I am never quite myself in my correspondence. These letters are to me a source of repentance, and often of agonising regret. When I read the correspondence of great men, published after their death, I am always disturbed by a vague sense of insincerity and falsehood.

" I will go on with the record of my musical predilections which I began some time ago. What are my feelings towards the Russian composers?

GLINKA.

" An unheard-of and astonishing apparition in the world of art. A dilettante who played the violin and the piano a little ; who concocted a few insipid quadrilles and fantasias upon Italian airs ; who tried his hand at more serious musical forms (songs, quartets, sextets, etc.), but accomplished nothing which rose superior to the jejune taste of the thirties ; suddenly, in his thirty-fourth year, creates an opera, which for inspiration, originality, and irreproachable technique, is worthy to stand beside all that is loftiest and most profound in musical art ! We are still more astonished when we reflect that the composer of this work is the author of the *Memoirs* published some twenty years later. The latter give one the impression of a nice, kind, commonplace man, with not much to say for himself. Like a nightmare, the questions continually haunt me : How could such colossal artistic force be united to such emptiness ? and how came this average amateur to catch up in a single stride such men as Mozart and Beethoven ? Yes, for he *has* overtaken them. One may say this without exaggeration of the composer of the

'Slavsia.' This question may be answered by those who are better fitted than myself to penetrate the mysteries of the artistic spirit which makes its habitation in such fragile and apparently unpromising shrines. I can only say no one loves and appreciates Glinka more than I do. I am no indiscriminate worshipper of *Russlan;* on the contrary, I am disposed to prefer *A Life for the Tsar*, although *Russlan* may perhaps be of greater musical worth. But the elemental force is more perceptible in his earlier opera; the 'Slavsia' is overwhelming and gigantic. For this he employed no model. Neither Glück nor Mozart composed anything similar. Astounding, inconceivable! *Kamarinskaya* is also a work of remarkable inspiration. Without intending to compose anything beyond a simple, humorous trifle, he has left us a little masterpiece, every bar of which is the outcome of enormous creative power. Half a century has passed since then, and many Russian symphonic works have been composed; we may even speak of a symphonic school. Well? The germ of all this lies in *Kamarinskaya*, as the oak tree lies in the acorn. For long years to come Russian composers will drink at this source, for it will need much time and much strength to exhaust its wealth of inspiration. Yes! Glinka was a true creative genius!"

To N. F. Von Meck.

"FROLOVSKOE, *July 17th (29th)*, 1888.

" . . . . My name-day was a great interruption to my work, for my visitors arrived the day before and only left yesterday evening. My guests were Laroche and his wife, Jurgenson, Albrecht, Siloti, and Zet,[1] who arrived quite unexpectedly from Petersburg. The last named (who has been highly recommended to me) has been my concert agent since May. . . . He is a great admirer of my work, and cares less to make money out of his position than to forward my interests in Europe and America. . . . "

---

[1] Julius Zet had been secretary to Sophie Menter, and so became acquainted with Tchaikovsky. Their friendship lasted until the latter's death, but their business relations were of brief duration. Zet was not sufficiently calculating. Rather an enthusiast than a man of business, he was unpractical and inaccurate.

At this time Tchaikovsky received an offer from an American impresario offering him a three months' concert tour at a fee of 25,000 dollars. The sum appeared to the Russian composer fabulous in its amount. "Should this really come off," he says, " I could realise my long-cherished wish to become a landowner."

Diary.

"*July* 13*th* (25*th*), 1888.

" Dargomijsky? Certainly he was a gifted man. But never was the type of amateur musician more strikingly realised than in him. Glinka, too, was a dilettante, but his immense inspiration served him as a defence from amateurishness. Except for his fatal *Memoirs*, we should not have realised his dilettantism. It is another matter with Dargomijsky: his amateurishness lies in his creative work, in his very forms themselves. To possess an average talent, to be weak in technique and yet to pose as an *innovator*—is pure amateurishness. When, at the close of his life, Dargomijsky composed *The Stone Guest*, he seriously believed he had overturned the old foundations and erected something new and colossal in their place. A piteous error; I saw him in this last period of his life, and in view of his suffering condition (he had a heart disease) there could be no question of a discussion. But I have never come in contact with anything more anti-pathetic and false than this unsuccessful attempt to drag *truth* into this sphere of art, in which everything is based upon falsehood, and " truth," in the everyday sense of the word, is not required at all. Dargomijsky was no *master* (he had not a tenth part of Glinka's mastership). He possessed a certain originality and piquancy. He was most successful in *curiosities*. But artistic beauty does not lie in this direction, as so many of us think.

" I might speak personally of Dargomijsky (I frequently saw him in Moscow at the time of his success there), but I prefer not to recall my acquaintance. He was very cutting and unjust in his judgments (when he raged against the brothers Rubinstein, for instance), but was pleased to talk of himself in a tone of self-laudation. During his fatal illness he became far more kindly disposed, and showed much cordial feeling to his younger colleagues. I will only keep this memory of him. Unexpectedly he showed me great sympathy (in respect of my opera *The Voyevode*).[1] Apparently he did not believe the report that I had hissed at the first performance of his *Esmeralda* in Moscow."

To N. F. von Meck.

"FROLOVSKOE, *July 25th* (*August 6th*), 1888.

" . . . The real summer weather has not lasted long, but how I enjoyed it! My flowers, which I feared would die, have nearly all recovered, and some have blossomed luxuriantly. I cannot tell you what a pleasure it has been to watch them grow and to see daily—even hourly—new blossoms coming out. Now I have as many as I want. When I am quite old, and past composing, I shall devote myself to growing flowers. I have been working with good results, and half the symphony is orchestrated. My age—although not very advanced—begins to tell. I get very tired now, and can no longer play or read at night as I used. Lately I miss the chance of a game of *vint*[2] in the evenings; it is the one thing that rests and distracts me."

To N. F. von Meck.

"FROLOVSKOE, *August 14th* (*26th*), 1888.

" Again I am not feeling well . . . but I am so glad to have finished the Symphony (No. 5) that I can forget all physical ailments. I have made no settled plans for the winter. There is a prospect of a tour in Scandinavia and also in America. But nothing is decided as to the first, and the second seems so fantastic that I can hardly give it a serious thought. I have promised to conduct at Dresden, Berlin, and Prague. . . . In November I am to conduct a whole series of my works in Petersburg (at the Philharmonic), including the new Symphony. They also want me in Tiflis, but I do not know if it will come off."

[1] Unfortunately it will always remain unknown in what way this sympathy was shown to Tchaikovsky.

[2] A favourite game of cards in Russia.

IV

1888–1889

The winter season 1888–1889 opened with much arduous work and personal anxiety. Tchaikovsky's niece, Vera, the second daughter of his sister Alexandra Davidov, was in a dying condition, and his old friend Hubert was suffering from a terrible form of intermittent fever. One gleam of joy shone through the darkness. His Moscow friends, Taneiev in particular, were delighted with the Fifth Symphony, a work which had filled Tchaikovsky himself with gloomy misgivings. At this time he was engaged in an active correspondence upon music and poetry with the Grand Duke Constantine.

To the Grand Duke Constantinovich.

"FROLOVSKOE, *September* 21st (*October 3rd*), 1888.

" . . . Fet[1] is quite right in asserting, as you say he does, that 'all which has no connection with the leading idea should be cast aside, even though it is beautiful and melodious.' But we must not deduce from this that only what is terse can be highly artistic ; therefore, to my mind, Fet's rule that an exemplary lyric must not exceed a certain limit is entirely wrong. All depends upon the nature of the leading idea and the poet who expresses it. Of two equally inspired poets, or composers, one, by reason of his artistic temperament, will show greater breadth of treatment, more complexity in the development of the leading idea, and a greater inclination for luxuriant and varied elaboration ; while the other will express himself concisely. All that is good, but superfluous, we call 'padding.' Can we say we find this padding in Beethoven's works ? I think most decidedly we do not. On the contrary, it is astonishing how equal, how significant and forceful, this giant among musicians always remains, and

---

[1] A well-known Russian poet.

how well he understands the art of curbing his vast inspiration, and never loses sight of balanced and traditional form. In his last quartets, which were long regarded as the productions of an insane and deaf man, there seems to be some padding, until we have studied them thoroughly. But ask someone who is well acquainted with these works, a member of a quartet who plays them frequently, if there is anything superfluous in the C♯ minor Quartet. Unless he is an old-fashioned musician, brought up upon Haydn, he would be horrified at the idea of abbreviating or cutting any portion of it. In speaking of Beethoven I was not merely thinking of his latest period. Could anyone show me a bar in the *Eroica*, which is very lengthy, that could be called superfluous, or any portion that could really be omitted as padding? So everything that is long is not *too long;* many words do not necessarily mean empty verbiage, and terseness is not, as Fet asserts, the essential condition of beautiful form. Beethoven, who in the first movement of the *Eroica* has built up a superb edifice out of an endless series of varied and ever new architectural beauties upon so simple and seemingly poor a subject, knows on occasion how to surprise us by the terseness and exiguity of his forms. Do you remember the Andante of the Pianoforte Concerto in B flat? I know nothing more inspired than this short movement; I go cold and pale every time I hear it.

"Of course, the classical beauty of Beethoven's predecessors, and their art of keeping within bounds, is of the greatest value. It must be owned, however, that Haydn had no occasion to limit himself, for he had not an inexhaustible wealth of material at command. As to Mozart, had he lived another twenty years, and seen the beginning of our century, he would certainly have sought to express his prodigal inspiration in forms less strictly classical than those with which he had to content himself.

"While defending Beethoven from the charge of long-windedness, I confess that the post-Beethoven music offers many examples of prolixity which is often carried so far as to become mere padding. That inspired musician who expresses himself with such breadth, majesty, force, and even brusqueness, has much in common with Michael

Angelo. Just as the Abbé Bernini has flooded Rome with his statues, in which he strives to imitate the style of Michael Angelo, without possessing his genius, and makes a caricature of what is really powerful in his model, so Beethoven's musical style has been copied over and over again. Is not Brahms in reality a caricature of Beethoven? Is not this pretension to profundity and power detestable, because the content which is poured into the Beethoven mould is not really of any value? Even in the case of Wagner (who certainly has genius), wherever he oversteps the limits it is the spirit of Beethoven which prompts him.

"As regards your humble servant, I have suffered all my life from my incapacity to grasp form in general. I have fought against this innate weakness, not—I am proud to say —without good results; yet I shall go to my grave without having produced anything really perfect in form. There is frequently *padding* in my works; to an experienced eye the stitches show in my seams, but I cannot help it. As to *Manfred*, I may tell you—without any desire to pose as being modest—that this is a repulsive work, and I hate it, with the exception of the first movement. I intend shortly, with the consent of my publisher, to destroy the remaining three movements and make a symphonic poem out of this long-winded symphony. I am sure my *Manfred* would then please the public. I enjoyed writing the first movement, whereas the others were the outcome of strenuous effort, in consequence of which—as far as I remember—I felt quite ill for a time. I should not think of being offended at what your Highness says about *Manfred*. You are quite right and even too indulgent."

To the Grand Duke Constantine Constantinovich.

"FROLOVSKOE, *October 2nd* (14*th*), 1888.

"YOUR IMPERIAL HIGHNESS,—Just returned from Moscow, where I have seen my poor friend Hubert laid in his grave, and still depressed by my painful experiences, I hasten to answer your letter. . . . Your Highness must bear in mind that although one art stands in close relationship to the other, at the same time each has its peculiarities. As such we must regard the "verbal repetitions" which are only possible to a limited extent in literature, but are a necessity in music. Beethoven never repeats an entire movement without a special reason, and, in doing so, rarely fails to introduce something new; but he has recourse to this characteristic method in his instrumental music, knowing that his idea will only be understood after many statements. I cannot understand why your Highness should object to the constant repetition of the subject in the Scherzo of the Ninth Symphony. I always want to hear it over and over again. It is so divinely beautiful, strong, original, and significant! It is quite another matter with the prolixity and repetitions of Schubert, who, with all his genius, constantly harps upon his central idea—as in the Andante of the C major Symphony. Beethoven develops his first idea fully, in its entirety, before repeating it; Schubert seems too indolent to elaborate his first idea, and—perhaps from his unusual wealth of thematic material—hurries on the beginning to arrive at something else. It seems as though the stress of his inexhaustible inspiration hindered him from the careful elaboration of the theme, in all its depth and delicacy of workmanship.

"God grant I may be in Petersburg to hear the performance of Mozart's *Requiem* in the Marble Palace. I hope your Highness will permit me to be present at this concert. The *Requiem* is one of the most divine creations, and we can but pity those who are unable to appreciate it.

"As regards Brahms, I cannot at all agree with your Highness. In the music of this master (it is impossible to deny his mastery) there is something dry and cold which repulses me. He has very little melodic invention. He never speaks out his musical ideas to the end. Scarcely do we hear an enjoyable melody, than it is engulfed in a whirlpool of unimportant harmonic progressions and modulations, as though the special aim of the composer was to be unintelligible. He excites and irritates our musical senses without wishing to satisfy them, and seems ashamed to speak the language which goes straight to the heart. His depth is not real: *c'est voulu*. He has set

before himself, once and for all, the aim of trying to be
profound, but he has only attained to an appearance of
profundity. The gulf is void. It is impossible to say
that the music of Brahms is weak and insignificant. His
style is invariably lofty. He does not strive after mere
external effects. He is never trivial. All he does is
serious and noble, but he lacks the chief thing—beauty.
Brahms commands our respect. We must bow before the
original purity of his aspirations. We must admire his
firm and proud attitude in the face of triumphant
Wagnerism ; but to love him is impossible. I, at least, in
spite of much effort, have not arrived at it. I will own
that certain early works (the Sextet in B♭) please me far
more than those of a later period, especially the symphonies, which seem to me indescribably long and colourless. . . . Many Brahms lovers (Bülow, among others)
predicted that some day I should see clearer, and learn to
appreciate beauties which do not as yet appeal to me.
This is not unlikely, for there have been such cases. I do
not know the *German Requiem* well. I will get it and
study it. Who knows?—perhaps my views on Brahms
may undergo a complete revolution."

To Ippolitov-Ivanov.

" *October 27th* (*November 8th*), 1888.

" I cannot possibly give you any definite news as to my
journey to Tiflis. It will be two or three weeks, at the
earliest, before I know when I shall have to go abroad.
. . . I only know that *I will come to Tiflis, even if I am
dying*. As to my fee, we will not speak of it. Before I
take anything from you, something must be there. Let us
see how the concert succeeds, and then we can settle how
much you shall give me as ' a tip.' If it is not a success,
I shall accept nothing."

To N. F. von Meck.

" FROLOVSKOE, *October 27th* (*November 8th*), 1888.

" Now we are having sharp frosts, without snow, and
fine, sunny days. It depresses me to think that I must

soon leave my quiet home, my regular life, and daily con-stitutionals. Three days hence I go to Petersburg, where my concert takes place on November 5th (17th). On the 12th (24th) I take part in the Musical Society's concert, and leave for Prague the next day to attend the rehearsals for *Eugene Oniegin*. I have been working very hard lately. The orchestration of the *Hamlet* overture is now finished. I have made innumerable corrections in the Symphony, and have been preparing everything I have to conduct at the forthcoming concerts.

"I hope to spend December here, for I have to return direct from Prague in order to conduct the new Sym-phony in Moscow, and then I shall hasten to my harbour of refuge."

The Philharmonic concert in St. Petersburg was ap-parently a great success, but the Press notices of the new Symphony (No. 5) were far from satisfactory. On November 12th (24th) Tchaikovsky conducted it once more at the Musical Society, and on this occasion the fantasia-overture *Hamlet* was heard for the first time. Both works were well received by the public.

V

On this occasion Prague received Tchaikovsky less hospitably than on his first visit. "The rehearsal," he wrote to Nadejda von Meck, "took place the very day I arrived. Last year, if you remember, I conducted two grand patriotic concerts, without a fee. To show their gratitude for my having come to the performance of the opera here, the management of the Prague Theatre organised a concert, of which I was to receive half the profits. But they chose such a bad day, and arranged everything so stupidly, that the concert only realised three hundred florins. After being received like a prince last year, when the enthusiasm which greeted me almost amounted to a frenzy, I felt somewhat hurt at this meagre offering on the part of the Prague public. I therefore declined the money, and made it over to the Musicians' Pension Fund. This was soon made public, and the Theatre Direction was overwhelmed with reproaches. The whole Press took up the matter, and thanks to this, the performance of *Oniegin*, which I conducted the evening before last, gave rise to a series of enthusiastic ovations. Yesterday I left Prague, crowned with laurels; but, alas! my laurel wreaths were all I carried away. I do not know how to look after my pecuniary interests."

The success of *Oniegin* in Prague was extraordinary, and the opera has kept its place in the repertory up to the present time.

Amid the chorus of praise, in which both the public and the Press united, one voice was especially valued by Tchaikovsky—that of his famous colleague, Anton Dvořák.

A. Dvořák to P. Tchaikovsky.

" PRAGUE, *January 2nd* (14*th*), 1889.

" DEAR FRIEND,—When you were lately with us in Prague I promised to write to you on the subject of your opera *Oniegin*. I am now moved to do so, not only in answer to your request, but also by my own impulse to express all I felt on hearing your work. I confess with joy that your opera made a profound impression on me— the kind of impression I expect to receive from a genuine work of art, and I do not hesitate to tell you that not one of your compositions has given me such pleasure as *Oniegin*.

" It is a wonderful creation, full of glowing emotion and poetry, and finely elaborated in all its details; in short, this music is captivating, and penetrates our hearts so deeply that we cannot forget it. Whenever I go to hear it I feel myself transported into another world.

" I congratulate both you and ourselves upon this work. God grant you may give us many another like it.

" I embrace you, and remain your sincerely devoted

"ANTON DVOŘÁK."

On his way home from Prague to Vienna, Tchaikovsky heard of the death of his niece, Vera Rimsky-Korsakov, *née* Davidov. Although he had long since given up all hope of her recovery, this news affected him deeply.

From Prague he returned to Frolovskoe for a short time. On December 10th (22nd) he conducted his new works at a Symphony Concert in Moscow. These included the new Symphony (No. 5, E minor) and the second Pianoforte Concerto, with Sapellnikov as soloist ; both works achieved great success.

December 17th (29th) found him again in Petersburg, where, at the fourth of Belaiev's "Russian Symphony Concerts," he conducted his *Tempest* overture, and on the following day was present at a performance of the *Oprichnik* given by the pupils of the Petersburg Conservatoire. Tchaikovsky was interested to renew his impressions of this work, and to prove whether his prejudice against it was well founded. In spite of a very good performance, his opinion of the opera remained unaltered.

The next work which Tchaikovsky took in hand after his return from Prague was the music of the ballet, *The Sleeping Beauty*, the programme of which had been prepared by Vsievolojsky, Director of the Imperial Opera. Tchaikovsky was charmed with the subject and the proposed mounting of the work, and retired to Frolovskoe late in December, in order to devote himself to the task.

In view of the great popularity to which his Fifth Symphony has since attained, it is interesting to read the composer's own judgment of the work, recorded within a few weeks of its first performance. Writing to Nadejda von Meck, in December, 1888, he says :—

" . . . After two performances of my new Symphony in Petersburg, and one in Prague, I have come to the conclusion that it is a failure. There is something repellent, something superfluous, patchy, and insincere, which the public instinctively recognises. It was obvious to me that the ovations I received were prompted more by my earlier work, and that the Symphony itself did not really please the audience. The consciousness of this brings me a sharp twinge of self-dissatisfaction. Am I really played out, as they say? Can I merely repeat and ring the changes on my earlier idiom? Last night I looked through *our* Symphony (No. 4). What a difference! How immeasurably superior it is! It is very, very sad!"

Such attacks of pessimism as to his creative powers were often, as we have already seen, the forerunner of a new tide of inspiration. This was now the case. Since *Eugene Oniegin* Tchaikovsky had never worked at anything with the ease and enthusiasm which inspired him in the first four tableaux of this ballet, *The Sleeping Beauty*, the sketch of which was completely finished by January 18th (30th).

The monotony of these six weeks' work was relieved by news of the success of the Fifth Symphony in Moscow, and also by the kindness of his friend, Peter Jurgenson, who surprised him at Christmas with a beautiful and valuable gift—the complete edition of Mozart's works. These he commissioned Alexis to present to his master, together with a tiny Christmas-tree.

On January 24th (February 5th), 1889, Tchaikovsky started on his second concert tour abroad. He experienced "the usual feelings of home-sickness," and began to anticipate the joy of his return. He remained three days in Berlin, and arrived in Cologne on January 29th (February 10th), where he was to make his first appearance as composer and conductor, with his Third Suite (in G), at a so-called "Gürzenich" concert.

To M. Tchaikovsky.

"COLOGNE, *January* 30*th* (*February* 11*th*), 1889.

". . . To-day was my first rehearsal. It went very well, and the orchestra is excellent, so that the three hours passed very pleasantly, excepting for the agitation at the start. Hardly had I got back to my hotel before I was seized with home-sickness and a wild longing for April 8th. . . ."

Tchaikovsky made his début at Cologne on January 31st (February 12th). He thus describes his impressions to Glazounov :—

"I arrived shortly before the first of the three re-hearsals. One hardly expects to find a first-class orchestra in a town of secondary importance, and I was convinced it would only be a very poor one. The local conductor, Wüllner, has, however, worked with such care and energy that he has succeeded in organising a magnificent orchestra, which filled me with astonishment and admiration from the very opening of my Third Suite. Twenty first violins! And such violins! The wind, too, is admirable. They read the Scherzo, which is particularly difficult, as if they were playing it for the tenth time. With such an orchestra and three rehearsals, it was easy to achieve an admirable performance. The concert-hall is also excellent; the audience equally so, and not so stupidly conservative as in many German towns. The success was great, and when I was recalled the musicians greeted me with a fanfare.

"Early on February 1st (13th)," the letter continues, "I started for Frankfort. Here the orchestra is equally large and excellent. The violins did not seem to me quite as good as those in Cologne, although they consist mostly of leaders from the neighbouring towns—so I was told—who come here to play at the great concerts. There are twelve 'cellos. One of them, Kossmann, the celebrated virtuoso, was once professor at Moscow. My Overture "*1812*" was in the programme. At the first rehearsal, however, the managers of the concert took fright at the noisy Finale, and timidly requested me to choose another piece. Since, however, I had no other piece at hand, they decided to confine themselves to the Suite. The success here was as great as it was unexpected, for the Frankfort public is very classical, and I am regarded in Germany as a notorious revolutionary."

Of those in Frankfort whose society Tchaikovsky most enjoyed, he mentions in his diary the family of the celebrated music publisher, pianist, and composer, Otto Neitzel, and Ivan Knorr, Professor at the Frankfort Conservatoire, besides the 'cellist Kossmann.

Tchaikovsky reached Dresden on February 4th (16th). Here disappointment awaited him. The orchestra proved to be only "third-rate," to use his own words, and the work he had to rehearse made even greater technical demands than the Third Suite; it was his favourite composition—the Fourth Symphony. The *Dresdner Zeitung* spoke of "a very poor rendering of several passages, the result of insufficient rehearsal." The concert took place on February 8th (20th). The first Pianoforte Concerto (Emil Sauer) was included in the programme. According to Tchaikovsky's account, "the first movement pleased the audience a little, the Andante pleased better, the Scherzo still more, while the Finale had a real success. The musicians honoured me with a fanfare. Sauer played incomparably."

To P. Jurgenson.

"DRESDEN, *February 5th* (17*th*), 1889.

"DEAR FRIEND,—I had forgotten to answer you about Paris. Please remember that it is impossible to give a concert there unless support is guaranteed by the French. I hear that Slaviansky, Bessel, and others want to have a finger in the pie. I have not the least wish to associate myself with them. You can simply say that, without a

2 P

guarantee, we are not in a position to undertake anything.'[1] Heavens, how tired I am, and how bored by all this!

" . . . I expect soon to hear decisively from Klindworth and Dvořák. A letter to hand from Massenet. He accepts with enthusiasm, but begs to keep the date open for the present, as it depends on the fate of his new opera."

To N. F. von Meck.

"BERLIN, *February* 11*th* (23*rd*), 1889.

" After an exhausting tour I arrived here yesterday. In one week I had three concerts and nine rehearsals. I cannot conceive whence I draw strength for all this. Either these fresh exertions will prove injurious, or this feverish activity will be an antidote to my troubles, which are chiefly the result of the constant sitting my work entails. There is no medium; I must return to Russia *'either with my shield or upon it.'* I am inclined to think that, in spite of hard moments and the continual self-conflict, all this is good for me."

To A. Glazounov.

"BERLIN, *February* 15*th* (27*th*), 1889.

" . . . If my whole tour consisted only of concerts and rehearsals, it would be very pleasant. Unhappily, however, I am overwhelmed with invitations to dinners and suppers. . . . I much regret that the Russian papers have said nothing as to my victorious campaign. What can I do? I have no friends on the Russian Press. Even if I had, I should never manage to advertise myself. My Press notices abroad are curious : some find fault, others flatter ; but all testify to the fact that Germans know very little about Russian music. There are exceptions, of course. In Cologne and in other towns I came across people who took great interest in Russian music and were well acquainted with it. In most instances Borodin's E flat Symphony is well known. Borodin seems to be a special favourite in Germany (although they only care for this symphony). Many people ask for information about you.

---

[1] Thus ended the plan for sending Tchaikovsky as musical representative of Russia to the Paris Exhibition of 1889.

They know you are still very young, but are amazed when I tell them you were only fifteen when you wrote your Symphony in E flat, which has become very well known since its performance at the festival. Klindworth intends to produce a Russian work at his concert in Berlin. I recommended him Rimsky-Korsakov's *Caprice Espagnol* and your *Stenka Razin.*"

To P. Jurgenson.

" LEIPZIG, *February* 17*th* (*March* 1*st*), 1889.

" Klindworth says that I am an 'excellent conductor.' First-rate, isn't it?

" Klindworth is prepared to appear next season at our concerts for anything we like to offer. He will give a Wagner programme. Dvořák promises to conduct a whole concert ; but he cannot travel alone, and brings his wife, so he asks a higher fee. Never mind. In the spring it would be well to get out an advertisement with such names as Massenet, Dvořák, Klindworth. I shall make an attempt to invite Brahms. That would be grand !

" When in Berlin, Artôt and dear Hugo Bock were my great comfort."

To N. F. von Meck.

" GENEVA, *February* 21*st* (*March* 5*th*), 1889.

" I am engaged to give a concert of my own compositions here. It takes place on Saturday, March 9th. The orchestra is very small, only third-rate. Had I known, I never would have come, but the theatrical Director (he is no musician) probably believes that the quality and number of an orchestra are of no importance to a wandering musician. How I shall get through with this small provincial band, I really do not know. However, I must confess that they showed great zeal at yesterday's rehearsal. . . ."

After all, this concert was a success. The room was crowded, and the Russian colony presented Tchaikovsky with a gilt laurel-wreath.

On February 27th (March 11th) Tchaikovsky arrived in

Hamburg. Brahms was at his hotel, occupying the room next his own. Peter Ilich felt greatly flattered on learning that the famous German composer was staying a day longer on purpose to hear the rehearsal of his Fifth Symphony. Tchaikovsky was very well received by the orchestra. Brahms remained in the room until the end of the rehearsal. Afterwards, at luncheon, he gave his opinion of the work "very frankly and simply." It had pleased him on the whole, with the exception of the Finale. Not unnaturally, the composer of this movement felt "deeply hurt" for the moment; but happily the injury was not incurable, as we shall see. Tchaikovsky took this opportunity to invite Brahms to conduct one of the Symphony Concerts in Moscow, but the latter declined. Nevertheless Tchaikovsky's personal liking for the composer of the *German Requiem* was increased, although his opinion of his compositions was not changed. Tchaikovsky played no part in the conflict between Brahms and Wagner, which divided all musical Germany into two hostile camps. Brahms's personality as man and artist, his purity and loftiness of aim, and his earnestness of purpose won his sympathy. Wagner's personality and tendencies were antipathetic to him; but while the inspired music of the latter found an echo in his heart, the works of Brahms left him cold.

At the second rehearsal all went "excellently," and at the third Tchaikovsky observed that the Symphony pleased the musicians. At the public rehearsal "there was real enthusiasm," and although the demonstration at the concert on March 3rd (15th) was less noisy, the success of the Symphony was no less assured.

The pleasant impressions of the evening were slightly marred by the absence—on account of illness—of Ave-Lallemant, to whom the Symphony is dedicated.

To V. Davidov.

"HANOVER *March* 5*th* (17*th*), 1889.

" . . . The concert at Hamburg has taken place, and I may congratulate myself on a great success. The Fifth Symphony was magnificently played, and I like it far better now, after having held a bad opinion of it for some time. Unfortunately the Russian Press continues to ignore me. With the exception of my nearest and dearest, no one will ever hear of my successes. In the daily papers here one reads long telegrams about the Wagner performances in Russia. Certainly I am not a second Wagner, but it would be desirable for Russia to learn how I have been received in Germany."

To M. Tchaikovsky.

" . . . Success is very pleasant at the time, but when there is neither rehearsal nor concert, I immediately relapse into my usual state of depression and boredom. Only one concert remains, the one in London, but not for another month. How on earth shall I kill time till then? Possibly I may go straight to Paris. Rushing about there ought to drive away *ennui*. How one wastes time!"

The three days' visit to Hanover only differed from Tchaikovsky's sojourn in other towns in that he missed the only thing that could help him to conquer his chronic home-sickness—concerts and rehearsals.

"Curious fact," he remarks in his diary, "I seek solitude, and suffer when I have found it." In this state of fluctuation between *bad* and *worse* Tchaikovsky had spent his time since he left Russia; but the *worst* was reserved for Hanover, where he experienced "extreme loneliness."

On March 8th (20th) he arrived in Paris, and remained there until the 30th (April 11th).

As his present visit to the French capital was not undertaken in a public capacity, it was neither so brilliant, nor so fatiguing, as that of the previous year. At the same time he came in contact with many people and received a number of invitations. On March 19th (31st) he was present at one of Colonne's concerts, when three numbers from his Third Suite were played.

During this holiday in Paris Tchaikovsky had only two aims in view: to secure Massenet for one of the Moscow Symphony Concerts and to use his influence in favour of Sapellnikov, whose gifts as a pianist he valued very highly.

To P. Jurgenson.

"*March 21st (April 2nd),* 1889.

"I have seen Massenet several times; he is very much flattered and prepared to come. The spring will suit him best. I have engaged Paderewski, who has had a colossal success in Paris. He is not inferior to D'Albert, and one of the very first pianists of the day.

"The Third Suite had a splendid success at Colonne's concert."

To Modeste Tchaikovsky.

"PARIS, *April 7th* (19*th*), 1889.

"MODI,—Vassia[1] played to Colonne yesterday evening. After the Chopin Polonaise Colonne was astonished, and said he would engage him next year and do '*les choses en grand.*' . . . Vassia has made a *furore.*"

To V. Davidov.

"LONDON, 1889.

" . . . The evening before I left Paris I went to Madame Viardot's. I heard an opera which she composed twenty years ago to a libretto by Tourgeniev.[2] The singers were her two daughters and her pupils, among whom was a Russian, who danced a national dance to the delight of all the spectators. I have seen the celebrated Eiffel Tower quite near. It is very fine . . . I very much enjoyed hearing the finest of Berlioz's works, *La Damnation de Faust.* I am very fond of this masterpiece, and wish you knew it.

---

[1] Vassily Sapellnikov.
[2] The opera is entitled *Le Dernier Sorcier.*

Lalo's opera, *Le Roi d'Ys*, also pleased me very much. It has been decided that I shall compose an opera to a French book, *La Courtisane*.[1] I have made acquaintance with a number of the younger French composers;[2] they are all the most rabid Wagnerites. But Wagnerism sits so badly on the French! With them it takes the form of a childishness which they pursue in order to appear earnest."

To the same.

" LONDON, *March* 30*th* (*April* 11*th*), 1889.

". . . Before all else, let me inform you that I have made acquaintance with London fog. Last year I enjoyed the fog daily, but I never dreamt of anything like the one we had to-day. When I went to rehearsal this morning it was rather foggy, as it often is in Petersburg. But when at midday I left St. James's Hall with Sapellnikov and went into the street, it was actually night—as dark as a moonless, autumn night at home. It made a great impression upon us both. I felt as though I were sitting in a subterranean dungeon. Now at 4 p.m. it is rather lighter, but still gloomy. It is extraordinary that this should happen half-way through April. Even the Londoners are astonished and annoyed.

" Ah, Bob, how glad I shall be to get back to Frolovskoe! I think I shall never leave it again.

" The rehearsal went off very well to-day ; the orchestra here is very fine. Sapellnikov has not played yet. To-morrow he will certainly make a sensation among the musicians. . . ."

At the London Philharmonic Tchaikovsky conducted his first Pianoforte Concerto (with Sapellnikov as soloist) and the Suite No. 1. Both works had a brilliant success. This was evident from the opinions of the Press, although the lion's share of praise fell to the lot of Sapellnikov. *The Musical Times* regretted that one of Tchaikovsky's

---

[1] This work, the libretto of which was by Galée and Detroyat, was never actually begun.

[2] In his diary Tchaikovsky only mentions V. d'Indy and Chaminade.

symphonies had not been given instead of the Suite, and considered this work was not sufficiently characteristic to give a just idea of the composer's talent.

Tchaikovsky left London very early on the morning of March 31st (April 12th), and arrived at Marseilles on the following day, where he embarked for Batoum by the Messageries Maritimes.

To Modeste Tchaikovsky.

"CONSTANTINOPLE, *April 8th* (20th), 1889.

". . . We left Marseilles a week ago. The ship is a good one, the food excellent. It was sometimes very rough. Between Syra and Smyrna there was quite a storm, to which I cannot look back without horror. Both these places pleased me very much. I got to know two Russians on board : a lad of fourteen, Volodya Sklifas-sovsky (son of the celebrated surgeon), and Hermanovich, a student at the Moscow University, who was travelling with him. Both were charming beings, with whom I made fast friends. They were going to Odessa—I to Batoum. We spent the whole of the evening together in the town, but slept on board. I shall miss them very much. . . ."

When Tchaikovsky parted from his new friends he returned to his cabin and "cried bitterly," as though he had some premonition that he should never again see this lovable and highly gifted boy on earth. Volodya Sklifas-sovsky died in January, 1890.

To N. F. von Meck.

"TIFLIS, *April 20th* (*May 2nd*), 1889.

". . . A glorious land, the Caucasus! How indescribably beautiful is the valley of the Rion, for instance, with its rich vegetation, through which runs the railway from Batoum to this place! Imagine, my dear, a wide valley, shut in on either side by rocks and mountains of fantastic form, in which flourish rhododendrons and other spring flowers, besides an abundance of trees, putting forth their fresh green foliage; and, added to this, the noisy, winding, brimming waters of the Rion. . . . In Tiflis, too, it is wonderful just now; all the fruit trees are in blossom. The weather is so clear that all the distant snow-peaks are visible, and the air is full of the feeling of spring, fragrant and life-giving. After the London fog it seems so beautiful, I can find no words to express it. . . ."

By May 7th (19th) Tchaikovsky was back in Moscow. The following letter throws some light on the musical life of that town.

To Anatol Tchaikovsky.

"Moscow, *May 12th (24th)*, 1889.

". . . All were glad to see me again. Since my return I have attended the committee meetings of the Musical Society every day. There is a great accumulation of business. A *coup d'état* has taken place in the Conservatoire. Taneiev has resigned the direction, and Safonov is prepared to take his place, on condition that Karl Albrecht gives up the post of inspector. I backed Karl persistently and energetically, and finally declared that I would retire from the Board of Direction if he were allowed to leave without any decoration for long service. . . ."

From Moscow Tchaikovsky went to Petersburg for a few days, returning to Frolovskoe, where he remained for the next four months.

The summer of 1889 passed in peaceful monotony. Tchaikovsky was engaged in composing and orchestrating his ballet, *The Sleeping Beauty*. . . . The little parties he occasionally gave—when Jurgenson, Mme. A. Hubert, and Siloti were his usual guests—were the sole "events" of this period of his life. But no account of this summer — uneventful as it was — would be complete without some mention of Legoshin's[1] daughter, a child of three.

---

[1] The servant of his friend Kondratiev.

Tchaikovsky was altogether fascinated by her prettiness, her clear, bell-like voice, her charming ways, and clever little head. He would spend hours romping with the child, listening to her chatter, and even acting as nursemaid.

At this time Tchaikovsky's correspondence had not decreased, but many of his business letters are not forthcoming, and those of a more private nature which date from this summer are for the most part short and uninteresting.

To Edward Napravnik.

"KLIN, *July 9th (21st)*, 1889.

". . . You have not forgotten your promise to conduct one of the concerts of the Moscow Musical Society, dear friend ? . . .

"Now for the programme. It rests entirely with you both as regards the choice of music and of the soloists. . . . We beg you to lay aside your modesty, and to include at least two important works of your own. I implore you *most emphatically* not to do any of my compositions. As I am arranging this concert, it would be most unseemly were the conductor I engaged to perform any work of mine. I would not on any account have it suspected that I was looking after my own interests. But people would be sure to put this interpretation upon the matter, if the conductor invited for the occasion were to include any of my music in the programme. I think Dvořák will only bring forward his own works, so I will ask you as a Russo-Bohemian to give us something of Smetana's, *Vishergrad,* or *Moldava.* . . ."

To N. F. von Meck.

"FROLOVSKOE, *July 25th (August 6th)*, 1889.

". . . My ballet will be published in November or December. Siloti is making the pianoforte arrangement. I think, dear friend, that it will be one of my best works. The subject is so poetical, so grateful for musical setting, that I have worked at it with all that enthusiasm and goodwill upon which the value of a composition so much depends. The instrumentation gives me far more trouble than it used to do; consequently the work goes slowly, but perhaps all the better. Many of my earlier compositions show traces of hurry and lack of due reflection."

VI

1889–1890

At the close of September, 1889, Tchaikovsky went to Moscow, where very complicated business in connection with the Russian Musical Society awaited his attention. For each symphony concert during the forthcoming season a different conductor was to be engaged.[1] Besides this, he had to superintend the rehearsals for *Eugene Oniegin*. This opera was to be newly and sumptuously remounted on September 18th (30th), when the composer had undertaken to conduct his own work.

From Moscow Tchaikovsky went to Petersburg for a few days, to attend a meeting of the committee appointed to arrange the Jubilee Festival for Anton Rubinstein. Tchaikovsky had undertaken to compose two works for this occasion.

While he was in Petersburg, Alexis prepared the new quarters in Moscow, which he had taken for the whole winter.

The lack of society in the evening, and the heavy duties which awaited him in connection with the Musical Society, were Tchaikovsky's sole reasons for wintering in Moscow rather than in the neighbourhood of Klin.

---

[1] Massenet and Brahms having declined their invitations, the following conductors were engaged for 1889–90 :—Rimsky - Korsakov, Tchaikovsky, Siloti, Arensky, Klindworth, A. Rubinstein, Slatin, Dvořák, Altani, Ippolitov-Ivanov, Napravnik, and Colonne.

During the summer the idea of trying town life once more seemed to attract him, and he spoke with enthusiasm of his new apartment, and took the greatest interest in getting it ready ; but, as the day of departure drew near, he felt less and less inclined to leave his country home.

Two circumstances contributed to make the first days after his arrival in Moscow depressing : first, he greatly missed the society of Laroche, who had gone to live in Petersburg ; and, secondly, his friend, the 'cellist Fitzen-hagen, was on his death-bed.

His winter quarters were small, but comfortable. The work to which he looked forward with most apprehension was the direction of the two festival concerts for Rubin-stein's jubilee. For two and a half years he had been conducting his own compositions, but had comparatively little experience of other music. Therefore these long and heavy programmes, including as they did several of Rubinstein's own works, filled him with anxious fore-boding.

To N. F. von Meck.

" Moscow, *October 12th (24th),* 1889.

" I am very glad you are at home, and I envy you. By nature I incline *very, very* much to the kind of life you lead. I long to live completely away from society, as you do, but during recent years circumstances have made it impossible for me to live as I please. I consider it my duty, while I have strength for it, to fight against my destiny and not to desert my fellow-creatures so long as they have need of me. . . .

"But, good God, what I have to get through this winter ! It frightens me to think of all that lies before me, here and in Petersburg. Directly the season is over I shall go to Italy for a rest. I have not been there since 1882."

To Modeste Tchaikovsky.

"*October* 16*th* (28*th*), 1889.

" Just think : I have heard from Tchekov.[1]   He wants to dedicate his new stories to me.   I have been to thank him.   I am very proud and pleased."

Tchaikovsky first became acquainted with Tchekov's works in 1887. His enthusiasm was such that he felt impelled to write to the author, expressing his delight at having come across a talent so fresh and original.   His first personal acquaintance with his literary favourite probably dated from the autumn of the same year.   At any rate, they had known each other previous to 1889.

To the Grand Duke Constantine Constantinovich.[2]

" MOSCOW, *October* 29*th* (*November* 10*th*), 1889.

" YOUR IMPERIAL HIGHNESS,—I feel a certain pride in knowing that your admirable poem is partly the outcome of my letter to you last year.   I cannot think why you should fancy that the idea of your poem does not please me.   On the contrary, I like it very much.   I cannot say that I have sufficient love and forbearance in my own nature always to love 'the hand that chastises.'   Very often I want to parry the blows, and play the rebellious child in my turn.   Nevertheless, I cannot but incline before the strength of mind and lofty views of such rare natures as Spinoza, or Tolstoi, who make no distinction between good and bad men, and take the same attitude towards every manifestation of human wickedness that you have expressed in your poem.   I have never read Spinoza, so I speak of him from hearsay ; but as regards Tolstoi, I have read and re-read him, and consider him the greatest writer in the world, past or present.   His writings awake in me— apart from any powerful artistic impression — a peculiar

---

[1] A celebrated Russian novelist and writer of short stories.

[2] The Grand Duke had dedicated his last volume of verse to Tchaikovsky.

emotion. I do not feel so deeply touched when he describes anything really emotional, such as death, suffering, separation, etc., so much as by the most ordinary, prosaic events. For instance, I remember that when reading the chapter in which Dolokhov plays cards with Rastov and wins, I burst into tears. Why should a scene in which two characters are acting in an unworthy manner affect me in this degree? The reason is simple enough. Tolstoi surveys the people he describes from such a height that they seem to him poor, insignificant pigmies who, in their blindness, injure each other in an aimless, purposeless way —and he pities them. Tolstoi has no malice; he loves and pities all his characters equally, and all their actions are the result of their own limitations and naïve egotism, their helplessness and insignificance. Therefore he never punishes his heroes for their ill-doings, as Dickens does (who is a great favourite of mine), because he never depicts anyone as absolutely bad, only blind people, as it were. His humanity is far above the sentimental humanity of Dickens; it almost attains to that view of human wickedness which is expressed in the words of Christ: 'they know not what they do.'

"Is not your Highness's poem an echo of this lofty feeling of humanity which so dominates me, and how can I therefore fail to admire the fundamental idea of your verses?

"The news that the Emperor has deigned to inquire after me gives me great pleasure. How am I to understand the Emperor's question about little pieces? If it is an indirect incitement to compose something in this style, I will take the first opportunity of doing so. I should immensely like to compose a great symphony, which should be, as it were, the crown of my creative work, and dedicate it to the Tsar. I have long since had a vague plan of such a work in my mind, but many favourable circumstances must combine before I can realise my idea. I hope I shall not die before I have carried out this project. At present I am entirely absorbed in the concerts here and the preparations for Rubinstein's jubilee."

In the same year in which my brother began to study

with Zaremba, in 1861 (or perhaps the previous year—I cannot remember for certain), he took Anatol and myself to an amateur performance in aid of some charity, given in the house of Prince Bieloselsky. Anton Rubinstein, already at the height of his fame, was among the audience. Peter Ilich pointed him out to me for the first time, and I still remember the excitement, rapture and reverence with which the future pupil gazed on his future teacher. He entirely forgot the play, while his eyes followed his "divinity," with the rapt gaze of a lover for the unattainable beauty of his fancy. During the intervals he stood as near to him as possible, strove to catch the sound of his voice, and envied the fortunate mortals who ventured to shake hands with him.

This feeling (I might say "infatuation" had it not been based upon a full appreciation of Rubinstein's value as a man and artist) practically lasted to the end of Tchaikovsky's life. Externally he was always "in love" with Rubinstein, although—as is always the case in love affairs —there were periods of coolness, jealousy, and irritation, which invariably gave place in turn to a fresh access of that sentiment which set me wondering in Prince Bieloselsky's reception-room. In Rubinstein's presence Tchaikovsky became quite diffident, lost his head, and seemed to regard him as a superior being. When at a supper, given during the pianist's jubilee, someone, in an indelicate and unseemly way, requested Rubinstein and Tchaikovsky to drink to each other "as brothers," the latter was not only confused and indignant, but, in his reply to the toast, protested warmly, saying that his tongue would never consent to address the great artist in the second person singular—it would be entirely against the spirit of their relations. He would be happy if Rubinstein addressed him by the familiar "thou," but for his own part, the more ceremonious form better expressed a sense of reverence from the pupil to his teacher, from the man to the embodiment of his ideal. These were no empty words. Rubinstein had been the first to give the novice in his art an example of the untiring devotion and disinterested spirit which animates the life of the true artist. In this sense Tchaikovsky was far more the pupil of Rubinstein than in questions of orchestration and composition. With his innate gifts and thirst for knowledge, any other teacher could have given him the same instruction. It was in his character as an energetic, irreproachably clean-minded and inspired artist, as a man who never compromised with his conscience, who had all his life detested every kind of humbug and the successes of vulgarity, as an indefatigable worker, that Rubinstein left really deep traces upon Tchaikovsky's artistic career. The latter, writing to the well-known German journalist, Eugen Zabel, said : "Rubinstein's personality shines before me like a clear, guiding star."

But there were times when clouds obscured this "guiding star." While recognising Rubinstein's great gifts as a composer, and valuing some of his works very highly— such as the "Ocean Symphony," *The Tower of Babel* the Pianoforte Concerto, *Ivan the Terrible*, the violoncello sonatas, and many of the pieces for pianoforte— Tchaikovsky grew angry and impatient over the vast majority of the virtuoso's mediocre and empty creations. He frequently expressed himself so sarcastically on this subject that I have cut out certain passages in his letters, lest they might give the reader a false impression of his attitude towards Rubinstein. But he soon forgot and forgave these momentary eclipses of "his star," and always returned to his old spirit of veneration.

The deepest, keenest, and most painful aspect of their relations—and here artistic self-esteem doubtless played a part—was the knowledge of Rubinstein's antipathy to him as a composer, which he never conquered to the end of his life. The virtuoso never cared for Tchaikovsky's music. Many of Rubinstein's intimate friends, and also his wife, maintained the reverse. But in that case it was the love of Wotan for the Wälsungs. Secretly rejoicing in the success of Tchaikovsky-Siegmund, and sympathising in his heart with Tchaikovsky-Siegfried, Wotan-Rubinstein never did anything to forward the performance of his works, nor held out a helping hand. . . . From the earliest exercises at the Conservatoire, to the "Pathetic Symphony," he never praised—and seldom condemned—a single work of Tchaikovsky's. All of them, without exception, were silently ignored—together with all the music which came after Schumann—as unworthy of serious attention.

The legend of Rubinstein's envy, which had absolutely no foundation in fact, always annoyed Tchaikovsky and aroused his wrath. Even if it might be to a certain extent true as regards the eighties, when my brother was recognised and famous, it could not apply to the attitude of a teacher towards a pupil who—although undoubtedly gifted—had a doubtful future before him. To the composer of the "Ocean Symphony" Tchaikovsky's earliest essays in composition were as antipathetic as *Eugene Oniegin* and the Fifth Symphony. Envy can only exist between two equally matched rivals, and could not have influenced a giant—as Rubinstein was in the sixties—in his relations with anyone so insignificant as the Tchaikovsky of those days.

The feeling was simply the same which Tchaikovsky himself cherished for the works of Chopin and Brahms; a sentiment of instinctive and unconquerable antipathy. Rubinstein felt like this, not only towards Tchaikovsky's music, but to all musical works which came after Chopin and Schumann.

In any case, however much Tchaikovsky may have been wounded by Rubinstein's indifference, he remained loyal to his enthusiasm for his former teacher. When the

2 Q

Duke of Mecklenburg-Strelitz requested him to take part in organising the celebration of Rubinstein's jubilee, he expressed himself willing to put himself at the disposal of the committee. It was decided that he should conduct the jubilee concerts and compose a chorus *a capella* to words by Polonsky. The chorus was to be sung at the festival given in the hall of the Nobles' Club, November 18th (30th), 1889. In addition he undertook to contribute something to the album which Rubinstein's former pupils at the Petersburg Conservatoire were going to present him on the same occasion.

The second half of his task was easily fulfilled. In a few days both compositions—the chorus and an Impromptu for pianoforte—were ready. The conducting of the concerts was another matter. The labour it involved, and the difficulties in connection with it, made real demands upon Tchaikovsky's devotion for his old teacher.

The programme of the first concert consisted entirely of symphonic works, including the Konzertstück (op. 113), with Rubinstein himself at the piano, and the Symphony No. 5 (op. 107). At the second concert, besides the dances from *Feramors* and the *Roussalka* songs, the chief item was the Biblical opera, *The Tower of Babel.*

This programme would have made very heavy demands upon the most experienced conductor; it was a still heavier task for one who—only a month previously—had conducted for the first time any works other than his own.

"There were moments," he wrote to Nadejda von Meck, "when I experienced such a complete loss of strength that I feared for my life. The working up of *The Tower of Babel*, with its chorus of seven hundred voices, gave me the most trouble. On the evening of November 10th (22nd), just before the oratorio began, I had an attack of nerves, which they feared might prevent my returning to the conductor's desk. But—perhaps thanks to this crisis—I pulled myself together in time, and all went well to the end. You will learn all details about the festival from the newspapers. I will only add that from the 1st to the 19th of November I endured martyrdom, and I am still marvelling how I lived through it all."

To the period between the end of October, 1889, to the middle of January, 1890, belong but twelve letters, only two of which have any biographical interest. The rest are merely short notes of no importance. Such a decrease in Tchaikovsky's correspondence is a symptom of the highly nervous and distracted phase which he was now passing through. For a long time past letter-writing had ceased to be a pleasant duty; still, it remained a *duty*, which he could only neglect under special circumstances, such as overwhelmed him at the commencement of this season.

He had scarcely got over the jubilee concerts, when he had to return to Moscow to conduct Beethoven's Ninth Symphony at an extra Symphony Concert, given in aid of the fund for the widows and orphans of musicians.

Only two published notices of this concert are in existence at Klin. Both emanate from staunch admirers of Tchaikovsky: Kashkin and Konius, who, in spite of all their justice, probably show some partisanship in their praise.

On the same occasion Brandoukov played Tchaikovsky's Pezzo Capriccioso for violoncello with great success.

It was unfortunate that after all this strain and anxiety the composer was not able to return to his country retreat, where the peaceful solitude invariably restored him to health and strength. In spite of all precautions, he was overrun with visitors; and his Moscow quarters were so small that he sighed perpetually for his roomy home at Frolovskoe. Added to which, Alexis Safronov's wife was dying of consumption. We know Tchaikovsky's attitude to those who served him. He never regarded them as subordinates, mere machines for carrying out his wishes, but rather as friends, in whose joys and sorrows he felt the keenest sympathy. The illness of his servant's young wife caused him great sorrow ; the more so that he saw no way of saving her life. The knowledge that he was of no use, but rather a hindrance to the care of the invalid—for Alexis was the poor soul's only nurse—made Tchaikovsky anxious to save his man all the personal services with which he could possibly dispense. For this reason he cut short his stay in Moscow and returned to Petersburg at the end of November, where his ballet, *The Sleeping Beauty*, was already in rehearsal.

To N. F. von Meck.

" PETERSBURG, *December* 17*th* (29*th*), 1889.

" MY DEAR, KIND, INCOMPARABLE FRIEND,—Where are you now ? I do not know. But I have such a yearning to talk to you a little that I am beginning this letter with the intention of posting it to you in Moscow, as soon as I can find your address. For three weeks I have been doing nothing in Petersburg. I say 'doing nothing' because my real business is to compose ; and all this conducting, attending rehearsals for my ballet, etc., I regard as something purposeless and fortuitious, which only shortens my days, for it needs all my strength of will to endure the kind of life I have to lead in Petersburg. . . . On January 6th I must be back in Moscow to conduct a concert of the Musical Society, at which Anton Rubinstein will play his new compositions, and on the 14th I have a popular concert here; after that I shall be at the end of my forces. I have made up my mind to refuse all engagements at home and abroad, and perhaps to go to Italy for four months to rest and work at my future opera, *Pique Dame*. I have chosen this subject from Poushkin. It happened in this way : three years ago my brother Modeste undertook to make a libretto for a certain Klenovsky, and gradually put together a very successful book upon this subject.

"Moscow, *December 26th* (*January 7th*), 1889.

" I continue my letter. The libretto of *Pique Dame* was written by Modeste for Klenovsky, but for some reason he declined to set it to music. Then Vsievolojsky, the Director of the Opera, took it into his head that I should write a work on this subject and have it ready by next season. He communicated his wish to me, and as the business fitted in admirably with my determination to escape from Russia for a time and devote myself to composition, I said 'yes.' A committee meeting was improvised, at which my brother read his libretto, its merits and demerits were discussed, the scenery planned, and even the parts distributed. . . . I feel very much inclined to work. If only I can settle myself comfortably in some corner abroad, I should be equal to my task, and could let the Direction have the pianoforte score in May. In the course of the summer the orchestration would be finished."

On January 1st (13th) Tchaikovsky was back in St. Petersburg, and on the following day attended a gala rehearsal of *The Sleeping Beauty*, at which the Imperial Court was present.

Practically it was the first night, for while the *parterre* was reserved for the Imperial party, the boxes on the first tier were crowded with aristocratic spectators. The Imperial family were pleased, but not enthusiastic in their appreciation of the music, although afterwards they grew very fond of this Ballet. "Very nice" was the only expression of opinion Tchaikovsky received from the Emperor's lips. This scanty praise—judging from the entry in his diary—greatly mortified the composer.

It is interesting to observe that at the first public performance, on the following day, the public seems to have shared the Emperor's opinion, for the applause, which was lacking in warmth, seemed to pronounce the same lukewarm verdict, "Very nice." The composer was still further depressed and embittered. "Embittered," because, during the rehearsals, Tchaikovsky had learnt to appreciate the splendour and novelty of the scenery and costumes, and the inexhaustible taste and invention of M. Petipa, and expected that all this talent and taste, combined with his music—which came only second to *Oniegin* in his affections—would arouse a storm of enthusiasm in the public.

This was not the case, because the novelty of the programme and the dazzling wealth of detail blinded the public to the musical beauties of the work. They could not appreciate the Ballet at the first performance, as they afterwards learnt to do. Its success was immense, and was proved in the same way as that of *Eugene Oniegin*—not by frantic applause during the performance, but by a long series of crowded houses.

On January 4th (16th) Tchaikovsky went to Moscow, where he conducted on the 6th. Convinced that no repose was possible in that town, he decided to start abroad immediately, and to take his brother Modeste's servant, Nazar, in place of Alexis, who remained by his wife's death-bed. Tchaikovsky left Petersburg on January 14th (26th) without any plans as to his destination.

VII

Not until he reached Berlin did Tchaikovsky decide in favour of Florence, where he arrived early on January 18th (30th), 1890, Italy did not interest him at the moment. He was actuated only by one motive—to get away. Soon he was at work upon *Pique Dame*. His surroundings were favourable, and he made rapid progress. His condition of mind was not cheerful, however, as may he gathered from the following letter to Glazounov, dated January 30th (February 11th), 1890.

"DEAR ALEXANDER CONSTANTINOVICH,—Your kind letter touched me very much. Just now I am sadly in need of friendly sympathy and intercourse with people who are intimate and dear. I am passing through a very enigmatical stage on my road to the grave. Something strange, which I cannot understand, is going on within me. A kind of life-weariness has come over me. Sometimes I feel an insane anguish, but not that kind of anguish which is the herald of a new tide of love for life; rather something hopeless, final, and—like every *finale*— a little commonplace. Simultaneously a passionate desire to create. The devil knows what it is! In fact, sometimes I feel my song is sung, and then again an unconquerable impulse, either to give it fresh life, or to start a new song. . . . As I have said, I do not know what has come to me. For instance, there was a time when I loved Italy and Florence. Now I have to make a great effort to emerge from my shell. When I do go out, I feel no pleasure whatever, either in the blue sky of Italy, in the sun that shines from it, in the architectural beauties I see around me, or in the teeming life of the streets. Formerly all this enchanted me, and quickened my imagination. Perhaps my trouble actually lies in those fifty years to which I shall attain two months hence, and my imagination will no longer take colour from its surroundings?

"But enough of this! I am working hard. Whether what I am doing is really good, is a question to which only posterity can give the answer.

"I feel the greatest sympathy for your misgivings as to the failure of your 'Oriental Fantasia.' There is nothing more painful than such doubts. But all evil has its good side. You say your friends did not approve of the work, but did not express their disapproval at the right time— at a moment when you could agree with them. It was wrong of them to oppose the enthusiasm of the author for his work, before it had had time to cool. But it is better that they had the courage to speak frankly, instead of giving you that meaningless, perfunctory praise some friends consider it their duty to bestow, to which we listen, and which we accept, because we are only too glad to believe. You are strong enough to guard your feelings as composer in those moments when people tell you the truth. . . . I, too, dear Alexander Constantinovich, have sometimes wished to be quite frank with you about your work. I am a great admirer of your gifts. I value the earnestness of your aims, and your artistic sense of honour. And yet I often think about you. I feel that, as an older friend who loves you, I ought to warn you against certain exclusive tendencies, and a kind of one-sidedness. Yet how to tell you this I do not quite know. In many respects you are a riddle to me. You have genius, but something prevents you from broadening out and penetrating the depths. . . . In short, during the winter you may expect a letter from me, in which I will talk to you after due reflection. If I fail to say anything apposite, it will be a proof of my incapacity, not the result of any lack of affection and sympathy for you."

To Modeste Tchaikovsky.

"FLORENCE, *February 2nd* (14*th*), 1890.

"You have arranged the death scene of *The Queen of Spades* very well, and suitably for musical setting. I am very pleased with you as a librettist, only keep conciseness in view and avoid prolixity. As to the scene on the bridge, I have thought it over. You and Laroche are quite opposed, and in spite of my wish to have as few scenes as possible, and to be concise, I fear the whole of Act III. will be without any women actors, and that would be dull. Lisa's part cannot be finished in the fourth scene ; the audience must know what becomes of her."

To Modeste Tchaikovsky.

"FLORENCE, *February 6th* (18*th*), 1890.

". . . . To-day, for the first time, I enjoyed my visit to Italy. So far I have felt indifferent—even hostile to it. But to-day the weather was so divine, and it was such a joy to gather a few violets in the Cascine ! At Kamenka they only appear in April.

"Now to return to *Pique Dame*. How can we manage to make the part lighter for poor Figner ? Seven scenes, in which he has to sing without intermission! Do think it over.

"I am anxiously awaiting the ball scene. For Heaven's sake lose no time, Modi, or I shall find myself without any text to set."

To A. P. Merkling.

"FLORENCE, *February 7th (19th)*, 1890.

"To-day I wrote the scene in which Hermann goes to the old *Queen of Spades*. It was so gruesome that I am still under the horrible spell of it."

To Modeste Tchaikovsky.

"FLORENCE, *February 12th (24th)*, 1890.

"If, God willing, I finish the opera, it will be something *chic*. The fourth scene will have an overwhelming effect."

Meanwhile, on February 4th (16th), *The Enchantress* had been produced in Moscow for the first time. Kashkin wrote of it as follows :—

"That the opera had been very superficially studied was evident from the entire performance, which was most un-satisfactory. I will not blame the artists, who did what they could, while some of them were very good ; but the ensemble was bad, in consequence of insufficient rehearsal. All went in a more or less disconnected way. The orchestra accompanied very roughly, without light or shade, the brass playing $f\!f$ throughout and drowning everything else with their monotonous noise. Madame Korovina, who took the chief part, was ill, and should not have been allowed to sing. We see from the repertory published in the newspapers that *The Enchantress* will not be put on again before Lent. Thank goodness! The repetition of such a performance is most undesirable. An opera should be studied before it is put on the stage."

The Enchantress, however, was not repeated, even after Lent. With this solitary performance its career came to an end as regards the Imperial Opera House.

Diary.

"February 21*st* (*March* 5*th*), 1890.

" This morning I had a letter from Alexis. He says Theklousha (his wife) prays God to take her soon. Poor, poor sufferer !

" Began the fifth scene, and in imagination I finished it yesterday, but in reality only got through it early to-day."

"February 24*th* (*March* 8*th*), 1890.

" Heard from Alexis. Theklousha is dead. I wept. Altogether a sad morning. . . . In the evening an act from *Puritani.* With all his glaring defects, Bellini is fascinating ! "

"March 3*rd* (15*th*), 1890.

" *Finished everything* this morning. God be praised, Who has let me bring my work to an end."

To Modeste Tchaikovsky.

" FLORENCE, *March* 3*rd* (15*th*), 1890.

" Yesterday I set your own closing scene to music. When I came to Hermann's death and the final chorus, I was suddenly overcome by such intense pity for Hermann that I burst out crying. Afterwards I discovered the reason for my tears (for I was never before so deeply moved by the sorrows of my hero, and I tried to explain to myself why it should be so now). I came to the conclusion that Hermann was to me not merely a pretext for writing this or that kind of music, but had been all the while an actual, living, sympathetic human being. Because I am very fond of Figner, and I always see Hermann in the form of Figner, therefore I have felt an intimate realisation of his fate.[1] Now I hope my warm and lively feeling for the hero of my opera may be happily reflected in my music. In any case, I think *Pique Dame* by no means a bad opera. We shall see. . . .

" Laroche writes that he and Napravnik do not approve of my having composed an opera in so short a time. They

[1] For the story of *Pique Dame* see Appendix B, p. 759.

will not realise that to rush through my work is an essential feature of my character. I only work quickly. I took my time over *The Enchantress* and the Fifth Symphony, and they were failures, whereas I finished the Ballet in three weeks, and *Oniegin* was written in an incredibly short time. The chief thing is to love the work. I have certainly written with love. How I cried yesterday when they sang over my poor Hermann!"

Tchaikovsky had decided to leave Florence early in March for Rome. But failing to find rooms in any of the hotels, he stayed on in Florence for two or three weeks longer.

To Anna Merkling.

"FLORENCE, *March 5th (17th)*, 1890.

". . . Heavens, what charming creatures children are! But little dogs are even more beautiful. They are simply the pearls of creation! . . . There is a breed here, almost unknown with us, called 'Lupetto.' You can often buy puppies of this kind on the Lungarno. If my Alexis did not hate dogs (they have a wretched life when the servants dislike them), I could not resist buying one of them."

To Modeste Tchaikovsky.

"FLORENCE, *March 19th (31st)*, 1890.

"Just two months ago I began the composition of the opera. To-day I finished the pianoforte score of the second act. This is to me the most dreadful and nerve-exasperating occupation. I composed the opera with pleasure and self-oblivion; I shall orchestrate with delight; but to make an arrangement! All the time one has to keep undoing what is intended for orchestra. I believe my ill-health is simply the result of this confounded work. Nazar says I have very much altered the last week or two, and have been in a dreadful state of mind. Whether it is that the worst and most wearisome part of my work is nearing an end, or that the weather is finer, I cannot say, but since yesterday I feel much better. . . . Modi, either I am greatly mistaken or *Pique Dame* is a masterpiece. At one place in the fourth scene, which I was arranging to-day, I felt such horror, such gruesome thrills, that surely the listeners cannot escape the same impressions.

"Understand, that I shall certainly spend my fiftieth birthday in Petersburg. Besides yourself, Anatol, and Jurgenson, I shall write to no one."

On March 27th (April 8th), Tchaikovsky completed the pianoforte arrangement of *Pique Dame*, and resolved to move on to Rome. "I am going there chiefly for Nazar's sake," he writes, "I want him to see the place." For the first time, after nine weeks of continuous work, the composer enjoyed a little leisure, and spent one of his last days in the Uffizi and Pitti galleries. "In spite of my efforts," he says, "I cannot acquire any appreciation of painting, especially of the older masters—they leave me cold."

To Modeste Tchaikovsky.

"ROME, *March 27th (April 8th).*

". . . The cheerful feelings that came over me to-day as soon as I stepped into the streets, breathed the well-known air of Rome, and saw the old familiar places, made me realise how foolish I had been not to come here first of all. However, I must not blame poor Florence, which for no particular reason grew so detestable to me, since I was able to compose my opera there unmolested. Rome is much changed. Parts of it are unrecognisable. Yet, in spite of these alterations, it is a joy to be back in the dear place. I think of the years that have dropped into eternity, of the two Kondratievs, gone to their rest. It is very sad and yet it has a melancholy pleasure. . . . Nazar is enchanted with Rome. I seem to see you and Kolya at every turn. I shall stay here three weeks."

To P. Jurgenson.

"ROME, *March 28th (April 9th),* 1890.

"All I hear about Safonov[1] does not surprise me in the least. But in any case it must be confessed that he may

---

[1] He had succeeded Taneiev as Director of the Moscow Conservatoire.

be useful at this critical juncture. A man of such child-like guilelessness and rectitude as Taneiev can hardly uphold the prestige of the Conservatoire. A Safonov is useful when there is no longer a Rubinstein. Such a man as Nicholas Rubinstein, who had furious energy, and at the same time could quite forget himself in the work he loved, is rare indeed."

To N. F. von Meck.

" ROME, *April 7th* (*19th*), 1890.

" DEAR FRIEND,—I am forced to flee from Rome. I could not preserve my incognito. A few Russians have already called to ask me to dinners, soirées, etc. I have refused every invitation, but my liberty is done for, and all pleasure in my visit at an end. Sgambati, the leading musician here, having heard from the Russians that I was in Rome, put my First Quartet into the programme of his chamber concert, and came to request my attendance. I could not possibly be ungracious, so I had to sacrifice one of my working hours in order to sit in a stuffy room and listen to a second-rate performance of my work ; while all the time I was an object of curiosity to the audience, whom Sgambati had informed of my presence, and who seemed very curious to see what a Russian musician could be like. It was most unpleasant. As these occurrences are certain to be repeated, I have decided to return to Russia in two or three days by way of Venice and Vienna.

" You cannot imagine how I long for Russia, and with what joy I look forward to my rural solitude. Just now something wrong is going on in Russia. But nothing hinders my passionate love of my own land. I cannot imagine how formerly I was contented to stay so long away from it, and even to take some pleasure in being abroad."

To Modeste Tchaikvosky.

" ROME, *April 7th* (*19th*), 1890.

". . . . The Quartet had a tremendous success ; the papers praise it to the skies. But the papers here praise everything. Home, quick, quick, home ! "

VIII

To Modeste Tchaikovsky.

"FROLOVSKOE, *May 5th (17th)*, 1890.

" I have been back four days. The house is almost un-recognisable: the parlour (it is also the dining-room) has become a beautiful apartment, thanks to the addition of Siloti's furniture to mine.[1] . . . But outside the house, O horror! *The whole—literally every stick—of the forest has been cut down!* Only the little thicket behind the church is left. Where is one to walk? Heavens, how entirely the disappearance of a wood changes the character of a place, and what a pity it is! All those dear, shady spots that were there last year are now a bare wilderness. Now we are sowing our flowering seeds. I am doing double work, that is to say, out of working hours I am correcting proofs. . . ."

To Ippolitov-Ivanov.

"FROLOVSKOE, *May 5th (17th)*, 1890.

" My visit abroad brought forth good fruit. I com-posed an opera, *Pique Dame*, which seems to me a success, that is why I speak of 'good fruit'. . . . My plans for the future are as follows: to finish the orchestration of the opera, to sketch out a string sextet, to go to my sister at Kamenka for the end of the summer, and to spend the whole autumn with you at Tiflis. Is your opera *Asra* finished? I saw none of the musical world in Moscow, and know nothing of what is going on. Safonov is a capable director, but—— However, we will talk this over when we meet."

---

[1] Siloti had taken a smaller house, and made over part of his furniture to Tchaikovsky, thinking it would be a kindness to him, for the composer's household lacked many comforts. Siloti did not reclaim the furniture after Tchaikovsky's death, and it stands at present in the house at Klin.

To the Grand Duke Constantine Constantinovich.

"FROLOVSKOE, *May* 18*th* (30*th*), 1890.

"YOUR IMPERIAL HIGHNESS,—. . . I should be delighted to meet Maikov[1] at your house to discuss the relations between art and craftsmanship. Ever since I began to compose I have endeavoured to be in my work just what the great masters of music—Mozart, Beethoven, and Schubert—were in theirs; not necessarily to be as great as they were, but to work as they did—as the cobbler works at his trade; not in a gentlemanly way, like Glinka, whose genius, however, I by no means deny. Mozart, Beethoven, Schubert, Mendelssohn, Schumann, composed their immortal works just as a cobbler makes a pair of boots—by daily work; and more often than not because they were ordered. The result was something colossal. Had Glinka been a cobbler, rather than a gentleman, besides his two (very beautiful) operas, he would have given us perhaps fifteen others, and ten fine symphonies into the bargain. I could cry with vexation when I think what Glinka might have left us, if he had not been born into an aristocratic family before the days of the Emancipation. He showed us what he could have done, but he never actually accomplished a twentieth part of what it was in him to do. For instance, in symphonic music (*Kamarinskaya*, and the two Spanish overtures) he simply played about like an amateur—and yet we are astonished at the force and originality of his gifts. What would he not have accomplished had he worked in the same way as the great masters of Western Europe?

"Although I am convinced that if a musician desires to attain to the greatest heights to which his inspiration will carry him he must develop himself as a craftsman, I will not assert that the same thing applies to the other arts. For instance, in the sphere you have chosen I do not think a man can force himself to create. For a lyrical poem, not only the mood, but the idea, must be there. But the idea will be evoked by some fortuitous phe-

---

[1] One of the most eminent of Russian poets.

nomenon. In music it is only necessary to evoke a certain general mood or emotion. For example, to compose an elegy I must tune myself to a melancholy key. But in a poet this melancholy must take some concrete expression so to speak; therefore in his case an external impulse is indispensable. But in all these things the difference between the various creative temperaments plays a great part, and what is right for one would not be permissible for another. The majority of my fellow-workers, for instance, do not like working to order; I, on the other hand, never feel more inspired than when I am requested to compose something, when a term is fixed and I know that my work is being impatiently awaited."

At the beginning of June, Ippolitov-Ivanov wrote to Tchaikovsky that the usual opera season would take place at Tiflis, and that, besides works by Tchaikovsky, his own opera *Asra* would be performed there. At the same time, he seems to have sounded his friend as to his prospects of succeeding to Altani's post in Moscow.

"The rumours of Altani's resignation were false," replied Tchaikovsky, "and the work of his enemies. . . . But you have no notion of all the disagreeables and annoyances you would have to endure. A more suitable position for you would be a professorship at the Moscow Conservatoire. But Safonov, it appears, makes no propositions. Write to me : yes or no."

To N. F. von Meck.

"FROLOVSKOE, *June* 30*th* (*July* 12*th*), 1890.

". . . I find more and more delight in the cultivation of flowers, and comfort myself with the thought of devoting myself entirely to this occupation when my powers of composition begin to decay. Meanwhile I cannot complain. Scarcely was the opera finished before I took up a new work, the sketch of which is already completed. I hope you will be pleased to hear I have composed a sextet for strings. I know your love of chamber music, and I am glad you will be able to hear my sextet; that will not necessitate your going to a concert, you can easily arrange a performance of it at home. I hope the work will please you: I wrote it with the greatest enthusiasm and without the least exertion."

To Modeste Tchaikovsky.

"FROLOVSKOE, *June* 30*th* (*July* 12*th*), 1890.

"Yesterday was my name-day. I had eleven guests to dinner, which was served in the garden. The peasants came again to get their money, and brought cracknels, etc. The summer is wonderful. My flowers have never been so luxuriant. Quantities of everything. Yesterday morning I had hardly left the house before I came upon two splendid white mushrooms."

To N. F. von Meck.

"FROLOVSKOE, *July* 2*nd* (14*th*), 1890.

"DEAR, KIND FRIEND,—At the same time as your letter yesterday, the composer Arensky came to see me, which delayed my immediate reply. I am afraid I did not fully express my thanks. But then, words are wanting to tell you of my eternal gratitude, and to say how deeply touched I am by your care and attention. Acting upon your advice, I have paid two-thirds of the sum to my current account. I have firmly resolved to begin to put by this year, so that in time I may buy a small landed property—perhaps Frolovskoe itself, since I am very fond of it, in spite of the demolition of the woods.

"Arensky has written an opera,[1] which Jurgenson has published. I had gone through it carefully and felt I must tell him exactly what I thought of this fine work. My letter touched him so deeply that he came here to thank me in person. Arensky is a man of remarkable gifts, but morbidly nervous and lacking in firmness—altogether a strange man."

[1] *A Dream on the Volga.*

2 R

To P. Jurgenson.

"*July 2nd* (14*th*), 1890.

"DEAR FRIEND,—The manuscript of the cantata is in the Petersburg Conservatoire. I cannot consent to its publication, because it is an immature work, for which there is no future. Besides, it is written to Schiller's *Ode to Joy*. It is not seemly to enter into competition with Beethoven.

"As to the fate of *The Little Shoes* (*Les Caprices d'Oxane*), I fully believe it will come to have a place in the repertory, and regard it, musically speaking, as my best operatic work.

"Arensky was here yesterday, and showed me a book of theory. It is admirably put together, and would be very useful for teaching purposes. I strongly recommend you to buy it."

To the Grand Duke Constantine Constantinovich.

"FROLOVSKOE, *August 3rd* (15*th*), 1890.

"YOUR IMPERIAL HIGHNESS,—Your kind and charming letter has reached me on the eve of my departure for a long journey, so forgive me if I do not answer it as fully as I ought. But I have much to say in answer to your remarks about *Pique Dame*. . . . Your criticisms of my sins as regards declamation are too lenient. In this respect I am past redemption. I do not think I have perpetrated many blunders of this kind in recitative and dialogue, but in the lyrical parts, where my mood has carried me away from all just equivalents, I am simply unconscious of my mistakes—you must get someone to point them out to me. . . .

"As regards the repetition of words and phrases, I must say that my views differ entirely from those of your Imperial Highness. There are cases in which such repetitions are quite natural and in accordance with truth of expression. . . . But even were it not so, I should not hesitate for an instant to sacrifice the literal to the artistic truth. These truths differ fundamentally, and I could not forget the second in pursuit of the first, for, if we aimed at pushing realism in opera to its extreme limits, we should finally have to abandon opera itself. To sing instead of speaking—that is the climax of falsehood in the accepted sense of the word. Of course, I am the child of my generation, and I have no wish to return to the worn-out traditions of opera ; at the same time I am not disposed to submit to the despotic requirements of realistic theories. I should be most grieved to think that any portions of *Pique Dame* were repellent to you—for I hoped the work might please you—and I have made a few changes in the scene where the governess scolds the girls, so that all the repetitions have some good reason. . . ."

IX

1890–1891

On December 13th (25th), 1890, Tchaikovsky received a letter from Nadejda von Meck, informing him that in consequence of the complicated state of her affairs she was on the brink of ruin, and therefore no longer able to continue his allowance.

In the course of their correspondence, which extended over thirteen years, Nadejda Filaretovna had referred more than once to her pecuniary embarrassments and to her fears of becoming bankrupt. But each time she had added that the allowance made to Tchaikovsky could be in no way affected, since she had assured it to him for life, and that the sum of 6,000 roubles a year was of no consequence to her one way or the other. In November, 1889, she had spoken again of her business anxieties, but, as usual, without any reference to Tchaikovsky's pension. On the contrary, in the summer of 1890 she showed her willingness to help him still further by advancing him a considerable sum. Consequently this news fell upon the composer like a bolt from the blue, and provoked the following reply :—

To N. F. von Meck.

"TIFLIS, *September 22nd* (*October 4th*), 1890.

"DEAREST FRIEND,—The news you communicated to me in your last letter caused me great anxiety; not on my account, however, but on your own. It would, of course, be untrue were I to say that such a radical change in my budget did not in any way affect my financial position. But it ought not to affect me so seriously as you apparently fear. In recent years my earnings have considerably increased, and there are indications that they will continue to do so. Therefore, if I am accountable for any fraction of your endless cares and anxieties, I beg you, for God's sake, to be assured that I can think of this pecuniary loss without any bitterness. Believe me, this is the simple truth; I am no master of empty phraseology. That I shall have to economise a little is of no importance. What really matters is that you, with your requirements and large ways of life, should have to retrench. This is terribly hard and vexatious. I feel as though I wanted to lay the blame on someone (you yourself are certainly above reproach), but I do not know who is the real culprit. Besides, not only is my indignation quite useless, but I have no right to interfere in your family affairs. I would rather ask Ladislaw Pakhulsky to tell me what you intend to do, where you will live, and how far you will be straitened as to means. I cannot think of you except as a wealthy woman. The last words of your letter have hurt me a little,[1] but I do not think you meant them seriously. Do you really think me incapable of remembering you when I no longer receive your money? How could I forget for a moment all you have done for me, and all for which I owe you gratitude? I may say without exaggeration that you saved me. I should certainly have gone out of my mind and come to an untimely end but for your friendship and sympathy, as well as for the material assistance (then my safety anchor), which enabled me to rally my forces and take up once more my chosen vocation. No, dear friend, I shall always remember and bless you with my last

[1] "Do not forget, and think of me sometimes."

breath. I am glad you can now no longer spend your means upon me, so that I may show my unbounded and passionate gratitude, which passes all words. Perhaps you yourself hardly suspect how immeasurable has been your generosity. If you did, you would never have said that, now you are poor, I am to think of you '*sometimes*.' I can truly say that I have never forgotten you, and never shall forget you for a moment, for whenever I think of myself my thoughts turn directly to you.

"I kiss your hands, with all my heart's warmth, and implore you to believe, once and for all, that no one feels more keenly for your troubles than I do.

"I will write another time about myself and all I am doing. Forgive my hasty, badly written letter: I am too much upset to write well."

To the above letter we need only add that Tchaikovsky, with his usual lack of confidence, greatly exaggerated to himself the consequences of this loss. A few days later he wrote to Jurgenson :—

"Now I must start quite a fresh life, on a totally different scale of expenditure. In all probability I shall be compelled to seek some occupation in Petersburg which will bring me in a good salary. This is very, very humiliating—yes, humiliating is the word !"

But this "humiliation" soon passed away. About this time his pecuniary situation greatly improved, and the success of *Pique Dame* more than covered the loss of his pension.

Soon, too, he was relieved as to the fate of Nadejda Filaretovna, for he learnt that her fears of ruin had been unfounded, and her financial difficulties had almost completely blown over. But with this relief—strange as it may appear—came also a sense of injury which Tchaikovsky carried to the grave. No sooner was he assured that his friend was as well off as before, than he began to persuade himself that her last letter had been nothing

" but an excuse to get rid of him on the first opportunity " ; that he had been mistaken in idealising his relations with his " best friend " ; that the allowance had long since ceased to be the outcome of a generous impulse, and that Nadejda Filaretovna was no longer as grateful to him for his ready acceptance of her help, as he was to receive it.

" Such were my relations with her," he wrote to Jurgenson, " that I never felt oppressed by her generous gifts ; but now they weigh upon me in retrospect. My pride is hurt ; my faith in her unfailing readiness to help me, and to make any sacrifice for my sake is betrayed."

In his agony of wounded pride Tchaikovsky was driven to wish that his friend had really been ruined, so that he " might help her, even as she had helped him." To these painful feelings was added all the bitterness involved in seeing their ideal connection shattered and dissolved. He felt as though he had been roughly awakened from some beautiful dream, and found in its stead " a commonplace, silly joke, which fills me with disgust and shame."

But the worst blow was yet to come. Shortly after receiving Nadejda von Meck's letter, Tchaikovsky's circumstances—as we have already said—improved so greatly that it would not have been difficult for him to have returned her the sum she had allowed him. He believed, however, that this would have hurt her feelings, and he could not bring himself to mortify in the smallest degree the woman who had actually been his saviour at the most critical moment of his life. The only way out of this painful situation seemed the continuance of his correspondence with her, as though nothing had happened. His advances, however, met with nothing but silent opposition on the part of Nadejda Filaretovna, and this proved the unkindest cut of all. Her indifference to his fate, her lack of interest in his work, convinced him that things had never been what they seemed, and all the old ideal friendship now appeared to him as the whim of a wealthy woman—the commonplace ending to a fairy tale; while her last letter remained like a blot upon the charm and beauty of their former intercourse. Neither the great success of *Pique Dame*, nor the profound sorrow caused by the death of his beloved sister, in April, 1891, nor even his triumphs in America, served to soften the blow she had inflicted.

On June 6th (18th), 1891, he wrote from Moscow to Ladislaw Pakhulsky:—

"I have just received your letter. It is true Nadejda Filaretovna is ill, weak, and her nerves are upset, so that she can no longer write to me as before. Not for the world would I add to her sufferings. I am grieved, bewildered, and—I say it frankly—deeply hurt that she has ceased to feel any interest in me. Even if she no longer desired me to go on corresponding directly with her, it could have been easily arranged for you and Julia Karlovna to have acted as links between us. But she has never once inquired through either of you how I am living, or what I am doing. I have endeavoured, through you, to re-establish my correspondence with Nadejda Filaretovna, but not one of your letters has contained the least courteous reference to my efforts. No doubt you are aware that in September last she informed me that she could no longer pay my pension. You must also know how I replied to her. I *wished* and *hoped* that our relations might remain unchanged. But unhappily this seemed impossible, because of her complete estrangement from me. The result has been that all our intercourse was brought to an end *directly I ceased to receive her money*. This situation lowers me in my own estimation; makes the remembrance of the money I accepted from her wellnigh intolerable; worries and weighs upon me more than I can say. When I was in the country last autumn I reread all her letters to me. No illness, no misfortune, no pecuniary anxieties could ever—so it seemed to me—change the sentiments which were expressed in these letters. And yet they have changed. Perhaps I idealised Nadejda Filaretovna because I did not know her personally. I could not conceive change in anyone so *half-divine*. I would sooner have believed that the earth could fail beneath me than that our relations could suffer change. But the inconceivable has happened, and all my ideas of human nature, all my faith in the best of mankind, have been turned upside down. My peace is broken, and the share of happiness fate has allotted me is embittered and spoilt.

" No doubt Nadejda Filaretovna has dealt me this cruel blow unconsciously and unintentionally. Never in my life have I felt so lowered, or my pride so profoundly injured as in this matter. The worst is that, on account of her shattered health, I dare not show her all the troubles of my heart, lest I should grieve or upset her.

" I may not speak out, which would be my sole relief. However, let this suffice. Even as it is, I may regret having said all this—but I felt the need of giving vent to some of my bitterness. Of course, I do not wish a word to be said to her.

" Should she ever inquire about me, say I returned safely from America and have settled down to work in Maidanovo. You may add that I am well.

" Do not answer this letter."

Nadejda Filaretovna made no response to this communication. Pakhulsky assured Tchaikovsky that her apparent indifference was the result of a serious nervous illness, but that in her heart of hearts she still cared for her old friend. He returned the above letter to Tchaikovsky, because he dare not give it to Nadejda Filaretovna during her illness, and did not consider himself justified in keeping it.

This was Tchaikovsky's last effort to win back the affection of his " best friend." But the wound remained unhealed, a cause of secret anguish which darkened his life to the end. Even on his death-bed the name of Nadejda Filaretovna was constantly on his lips, and in the broken phrases of his last delirium these words alone were intelligible to those around him.

Before taking leave of this personality who played so

benevolent a part in Tchaikovsky's existence, let it be said, in extenuation of her undeserved cruelty, that from 1890 Nadejda von Meck's life was a slow decline, brought about by a terrible nervous disease, which changed her relations not only to him, but to others. The news of his end reached her on her death-bed, and two months later she, too, passed away, on January 13th (25th), 1894.

X

Early in September, 1890, Tchaikovsky spent a day or two in Kiev on his way to Tiflis. In the former town he learnt that Prianichnikov, a favourite singer and theatrical impresario, was anxious to produce *Dame de Pique*. The idea pleased Tchaikovsky, for, thanks to Prianichnikov's energy, the opera at Kiev almost surpassed that of Moscow as regards *ensemble* and the excellence of the staging in general.

On October 20th (November 1st) Tchaikovsky conducted a concert given by the Tiflis branch of the Musical Society, the programme of which was drawn exclusively from his own works. The evening was a great success for the composer, who received a perfect ovation and was "almost smothered in flowers," besides being presented with a bâton.

Tiflis was the first town to welcome Tchaikovsky with cordiality and enthusiasm ; it was also the first to accord him a warm and friendly farewell, destined, alas ! to be for eternity.

On his return to Frolovskoe he busied himself with the collected edition of his songs, which Jurgenson proposed to issue shortly. The composer stipulated that the songs should be reprinted in their original keys, for, as he writes to Jurgenson : "I have neither strength nor patience to look through all the transpositions, which have been very badly done, and are full of the stupidest mistakes."

From Frolovskoe Tchaikovsky went to Petersburg, about the middle of November, to attend the rehearsals for his latest opera, *Pique Dame*. During his stay at the Hôtel Rossiya he arranged an *audition* of his newly composed sextet. The instrumentalists were : Albrecht, Hildebrandt, Wierzbilowicz, Hille, Kouznietsov and Heine. As audience, he invited Glazounov, Liadov, Laroche, and a few friends and relatives. Neither his hearers, nor the composer himself, were equally pleased with all the movements of the sextet, so that he eventually resolved to rewrite the Scherzo and Finale. Apart from this one disappointment, the rest of his affairs—including the rehearsals —went so well that his prevailing mood at this time was cheerful ; although the numerous festivities given in his honour hindered him from keeping up his correspondence during this visit to Petersburg. Not a single letter appears to exist dating from these weeks of his life.

On December 6th (18th) a rehearsal of the opera was given before their Imperial Majesties and many leaders of society in the capital. The success of the work was very evident ; yet Tchaikovsky had an idea that the Emperor did not care for it. As we shall see, later on, he was quite mistaken in coming to this conclusion.

The first public representation took place on December 7th (19th), 1890, just a year after the commencement of the work. Not one of Tchaikovsky's operas had a better caste than *Pique Dame*. The part of Hermann was taken by the celebrated singer Figner, while the heroine was represented by his wife. The rôles of the old Countess and Paulina were respectively allotted to Slavina and Dolina. Each of these leading singers distinguished themselves in some special quality of their art. Throughout the entire evening artists and audience alike experienced a sense of complete satisfaction, rarely felt during any operatic performance. Napravnik as conductor, and Figner in the part of hero, surpassed themselves, and did most to ensure the success of the opera. The scenery and dresses, by their beauty and historical accuracy, were worthy of the fine musical interpretation.

The applause increased steadily to the end of the work, and composer and singers were frequently recalled. At the same time, no one would have ventured to predict that the opera would even now be holding its own in the repertory, for there was no question of a great ovation.

The critics not only unanimously condemned the libretto, but did not approve of the music. One remarked : " As regards instrumentation, Tchaikovsky is certainly a great poet ; but in the actual music *he not only repeats himself, but does not shrink from imitating other composers.*" Another thought this " the weakest of all his efforts at opera." A third called the work " a card problem," and declared that, musically speaking, " the accessories prevailed over the essential ideas, and external brilliance over the inner content."

A few days after the first performance of *Pique Dame* in St. Petersburg, Tchaikovsky went through the same experience in Kiev, with this difference, that the reception of the opera in the southern city far surpassed in enthusiasm that which had been accorded to it in the capital.

" It was indescribable," he wrote to his brother on December 21st (January 2nd, 1891). " I am very tired, however, and in reality I suffer a great deal. My uncertainty as to the immediate future weighs upon me. Shall I give up the idea of wandering abroad or not ? Is it wise to accept the offer of the Opera Direction,[1] for the sextet seems to point to the fact that I am going downhill ? My brain is empty ; I have not the least pleasure in work. *Hamlet*[2] oppresses me terribly."

---

[1] To compose an opera in one act and a ballet for the season 1891-2.
[2] Incidental music to the tragedy *Hamlet*, for Guitry's benefit.

To Ippolitov-Ivanov.

"KAMENKA, *December 24th*, 1890 (*January 5th*, 1891).

"In Petersburg I frequently saw the Intendant of the Opera, and tried to throw out a bait with regard to your *Asra*. I shall be able to go more closely into the matter in January, but I can tell you already there is little hope for next year. Rimsky-Korsakov's *Mlada* is being considered, and I am commissioned to write a one-act opera and a ballet. . . . In this way I am involuntarily a hindrance to the younger composers, who would be glad to see their works performed at the Imperial Opera. This troubles me, but the temptation is too great, and I am not yet convinced that the time has come for me to make room for the younger generation. . . . As I have also asked Kondratiev—at Arensky's request—to persuade the Direction into giving a performance of his *Dream on the Volga*, I must warn you that you will meet with great difficulties in gaining your end. . . . No one knows better than I do how important it is for a young composer to get his works performed at a great theatre, therefore I would be willing to make some sacrifice, if I were sure it would be of any use. But supposing I were to relinquish my commission to compose an opera and a ballet. What would be the result? They would rather put on three foreign operas than risk a new Russian one by a young composer."

To Modeste Tchaikovsky.

"KAMENKA, *January 1st* (13*th*), 1890.

"Do you sometimes give a thought to *King René's Daughter?* [1] It is very probable that I shall end by going to work in Italy. In that case the libretto ought to be in my hands by the end of January. And the ballet? I shall spend a fortnight at Frolovskoe."

The time Tchaikovsky now spent at Frolovskoe was devoted to the *Hamlet* music, which he had promised Guitry should be ready in February.

---

[1] An opera in one act, afterwards known as *Iolanthe*.

Not one of his works inspired him with less enthusiasm than this. As a rule he rather enjoyed working to order, but he took up this task with great repugnance, because he had to begin by arranging the existing *Hamlet* overture, originally written for full orchestra, for the small band of the Michael Theatre. At his request the orchestra of twenty-nine was increased by seven musicians, but there was no room to accommodate a larger number. In spite of his disinclination for the work, Tchaikovsky succeeded in composing several numbers which delighted the public; while one movement (*The Funeral March*) became exceedingly popular.

Tchaikovsky arrived at Frolovskoe on January 6th (18th), and immediately telegraphed to the concert agent, Wolf, that he would be unable to fulfil the engagements made for him at Mainz, Buda-Pesth, and Frankfort.

It was not merely the composition of the *Hamlet* music which caused him to relinquish these engagements; at this time he was suffering from a nervous affection of the right hand, which made conducting a matter of considerable difficulty.

To S. I. Taneiev.

"*January* 14*th* (26*th*), 1891.

"The question: How should opera be written? is one I answer, have answered, and always shall answer, in the simplest way. Operas, like everything else, should be written just as they come to us. I always try to express in the music as truthfully and sincerely as possible all there is in the text. But truth and sincerity are not the result of a process of reasoning, but the inevitable outcome of our inmost feelings. In order that these feelings should have warmth and vitality, I always choose subjects in which I have to deal with real men and women, who share the same emotions as myself. That is why I cannot bear the Wagnerian subjects, in which there is so little human interest. Neither would I have chosen your subject, with its supernatural agencies, its inevitable crimes, its Eumenides and Fates as *dramatis personæ*. As soon as I have found a subject, and decided to compose an opera, I give free rein to my feelings, neither trying to carry out Wagner's principles, nor striving after originality. At the same time I make no conscious effort to go against the spirit of my time. If Wagner had not existed, probably my compositions would have been different to what they are. I may add that even the 'Invincible Band' has had some influence on my operas. Italian music, which I loved passionately from my childhood, and Glinka, whom I idolised in my youth, have both influenced me deeply, to say nothing of Mozart. But I never invoked any one of these musical deities and bade him dispose of my musical conscience as he pleased. Consequently I do not think any of my operas can be said to belong to a particular school. Perhaps one of these influences may occasionally have gained the upper hand and I have fallen into imitation; but whatever happened came of itself, and I am sure I appear in my works just as God made me, and such as I have become through the action of time, nationality, and education. I have never been untrue to myself. What I am, whether good or bad, others must judge for me. . . .

"Arensky's opera[1] did not please me much when he played me fragments of it in Petersburg after his illness. I liked it a little better when he played it to you at Altani's; far more when I went through it myself this summer; and now, having seen it actually performed, I think it one of the best of Russian operas. It is very elegant and equal throughout; only the end lacks something of inspiration. It has one defect: a certain monotony of method which reminds me of Korsakov. . . . Arensky is extraordinarily clever in music; everything is so subtly and truly thought out. He is a very interesting musical personality."

To P. Jurgenson.

"*January* 15*th* (27*th*), 1891.

"DEAR FRIEND,—Wolf has sent me the letter from that American gentleman who has arranged for my en-

[1] *A Dream on the Volga* (the Voyevode).

gagement. It is so easy and profitable that it would be foolish to lose this opportunity of an American tour, which has long been one of my dreams. This explains my telegram to you yesterday. In America, the news that I could not go, because my right hand was disabled, reached them by cable, and they were very much upset. Now they are awaiting an answer—yes or no."

To the same.

"*January* 17*th* (29*th*), 1891.

"DEAR SOUL,—Send me immediately my *Legend* for chorus, and the *Liturgy* and other church works, with the exception of the Vespers. I must make a selection for the American festival.[1] Have you the *Children's Songs* in Rahter's edition? I want the German text for the *Legend.*"

At the close of January Tchaikovsky went to St. Petersburg. Early in February he had to conduct at a concert in aid of the school founded by the Women's Patriotic League. This annual concert drew a fashionable audience, who only cared for the singing of such stars as Melba and the De Reszkes. Consequently Tchaikovsky's Third Suite merely served to try their patience.

His reception on the 9th, at the performance of *Hamlet* (at the Michael Theatre), was equally poor. But he was agreeably surprised at the individual criticisms of his music which reached his ears. "I am not averse from your idea of publishing the *Hamlet* music," he wrote to Jurgenson, "for it pleased, and everyone is delighted with the March."

Meanwhile the Direction of the Imperial Opera were discussing the opera and ballet which Tchaikovsky had been commissioned to compose. For the former, Herz's play, *King René's Daughter*—translated into Russian by Zvanstiev—was chosen ; and for the ballet, *Casse-Noisette*

---

[1] The opening ceremony of the new Carnegie Hall in New York.

("The Nut-cracker"). Neither of these subjects awoke in Tchaikovsky that joy of creation he had experienced while composing *The Sleeping Beauty* and *Pique Dame.* There were several reasons for this. The *Casse-Noisette* subject did not at all please him. He had chosen *King René's Daughter* himself, but he did not know as yet how the libretto would suit him. He was also annoyed with the Direction because they had engaged foreign singers, and were permitting them to sing in French and Italian at the Russian Opera. Thirdly, in view of the American tour, he did not feel master of his time, and really had no idea how he should get through so much music by December, 1891. Finally, he was very deeply mortified.

The source of his vexation lay in the fact that after its thirteenth performance *Pique Dame* was unexpectedly withdrawn until the autumn, although almost all the tickets had been secured beforehand for at least another ten performances. No definite reason was assigned for this action, which was the outcome of mere caprice on the part of some unknown person. Tchaikovsky's anxiety was aggravated by the fear that his favourite work might disappear altogether from the repertory. He suspected that its withdrawal was ordered at the desire of the Emperor, who—so he fancied—did not like the opera. Anyone else would have discovered the real reason by the medium of inquiry, but Tchaikovsky was prevented from speaking of it in Petersburg "by pride and fear," as he wrote to Jurgenson, "lest people should think I was regretting the royalty; and, on their part, the members of the operatic Direction carefully avoided mentioning the subject to me." After a while he poured out his heart in a letter to Vsievolojsky, who, in reply, entirely reassured him as to his fears. The Emperor, he said, was very pleased with *Pique Dame,* and all that Tchaikovsky composed for the opera in Petersburg awakened a lively interest in the Imperial box. "Personally, I need not 'lay floral tributes' before you," he concludes, "for you know how greatly I admire your talents. . . . In *Pique Dame* your dramatic power stands out with startling effect in two scenes: the death of the Countess and Hermann's madness. I think you should keep to intimate drama and avoid grandiose subjects. *Jamais, au grand jamais, vous ne m'avez impressioné comme dans ces deux tableaux d'un réalisme saississant.*"

Comforted by this letter, Tchaikovsky set to work upon his new ballet, *Casse-Noisette.* "I am working with all my might," he wrote to his brother from Frolovskoe, "and I am growing more reconciled to the subject. I hope to finish a considerable part of the first act before I go abroad."

Early in March he left Frolovskoe and travelled to Paris, *viâ* St. Petersburg.

To Vladimir Davidov.

"BERLIN, *March 8th (20th)*, 1891.

"Against this form of home-sickness, that you have hardly experienced as yet, which is more agonising than anything in this world, there is but one remedy—to get drunk. Between Eydkuhnen and Berlin I consumed an incredible amount of wine and brandy; consequently I slept, though badly. . . . To-day I am less home-sick, yet all the while I feel as though some vampire were sucking at my heart. I have a headache, and feel weak, so I shall spend the night in Berlin. . . . After the midday meal I shall take a long walk through the town and go to a concert where my '*1812*' overture is being played.

"It is great fun to sit incognito among a strange audience and listen to one's own works. I leave to-morrow, and my next letter will be written from Paris. Bob, I idolise you! Do you remember how I once told you that the happiness your presence gave me was nothing compared to all I suffered in your absence? Away from home, with the prospect of long weeks and months apart, I feel the full meaning of my affection for you."

2 S

" I had already been in Paris a month when my brother arrived on March 10th (22nd)," says Modeste Tchaikovsky. " This was the first time I had seen him abroad, except in a very intimate circle. Now I saw him as the artist on tour. This period has left an unpleasant impression on my memory. He had not told me the hour of his arrival, and I only knew of it when I returned one evening to my hotel. He was already asleep, and the servants told me he did not wish to be aroused. This, in itself, was a symptom of an abnormal frame of mind. As a rule he was eager for the first hour of meeting. We met the next morning, and he evinced no sign of pleasure, only wondered how I—who was under no obligation—could care to stay so long away from Russia. A chilling and gloomy look, his cheeks flushed with excitement, a bitter laugh upon his lips—this is how I always remember Peter Ilich during that visit to Paris. We saw very little of each other ; he was continually occupied either with Colonne, or Mackar, or somebody. Or he sat in his room surrounded by visitors of all kinds. The real Peter Ilich only reappeared in the evening when, in the society of Sophie Menter, Sapellnikov, and Konius—a young violinist in Colonne's orchestra, formerly his pupil in Moscow—he rested after the rush and bustle of the day."

The concert which Tchaikovsky was to conduct in Paris on March 24th (April 5th) was the twenty-third of Colonne's series, and the French conductor had relinquished his place for the occasion because he himself was engaged in Moscow. The colossal programme included : (1) the Third Suite, (2) Pianoforte Concerto No. 2 (Sapellnikov), (3) *Sérénade Mélancolique* (Johann Wolf), (4) Songs, (5) Andante from the First Quartet (arranged for string orchestra), (6) Symphonic Fantasia, *The Tempest*, (7) Slavonic March. The room was crowded, and all the works met with notable success. The Press was also unanimous in its favourable verdict.

But nothing could appease Tchaikovsky's home-sickness. There still remained twelve days before he sailed from Havre for America. Partly to work at his opera and ballet, partly to have a little rest and freedom, he decided to spend ten days at Rouen. On April 4th Sophie Menter, Sapellnikov, and myself were to meet him there, and see him off the following day from Havre.

This plan was not carried out, however, for on March 29th I received a telegram informing me of the death of our sister Alexandra Davidov.

For some years past, in consequence of a serious illness, which gradually cut her off from her relations with others, this sister had not played so important a part in the life of Peter Ilich. Continually fighting against her malady, sorely tried by the death of her two elder daughters, she could not keep up the same interest as of old in her brother's existence. Yet he loved her dearly, and she was as essential to his happiness as ever. She, who had been to him a haven and a refuge from all the troubles of life, was still the holiest reliquary of his childhood, his youth, and the Kamenka period of his life; for, together with Nadejda von Meck, she had been his chief support, making him welcome, and bestowing upon him the most affectionate attention.

I was aware that the news of her death would come as a crushing blow to my brother, and felt it imperative to break it to him in person. The same day I set out for Rouen. Peter Ilich was as delighted to see me as though we had not met for ages. It was not difficult to guess at the overwhelming loneliness which he had experienced during his voluntary exile. Apart from the fact that I found it hard to damp his cheerful mood, I became more and more preoccupied with the idea: was it wise to tell him of our loss under the present circumstances? I knew it was too late for him to give up his journey to America. He had already taken his ticket to New York. What would he have done during the long voyage alone, which he already dreaded, had he been overweighted with this grief? In America, distracted by the anxieties of his concerts, the sad news would not come as so great a shock. Therefore, in answer to his question, why had I come, I did not reveal the truth, but simply said that I, too, felt home-sick, and had come to say good-bye before starting for Russia the next day. He seemed almost pleased at my news. . . . Incomprehensible to others, I understood his satisfaction. He had often said: "Modeste is too closely akin to myself." In Paris, it vexed him to realise that I did not yearn for our native land. Now that he believed I was content to cut short my stay abroad, he forgave me, and our meeting was as hearty as though we had come together after a long separation. This made it all the more difficult to tell him what had happened, and I returned to Paris after a touching farewell, without having broken the news to him. I had warned our friends in Paris, and there were no Russian newspapers to be had in Rouen. All letters from home were to be addressed to the Hôtel Richepanse, whence I requested that they should be forwarded straight to America.

Firmly convinced that my brother would not receive the melancholy news until he reached New York, I started for St. Petersburg.

But no sooner had his brother left Rouen than Tchaikovsky's depression reached a climax. First of all he wrote to Vsievolojsky that he could not possibly have the ballet and opera ready before the season of 1892–3; and then he resolved to return to Paris for a couple of days, to distract his anxiety as to the approaching journey.

On his arrival the truth became known to him, and he wrote the following letter to his brother :—

"Modi, yesterday I went to Paris. There I visited the reading-room in the Passage de l'Opéra, took up the

Novoe Vremya and read the announcement of Sasha's death. I started up as though a snake had stung me. Later on I went to Sophie Menter's and Sapellnikov's. What a fortunate thing they were here! I spent the night with them. To-day I start, *viâ* Rouen and Le Havre. At first I thought it was my duty to give up America and go to Petersburg, but afterwards I reflected that this would be useless. I should have had to return the 5,000 francs I had received, to relinquish the rest, and lose my ticket. No, I must go to America. Mentally I am suffering much. I am very anxious about Bob, although I know from my own experience that at his age we easily recover from such blows.

". . . . For God's sake write all details to New York. To-day, even more than yesterday, I feel the absolute impossibility of depicting in music the ' Sugar-plum Fairy.' "

XI

To Modeste Tchaikovsky.

"S.S. 'LA BRETAGNE,' ATLANTIC OCEAN,
"April 6th (18*st*), 1891.

" During the voyage I shall keep a diary, and send it to you when I get to New York. Please take care of it, for I mean to write an article later on, for which my diary will serve as material. . . . The ship is one of the largest and most luxurious. I dined in Le Havre, walked about a little, and at 10 p.m. made myself comfortable in my cabin. . . . There I suddenly felt more miserable than ever. Principally because I had received no answer to my telegram to Petersburg. I cannot think why. Probably the usual telegraphic blunder, but it is very hard to leave without any news. . . . I curse this voyage.

" The ship is superb. A veritable floating palace. There are not a great number of passengers, about eighty in the first class. . . . At dinner I sit at a little table with an American family. Very uncomfortable and wearisome.

"At five o'clock there was a tragic occurrence, which had a depressing effect upon me and all the other passengers.

I was below, when suddenly a whistle was heard, the ship hove to, and everyone was greatly excited. A boat was lowered. I went on deck and heard that a young man, a second-class passenger, had suddenly taken out his pocket-book, scribbled a few words in haste, thrown himself overboard and disappeared beneath the waves. A life-belt was flung to him, and a boat was lowered immediately, which was watched with the greatest anxiety by all of us. But nothing was to be seen on the surface of the sea, and after half an hour's search we continued our course. In his pocket-book was found thirty-five francs, and on a sheet of paper a few words hardly decipherable. I was the first to make them out, for they were written in German, and all the passengers were French or Americans. '*Ich bin unschuldig, der Bursche weint . . .*' followed by a few scrawls no one could read. Afterwards I heard that the young man had attracted attention by his strange conduct, and was probably insane.

"The weather is beautiful, and the sea quite calm. The ship moves so quietly that one can hardly believe oneself on the water. We have just seen the lighthouse at the Lizard. The last sight of land before we reach New York."

To Modeste Tchaikovsky.

"*April 7th* (19*th*), 1891.

"Early this morning the tossing began, and grew gradually worse, until at times I felt horribly nervous. It was a comfort that most of the passengers had made the voyage very often, and were not in the least afraid of going down, as I was, only of being sea-sick. I was not afraid of that, for I felt no symptoms whatever. The steward to whom I spoke called it '*une mer un peu grosse.*' What must '*une mer très grosse*' be like? The aspect of the sea is very fine, and when I am free from alarm I enjoy watching the grand spectacle. I am interested in three huge sea-gulls which are following us. They say they will go with us to Newfoundland. When do they rest, and where do they spend the night? I read all day, for there is nothing else to do. Composition goes against the grain. I am very depressed. When I opened my heart to my acquaintance, the commercial traveller in the second class, he replied, 'Well, at your age it is very natural,' which hurt my feelings. . . . I would rather not say what I feel. . . . It is for the last time. . . . When one gets to my years it is best to stay at home, close to one's own folk. The thought of being so far from all who are dear to me almost kills me. But otherwise I am quite well, thank God. A 'miss' has been singing Italian songs the whole evening, and her performance was so abominable, such an effrontery, that I was surprised no one said anything rude to her."

To M. Tchaikovsky.

"*April 8th* (*20th*), 1891.

" I had a good night. When everyone had gone to bed I walked for a long time on deck. The wind went down, and it was quite calm by the time I went to my cabin. To-day it is sunny, but the wind has been getting up since midday. There is now a head sea instead of the waves coming broadside on. But the ship is so big that very few have been sea-sick. My friendship with the commercial traveller and his companions grows more intimate. They are very lively, and entertain me more than the correct and respectable first-class passengers. . . . The most interesting of these is a Canadian bishop with his secretary, who has been to Europe to receive the Pope's blessing. Yesterday he celebrated mass in a private cabin, and I chanced to be present. While I am writing, the ship is beginning to pitch more, but now I realise it must be so in mid-ocean, and I am getting used to it."

"*April 9th* (*21st*), 1891.

" In the night the ship pitched so that I awoke, and had palpitations and almost nervous fever. A glass of brandy soon picked me up and had a calming effect. I put on my overcoat and went on deck. It was a glorious moonlight night. When I saw that everything was going on as usual, I realised that there was no cause for fear. . . . By morning the wind had dropped. We were in the Gulf

Stream. This was evident, because suddenly it became much warmer. There are about a hundred emigrants on board, mostly Alsatians. As soon as the weather improves they give a ball, and it is amusing to see them dancing to the strains of their concertinas. These emigrants do not appear at all unhappy. The unsympathetic lady who sits near me at table is the wife of a member of the Boston orchestra. Consequently to-day the conversation turned upon music. She related some interesting things about the Boston concerts and musical life there.

" To-day we passed a few sailing vessels, and a huge whale which sent up a spout of water into the air."

To Modeste Tchaikovsky.

"*April* 10*th* (*22nd*), 1891.

" I believed I was quite immune from sea-sickness. It appears that I am not. Last night the weather got worse and worse. When I got up at seven a.m. it was so bad, and the sea so rough, that I enjoyed watching it, in spite of the huge ocean waves. It continued to blow until two o'clock, when it was so terrible that I expected every moment the ship would go down. Of course there was really no question whatever of our sinking. Not only the captain, but the sailors and all the stewards took it as a matter of course. But to me, who only know the sea from the Mediterranean, it was like hell let loose. Everything cracked and groaned. One minute we were tossed up to the clouds, the next we sank into the depths. It was impossible to go on deck, for the wind almost blew one overboard—in short, it was terrible. Most of the passengers were ill, but some enjoyed it, and even played the piano, arranged card-parties, etc. I had no appetite for breakfast, afterwards I felt *very uncomfortable*, and at dinner I could not bear the sight of the food. I have not really been ill, but I have experienced disagreeable sensations. It is impossible to sleep. *Brandy* and *coffee* are the only nourishment I have taken to-day."

To Modeste Tchaikovsky.

"*April* 12*th* (24*th*), 1891.

" The night was horrible. Towards morning the weather improved, and remained bearable until four o'clock. Then came a fresh misery. As we approached the 'sand banks' of Newfoundland we passed into a belt of dense fog—which seems the usual experience here. This is the thing most dreaded at sea, because a collision, even with a small sailing vessel, may sink the ship. Our speed was considerably slackened, and every few seconds the siren was heard ; a machine which emits a hideous roar, like a gigantic tiger. It gets terribly on one's nerves. . . . Now the people on board have discovered who I am, and amiabilities, compliments, and conversations have begun. I can never walk about by myself. Besides, they press me to play. I refuse, but apparently it will never end until I have played something on the wretched piano. . . . The fog is lifting, but the rolling is beginning again."

To Modeste Tchaikovsky.

"*April* 12*th* (24*th*), 1891.

" I absolutely cannot write. Since yesterday evening I have been a martyr. It is blowing a fearful gale. They say it was predicted by the Meteorological Observatory. It is horrible ! Especially to me, a novice. They say it will last till we get to New York. I suffer as much mentally as physically ; simply from fright and anxiety."

"*April* 13*th* (25*th*), 1891.

" After writing the above lines I went into the smoking-room. Very few passengers were there, and they sat idle, with gloomy, anxious faces. . . . The gale continually increased. There was no thought of lying down. I sat in a corner of the sofa in my cabin and tried not to think about what was going on ; but that was impossible, for the straining, creaking, and shivering of the vessel, and the howling of the wind outside, could not be silenced. So I sat on, and what passed through my mind I cannot describe to you. Unpleasant reflections. Presently I noticed that the horrible shocks each time the screw was lifted out of the water came at longer intervals, the wind howled less. Then I fell asleep, still sitting propped between my trunk and the wall of the cabin. . . . In the morning I found we had passed through the very centre of an unusually severe storm, such as is rarely experienced. At two o'clock we met the pilot who had long been expected. The whole bevy of passengers turned out to see him waiting for us in his tiny boat. The ship hove to, and we took him on board. There are only about twenty-four hours left. In consequence of the gale we are a few hours late. I am very glad the voyage is nearing its end: I simply could not bear to remain any longer on board ship. I have decided to return from New York by a German liner on April 30th (May 12th). By May 10th (22nd), or a little later, I shall be in Petersburg again, D.V."

XII

To Modeste Tchaikovsky.

"NEW YORK, *April* 15*th* (27*th*), 1891.

"The remainder of the journey was happily accomplished. The nearer we came to New York, the greater grew my fear and home-sickness, and I regretted ever having undertaken this insane voyage. When all is over I may look back to it with pleasure, but at present it is not without suffering. Before we reached New York— endless formalities with passports and Customs. A whole day was spent in answering inquiries. At last we landed at 5 p.m. I was met by four very amiable gentlemen and a lady, who took me straight to the Hotel Normandie. Here I explained to Mr. Morris Reno[1] that I should leave on the 12th. He said that would not be feasible, because an extra concert had been fixed for the 18th, of which Wolf had not said a word to me. After all these people had gone, I began to walk up and down my

---

[1] President of the Music Hall Company of New York, upon whose initiative Tchaikovsky had been engaged in America.

rooms (I have two) and shed many tears. I declined their invitations to dinner and supper, and begged to be left to myself for to-night.

"After a bath, I dressed, dined against my inclination, and went for a stroll down Broadway. An extraordinary street! Houses of one and two stories alternate with some nine-storied buildings. Most original. I was struck with the number of nigger faces I saw. When I got back I began crying again, and slept like the dead, as I always do after tears. I awoke refreshed, but the tears are always in my eyes."

Diary.

"*Monday, April* 15*th* (27*th*).

"Mayer[1] was my first visitor. The cordial friendliness of this pleasant German astonished and touched me. For, being the head of a pianoforte firm, he had no interest in paying attentions to a musician who is not a pianist. Then a reporter appeared, and I was very thankful for Mayer's presence. Many of his questions were very curious. Reno next arrived, bringing an interesting friend with him. Reno told me I was expected at the rehearsal. After we had got rid of the interviewer we went on foot to the music hall.[2] A magnificent building. We got to the rehearsal just at the end of Beethoven's Fifth Symphony. Damrosch[3] (who was conducting without his coat) appeared very pleasant. I wanted to speak to him at the finish of the Symphony, but had to wait and answer the cordial greetings of the orchestra. Damrosch made a little speech. More ovations. I could only rehearse the first and third movements of the First Suite. The orchestra is excellent. After the rehearsal I breakfasted with Mayer, who then took me up Broadway, helped me to buy a hat, presented me with a hundred cigarettes, showed me the very

[1] The head of the Knabe Pianoforte Manufactory.

[2] This hall was built principally with the help of Mr. Carnegie. Tchaikovsky was invited to the opening festivities.

[3] Walter Damrosch, son of the founder of the "Symphony Society" in New York, one of the directors of the Music Hall Company of New York, and conductor of the Symphony Concerts and of the opera.

interesting Hoffman Bar, which is decorated with the most beautiful pictures, statues and tapestries, and finally brought me home. I lay down to rest, completely exhausted. Later on I dressed, for I was expecting Reno, who soon turned up. I tried to persuade him to let me give up Philadelphia and Baltimore, but he did not seem inclined to grant my request. He took me to his house and introduced me to his wife and daughters, who are very nice. Afterwards he went with me to Damrosch's. A year ago Damrosch married the daughter of a very rich and distinguished man. They are a very agreeable couple. We sat down three to dinner. Then Damrosch took me to visit Carnegie,[1] the possessor of 30,000,000 dollars, who is very like our dramatist Ostrovsky. I was very much taken with the old man, especially as he is an admirer of Moscow, which he visited two years ago. Next to Moscow, he admires the national songs of Scotland, a great many of which Damrosch played to him on a magnificent Steinway grand. He has a young and pretty wife. After these visits I went with Hyde[2] and Damrosch to see the Athletic Club and another, more serious in tone, which I might perhaps compare with our English Club. The Athletic Club astonished me, especially the swimming bath, in which the members bathe, and the upper gallery, where they skate in winter. We ordered drinks in the serious club. I reached home about eleven o'clock. Needless to say, I was worn out.

"*April* 16*th* (28*th*).

"Slept very well. A messenger came from * * * * to know if I wanted anything. These Americans strike me as very remarkable, especially after the impression the Parisians left upon me : there politeness or amiability to a stranger always savoured of self-interest ; whereas in this country the honesty, sincerity, generosity, cordiality, and readiness to help you without any *arrière-pensée*, is

---

[1] A. Carnegie, the greatest ironmaster in America, perhaps in the world ; orator, author, politician ; a most generous benefactor and founder of many schools, libraries and museums.

[2] Francis Hyde, Director of the Trust Company, and President of the New York Philharmonic Society.

very pleasant. I like this, and most of the American ways and customs, yet I enjoy it all in the same spirit as a man who sits at a table laden with good things and has no appetite. My appetite will only come with the near prospect of my return to Russia.

"At eleven a.m. I went for a walk, and breakfasted in a very pretty restaurant. Home again by one o'clock and reflected a little. Reinhard,[1] an agreeable young man, came to take me to Mayer's. On the way we turned into the Hoffman Bar. Saw Knabe's warehouse. Mayer took me to a photographic studio. We went up by the lift to the ninth or tenth floor, where a little old man (the owner of the studio) received us in a red nightcap. I never came across such a droll fellow. He is a parody of Napoleon III. (very like the original, but a caricature of him). He turned me round and round while he looked for the *best* side of my face. Then he developed rather a tedious theory of the *best side of the face* and proceeded to experiment on Mayer. Finally I was photographed in every conceivable position, during which the old man entertained me with all kinds of mechanical toys. But, with all his peculiarities, he was pleasant and cordial in the American way. From the photographer I drove with Mayer to the park, which is newly laid out, but very beautiful. There was a crowd of smart ladies and carriages. We called for Mayer's wife and daughter and continued our drive along the high bank of the Hudson. It became gradually colder, and the conversation with these good German-Americans wearied me. At last we stopped at the celebrated Restaurant Delmonico, and Mayer invited me to a most luxurious dinner, after which he and the ladies took me back to my hotel. I hurried into my dress-coat and waited for Mr. Hyde. Then, together with him and his wife, Damrosch, and Mr. and Mrs. Reno, we all went to a somewhat tedious concert at the great Opera House. We heard an oratorio, *The Captivity*, by the American composer Max Vogrich. Most wearisome. After this I wanted to go home, but the dear Hydes carried me off to supper at Delmonico's. We ate oysters with a sauce of small turtles (! ! !), and cheese. Champagne, and an

---

[1] A representative from the firm of Knabe.

iced peppermint drink, supported my failing courage. They brought me home at twelve o'clock. A telegram from Botkin summoning me to Washington.

"*April* 17*th* (29*th*).

" Passed a restless night. After my early tea I wrote letters. Then I sauntered through Fifth Avenue. What palaces! Breakfasted alone at home. Went to Mayer's. The kindness and attentiveness of this man are simply wonderful. According to Paris custom, I try to discover what he wants to get out of me. But I can think of nothing. Early this morning he sent Reinhard to me again, in case I wanted anything, and I was very glad of his help, for I did not know what to do about the telegram from Washington. By three o'clock I was at home, waiting for William de Sachs, a very amiable and elegant gentleman, who loves music and writes about it. He was still here when my French friends from the steamer arrived. I was very glad to see them and we went out together to have some absinthe. When I got back I rested for a while. At seven o'clock Hyde and his wife called for me. What a pity it is that words and colours fail me to describe this most original couple, who are so extremely kind and friendly! The language in which we carry on our conversation is very amusing; it consists of the queerest mixture of English, French and German. Every word which Hyde utters in our conversation is the result of an extraordinary intellectual effort : literally a whole minute passes before there emerges, from an indefinite murmur, some word so weird-sounding that it is impossible to tell to which of the three languages it belongs. All the time Hyde and his wife have such a serious, yet good-natured air. I accompanied them to Reno's, who was giving a big dinner in my honour. The ladies—all in full evening dress. The table decorated with flowers. At each lady's place lay a bunch of flowers, while the men had lilies-of-the-valley, which we put in our buttonholes as soon as we were seated at table. Each lady had also a little picture of myself in a pretty frame. The dinner began at half-past seven, and was over at eleven. I am not exaggerating when I say this, for it is the custom here.

It is impossible to describe all the courses.   In the middle of the dinner ices were served in little cases, to which were attached small slates with pencils and sponges, on which fragments from my works were beautifully inscribed.   I had to write my autograph on these slates.   The conversation was very lively.   I sat between Mrs. Reno and Mrs. Damrosch.   The latter is a most charming and graceful woman.   Opposite to me sat Carnegie, the admirer of Moscow, and the possessor of forty million dollars. His likeness to Ostrovsky is astonishing.   Tormented by the want of a smoke, and almost ill with over-eating, I determined about eleven o'clock to ask Mrs. Reno's permission to leave the table.   Half an hour later we all took our leave."

To V. Davidov.

"NEW YORK, *April* 18*th* (30*th*), 1891.

" Have just received my letters.   It is impossible to say how precious these are under the present circumstances.   I was unspeakably glad.   I make copious entries every day in my diary and, on my return, you shall each have it to read in turn, so I will not go into details now. New York, American customs, American hospitality—all their comforts and arrangements—everything, in fact, is to my taste.   If only I were younger I should very much enjoy my visit to this interesting and youthful country. But now, I just tolerate everything as if it were a slight punishment mitigated by many pleasant things.   All my thoughts, all my aspirations, tend towards Home, Home!!! I am convinced that I am ten times more famous in America than in Europe.   At first, when others spoke about it to me, I thought it was only their exaggerated amiability.   But now I see that it really is so.   Several of my works, which are unknown even in Moscow, are frequently played here.   I am a much more important person here than in Russia.   Is not that curious?"

Diary.   "*April* 18*th* (30*th*).

" It is becoming more and more difficult to find time for writing.   Breakfasted with my French friends.   Interview with de Sachs. We went to see the Brooklyn Bridge. From there we went on to see Schirmer, who owns the largest music business in America; the warehouse—especially the metallography—resembles Jurgenson's in many respects. Schirmer begged to be allowed to publish some of my compositions. On reaching home, I received the journalist, Ivy Ross, who asked me for a contribution for her paper. When she had gone, I sank on the sofa like a log and enjoyed a little rest and solitude. By 8.30 I was already at the Music Hall for the first rehearsal. The chorus greeted me with an ovation. They sang beautifully. As I was about to leave, I met the builder of the hall in the doorway; he presented to me a pleasant, rather stout, man, his chief assistant, whose talent and cleverness he could not sufficiently praise. This man was—as it turned out—a pure-blooded Russian, who had become a naturalised American. The architect told me he was an anarchist and socialist. I had a little conversation with my fellow-countryman, and promised to visit him. After a light supper I took a walk. Read over and over again the letters I had received and, naturally, shed a few tears.

"*April* 19th (*May* 1st).

"Awoke late and sat down to write a little article for Miss Ross. Reno appeared, with the news that he had engaged a cabin for me on board the *Fürst Bismarck*, which sails on May 2nd (14th). Oh God, what a long way off it still seems! I called for my good friend Mayer and breakfasted with him in an excellent little Italian restaurant, after which we went down town. Here I saw for the first time what life means at certain hours on Broadway. So far I had only been able to judge this street from the neighbourhood of the hotel, where there is little traffic. But this is only a very small portion of this street, which is seven versts (over four miles) long. The houses down town are simply colossal; I cannot understand how anyone can live on the thirteenth floor. Mayer and I went out on the roof of one such house. The view was splendid, but I felt quite giddy when I looked down into Broadway. Then Mayer obtained permission for me to visit the cellars of the mint, where hundreds of millions of gold and silver coins, as well as paper money, are kept. Very good-natured, but fussy and important, officials conducted us round these cellars, and opened monumental doors with mysterious keys and no less mysterious pressings of various springs and knobs. The sacks of gold, which look just like sacks of corn in a granary, are kept in clean, tidy rooms lit by electric light. I was allowed to hold in my hand a packet of new shining coins worth about 10,000,000 dollars.[1] Then I understood why so little gold and silver are in circulation. The Americans prefer dirty, unpleasant paper notes to metal, because they find them so much more practical and useful. Therefore, these paper notes—quite the reverse to our country— thanks to the vast amount of metals kept in the mint, are valued far more than gold and silver. From the mint we visited the scene of activity of good Mr. Hyde. He is a director of one of the banks, and took me round his strong-rooms, in which mountains of paper money are stored away. We also visited the Exchange, which struck me as quieter than the Paris Bourse. Hyde treated us to lemonade at a café. On my return home I had to finish my newspaper article on Wagner for Miss Ross, and at five o'clock I was ready to visit William de Sachs. He lives in a very large house, where rooms are let to bachelors only. Ladies are only admitted as guests into this curious American monastery. I found a small gathering, which gradually grew larger. It was "five o'clock tea." The pianist, Miss Wilson (who called on me yesterday, and is a staunch adherent of Russian music), played Borodin's beautiful Serenade. After refusing several invitations I spent the evening alone. How pleasant it was! Dined in the Restaurant Hoffmann, as usual, without any enjoyment. During my walk further along Broadway I came upon a meeting of Socialists in red caps. Next morning I learnt from the newspapers that about five thousand men had assembled, carrying banners and huge lanterns, on which were inscribed these words: 'Comrades! We are slaves in free America. We

[1] This would have been an impossible athletic feat, probably the equivalent in notes is intended.—R. N.

2 T

will no longer work more than eight hours!' The whole demonstration seemed to me a farce; I think the inhabitants also look on it as such, for very few people had the curiosity to stand and watch; the others walked about as usual. I went to bed bodily tired, but mentally refreshed.

"*April 20th (May 2nd)*.

"By 10.30 a.m. I was at the rehearsal in the Music Hall. It was held in the large hall, where several workmen were hammering, shouting, and running hither and thither. The orchestra is placed across the whole breadth of the huge platform; consequently the sound is bad and unequal. This got on my nerves until, in my rage, I was several times on the point of making a scene, leaving everything in the lurch and running away. I played through the Suite and the March very carelessly, and stopped the Pianoforte Concerto at the first movement, as the parts were in confusion and the musicians exhausted. The pianist, Adèle Aus-der-Ohe, came at five o'clock and played over the Concerto, which had gone so badly at rehearsal.

"*April 21st (May 3rd)*.

"Telegram from Jurgenson: 'Christos vosskresse.'[1] Rain outside. Letters from Modi and Jurgenson. 'Nur wer die Sehnsucht kennt'—realises what it means to receive letters in a strange country. I have never before experienced similar sensations. Mr. N. and his wife came to call upon me. He—a tall, bearded man, with iron-grey hair, very elegantly dressed, always bewailing his spinal complaint, speaking very good Russian and abusing the Jews (although he himself looks very like one); she—a very plain Englishwoman (not American), who can speak nothing but English. She brought a great pile of newspapers with her, and showed me her articles. I cannot make out what these people want. He asked me if I had composed a fantasia on the *Red Sarafan*. On my replying in the negative, he was very much astonished, and added: 'I will send you Thalberg's fantasia; pray copy his style.' I had great trouble in politely getting rid of this

[1] "Christ is risen "—a Russian Easter greeting.

curious couple. De Sachs came to fetch me at twelve o'clock. We walked into the park. Then we went up by the lift to the fourth floor of an immense house where Schirmer lives. Besides myself and Sachs, there were at table the conductor Seidl, a Wagnerian and well known in this country, his wife, the pianist Adèle Aus-der-Ohe, who is going to play at my concert, her sister, and the Schirmer family. Seidl told me that my *Maid of Orleans* would be produced next season. I had to be at rehearsal by four o'clock. De Sachs accompanied me to the Music Hall in the Schirmers' carriage. It was lit up and in order for the first time to-day. I sat in Carnegie's box, while an oratorio, *The Shulamite*, by the elder Damrosch, was being rehearsed. Before my turn came they sang a wearisome cantata by Schütz, *The Seven Words*. My choruses[1] went very well. After it was over, I accompanied Sachs very unwillingly to the Schirmers', as he had made me promise to come back. We found a number of people there who had come merely to see me. Schirmer took us on the roof of his house. This huge, nine-storied house has a roof so arranged that one can take quite a delightful walk on it and enjoy a splendid view from all sides. The sunset was indescribably beautiful. When we went downstairs we found only a few intimate friends left, with whom I enjoyed myself most unexpectedly. Aus-der-Ohe played beautifully. Among other things, we played my Concerto together. We sat down to supper at nine o'clock. About 10.30 we, that is, Sachs, Aus-der-Ohe, her sister, and myself, were presented with the most splendid roses, conveyed downstairs in the lift and sent home in the Schirmers' carriage. One must do justice to American hospitality ; there is nothing like it—except, perhaps, in our own country.

" *April 22nd* (*May 4th*).

" Received letters. A visit from Mr. Romeike, the proprietor of the bureau for newspaper cuttings. Apparently, he, too, is one of our Anarchists, like those mysterious Russians who spoke to me yesterday at the rehearsal. Wrote letters and my diary. Called for Mayer, and went

---

1 " Legend " and " Our Father."

with him to see Hyde, who invited us to breakfast at the Down Town Club. After a most excellent breakfast I walked down Broadway, alas—still with Mayer. Then we went to the concert given by the celebrated English singer Santley. The celebrated singer turned out to be an elderly man, who sang arias and songs in a fairly rhythmic manner, but without any tone, and with truly English stiffness. I was greeted by several critics, among them Finck, who had written to me last winter so enthusiastically about *Hamlet*. I went home without waiting for the end of the concert, as I had to go through my Pianoforte Concerto with Adèle Aus-der-Ohe. She came with her sister, and I showed her various little nuances and delicate details, which—after yesterday's rehearsal—I considered necessary, in view of her powerful, clean, brilliant, but somewhat rough, style of playing. Reno had told me some interesting facts about Aus-der-Ohe's American career. Four years ago she obtained an engagement at one of the Symphony Concerts to play a Concerto by Liszt (she was one of his pupils), and came over without a penny in her pocket. Her playing took with the public. She was engaged everywhere, and was a complete success. During these four years she has toured all over America, and now possesses a capital of over £20,000!!! Such is America! After they had left, I hurried into my evening clothes and went to dinner at the Renos'. This time it was quite a small family party. Damrosch came in after dinner. I played duets with charming Alice Reno. The evening passed very pleasantly. Reno saw me to the tramway. It has suddenly turned very cold.

"April 23rd (May 5th).

"The waiter Max, who brings me my tea in the morning, spent all his childhood in Nijni-Novogorod and went to school there. Since his fifteenth year he has lived partly in Germany, partly in New York. He is now twenty-three, and has so completely forgotten his native tongue that he can only mangle it, although he still remembers the most common words. I find it very pleasant to talk a little Russian with him. At eleven a.m. the pianist Rummel (an old acquaintance from Berlin) came to ask me again if I would conduct his concert on the 17th; he has been once before. Next came a very pleasant and friendly journalist, who asked how my wife liked New York. I have been asked this question before. One day, shortly after my arrival, it was announced in some of the newspapers that I had arrived with a young and pretty wife. This arose from the fact that two reporters on the pier had seen me get into a carriage with Alice Reno. At 7.30 Reno's brother-in-law came. We drove to the Music Hall in a carriage, filled to overflowing. The appearance of the hall in the evening, lit up and crowded with people, was very fine and effective. The ceremony began with a speech by Reno (this had caused the poor fellow much perturbation all the day before). After this the National Anthem was sung. Then a clergyman made a very long and wearisome speech, in which he eulogised the founders of the Hall, especially Carnegie. The Leonore Symphony was then beautifully rendered. Interval. I went downstairs. Great excitement. I appeared, and was greeted with loud applause. The March went splendidly. Great success. I sat in Hyde's box for the rest of the concert. Berlioz's *Te Deum* is somewhat wearisome; only towards the end I began to enjoy it thoroughly. Reno carried me off with him. An improvised supper. Slept like a log.

"*April 24th (May 6th)*, 1891.

"'Tchaikovsky is a man of ample proportions, with rather grey hair, well built, of a pleasing appearance, and about sixty years of age (!!!). He seemed rather nervous, and answered the applause with a number of stiff little bows. But as soon as he had taken up the bâton he was quite master of himself.' I read this to-day in the *Herald*.[1] It annoys me that, not content with writing about my music, they must also write about my personal appearance. I cannot bear to think that my shyness is noticeable, or that my 'stiff little bows' fill them with astonishment. I went to rehearsal at 10.30. I had to get a workman to show me the entrance to the Hall. The rehearsal went very well. After the Suite the musicians called out something which

---

[1] *The New York Herald*, 6th May, 1891.

sounded like 'hoch.' Simply bathed in perspiration, I had to go and talk to Mme. Reno, her eldest daughter and two other ladies. Went to see Reno. The steamboat ticket. Instructions for the journey to Philadephia and Boston. Then I hurried over to Mayer's, where Rummel had already been waiting half an hour to play me the Second Concerto. But we did not play it. I practised my powers of eloquence instead. I tried to prove to him that there was no reason why I should accede to his proposal—to conduct his concert gratuitously on the 17th. Breakfasted with Mayer at the Italian Restaurant. P. Botkin[1] from Washington turned up quite unexpectedly about seven o'clock. He has come on purpose to be at the concert. Hyde and his wife fetched me about 7.30. The second concert. Mendelssohn's oratorio, *Elijah*, was given. A splendid work, but rather too long. During the interval, I was dragged the round of the boxes of various local magnates.

"*April 25th (May 7th).*

" I am fifty-one to-day. I feel very excited. The concert begins at two o'clock, with the Suite. This curious fright I suffer from is very strange. How many times have I already conducted the Suite, and it goes splendidly. Why this anxiety? I suffer horribly, and it gets worse and worse. I never remember feeling so anxious before. Perhaps it is because over here they pay so much attention to my outward appearance, and consequently my shyness is more noticeable. However that may be, after getting over some painful hours (the last was worst of all, for before my appearance I had to speak to several strangers) I stepped into the conductor's desk, was received most enthusiastically, and made a sensation—according to to-day's papers. After the Suite I sat in Reno's private room, and was interviewed by several reporters. (Oh, these reporters!) Among others, the well-known journalist, Jackson. I paid my respects to Mrs. Reno in her box; she had sent me a quantity of flowers in the morning, almost as if she had guessed it was my birthday. I felt

[1] Son of the celebrated scientist, S. Botkin, and Secretary to the Russian Embassy in Washington.

I must be alone, so refused Reno's invitation, pushed my way through a crowd of ladies, who were standing in the corridor to stare at me, and in whose eyes I read with involuntary pleasure signs of enthusiastic sympathy—and hastened home. I wrote Botkin a card, telling him that I could not keep my promise to dine with him. Relieved and—in a measure—happy, I went out to stroll about, to eat my dinner, and lounge in a café, to enjoy silence and solitude.

"*April* 26*th* (*May* 8*th*).

" I can scarcely find time to keep up my diary and correspondence. I am simply overrun with visitors—reporters, composers, and librettists. Among the latter was one who brought me the text of an opera, *Vlasta*, and touched me very deeply by the account of the death of his only son. Moreover, from every part of America I receive a heap of letters asking for my autograph ; these I answer most conscientiously. Went to the rehearsal of the Pianoforte Concerto. Damrosch annoyed me very much by taking up the best of the time for himself and leaving the rest of the rehearsal to me. However, all went well. Went to Knabe's to thank him for the beautiful present (a statue of Freedom) which he sent me yesterday. Shall I be allowed to take it into Russia ? Then I hastened home. Visitors without end, among others two Russian ladies. One of them was Mrs. MacMahan, widow of the celebrated war correspondent of 1877, and herself the correspondent of the *Russky Viedomosti* and the *Severny Vestnik*. This was the first time I had had the pleasure of talking to a Russian lady ; consequently I made a fool of myself. Suddenly the tears came into my eyes, my voice broke, and I could not suppress my sobs. I fled into the next room, and could not show myself again for a long time. I blush with shame to think of this unexpected episode. . . . Rested a little before the concert. The chorus went well, but might have gone better if I had not been so upset. Sat in the box with Reno and Hyde during the beautiful oratorio, *The Shulamite*. Walked with Reno and Carnegie to sup with Damrosch. This arch-millionaire is very kind to me, and constantly talks of an engagement for next year. . . . A good deal of champagne was drunk. I sat between the host and the conductor, Dannreuther. While I was talking to him about his brother he must have had the impression, for at least two hours, that I was either a madman or an impudent liar. He sat with his mouth open, and looked quite astonished. It seems that I had confused the pianist Dannreuther with the pianist Hartvigson. My absent-mindedness is becoming almost unbearable, and is a sign of advancing age. However, everyone was surprised to learn that I was only fifty-one yesterday. Carnegie especially was very much astonished. They all thought, except those who knew something of my life, that I was much older. Probably I have aged very much in the last few years. I feel I have lost vitality. I returned in Carnegie's carriage. This talk about my age resulted in dreadful dreams; I thought I slipped down a tremendously steep wall into the sea, and then climbed on to a little rocky projection. Probably this was the result of our conversation yesterday.

"Every day Romeike sends me a heap of newspaper cuttings about myself. All, without exception, are written in terms of the highest praise. The Third Suite is praised to the skies, and, what is more, my conducting also. Am I really such a good conductor, or do the Americans exaggerate?

"*April 27th (May 9th).*

"The manager of the Composers' Club called upon me and wished to arrange an evening for my compositions. Mrs. White[1] sent me such a quantity of lovely flowers that, owing to lack of room and vases, I had to give some to Max, who was highly delighted, as his wife is passionately fond of them. Ritzel, the violinist, also called upon me. He would like to have my portrait, and told me that the members of the orchestra were quite delighted with me. This touched me very much. I changed my things, and took Mayer my large portrait. From there I went to Schirmer's, and then hurried to the Music Hall, where I was to make my last appearance before the public. All

---

[1] Schirmer's married daughter.

these visits made before the concert show how calm I was at this time. Why, I do not know. In the artists' room I made the acquaintance of a singer who sang one of my songs yesterday. A very fine artist and a charming woman. My Concerto went magnificently, thanks to Aus-der-Ohe's brilliant interpretation. The enthusiasm was far greater than anything I have met with, even in Russia. I was recalled over and over again ; handkerchiefs were waved, cheers resounded—in fact, it is easy to see that I have taken the Americans by storm. But what I valued most of all was the enthusiasm of the orchestra. Owing to the heat and my exertions, I was bathed in perspiration, and could not, unfortunately, listen to the scenes from *Parsifal.* At the last evening concert of the Festival I sat alternately in the boxes of Carnegie, Hyde, and Reno. The whole of Handel's oratorio, *Israel in Egypt,* was given. During the course of the evening the architect of the Hall received an ovation. Afterwards I had supper with Damrosch at the Sachs'. . . .

"*April* 28*th* (*May* 10*th*).

" This has been a very heavy day. In the morning I was besieged by visitors. The interesting Korbay, the young, good-looking composer Klein, the pianist F.— with gold-stopped teeth—and others I do not remember. I went out at one o'clock to call on the nihilist Starck-Stoleshnikov, but he lives so far away, and the heat was so oppressive, that I gave it up. I hastened instead to Dr. N.'s, and arrived there in good time. Dr. N. is a Russian—at least he was brought up in Russia. His wife, as I finally discovered, is Countess G. They have lived in America since 1860, and often go to Europe, but never visit Russia. I did not like to ask their reason for avoiding it. They are both ardent patriots, and have a genuine love of Russia. In speaking of our country he seems to think that despotism and bureaucracy hinder it from becoming a leading nation. It strikes me that he is a freethinker who has at some time brought down the wrath of the Government on himself, and fled just at the right moment. But his liberalism is not in the least akin to Nihilism or Anarchism. Both frequently asserted that they had nothing to do with the nihilists in this country. I lunched with them about three o'clock, and then rushed off to B. MacMahan's (owing to a lack of cabs one has to walk everywhere). While the N.s' house is almost luxuriously furnished, this Russian correspondent lives quite in the student style. Somewhat later the celebrated sculptor Kamensky came in ; he has lived in America for the last twenty years, but I do not know why. He is an old, somewhat invalidish-looking man, with a deep scar on his forehead. He confused me very much by asking me to tell him *everything* that I knew about the Russia of to-day. I did not quite know how to accomplish such a vast undertaking, but Barbara Nikolaevna (Mrs. MacMahan) began to talk about my music, and I soon took my departure, as I had to go home and dress before dining with Carnegie. All the cafés are closed on Sundays. This English Puritanism, which shows itself in such senseless trivialities (for instance, one can only obtain a glass of whisky or beer on Sunday by means of some fraud), irritates me very much. It is said that the men who brought this law into force in the State of New York were themselves heavy drinkers. I had scarcely time to change and drive to Carnegie's in a carriage, which had to be fetched from some distance, and was very expensive. This millionaire really does not live so luxuriously as many other people. Mr. and Mrs. Reno, Mr. and Mrs. Damrosch, the architect of the Music Hall and his wife, an unknown gentleman and a stout friend of Mrs. Damrosch's were at dinner. I sat beside this aristocratic and evidently distinguished lady. This singular man, Carnegie, who rapidly rose from a telegraph apprentice to be one of the richest men in America, while still remaining quite simple, inspires me with unusual confidence, perhaps because he shows me so much sympathy. During the evening he expressed his liking for me in a very marked manner. He took both my hands in his, and declared that, though not crowned, I was a genuine king of music. He embraced me (without kissing me : men do not kiss over here), got on tiptoe and stretched his hand up to indicate my greatness, and finally made the whole company laugh by imitating my conducting. This he did so solemnly, so well, and so like me, that I myself was quite delighted. His wife is also an extremely simple and charming young lady, and showed her interest in me in every possible way. All this was very pleasant, but still I was glad to get home again at eleven, as I felt somewhat bored.

" *April 29th (May 11th)*.

" Mayer fetched me at a quarter-past eight. How should I have got on without Mayer? I got a seat in a saloon carriage. . . . We reached Buffalo at 8.30. I was met by two gentlemen whom Mayer had instructed to look after me, as I had to change here, and it is very difficult to find one's way in this labyrinth of lines. I reached Niagara fifty minutes after leaving Buffalo, and went to the hotel in which a room—also thanks to Mayer—was reserved for me. The hotel is quite unpretentious—after the style of the small Swiss inns—but very clean and convenient, as German is spoken. I went to bed early. The roaring of the waterfall is very audible in the stillness of the night.

" NIAGARA, *April 30th (May 12th)*.

" The carriage was here at nine o'clock. There was no guide, which was very pleasant. I will not try to describe the beauties of the Falls; it is hard to find words for these things. In the afternoon I walked again to the Falls and round the town. During this walk—as in the morning—I could not get rid of a curious—probably entirely nervous—lassitude, which prevented my full enjoyment of this beautiful scenery. I started again at a quarter-past six in a special sleeping-carriage.

" NEW YORK, *May 1st (13th)*.

" At five o'clock I awoke, my mind full of anxious thoughts about the approaching week, which I dread so much. I was home by 8 a.m., and very glad to see Max again. The news of the attempt on the Tsarevich made me feel very sad. I was also grieved to find that there were no letters from home—and I had hoped to find a number. Many visitors. I hired a carriage from the hotel, on account of the great distances which I had to get over to-day. First I went to say good-bye to Damrosch, as he is going to Europe. He asked me to take him as a pupil. Of course I refused, but am afraid involuntarily I showed far too plainly my horror at the idea of Damrosch arriving at my country home to study with me. From there I hastened to lunch at the Renos'. The coachman was quite drunk, and would not understand where I wanted him to drive. It was lucky I knew the way myself. The Renos received me as cordially as ever. Afterwards I went to Mayer's. Then the same drunken coachman drove Mayer and myself to the great steam-ferry which conveys carriages, horses, and foot-passengers over the East River. Thence we went by train to Mayer's summer residence. I felt so tired, so irritable and unhappy, I could hardly restrain my tears. His family is good and kind, but all the same I was bored, and longed to get away. In the afternoon we walked along the shore ; the sea was rather rough. The air is so fresh and pure here that my walk really gave me pleasure and did me good. I stayed the night at Mayer's, but slept badly.

"*May 2nd* (14*th*).

"I got up at six o'clock. Went down to the sea, and was delighted. After breakfast we drove into the town. I should have liked to be alone. Miss Ross came to see me. My letter on Wagner has been published, and created quite a sensation. Anton Seidl, the celebrated conductor and Wagnerian, had published a lengthy reply, in which he attacked me, but in quite a friendly tone. Miss Ross came to ask me to write an answer to Seidl's reply. I set to work upon it, but was interrupted by X., who stayed an endless time, and told me all kinds of uninteresting musical gossip, which I had heard a hundred times before. The next to come was the correspondent of a Philadelphia newspaper, who is one of my most fervent admirers. I had to speak English with him : I have made progress, and can say a few phrases very well. Wrote letters. Breakfasted alone in my hotel. Wandered through the Central Park. According to my promise, I went over to Z.'s to write a testimonial for the * * * pianofortes. Was this the object of all Z.'s attentions? All these presents, all this time and money spent on me, all these unaccountable kindnesses, were these intended as a premium for a future puff? I proposed that Z. himself should write the testimonial. He sat for a long time, but could not think of anything; so we put it off until our next meeting. Then I paid a call on Tretbar, Steinway's representative, for whom I had a letter of introduction from Jurgenson. He had waited till now without calling upon me because he did not wish to make the first advances. I had purposely delayed my visit from similar motives. Home to pack. Shortly afterwards a messenger from Z. brought me the testimonial to sign. It read as follows: '*I consider the * * * pianofortes without doubt the best in America.*' Now as I do *not* think so at all, but value some other makers' far more highly, I declined to have my opinion expressed in this form. I told Z., that notwithstanding my deep gratitude to him, I could not tell a lie. The reporter from the *Herald* came to see me—a very interesting man. Drove to Hyde's. I wish I could find words to describe all the charm and originality of this interesting couple. Hyde greeted me with these words: 'Kak vasche sdorovie? sidite poschaljust.'[1] Then he laughed like a lunatic, and his wife and I joined in. He had bought a guide to Russian conversation, and learnt a few phrases as a surprise to me. Mrs. Hyde immediately invited me to smoke a cigarette in her drawing-room—the climax of hospitality in America. After the cigarette we went to dinner. The table was most exquisitely decorated with flowers; everyone received a bouquet. Then, quite unexpectedly, Hyde became very solemn, closed his eyes and said the Lord's Prayer. I did the same as the others: lowered my eyes and gazed on the ground. Then began an endlessly long dinner. . . . At ten o'clock I withdrew. At home a messenger from Knabe was waiting for me. We drank a glass of beer together, took my trunk, and went down town. We went over the Hudson in the steam ferry, and finally reached the station. Knabe's messenger (without whose help I should certainly have been lost) engaged a comfortable *coupé* for me; the friendly negro made the bed, I threw myself on it just as

[1] Broken Russian. "How are you? Please sit down."

I was, for I really had not the strength to undress, and sank at once into a deep sleep. I slept soundly, but not for long. The negro woke me an hour before my arrival at Baltimore.

"BALTIMORE, *May 3rd* (15*th*).

"As usual, I was received at the hotel with cool contempt. Sitting alone in my room, I suddenly felt so unhappy, chiefly because everyone around me speaks only English. I slept a little. Then I went into a restaurant for breakfast, and was quite annoyed because the waiter (a negro) would not understand that I wished for tea and bread-and-butter only. I had to go to the desk, where they did not understand me any better. At last a gentleman knowing a little German kindly came to my help. I had hardly sat down when Knabe, a stout man, came in. Very shortly after, Adèle Aus-der-Ohe and her sister joined us, too. I was very glad to see them, for they seem like connections, at least as regards music. We went to the rehearsal together. This was held on the stage of the Lyceum Theatre. The orchestra was small, only four first violins, but not bad. But the Third Suite was not to be thought of. It was decided to put the Serenade for strings in its place. The orchestra did not know this work. The conductor had not even played it through, although Reno had promised that this should be done. The Concerto with Adèle Aus-der-Ohe went very smoothly, but the Serenade needs many rehearsals. The orchestra was impatient. The young leader behaved in rather a tactless way, and made it too clearly evident that he thought it time to stop. It is true—this unhappy touring orchestra must be wearied by their constant travelling. After the rehearsal I went home with Adèle Aus-der-Ohe, dressed, and went immediately to the concert. I conducted in my frock-coat. Happily everything went very well, but there was little enthusiasm in comparison with New York. After the concert we both drove home to change. Half an hour later Knabe called for us. His hospitality is on the same colossal scale as his figure. This beardless giant had arranged a festivity in my honour at his own house. I found a number of people there. The dinner was endlessly long, but very tasteful and good, as were also the wines with which Knabe kept filling up our glasses. During the second half of the dinner I felt quite worn out. A terrible hatred of everything seemed to come over me, especially of my two neighbours. After dinner I conversed a little with everyone, and smoked and drank ceaselessly. At half-past twelve Knabe brought me home, and also the sisters Aus-der-Ohe.

"WASHINGTON, 4*th* (16*th*).

" I woke early, breakfasted downstairs, wrote my diary, and waited, rather in fear and trembling, for Knabe, who wanted to show me the sights of the town. At last he came and, together with the sisters Aus-der-Ohe, we drove round Baltimore. Weather bad and inclined to rain. Baltimore is a pretty, clean town. Then the good-natured giant helped me to pack my box, invited Aus-der-Ohe and myself to a champagne lunch, and finally put me in the carriage that was to take me to my destination. He himself was travelling to Philadelphia, while I was going to Washington. The journey lasted about three-quarters of an hour. I was met by Botkin, who accompanied me to the hotel, where a room was engaged for me. This was delightfully comfortable, and at the same time tastefully and simply furnished. I declined to receive Rennen, begged Botkin to call for me before the dinner, took a bath, and hurried into my dress clothes. The dinner was given in the Metropolitan Club, of which Botkin and his colleagues are members. The dinner was very gay, and I was so delighted to talk Russian once more, although this happiness was a little dimmed by the sad fact that my ' s,' ' sch,' ' tsch,' are beginning to sound rather indistinct from age. During the dinner we heard, first by telegram and then through the telephone, that the Ambassador Struve had returned from a journey to New York solely on my account. At ten o'clock we all repaired to the Embassy, where Botkin had arranged a musical evening. About a hundred persons were invited. The Ambassador also arrived, an old man, very cordial and also interesting. The company at the Embassy belonged principally to the diplomatic circle. There were ambassadors with their wives and daughters, and personages belonging to the highest class of the diplomatic service. Most of the ladies spoke French, so things were not so difficult for me. The programme consisted of my Trio and a Quartet by Brahms. Hausen, the Secretary to our Embassy, was at the piano, and he proved quite a respectable pianist. My Trio he played decidedly well. The violinist was only middling. I was introduced to everyone. After the music there was an excellent cold supper. When most of the guests had left, ten of us (the Belgian Ambassador and the Secretaries to the Swedish and Austrian Embassies, besides the Russians) sat for some time longer at a large round table, before an excellent flagon. Struve enjoys a glass of wine. He gave me the impression of a broken and unhappy man who finds it a consolation. It was three o'clock before I went home, accompanied by Botkin and Hausen.

"*May 5th* (17*th*).

"Awoke with pleasant memories of yesterday. I always feel well in Russian society when I am not obliged to speak a foreign tongue. At twelve o'clock Botkin called for me to lunch with the Ambassador, Struve. Afterwards I went with Botkin and Hausen to see the sights of Washington.

"Philadelphia, *May 6th* (18*th*).

"I reached Philadelphia at three o'clock. Breakfasted downstairs. A very importunate Jew from Odessa called and got some money out of me. Went for a walk. The concert at eight p.m. The enormous theatre was filled to overflowing. After the concert, according to long-standing promise, I went to the club. The return journey to New York was very wearisome.

"*May 7th* (19*th*).

"Feel quite stupid from exhaustion and constant travelling. I could stand no more, if it were not for the thought of my departure to-morrow, which buoys me up. I am inundated with requests for my autograph. At 12.30 I went over to Z.'s and wrote the testimonial, omitting the phrase which ranks these pianos as the first. Went home and waited for the composer Brummklein. He came and played me some very pretty things.

"*May 8th (20th).*

"The old librettist came. I was very sorry to have to tell him I could not compose an opera to his libretto. He seemed very sad. Scarcely had he gone before Dannreuther came in to take me to the rehearsal of the Quartets and Trios to be played this evening at the Composers' Club. It was rather a long distance. The Quartet was indifferently played and the Trio really badly, for the pianist, a shy, nervous man, was no good: he could not even count. I had no time to make any preparations for the journey. Drove to Renos'. They received me with more kindness and cordiality than ever, especially Madame Reno and her three daughters. The eldest (Anna, who is married) gave me a beautiful cigar-case, M. Reno a quantity of scent, and Alice and her sister cakes for the journey. Then I hurried to Hyde's. Mrs. Hyde was already expecting me. Here too I was received with great kindness and sincere enthusiasm. At last I got home to pack my box. Hateful business, which gave me a dreadful pain in my back. Tired out, I went over to Mayer's, and invited him to dinner at Martelli's. At eight o'clock I was taken to the Composers' Club. This is not a club of composers, as I first thought, but a special musical union which arranges, from time to time, evenings devoted to the works of one composer. Yesterday was devoted to me, and the concert was held in the magnificent Metropolitan House. I sat in the first row. They played the Quartet (E flat minor) and the Trio; some songs were very well sung, but the programme was too long. In the middle of the evening I received an address; I answered shortly, in French; of course an ovation. One lady threw an exquisite bouquet of roses straight in my face. I was introduced to a crowd of people, among others our Consul-General. At the conclusion I had to speak to about a hundred people and distribute a hundred autographs. I reached home half dead with fatigue. As the steamer left at five o'clock in the morning, I had to go on board that night, so I dressed with all speed, and

2 U

packed my things while Reno and Mayer waited for me. Downstairs we drank two bottles of champagne. I said good-bye to the servants of the hotel and drove off to the steamer. The drive was very long. The steamer is quite as fine as the *Bretagne ;* I have an officer's cabin. On this ship the officers are allowed to let their cabins, but they ask an exorbitant price. I had to pay 300 dollars (1,500 francs) for mine. . . . But it is really nice and very roomy. I said good-bye to my dear American friends and went straight to bed. I slept badly and heard all the noise when the steamer started at five o'clock. I came out of my cabin as we passed the statue of Freedom."

Altogether Tchaikovsky gave six concerts in America: four in New York, one in Baltimore, and one in Philadelphia. The following works were performed: (1) The Coronation March, (2) Third Suite, (3) two Sacred Choruses: the Lord's Prayer and the Legend, (4) Pianoforte Concerto No. 1, and (5) Serenade for string instruments.

I have before me sixteen American Press notices of Tchaikovsky, and all are written in a tone of unqualified praise ; the only difference lies in the degree of enthusiasm expressed. According to some he is " the first of modern composers after Wagner " ; according to others, " one of the first." His talent as a conductor is equally praised. Everywhere he had an unprecedented success, and many spoke of his interesting appearance. The interviews (especially those in *The New York Herald*) are reproduced with astonishing fidelity. As we read them we can almost fancy we can hear the voice of Tchaikovsky himself.

XIII

"'PRINCE BISMARCK,' *May 9th (21st)*.

" On account of the maddening pain in my back, I dressed with great difficulty, went below for my morning tea, and then walked about the ship to make myself better acquainted with the various quarters. A host of passengers, but of totally different appearance to those who travelled with me on the *Bretagne*. The most perceptible difference lies in the fact that there are no emigrants. At eight a.m. I was called to breakfast. My place had already been allotted to me. I had a middle-aged man for my neighbour, who immediately began to converse. Slept the whole morning. The sight of the sea leaves me indifferent. I think with horror of the rest of the journey, but also with longing: may it soon be over. This is a very fast ship; it is the magnificent new *Prince Bismarck*, and is making its first passage. Last week it only took six days and fourteen hours from Hamburg to New York. I trust we shall get over the horrible distance as quickly. The motion is not so smooth as that of the *Bretagne*. The weather is splendid just now. At breakfast I became better acquainted with my vis-à-vis. It is difficult to say to what nationality he belongs, as he speaks all languages wonderfully well; perhaps he is a Jew, so I told him on purpose the story of the importunate Jew. He lives in Dresden, and is a wholesale tobacco dealer. He has already discovered who I am. If he speaks the truth, he heard me conduct in New York; anyway, he improves on acquaintance. I have got so accustomed to talking in New York that, in spite of my preference for silence, I can stand his society without being bored. I am astonished to find I sleep so much. In the evening, soon after dinner, I was so overcome that I went to bed at ten o'clock and slept straight on until seven the next morning. Nothing particular happened during the day. A Mr. Aronson and his young wife introduced themselves to me. He is the proprietor of the Casino Theatre (favoured by Von Bülow), as I discovered by means of an autograph album which was sent to me that I might write my name and a few lines in it. Schröder, the man who attends to my cabin, is a good-natured young German; at table also there are two nice German stewards—this is very important for me. I am pleased with the ship, the cabin, and the food. As there are no emigrants I can walk on the lower deck; this is very pleasant, as I meet no first-class passengers there and can be quiet.

"*May 11th (23rd)*.

"I keep very much to myself and, thanks to my splendid cabin, in which there is plenty of room to move about, I feel much freer than on the *Bretagne*. I only use the drawing-room in the morning when no one is there. There is a nice Steinway grand, and not at all a bad musical library, including a few of my own productions. The day is divided as follows: Dress, ring my bell, and Schröder brings me a cup of tea; first breakfast, eight o'clock; walk on the lower deck, work, read. By work I mean the sketches for my next Symphony. At twelve o'clock the gong sounds for second breakfast. . . . I am reading a book by Tatistchev, *Alexandre et Napoléon*.

"*May 11th (23rd)*.

"In New York they so often assured me that the sea was calm at this time of year that I believed them. But what a disenchantment! Since early morning the weather has been getting worse: rain, wind, and towards evening quite a gale. A dreadful night, could not sleep, so sat on the sofa. Towards morning dozed a little.

"*May 12th (24th)*.

"A detestable day. The weather is frightful. Sea-sickness, could eat nothing but an orange.

"*May (13th) 25th*.

"I feel quite unnerved from exhaustion and sickness. Yesterday evening I fell asleep in my clothes on my sofa and slept there the whole night. To-day the motion is less, but the weather is still dreadful. My nerves are in-expressibly strained and irritated by this ceaseless noise and horrible cracking. Shall I ever make up my mind to endure such torment again?

"During the course of the day the motion grew still less and the weather improved. I have taken such a dis-like to the society of my fellow-passengers that the very sight of them annoys and irritates me. I constantly sit in my own cabin.

"*May* 14*th* (26*th*).

"The moon was magnificent to-night. I read in my cabin till I was tired, and then went out for a stroll on deck. Everyone, without exception, was asleep, and I was the only one of the 300 first-class passengers who had come out to enjoy the lovely night. It was beautiful beyond all words. It was strange to think of the terrible night on Sunday, when everything in my cabin, even my trunk, was hurled from one side to the other, and the vessel seemed to be fighting for life against the storm; when one was racked with terror, and, added to all, the electric lamp and bell fell with a crash on the floor and was smashed to pieces. That night I vowed never to make another sea-voyage. But Schröder, my steward, says he resolves to give up his place every time the weather is bad, but no sooner is he in harbour than he longs for the sea again. Perhaps it may be the same with me. The passengers are getting up a concert, and want me to play. Quite the worst part of a sea-voyage is having to know all the passengers.

"*May* 15*th* (27*th*).

"As we neared the Channel it became more lively. Hundreds of little ships came in sight. About two o'clock the English coast was visible; sometimes rocky and picturesque, sometimes flat and green with spring grass. . . . Soon afterwards we entered Southampton.

"*May* 16*th* (28*th*).

"After passing Southampton and the Isle of Wight, I went to sleep and awoke feeling rather chilly. . . . Enjoyed the views of the English coast and the sight of the many steamers and sailing vessels which enliven the Channel. We saw Folkestone and Dover. The North Sea is very lively. We passed Heligoland in the night.

"*May* 17*th* (29*th*).

"Arrived early this morning at Cuxhaven. . . . At 8 a.m. we went on board a small steamer that took us to the Custom House. Long wait and examination. Arrived at Hamburg by midday."

Tchaikovsky spent one day in Hamburg and one in Berlin; then travelled direct to Petersburg.

During his short stay there he was in a cheerful frame of mind. This was partly the result of his reunion with his friends and relatives, and partly the delightful impression of the early spring in Petersburg, which he always enjoyed. This time he was so charmed with the city that he had a great wish to settle in the neighbourhood, and commissioned us to look out for a suitable house, or a small country property.

Since Frolovskoe was becoming more and more denuded of its forests, and the demands of the landlord steadily increased, Tchaikovsky decided to leave. After many vain attempts to find a suitable country house, or to acquire a small property, he resolved to return to Maidanovo. While he was abroad, Alexis Safronov had moved all his belongings into the house he formerly occupied, and arranged it just as in 1886. Although Tchaikovsky was fond of this house and its surroundings, and looked forward to working there under the old conditions, his return somewhat depressed him. There was an air of decay about house and park; the walks did not please him; and then there was the prospect of an inroad of summer visitors.

Soon after settling in Maidanovo he was visited by his brother, Modeste Tchaikovsky, and his nephews, Vladimir Davidov and Count A. Litke. All four travelled to Moscow together, where he was greatly interested by the Franco-Russian Exhibition, and enjoyed acting as cicerone to his favourite nephews.

The chief musical works upon which he was engaged at this time were: the second act of the Ballet, *The Nutcracker;* the completion of the opera, *King René's Daughter;* the remodelling of the Sextet and the instrumentation of a symphonic poem, *The Voyevode*, composed the previous autumn while he was staying at Tiflis.

To P. Jurgenson.

"MAIDANOVO, *June 3rd* (15*th*), 1891.

"I have discovered a new instrument in Paris, something between a piano and a *glockenspiel*, with a divinely beautiful tone. I want to introduce this into the ballet and the symphonic poem. The instrument is called the 'Celesta Mustel,' and costs 1,200 francs. You can only buy it from the inventor, Mustel, in Paris. I want to ask you to order one of these instruments. You will not lose by it, because you can hire it out to the concerts at which *The Voyevode* will be played, and afterwards sell it to the Opera when my ballet is put on. . . . Have it sent direct to Petersburg; but no one there must know about it. I am afraid Rimsky-Korsakov and Glazounov might hear of it and make use of the new effect before I could. I expect the instrument will make a tremendous sensation."

To J. Konius.

"*June* 15*th* (27*th*), 1891.

" . . . The news that you are engaged (for America) with Brodsky rejoices me. Brodsky is one of the most sympathetic men I ever met. He is also a fine artist and the best quartet player I ever heard, not excepting Laub, who was so great in this line."

To V. Davidov.

"*June* 25*th* (*July* 7*th*), 1891.

"According to my promise, I write to let you know that I finished the sketch of the ballet yesterday. You will remember my boasting when you were here that I should get it done in about five days. But I have taken at least a fortnight. Yes, the old fellow is getting worn out. Not only is his hair turning white as snow and beginning to fall, not only is he losing his teeth, not only do his eyes grow weaker and get tired sooner, not only do his feet begin to drag—but he is growing less capable of accomplishing anything. This ballet is far weaker than *The Sleeping Beauty*—no doubt about it. We shall see how the opera turns out. Once I feel convinced that I can only contribute 'warmed-up' dishes to the musical bill of fare, I shall give up composing."

The following is quoted from a letter to Arensky, who had been consulting Tchaikovsky as to the advisability of taking the post of Director of the Tiflis branch of the Musical Society :—

"I hardly know how to advise you, dear Anton Stepanovich. I would prefer not to do so. If you had some private means, I could only rejoice in the prospect of your going to the Caucasus for a time. But it saddens me to think of you in the provinces, remote from musical centres, overburdened with tiresome work, solitary and unable to hear good music. You cannot imagine how it depresses me to think of men like Rimsky-Korsakov, Liadov, and yourself being obliged to worry with teaching. But how can it be helped? I think if you bear it for another two years, and work hard, little by little, you may manage to live by composition only. I know in my own case this is not impossible. I earn enough now to keep a large family, if need were. I may tell you in conclusion, that Tiflis is a fascinating town, and life there is pleasant."

To Anatol Tchaikovsky.

"MAIDANOVO, *July 8th (20th)*, 1891.

". . . Do not be vexed that I stayed so long in Petersburg without coming to see you in Reval.[1] . . . From your letter I gather that you are pretty comfortable there, although you mention many difficulties you have to contend with. I think one must be very politic and tactful in these things, then we can get over most difficulties. In the diplomatic service we must often *faire bonne mine au mauvais jeu.* There is nothing for it! I think you would find Valoniev's diary interesting. He was governor of one of the Baltic provinces, and relates a great deal that is

---

[1] Anatol was then Vice-Governor of Estland.

interesting. At that time Souvarov, the extreme Liberal, ruled in these provinces. In the long run the spirit of Pobiedonostsiev is better than the spirit of Souvorov."

Towards the end of July a misfortune befell Tchaikovsky which was the cause of much subsequent anxiety. While he was taking his afternoon constitutional, and Alexis was resting in his room, a thief, who probably entered through the window, carried off the clock which had been given to him by Nadejda von Meck in 1888. This clock, which was beautifully decorated with a figure of Joan of Arc on one side, and on the other with the Apollo of the Grand Opéra, upon a background of black enamel, had been specially made in Paris, and cost 10,000 francs. For years Tchaikovsky had hardly consented to be parted from this gift, even for the necessary cleaning and repairs. It was his chief souvenir of his relations with his friend and benefactress. The police of Moscow and Klin were communicated with at once, but to no purpose : the clock was never recovered.

To V. Davidov.

"*August 1st (13th)*, 1891.

". . . I am now reading your " Chevrillon on Ceylon,"[1] and thinking of you. I do not altogether share your enthusiasm. These modern French writers are terribly affected ; they have a kind of affectation of simplicity which disgusts me almost as much as Victor Hugo's highsounding phrases, epithets, and antitheses. Everything that your favourite recounts in such a clever and lively style might be told in very simple and ordinary language, neither in such brief and broken sentences, nor yet in long periods with the subject and predicate in such forced and unnatural positions. It is very easy to parody this gentleman :—

" Une serviette de table négligemment attachée à son cou, il dégustait. Tout autour des mouches, avides, grouil-

---

[1] In the *Revue des Deux Mondes*, 1891.

lantes, d'un noir inquiétant volaient. Nul bruit sinon un claquement de machoirs énervant. Une odeur moite, fétide, écœurante, lourde, répandait un je ne sais quoi d'animal, de carnacier dans l'air. Point de lumière. Un rayon de soleil couchant, pénétrant comme par hasard dans la chambre nue et basse, éclairait par-ci, par-là tantôt la figure blême du maître engurgitant sa soupe, tantôt celle du valet, moustachue, à traits kalmouks, stupide et rampante. On devinait un idiot servi par un idiot. 9 heures. Un morne silence régnait. Les mouches fatiguées, somnolentes, devenues moins agitées, se dispersaient. Et lá-bas, dans le lointain, par la fenêtre, on voyait une lune, grimaçante, enorme, rouge, surgir sur l'horizon embrasé. Il mangeait, il mangeait toujours. Puis l'estomac bourré, la face écarlate, l'œil hagard, il se leva et sortit, etc., etc., etc. I have described my supper this evening. I think Zola was the discoverer of this mode of expression."

To A. Alferaki.

"*August 1st* (13*th*), 1891.

". . . I have received your letter and the songs, and played through the latter. I have nothing new to add to what I have already said as to your remarkable creative gifts. It is useless to lament that circumstances have not enabled you to go through a course of strict counterpoint, which you specially needed. This goes without saying. Your resolve to confine yourself entirely to song-writing does not please me. A true artist, even if he possesses only a limited creative capacity, which hinders him from producing great works in certain spheres of art, should still keep the highest aim in view. Neither age, nor any other obstacle, should check his ambition. Why should you suppose one needs less than a complete all-round technique in order to compose a perfect song? With an imperfect technique you may limit your sphere of work as much as you please—you will never get beyond an elegant amateurism. . . . I dislike the system of putting the date of composition on each song. What is the use of it? What does it matter to the public when and where a work was composed?"

About August 20th Tchaikovsky left home for Kamenka, from whence he went on to stay with his brother Nicholas. Here he met his favourite poet, A. Fet, and became very friendly with him. Fet wrote a poem, "To Peter Ilich Tchaikovsky," an attention which touched the musician very deeply. At the end of August he returned to Moscow in a very contented frame of mind.

XIV

1891–1892

Through September, and the greater part of October Tchaikovsky remained at Maidanovo, working uninterruptedly upon the opera *Iolanthe* and the orchestration of *The Voyevode*. The work went easily, and his health was good. The evenings, which during the last years of his life brought home to him a sense of his loneliness, were enlivened by the presence of Laroche, who was staying in the house. The friends played arrangements for four hands, or Laroche read aloud. Everything seemed so ordered as to leave no room for dissatisfaction with his lot ; and yet his former contentment with his surroundings had vanished.

The theft of his clock was still a matter of anxiety. He might have partially forgotten it, had not the police announced the capture of the criminal. "I am living in the atmosphere of one of Gaboriau's novels," he wrote to his brother. "The police have caught the criminal, and he has confessed. But nothing will induce him to reveal where he has hidden the clock. To-day he was brought to me in the hopes that I might persuade him to tell the truth. . . . He said he would confess all, if he was left alone with me. We went into the next room. There he flung himself at my feet and implored forgiveness. Of course I forgave him, and only begged him to say where the clock was. Then he became very quiet and afterwards declared he had never stolen it at all! . . . You can imagine how all this has upset me, and how it has set me against Maidanovo."

Another cause of his passing discontent was wounded pride. So far he believed himself to have scored a great success in America ; he was convinced that his return was anxiously waited, and that his popularity had greatly increased. One day, however, he received a letter from Morris Reno, who had originally engaged him, offering him a three months' tour with twenty concerts at a fee of 4,000 dollars. Seeing that on the first occasion he had received 2,400 dollars for four concerts, Tchaikovsky immediately concluded that he had greatly overrated the importance of his previous visit, and was deeply mortified in consequence. He telegraphed in reply to Reno two words only : "Non. Tchaikovsky." Afterwards he came to recognise that there was nothing offensive in the proposal made to him, and that it in no way denoted any falling off in the appreciation of the Americans. But the desire to return was no longer so keen ; only a very substantial pecuniary advantage would have induced him to undertake the voyage.

Finally, he had another reason for feeling somewhat depressed at this moment. The will which he made in the month of September involuntarily caused him to think of that "flat-nosed horror," which was sometimes his equivalent for death. He had hitherto been under the impression that the law which existed before the accession of Alexander III. was still in force, and that at his death all his rights in his operas would pass into the hands of the Theatrical Direction. The discovery that he had more than a life interest in them was the reason for making a will. It proves how much attention Tchaikovsky must have given to his contracts for *Eugene Oniegin*, *Mazeppa*, and the later operas before signing them, since the clause relating to his hereditary rights was prominent in them all. When his brother Modeste called his attention to the fact, he would not believe him until he had inquired from the Direction, when he found himself agreeably mistaken. He was always anxious as to the fate of certain people whom he suppported during his lifetime, and was thankful to feel that this assistance would be continued after his death.

The number of those he assisted continually increased. " I was the most expensive pensioner," says Modeste Tchaikovsky, " for he allowed me about two thousand roubles a year." But he always met every request for money halfway. Here are a few specimens of his generosity, quoted from letters to Jurgenson and others :—

" DEAR FRIEND,—I want to help X. in some way. You are selling the tickets for his concert. Should they go badly, take fifteen or twenty places on my behalf and give them to whomsoever you please. Of course, X. must know nothing about it."

" If you are in pecuniary difficulties," he wrote to Y., " come to your sincere friend (myself), who now earns so much from his operas and will be delighted to help you. I promise not a soul shall hear of it; but it will be a great pleasure to me."

" Please write at once to K., that he is to send Y. twentyfive roubles a month. He may pay him three months in advance."

There would be no difficulty in multiplying such instances. Not only his neighbour's need, but the mere whim of another person, awoke in Tchaikovsky the desire of fulfilment. He always wished to give all and receive nothing. It is not surprising, therefore, that there were occasionally periods—as in September and October, 1891

—when he found himself penniless and felt the shortness of funds, chiefly because he was unable to help others.

His correspondence with concert agents, publishers and all kinds of applicants had become a great burden to him in those days.

All these things conduced to that mood of melancholy which is reflected in the letters written at this time.

At the end of October he went to Moscow, to be present at the first performance of *Pique Dame*, and to conduct Siloti's concert, at which his Symphonic Fantasia, *The Voyevode*, was brought out.

To the Grand Duke Constantine Constantinovich.

"MOSCOW, *October* 31*st* (*November* 12*th*), 1891.

"It is difficult to say how deeply your precious lines touched and delighted me. Naturally I felt in my heart of hearts that you had not forgotten me—but it is pleasant to have some clear evidence that amid all your varied and complicated occupations, and while under the impression of a profound family sorrow, you still found time to think of me.

"I was very pleased to make Fet's acquaintance. From his ' Reminiscences,' which were published in the *Russky Viestnik*, I fancied it would not be very interesting to converse with him. On the contrary, he is most agreeable company, full of humour and originality. If your Highness only knew how enchanting his summer residence is! The house and park—what a cosy retreat for a poet in his old age! Unluckily, as his wife complained to me, the poet does not enjoy life in these poetical surroundings at all. He sits at home all day, dictating verses, or his translation of Martial, to his lady secretary. He read me many new poems, and I was surprised at the freshness and youthfulness of his inspiration. We both regretted your Highness could not devote yourself entirely to poetry. If only you could repose in summer in just such a solitary spot! But, alas! it is not possible. . . .

"When I have finished my opera and ballet I shall give

up that kind of work for a time and devote myself to Symphony. . . . I often think it is time to shut up shop. A composer who has won success and recognition stands in the way of younger men who want to be heard. Time was when no one wanted to listen to my music, and if the Grand Duke, your father, had not been my patron, not one of my operas would ever have been performed. Now I am spoilt and encouraged in every way. It is very pleasant, but I am often tormented by the thought that I ought to make room for others."

The first performance of *Pique Dame* in Moscow took place on November 4th (16th), 1891, under Altani's bâton. It was merely a fair copy of the Petersburg performance, and presented no "special" qualities as regards musical rendering or scenery.

The opera met with a warmer and more genuine welcome than in the northern capital. Nevertheless the Press was not very pleased with the music. The *Moscow Viedomosti* thought "Tchaikovsky possessed a remarkable talent for imitation, sometimes going so far as to borrow wholesale from the older masters, as in his Suite *Mozartiana.*" Another newspaper considered the opera "more pleasing than inspired." The only serious and intelligent criticism of the work appeared in the *Russky Viedomosti*, from Kashkin's pen.

Siloti's concert, two days later, was marked by one of the most painful episodes in the composer's career. Kashkin, in his 'Reminiscences,' says that, even at the rehearsals, Tchaikovsky had shown a kind of careless indifference in conducting his latest orchestral work, the Symphonic Ballade, *The Voyevode.* After the rehearsal he asked several people for their opinion upon the work, among others Taneiev, who seems to have replied that the chief movement of the Ballade—the love episode—was not equal to similar episodes in *The Tempest, Romeo and Juliet,* or *Francesca.* Moreover, he considered that

Tchaikovsky had treated it wrongly, and that Poushkin's words could be *sung* to this melody, so that it was more in the style of a vocal than an orchestral work.

At the concert *The Voyevode* made little impression, notwithstanding the enthusiastic reception given to the composer. This was due to some extent to Tchaikovsky's careless rendering of the work.

Siloti relates that during the interval the composer came into the artists' room and tore his score to pieces, exclaiming: " Such rubbish should never have been written." To tear a thick score in pieces is not an easy feat, and possibly Siloti's memory may have been at fault. It is more probable that Tchaikovsky *wished* to destroy the score on the spot than that he actually did so. Besides, he himself wrote to V. Napravnik : " *The Voyevode* turned out such wretched stuff that I tore it up the day *after* the concert."

Siloti carefully concealed the parts of *The Voyevode*, so that after Tchaikovsky's death the score was restored from these and published by M. Belaiev, of Leipzig. When it was given for the first time in Petersburg, under Nikisch, it made a very different impression upon Taneiev, and he bitterly regretted his hasty verdict delivered in 1891.

Tchaikovsky remained two days longer in Moscow, in order to be present at a dinner given in his honour by the artists who had taken part in *Pique Dame*, and returned to Maidanovo worn out with the excitement he had experienced.

On December 17th (29th) he started upon his concert tour, which included not only foreign, but Russian towns. He was pledged to conduct in Kiev and Warsaw, as well as at the Hague and in Amsterdam,[1] and to attend the first performance of *Oniegin* in Hamburg and of *Pique Dame* in Prague.

[1] In July of this year he had been made a corresponding member of the " Maatschappij tot Bevorderung van Toonkunst."

At the time of the first performance of *Pique Dame* in Kiev, Tchaikovsky had become intimately acquainted with Prianichnikov, whose services to art he valued very highly. Not only the attitude of this artist towards him, but that of the entire opera company, had touched him very deeply. He was aware that the affairs of this company—one of the best in Russia—were not very flourishing, and he wanted to show his sympathy in some substantial form. He proposed, therefore, that the first performance of his *Iolanthe* should be transferred from Petersburg to Kiev, provided the Imperial Direction made no objections to the plan. Naturally they objected very strongly, and Tchaikovsky, by way of compensation, offered to conduct a concert for the benefit of Prianichnikov's company. The local branch of the Musical Society, which had made overtures to the composer on several occasions, was offended at his preference for the artists of the opera, and immediately engaged him for a concert of their own. In view of his former connection with the Society, Tchaikovsky could not refuse this offer. Both concerts were a great success, and evoked immense enthusiasm from the public and the Press.

From Kiev he went to Kamenka for a few days, but a feeling of sadness came over him at the sight of his old dwelling-place, so inseparably connected with the memory of the sister he had lost.

. . . At Warsaw, where he arrived on December 29th (January 10th), he was overcome with that terrible, despairing nostalgia, which, towards the close of his life, accompanied him like some sinister travelling companion whenever he left Russia. "I am counting—just as last year—the days, hours, and minutes till my journey is over," he wrote to Vladimir Davidov. "You are constantly in my thoughts, for at every access of agitation and homesickness, whenever my spiritual horizon grows dark, the thought that you are there, that I shall see you sooner or

2 X

later, flashes like a ray of sunlight across my mind. I am not exaggerating, upon my honour! Every moment this sun-ray keeps breaking forth in these or similar words: " Yes, it is bad, but never mind, Bob lives in the world"; " Far away in 'Peter'[1] sits Bob, drudging at his work"; " In a month's time I shall see Bob again."

To N. Konradi.

"WARSAW, *December* 31*st* (*January* 12*th*).

" I have been three days in Warsaw. I do not find this town as agreeable as many others. It is better in summer. The rehearsals are in progress, but the orchestra here is worse than second-rate. I spend my time with my former pupil, the celebrated violinist Barcewicz, and with the Friede[2] family. I shall stay here over the New Year. In the evening I generally go to the theatre. The opera is not bad here. Yesterday I saw the famous *Cavalleria Rusticana.* This opera is really very remarkable, chiefly for its successful subject. Perhaps Modi could find a similar libretto. Oh, when will the glad day of return be here!"

To Modeste Tchaikovsky.

"WARSAW, *January* 3*rd* (15*th*), 1892.

". . . I have only time for a few lines. Yesterday my concert took place in the Opera House, and went off brilliantly in every respect. The orchestra, which took a great liking to me, played admirably. Barcewicz played my Concerto with unusual spirit, and Friede[3] sang beautifully. The day before yesterday Grossmann[4] arranged a grand soirée in my honour. The Polish countesses were fascinatingly amiable to me. I have been fêted everywhere. Gurko[5] is the only person who has not shown me

---

[1] Diminutive of Petersburg.

[2] A. Friede, General of Infantry.

[3] Daughter of General A. Friede and a prima donna at the Maryinsky Theatre, St. Petersburg.

[4] The representative of the firm of Bechstein.

[5] The celebrated general.

the least attention. . . . Three weeks hence I go to Hamburg. I shall conduct *Oniegin* there myself; Pollini has made a point of it."

To A. Merkling.

"BERLIN, *January* 4*th* (16*th*), 1892.

". . . At Grossman's grand evening I observed that the Polish ladies (many very aristocratic women were there) are amiable, cultivated, interesting, and sympathetic. The farewell at the station yesterday was very magnificent. There is some talk of giving one of my operas in Polish next season. I am spending a day in Berlin to recover from the exciting existence in Warsaw. To-morrow I leave for Hamburg, where I conduct *Oniegin* on January 7th (19th). On the 29th (February 10th) my concert takes place in Amsterdam, and on the 30th (February 11th), at the Hague. After that—full steam homewards. I can only look forward with fearful excitement and impatience to the blessed day when I shall return to my adored Mother Russia."

Tchaikovsky arrived in Hamburg to find *Oniegin* had been well studied, and the preparations for its staging satisfactory on the whole. " The conductor here," he wrote to his favourite nephew, "is not merely passable, but actually has genius, and he ardently desires to conduct the first performance. Yesterday I heard a wonderful rendering of *Tannhäuser* under his direction. The singers, the orchestra, Pollini, the managers, and the conductor—his name is Mahler [1]—are all in love with *Oniegin ;* but I am very doubtful whether the Hamburg public will share their enthusiasm." Tchaikovsky's doubts as to the success of *Eugene Oniegin* were well founded. The opera was not much applauded.

---

[1] Gustav Mahler, afterwards conductor at the Vienna Opera, also produced *Eugene Oniegin* and *Iolanthe* in the Austrian capital.

To Vladimir Davidov.

"PARIS, *January* 12*th* (24*th*), 1892.

". . . I am in a very awkward position. I have a fortnight in prospect during which I do not know how to kill time. I thought this would be easier in Paris than anywhere else—but it was only on the first day that I did not feel bored. Since yesterday I have been wondering how I could save myself from idleness and ennui. If Sapellnikov and Menter would not be offended at my not going to Holland, how gladly I should start homewards! If the Silotis had not been here, I do not think I could have stayed. Yesterday I was at the 'Folies-Bergères,' and it bored me terribly. The Russian clown Durov brings on 250 dressed-up rats. It is most curious in what forms the Parisians display their Russophile propensities. Neither at the Opera, nor at any of the more serious theatres, is anything Russian performed, and while *we* are giving *Esclarmonde, they* show their goodwill towards Russian art by the medium of Durov and his rats! Truly, it enrages me—I say it frankly—partly on account of my own interests. Why cannot Colonne, who is now the head of the Opera, give my *Pique Dame*, or my new Ballet? In autumn he spoke of doing so, and engaged Petipa with a view to this. But it was all empty talk. . . . You will say : 'Are you not ashamed to be so envious and small-minded?' I am ashamed. Having nothing to do, I am reading Zola's *La bête humaine.* I cannot understand how people can seriously accept Zola as a great writer. Could there be anything more false and improbable than the leading idea of this novel? Of course, there are parts in which the truth is set forth with realism and vitality. But, in the main, it is so artificial that one never for a moment feels any sympathy with the actions or sufferings of the characters. It is simply a story of crime *à la* Gaboriau, larded with obscenities."

His increasing nostalgia and depression of spirits finally caused Tchaikovsky to abandon the concerts in Holland and return to Petersburg about the end of January. There he spent a week with his relatives, and went back to Maidanovo on the 28th (February 9th).

While in Paris, Tchaikovsky completed the revision of his Sextet, and on his return to Russia devoted himself to the orchestration of the *Nut-cracker* Ballet. He was in haste to finish those numbers from this work, which, in the form of a Suite, were to be played in St. Petersburg on March 7th (19th), instead of the ill-fated ballade, *The Voyevode.*

To Anatol Tchaikovsky.

" MAIDANOVO, *February 9th (21st)*, 1892.

" I am living very pleasantly here and enjoying the most beautiful of all the winter months. I love these clear, rather frosty days, when the sun sometimes begins to feel quite warm. They bring a feeling of spring. . . . Volodya Napravnik is staying with me just now, and has turned out to be excellent company. He is very musical, and that is a great pleasure. I often play pianoforte duets with him in the evening, or simply listen while he plays my favourite pieces. I have taken a house at Klin which will be my future home. . . . Later on I may buy it. Thank God, my financial position is excellent. *Pique Dame* was given nineteen times in Moscow, and the house was always sold out. Besides, there are the other operas. There is a good deal due to me from Petersburg."

Late in February Tchaikovsky went to St. Petersburg for a short visit. Here he received news which made a startling impression upon him. He had long believed his old governess Fanny to be dead. Suddenly he was informed that not only was she still alive, but had sent him her greetings. The first effect of these glad tidings came upon him as a kind of shock. In his own words, " he felt as though he had been told that his mother had risen from the dead, that the last forty-three years of existence were nothing but a dream, and that he had awakened to find himself in the upstairs rooms of the house at Votinsk." He dreaded, too, lest his dear teacher should now be only the shadow of her old self, a feeble and senile creature to whom death would be a boon. Nevertheless, he wrote to her at once, a kindly letter in which he asked if he could serve her in any way, and enclosed his photograph. Her reply, written in a firm handwriting, in which he recognised her old clearness of style, and the absence of all complaint, greatly assured him. Thus, between teacher and pupil the old affectionate relations were again renewed.

At the Symphony Concert of the Musical Society, on March 7th (19th), Tchaikovsky conducted his *Romeo and Juliet* Overture and the *Nut-cracker* Suite. The new work must have had an unprecedented success, since five out of the six movements had to be repeated.

At a concert given by the School of Jurisprudence, on March 3rd (15th), the composer had the honour of being introduced to the Tsarevich, now the reigning Emperor of Russia.

He returned to Maidanovo on March 9th.

To J. Konius.

"*March 9th (21st)*, 1892.

"In Petersburg I heard a very interesting violinist named (César) Thomson. Do you know him? He has a most remarkable technique; for instance, he plays passages of octaves with a rapidity to which no one has previously attained. I am telling you this on the assumption that you, too, will attempt this artistic feat. It makes a tremendous effect."

To P. Jurgenson.

"*March 18th (30th)*, 1892.

". . . I have no recollection of having promised you that I would never give away any of my manuscripts. I should have been very unwilling to make any such promise, because there are cases in which I could only be very pleased to present one of my scores to the Opera Direction—or in a similar instance.[1] . . . Your reproach that I give them away 'right and left' is without foundation. The Opera Direction, to which I owe my prosperity, is surely worthy to possess one of my scores in its superb library; and the same applies to the Russian Musical Society, from which originated the Conservatoire where I studied, and where I was invariably treated with kindness and indulgence. If you are really going to make it a *sine quâ non* that all my manuscripts must be your property, we must discuss the question . . . and should you convince me that your interests really suffer through the presentation of my scores, I will promise not to do it again. I have so rarely deprived you of the priceless joy of possessing my autograph scrawls! You have so many to the good! I cannot understand why you should be so annoyed!"

At the end of March Tchaikovsky spent a week with his relatives in Petersburg—now a very reduced circle—and afterwards went to Moscow. During the month Tchaikovsky spent in this city Alexis moved all his master's belongings from Maidanovo to the new house at Klin.

To Anatol Tchaikovsky.

"Moscow, *April 23rd* (*May 5th*), 1892.

"Moscow is unbearable, for there is scarcely a human being who does not bother me with visits or invitations; or ask me to look at an opera or songs, or—most unpleasant of all—try to get money out of me in one form or another. I shall look back upon this month spent in Moscow as upon a horrid nightmare. So far, I have conducted *Faust* and Rubinstein's *Demon; Oniegin* has yet to come.[2] But what are all these small inconveniences

---

[1] Tchaikovsky presented several autograph scores to the Imperial Public Library, Petersburg.

[2] Tchaikovsky was conducting for the benefit of Prianichnikov and the Kiev Opera Company, then in Moscow.

compared to what you have to do?[1] I have read your last letter with the greatest interest, and felt glad for your sake that you have such a fine opportunity of helping your fellow-creatures. I am sure that you will always cherish the memory of your mission to the famine-stricken Siberians."

XV

After the month's uncongenial work in Moscow, Tchaikovsky rested a few days in Petersburg, until Alexis had everything ready for him in the new home—which was destined to be his last. The house at Klin stood at the furthest end of the little town, and was completely surrounded by fields and woods; two-storied and very roomy. It particularly pleased Tchaikovsky, because—quite an unusual thing in a small country house in Russia—the upper rooms were large, and could be turned into an excellent bedroom and study for a guest. This was perhaps the only improvement upon Maidanovo and Frolovskoe. A small garden, the usual outlook across the country, the neighbourhood of endless kitchen-gardens on the one hand, and of the high-road to Moscow on the other, deprived the spot of all poetic beauty, and only Tchaikovsky, with his very modest demands for comfort or luxury, could have been quite satisfied—even enthusiastic—about the place.

After the composer's death, this house was purchased by his servant, Alexis Safronov, who sold it in 1897 to Modeste Tchaikovsky and his nephew, Vladimir Davidov. At the present moment—in so far as possible—every relic, and all documents connected with the composer, are preserved in the house.

---

[1] Anatol was one of the nine commissioners chosen by the Tsarevich to inquire into the failure of the crops and the sufferings of the starving peasants in Siberia.

THE HOUSE IN WHICH TCHAIKOVSKY LIVED AT KLIN

(HIS LAST HOME)

To Modeste Tchaikovsky.

"KLIN, *May 20th (June 1st)*, 1892.

" I have spent so much money lately (of course not upon myself alone) that all my hopes of laying aside something for George[1] have vanished."

To Eugen Zabel.

"KLIN, NEAR MOSCOW, *May 24th (June 5th)*, 1892.

" I have just received your esteemed letter, and feel it a pleasant duty to send you an immediate answer, but as I write German very badly I must have recourse to French. I doubt if you will find anything new, interesting, or of any value for your biography in the following lines; but I promise to say quite frankly all that I know and feel about Rubinstein.

" It was in 1858 that I heard the name of Anton Rubinstein for the first time. I was then eighteen, and I had just entered the higher class of the School of Jurisprudence, and only took up music as an amateur. For several years I had taken lessons on Sundays from a very distinguished pianist, M. Rodolphe Kundinger. In those days, never having heard any other virtuoso than my teacher, I believed him, in all sincerity, to be the greatest in the world. One day Kundinger came to the lesson in a very absent-minded mood, and paid little attention to the scales and exercises I was playing. When I asked this admirable man and artist what was the matter, he replied that, the day before, he had heard the pianist Rubinstein, just come from abroad; this man had impressed him so profoundly that he had not yet recovered from the experience, and everything in the way of virtuosity now seemed to him so poor that it was as unbearable to listen to my scales as to hear himself play the piano.

" I knew what a noble and sincere nature Kundinger possessed. I had a very high opinion of his taste and knowledge—and this caused his words to excite my

---

[1] George, the son of Nicholas Tchaikovsky, to whom the composer left his real estate and a life annuity of 1,200 roubles per annum.

imagination and my curiosity in the highest degree. In the course of my scholastic year I had the opportunity of hearing Rubinstein—and not only of *hearing* him, but of *seeing* him play and conduct. I lay stress upon this first *visual impression*, because it is my profound conviction that Rubinstein's prestige is based not only upon his rare talent, but also upon an irresistible charm which emanates from his whole personality; so that it is not sufficient to hear him in order to gain a full impression—one must see him too. I heard and saw him. Like everyone else, I fell under the spell of his charm. All the same, I finished my studies, entered the Government service, and continued to amuse myself with a little music in my leisure hours. But gradually my true vocation made itself felt. I will spare you details which have nothing to do with my subject, but I must tell you that about the time of the foundation of the St. Petersburg Conservatoire, in September, 1862, I was no longer a clerk in the Ministry of Justice, but a young man resolved to devote himself to music, and ready to face all the difficulties which were predicted by my relatives, who were displeased that I should voluntarily abandon a career in which I had made a good start. I entered the Conservatoire. My professors were: Zaremba for counterpoint and fugue, etc., Anton Rubinstein (Director) for form and instrumentation. I remained three and a half years at the Conservatoire, and during this time I saw Rubinstein daily, and sometimes several times a day, except during the vacations. When I joined the Conservatoire I was—as I have already told you—an enthusiastic worshipper of Rubinstein. But when I knew him better, when I became his pupil and we entered into daily relations with each other, my enthusiasm for his personality became even greater. In him I adored not only a great pianist and composer, but a man of rare nobility, frank, loyal, generous, incapable of petty and vulgar sentiments, clear and right-minded, of infinite goodness—in fact, a man who towered far above the common herd. As a teacher, he was of incomparable value. He went to work simply, without grand phrases or long dissertations; but always taking his duty seriously. He was only once angry with me. After the holidays I took him an overture entitled 'The Storm,' in which I had been guilty of all kinds of whims of form and orchestration. He was hurt, and said that it was not for the development of imbeciles that he took the trouble to teach the art of composition. I left the Conservatoire full of gratitude and admiration for my professor.

"For over three years I saw him daily. But what were our relations? He was a great and illustrious musician— I a humble pupil, who only saw him fulfilling his duties, and had no idea of his intimate life. A great gulf lay between us. When I left the Conservatoire I hoped that by working courageously, and gradually making my way, I might look forward to the happiness of seeing this gulf bridged over. I dared to aspire to the honour of becoming the friend of Rubinstein.

"It was not to be. Nearly thirty years have passed since then, but the gulf is deeper and wider than before. Through my professorship in Moscow I came to be the intimate friend of Nicholas Rubinstein; I had the pleasure of seeing Anton from time to time; I have always continued to care for him intensely, and to regard him as the greatest of artists and the noblest of men, but I never became, and never shall become, his friend. This great luminary revolves always in my heaven, but while I see its light I feel its remoteness more and more.

"It would be difficult to explain the reason for this. I think, however, that my *amour propre* as a composer has a great deal to do with it. In my youth I was very impatient to make my way, to win a name and reputation as a gifted composer, and I hoped that Rubinstein—who already enjoyed a high position in the musical world— would help me in my chase for fame. But painful as it is, I must confess that he did nothing, *absolutely nothing*, to forward my plans or assists my projects. Certainly he never injured me—he is too noble and generous to put a spoke in the wheel of a comrade—but he never departed from his attitude of reserve and kindly indifference towards me. This has always been a profound regret. The most probable explanation of this mortifying lukewarmness is that Rubinstein *does not care for my music, that my musical temperament is antipathetic to him.* Now

I still see him from time to time, and always with pleasure, for this extraordinary man has only to hold out his hand and smile for us to fall at his feet. At the time of his jubilee I had the happiness of going through much trouble and fatigue for him ; his attitude to me is always exceedingly correct, exceedingly polite and kind—but we live very much apart, and I can tell you nothing about his way of life, his views and aims—nothing, in fact, that could be of interest to the future readers of your book.

"I have never received letters from Rubinstein, and never wrote to him but twice in my life, to thank him for having, in recent years, included, among other Russian works in his programmes, one or two of my own.

"I have made a point of fulfilling your wish and telling you all I could about Rubinstein. If I have told too little, it is not my fault, nor that of Anton, but of fatality.

"Forgive my blots and smudges. To-morrow I have to leave home, and have no time to copy this.

"Your devoted

"P. T."

The sole object of the journey mentioned in this letter was to take a cure at Vichy. The catarrh of the stomach from which he suffered had been a trouble to Tchaikovsky for the last twenty years. Once, while staying with Kondratiev at Nizy, the local doctor had recommended him *natron* water. From that time he could not exist without it, and took it in such quantities that he ended by acquiring a kind of taste for it. But it did not cure his complaint, which grew worse and worse, so that in 1876 he had to undergo a course of mineral waters. The catarrhal trouble was not entirely cured, however, but returned at intervals with more or less intensity. About the end of the eighties his condition grew worse. Once during the rehearsals for *Pique Dame*, while staying at the Hôtel Rossiya in St. Petersburg, he sent for his brother Modeste, and declared he "could not live through the night." This turned his thoughts more and more to the "hateful but health-giving Vichy." But the periods of rest after his various tours, and of work in his "hermit's cave" at Klin, were so dear to him that until 1892 he could not make up his mind to revisit this watering-place. This year he only decided to go because the health of Vladimir Davidov equally demanded a cure at Vichy. He hoped in this congenial company to escape his usual home-sickness, and that it might even prove a pleasure to take his nephew abroad.

To Modeste Tchaikovsky.

"VICHY, *June* 19*th* (*July* 1*st*), 1892.

"We have been here a week. It seems more like seven months, and I look forward with horror to the fortnight which remains. I dislike Vichy as much as I did sixteen years ago, but I think the waters will do me good. In any case I feel sure Bob will benefit by them."

To P. Jurgenson.

"VICHY, *July* 1*st* (13*th*), 1892.

"I only possess one short note from Liszt, which is of so little importance that it is not worth your while to send it to La Mara. Liszt was a good fellow, and ready to respond to everyone who paid court to him. But as I never toadied to him, or any other celebrity, we never got into correspondence. I think he really preferred Messrs. Cui and Co., who went on pilgrimages to Weimar, and he was more in sympathy with their music than with mine. As far as I know, Liszt was not particularly interested in my works."

By July 9th (21st) Tchaikovsky and his nephew were back in Petersburg, from whence he travelled almost immediately to Klin, where he busied himself with the new Symphony (No. 6) which he wished to have ready in August.

At the outset of his career Tchaikovsky was somewhat indifferent as to the manner in which his works were published. He troubled very little about the quality of the pianoforte arrangements of his operas and symphonic works, and still less about printers' errors. About the end of the seventies, however, he entirely changed his attitude, and henceforth became more and more particular and insistent in his demands respecting the pianoforte arrangements and correction of his compositions. Quite half his correspondence with Jurgenson is taken up with these matters. . . . His requirements constantly increased. No one could entirely satisfy him. The cleverest arrangers, such as Klindworth, Taneiev, and Siloti did not please him, because they made their arrangements too difficult for amateurs. He was also impatient at the slowness with which they worked.

Now that for a year and a half Tchaikovsky has been in his grave, it is easy to attribute to certain events in his life (which passed unnoticed at the time) a kind of prophetic significance. His special and exclusive care as to the editing and publishing of his works in 1892 may, however, be compared to the preparations which a man makes for a long journey, when he is as much occupied with what lies before him as with. what he is leaving behind. He strives to finish what is unfinished, and to leave all in such a condition that he can face the unknown with a quiet conscience.

The words Tchaikovsky addressed to Jurgenson with reference to the Third Suite—"If all my best works were published in this style I might depart in peace"—offer some justification for my simile.

In the autumn of 1892 he undertook the entire correction of the orchestral parts of *Iolanthe* and the *Nutcracker* Ballet; the improvements and corrections of the pianoforte arrangement (two hands) of *Iolanthe;* the corrections of the pianoforte score of the Opera and Ballet, and a simplified pianoforte arrangement of the latter.

Tchaikovsky so often speaks in his letters of his dislike to this kind of work that he must have needed extraordinary self-abnegation to take this heavy burden upon his shoulders.

As with the spirits in Dante's *Inferno*, the dread of their torments by the will of divine justice "*si volge in disio*,"[1] so the energy with which Tchaikovsky attacked his task turned to a morbid, passionate excitement. "Corrections, corrections! More, more! For Heaven's sake, corrections!" he cries in his letters to Jurgenson, so that the casual reader might take for an intense desire that which was, in reality, only a worry to him, as the following letter shows.

To S. Taneiev.

"KLIN, *July* 13*th* (25*th*), 1892.

"Just now I am busy looking through the pianoforte score of *Iolanthe*. It bothers and annoys me indescribably. Before I went abroad in May I had sketched the first movement and finale of a Symphony. Abroad it did not progress in the least, and now I have no time for it."

To Anna Merkling.

"KLIN, *July* 17*th* (29*th*), 1892.

"DEAREST ANNA,—I have received your letter with the little additional note from dear Katy.[2] What extraordinary people you are! How can you imagine it would be a great pleasure for you if I were to come on a visit? If I were cheerful and pleasant company that would be a different matter. But I am no use for conversational purposes, and am often out of spirits, nor have I any resources in myself. I cannot help thinking that if I came you might afterwards say to yourselves: 'This old fool, we awaited him with such impatience, and he is not a bit nice after all!' Anna, I really do want to come to

---

[1] "Is changed to desire."

[2] Katharine Oboukhov, a second cousin of Tchaikovsky.

the Oboukhovs', but I cannot positively say 'yes' at present. . . . It will be sad to part from Bob, who is dearer to me than ever, since we have been inseparable companions for the last six weeks."

To Modeste Tchaikovsky.

" KLIN, *July* 17*th* (29*th*), 1892.

". . . I am sorry your comedy is ineffective and not suitable for the stage. Why do you think so? Authors are never good judges of their own work. Flaubert's letters—which I enjoy very much at present—are very curious in this respect. I think there is no more sympathetic personality in all the world of literature. A hero and martyr to his art. And so wise! I have found some astonishing answers to my questionings as to God and religion in his book."

At the end of July Russian art suffered a great loss in the death of the connoisseur and wealthy patron, S. M. Tretiakov, who had been Nicholas Rubinstein's right hand in the founding of the Moscow Conservatoire. To Tchaikovsky, Tretiakov's somewhat sudden end came as a severe blow, and he immediately travelled to Moscow to be present at the funeral of his friend.

A pleasanter incident during this summer of hard work came in the form of an invitation to conduct a concert at the Vienna Exhibition. "It is an advantage," he wrote to his brother Modeste, "because so far—on account of Hanslick—Vienna has been hostile to me. I should like to overcome this unfriendly opinion."

At last, at the very end of August, the vast accumulation of proof-correcting was finished, which, as he himself said, would have almost driven him out of his mind, but for his regular and healthy way of life. "Even in dreams," he wrote to Vladimir Davidov, "I see corrections, and flats and sharps that refuse to do what they are ordered. . . . I should like to see you at Verbovka after Vienna, but Sophie Menter, who is coming to my concert there, has given me a pressing invitation to her castle. Three times already I have broken my promise to go to Itter. I am really interested to see this 'marvel,' as everyone calls the castle."

In the course of this year, at the suggestion of the Grand Duke Constantine Constantinovich, President of the Academy of Sciences, Tchaikovsky was invited by the academician Y. K. Grote to contribute to the new *Dictionary of the Russian Language*, then appearing in a second edition. Tchaikovsky's duties were limited to the super-intendence of musical words, but he was flattered by his connection with such an important scientific work.

XVI

1892–1893

Tchaikovsky never travelled so much as during the foregoing season. It is true he was always fond of moving about. He could not remain long in one spot; but this was chiefly because it always seemed to him that "every place is better than the one in which we are." Paris, Kamenka, Clarens, Rome, Brailov, Simaki, Tiflis— all in turn were his favourite resorts, which he was delighted to visit and equally pleased to quit. But apart from the ultimate goal, travelling in itself was an enjoy-ment rather than a dread to Tchaikovsky.

From 1885, when he resolved "no longer to avoid man-kind, but to keep myself before the world so long as it needs me," his journeys became more frequent. When he began to conduct his own compositions in 1887, his journeys were undertaken with a fresh object: the propa-gation of his works abroad. As his fame increased, so also did the number of those who wished to hear him

2 Y

interpret his own music, and thus it was natural that by 1892 the number of his journeys was far greater than it had been ten years earlier.

When Tchaikovsky started upon his first concert tour he undoubtedly did violence to his "actual self," and did not look forward with pleasure, but rather with dread, to what lay before him. At the same time he was full of the expectation of happy impressions and brilliant results, and was firmly convinced of the importance of his undertaking, both for his own fame and for the cause of Russian art in general.

The events of his first tour would not have disappointed even a man less modest than Tchaikovsky. He had many consoling experiences, beginning with the discovery that he was better known abroad than he had hitherto suspected. His reception in Prague, with its "moment of absolute happiness," the sensation in Paris, the attention and respect with which he was received in Germany, all far surpassed his expectations. Nevertheless, he returned disillusioned, not by what had taken place, but by the price he had paid for his happiness.

But no sooner home again, than he forgot all he had gone through, and was planning his second tour with evident enjoyment.

This inexplicable discontent and disenchantment may, he thought, have been the result of a passing mood. The worst of his fears—the appearance before a crowd of foreigners—was over. He believed his second appearance would be far less painful, and expected even happier impressions than on his first tour. He was mistaken. He merely awoke to the "uselessness" of the sacrifice he was making for popularity's sake, and he asked himself whether it would not be better to stay at home and work. His belief in the importance of the undertaking vanished, and with it the whole reason for doing violence to his nature. In the early part of 1890 he declined all engagements to travel, and devoted himself to composition. But by the end of the year Tchaikovsky seems to have forgotten all the lessons of his two concert tours, for he began once more to conduct in Russia and abroad. Every journey cost him keener pangs of home-sickness, and each time he vowed it should be the last. Yet no sooner had he reached home again, than he began planning yet another tour. It seemed as though he had become the victim of some blind force which drove him hither and thither at will. This power was not merely complaisance to the demands of others, nor his old passion for travelling, nor the fulfilment of a duty, nor yet the pursuit of applause; still less was it the outcome of a desire for material gain. This mysterious force had its source in an inexplicable, restless, despondent condition of mind, which sought appeasement in any kind of distraction. I cannot explain it as a premonition of his approaching death; there are no grounds whatever for such a supposition. Nor will I, in any case, take upon myself to solve the problem of my brother's last psychological development. I will only call attention to the fact that he passed through a similar phase before every decisive change in his life. As at the beginning of the sixties, when he chose a musical career, and in 1885, when he resolved to "show himself in the eyes of the world," so also at this juncture, we are conscious of a feeling *that things could not have gone on much longer;* we feel on the brink of a change, as though something had come to an end, and was giving place to a new and unknown presence.

His death, which came to solve the problem, seemed fortuitous. Yet it is clear to me that it came at a moment *when things could not have gone on much longer;* nor can I shake off the impression that the years 1892 and 1893 were the dark harbingers of a new and serene epoch.

An unpleasant surprise awaited Tchaikovsky in Vienna. The concert, in connection with the Exhibition, which he had been engaged to conduct was to be given, so he discovered, in what was practically a large restaurant, reeking of cookery and the fumes of beer and tobacco. The composer immediately declined to fulfil his contract, unless the tables were removed and the room converted into something approaching a concert-hall. Moreover, the orchestra, though not very bad, was ridiculously small. Tchaikovsky's friends—Door, Sophie Menter, and Sapellnikov —were indignant at the whole proceeding, and realising the unpleasantness of his position, he decided to disregard his contract, and started with Mme. Menter for her castle at Itter.

Professor Door has related his reminiscences of Tchaikovsky's unlucky visit to Vienna,[1] when he met his old friend again after a long separation. "I was shocked at his appearance," he writes, "for he had aged so much that I only recognised him by his wonderful blue eyes. A man old at fifty! His delicate constitution had suffered terribly from his incessant creative work. We spoke of old days, and I asked him how he now got on in Petersburg. He replied that he was so overwhelmed with all kinds of attentions that he was perpetually embarrassed by them, and had but one trouble, which was that he never saw anything of Rubinstein, whom he had loved and respected from his student days. 'Do what I will,' he said, 'I can get no hold on him; he escapes me like an eel.' I laughed and said : 'Do not take the great man's ways too much to heart; he has his weaknesses like other mortals. Rubinstein, a distinctly lyrical temperament, has never had any great success in dramatic music, and avoids everyone who has made a name in this sphere of art. Comfort yourself, dear friend; he cut Richard Wagner and many others besides.' 'But,' he broke in with indignation, 'how can you compare me with Wagner and many others who have

[1] *Neue Freie Presse*, March 30th, 1901. The above is quoted from the German edition of *The Life and Letters of Tchaikovsky*.

created immortal works?' 'Oh, as to immortality,' I replied, 'I will tell you a good story about Brahms. Once when this question was being discussed, Brahms said to me: 'Yes, immortality is a fine thing, if only one knew how long it would last.' Tchaikovsky laughed heartily over this 'bull,' and his cheerfulness seemed quite restored. . . . After three hours' rehearsal he was greatly exhausted. He descended with great difficulty from the conductor's desk, the perspiration stood in beads on his forehead, and he hurried into his fur-lined coat, although it was as warm as a summer's day. He rested for a quarter of an hour, and then left with Sophie Menter and Sapellnikov."

During this short visit to Vienna, Tchaikovsky stayed in the same hotel as Pietro Mascagni, and their rooms actually adjoined. The Italian composer was then the most fêted and popular man in Vienna. As we have already mentioned, Tchaikovsky admired *Cavalleria Rusticana.* The libretto appealed to him in the first place, but he recognised much promising talent in the music. The rapidity with which the young musician had become the idol of the Western musical world did not in the least provoke Tchaikovsky's envy ; on the contrary, he was interested in the Italian composer, and drawn to him. Accident having brought him into such near neighbourhood, it occurred to him to make the acquaintance of his young colleague. But when he found himself confronted in the passage with a whole row of admirers, all awaiting an audience with the *maestro*, he resolved to spare him at least one superfluous visitor.

The Castle of Itter, which belongs to Madame Sophie Menter, is situated in Tyrol, a few hours from Munich. Besides its wonderfully picturesque situation, it has acquired a kind of reflected glory, not only from the reputation of its owner, but because Liszt often stayed there.

To Modeste Tchaikovsky.

"ITTER, *September* 15th (27th), 1892.

". . . Itter deserves its reputation. It is a devilish pretty nest. My rooms—I occupy a whole floor—are very fine, but a curious mixture of grandeur and bad taste : luxurious furniture, a wonderful inlaid bedstead and—some vile oleographs. But this does not affect me much. The great thing is the exquisite, picturesque neighbourhood. Peace and stillness, and not a trace of any other visitors. I am fond of Sapellnikov and Menter, and, altogether, I have not felt more comfortable for a long while. I shall stay five days longer and return to 'Peter' by Salzburg (where I want to see the Mozart Museum) and Prague (where I stay for the performance of *Pique Dame*). On the 25th (October 7th) I hope to put in an appearance upon the Quay Fontanka. The chief drawback here is that I get neither letters nor papers and hear nothing about Russia or any of you."

The performance of *Pique Dame* in Prague did not take place until October 8th. The opera, judging from the accounts of those present, had a brilliant success, and the composer was repeatedly recalled. Between 1892–1902 *Pique Dame* was given on forty-one occasions. When we bear in mind that opera is only given three times a week at the National Theatre in Prague, and that the chief object of this enterprise is to forward the interests of Czechish art, this number of performances points to the fact that the success of *Pique Dame* has proved as lasting as it was enthusiastic.

Tchaikovsky returned to Klin about the first week in October (Russian style), and was soon busy with preparations for the performance of *Iolanthe* in St. Petersburg. On the 28th (November 9th) he left home for the capital, in order to superintend the rehearsals of the new opera. Soon after his arrival he received two interesting communications. The first informed him that he had been

TCHAIKOVSKY'S BEDROOM AT KLIN

elected a Corresponding Member of the French Academy; the second, from the University of Cambridge, invited him to accept the title of Doctor of Music, *honoris causa*, on condition that he attended in person to receive the degree at the hands of the Vice-Chancellor.

Tchaikovsky acknowledged the first honour, and expressed his readiness to conform to the conditions of the second.

At the same time he had a further cause for congratulation in the success of his Sextet, *Souvenir de Florence*, which was played for the first time in public at the St. Petersburg Chamber Music Union, on November 25th (December 7th). The players were: E. Albrecht, Hille, Hildebrandt, Heine, Wierzbilowiez, and A. Kouznietsov. This time all were delighted: the performers, the audience, and the composer himself. The medal of the Union was presented to Tchaikovsky amid unanimous applause. During this visit the composer sat to the well-known sculptor, E. Günsburg, for a statuette which, in spite of its artistic value, is not successful as a likeness.

To Anatol Tchaikovsky.

" PETERSBURG, *November 24th* (*December 6th*), 1892.

". . . Modeste's play was given yesterday.[1] It was a complete failure, which does not surprise me in the least, for it is much too subtle for the public at the Alexander Theatre. It does not matter: may it be a lesson to Modeste. The pursuit of the unattainable hinders him from his real business—to write plays in the accepted form. The rehearsals for *Iolanthe* and the Ballet are endlessly dragged out. The Emperor will be present on the 5th, and the first public performance will take place the following day."

During this visit to the capital Tchaikovsky did his utmost to forward the interests of his friends, Taneiev

---

[1] *A Day in St. Petersburg.*

and Arensky, as will be seen from the following extract from a letter to the former, respecting the performance of his *Orestes* :—

" Vsievolojsky (Director of the Opera) took Napravnik aside and consulted him as to the advisability of proposing *Orestes* to the Emperor for next season. . . . I suggested that you should be sent for, in order to play over the work in their presence. Vsievolojsky was afraid if you were put to this trouble you might feel hurt should the matter fall through. I ventured to say that, as a true philosopher, you would not lose heart if nothing came of it. . . . I spoke not less eloquently of Arensky, but so far without success."

On December 5th (17th) *Iolanthe* and the *Nut-cracker* Ballet were given in the presence of the Imperial Court. The opera was conducted by Napravnik. The Figners distinguished themselves by their admirable interpretations of the parts of Vaudemont and Iolanthe. The scenery and costumes were beautiful. Nevertheless the work was only accorded a *succès d'estime.* The chief reason for this —according to Modeste Tchaikovsky—was the prolixity of the libretto and its lack of scenic interest.

The Ballet—admirably conducted by Drigo—was brilliantly staged, and received with considerable applause ; yet the impression left by the first night was not wholly favourable. The subject, which differed greatly from the conventional ballet programme, was not entirely to blame. The illness of the talented ballet-master, Petipa, and the substitution of a man of far less skill and imagination, probably accounted for the comparative failure of the work. The delicate beauty of the music did not appeal to the public on a first hearing, and some time elapsed before the *Nut-cracker* became a favourite item in the repertory.

The attitude of the Press appears from the following letter from the composer to Anatol, dated Petersburg, December 10th (22nd), 1892 :—

"This is the fourth day on which all the papers have been cutting up both my latest creations. . . . It is not the first time. The abuse does not annoy me in the least, and yet—as always under these circumstances—I am in a hateful frame of mind. When one has lived in expectation of an important event, as soon as it is over there comes a kind of apathy and disinclination for work, while the emptiness and futility of all our efforts becomes so evident. . . . The day after to-morrow I leave for Berlin. There I shall decide where to go for a rest (most probably to Nice). On December 29th I shall be in Brussels. From thence I shall go to Paris, and afterwards to see Mlle. Fanny at Montbeillard. About the 10th January I have to conduct the concerts at Odessa. At the end of the month I shall be in Petersburg. Later I shall spend some time in Klin, and go to you in Lent."

To Vladimir Davidov.

"BERLIN, *December* 16*th* (28*th*), 1892.

"Here I am, still in Berlin. To-day I have given myself up to serious reflections, which will have important results. I have been carefully, and as it were objectively, analysing my Symphony, which luckily I have not yet orchestrated and given to the world. The impression was not flattering : the work is written for the sake of writing, and is not interesting or moving. I ought to put it aside and forget it. . . . Am I done for and dried up? Perhaps there is yet some subject which could inspire me ; but I ought to compose no more absolute music, symphony or chamber works. To live without work would weary me. What am I to do? Fold my hands as far as composition is concerned and try to forget it? It is difficult to decide. I think, and think, and do not know how to settle the question. In any case, the outlook has not been cheerful the last three days."

To Modeste Tchaikovsky.

"BÂLE, *December* 19*th* (31*st*), 1902.

" . . . I have nothing to write about but fits of weeping. Really it is surprising that this phenomenal, deadly home-sickness does not drive me mad. Since this psychological phase grows stronger with every journey abroad, in future I shall never travel alone, even for a short time. To-morrow this feeling will give place to another (scarcely?) less painful emotion. I am going to Montbeillard, and I must confess to a morbid fear and horror, as though I were entering the kingdom of the dead and the world of those who had long since vanished."

To his brother, Nicholas Ilich Tchaikovsky.

" Paris, *December 22nd (January 3rd),* 1892. \ ?

" . . . I wrote to Mlle. Fanny from Bâle to let her know the time of my arrival, so that she should not be upset by my unexpected appearance. I reached Montbeillard at 3 p.m. on January 1st (new style), and went straight to her house. She lives in a quiet street in this little town, which is so quiet that it might be compared to one of our own Russian 'district' towns. The house contains but six rooms—two on each floor—and belongs to Fanny and her sister. Here they were born, and have spent their whole lives. Mlle. Fanny came to the door, and I knew her at once. She does not look her seventy years, and, curiously enough, has altered very little on the whole. The same high-coloured complexion and brown eyes, and her hair is not very grey. She has grown much stouter. I had dreaded tears and an affecting scene, but there was nothing of the sort. She greeted me as though we had not met for a year—joyfully and tenderly, but quite simply. It soon became clear to me why our parents, and we ourselves, were so fond of her. She is a remarkably clever, sympathetic creature, who seems to breathe an atmosphere of kindliness and integrity. Naturally we started upon reminiscences, and she re-called a number of interesting details from our childhood. Then she showed me our copybooks, my exercises, your letters and mine, and—what was of the greatest interest to me—a few dear, kind letters from our mother. I cannot tell you what a strange and wonderful feeling came over me while listening to her recollections and looking over these letters and books. The past rose up so clearly before me that I seemed to inhale the air of Votinsk and hear my mother's voice distinctly. . . . When she asked me which of my brothers I loved best, I replied evasively that I was equally fond of them all. At which she was a little indignant, and said that, as my playmate in childhood, I ought to care most for you. And truly at that moment I felt I loved you intensely, because you had shared all my youthful joys. I stayed with her from three until eight o'clock, without noticing how time went. I spent the whole of the next day in her society. . . .

" She gave me a beautiful letter from my mother, in which she writes of you with special tenderness. I will show it to you. The two sisters do not live luxuriously— but comfortably. Fanny's sister also lived a long time in Russia, and does not speak the language badly. Both of them still teach. They are known to the whole town, for they have taught all the educated people there, and are universally loved and respected. In the evening I embraced Fanny when I took leave of her, and promised to return some day. . . ."

To Modeste Tchaikovsky.

" PARIS, *January 4th* (*16th*), 189x.

". . . After my brilliant concert in Brussels I returned here yesterday. The orchestra was very good, but not highly disciplined. I was very cordially received, but this did not make things any easier for me. I suffered equally from agitation and the anguish of home-sickness. During the interval Gevaert, as President of the Artists' Benevolent Association, made a speech before the assembled orchestra, in which he thanked me on behalf of this society. As the concert was given in aid of a charity, I declined to accept any fee, which touched the artists very deeply."

The programme of the Brussels concert included, among other compositions by Tchaikovsky, the Pianoforte Concerto, op. 23 (Rummel as soloist), the *Nut-cracker* Suite, and the Overture " *1812*."

On January 12th (24th), 1893, Tchaikovsky arrived in Odessa, where for nearly a fortnight he was fêted with such enthusiasm that even the Prague festivities of 1888 dwindled into insignificance compared with these experiences.

The ovations began the day after his arrival, when, on his appearance at the rehearsal of *Pique Dame*, he was welcomed by the theatrical direction and the entire opera company. Not contented with vociferous cheering, he was "chaired" and borne around in triumph, much to his discomfort. On the 16th he conducted the following works at the concert of the Musical Society: *The Tempest*, the Andante cantabile from the Quartet, op. 11, and the *Nutcracker* Suite. The local section of the Musical Society presented him with a bâton, and the musicians gave him a laurel wreath. Some numbers on the programme had to be repeated three times in response to the vociferous applause.

This triumph was followed by a series of others: the first performance of *Pique Dame*, a soirée in his honour at the English Club, a charity concert, given by the Slavonic Association, and a second concert of the Musical Society, at which the Overture "*1812*" had to be repeated *da capo*.

Tchaikovsky left Odessa on January 25th (February 6th), and returned to Klin to recover from the strain and fatigue of his visit.

Among the many occupations which overwhelmed him there, he found time to sit to Kouznietsov for his portrait. "Although the artist knew nothing of Tchaikovsky's inner life," says Modeste, "he has succeeded, thanks to the promptings of inspiration, in divining all the tragedy of that mental and spiritual phase through which the composer was passing at that time, and has rendered it with profound actuality. Knowing my brother as I do, I can affirm that no truer, more living likeness of him exists. There are a few slight deviations from strict truth in the delineation of

SITTING-ROOM AT KLIN

the features; but they do not detract from the portrait as a whole, and I would not on any account have them corrected. Perhaps the vitality which breathes from the picture has been purchased at the price of these small defects."

Kouznietsov presented the portrait to Tchaikovsky, who, however, declined to accept it, partly because he could not endure a picture of himself upon his own walls, but chiefly because he did not consider himself justified in preventing the artist from making something out of his work. The portrait is now in the Tretiakov Gallery, Moscow.

To Modeste Tchaikovsky.

"KLIN, *February 5th* (17*th*), 1893.

". . . My journey from Kamenka here was not very propitious. I was taken so ill in the carriage that I frightened my fellow-passengers by becoming delirious, and had to stop at Kharkov. After taking my usual remedies, and a long sleep, I awoke quite well in the morning. . . .

"Next week I must pay a visit to Vladimir Shilovsky. The prospect fills me with fear and agitation. Tell me, has he greatly changed? How is the dropsy? I am afraid of a scene, and altogether dread our meeting. Is there really no hope for him? Answer these questions."

Vladimir Shilovsky, who had played an important part in my brother's life some twenty years earlier, had very rarely come in contact with his old teacher since his marriage with the only remaining child of Count Vassiliev. There had been no breach between them, but their lives had run in opposite directions. In January, 1893, I heard that Vladimir Shilovsky was seriously ill. I informed Peter Ilich, who visited his old pupil in Moscow, and was touched by the joy he showed at their reunion, and by the calm self-control with which he spoke of his hopeless condition. The old intimacy was renewed, and only ended with the Count's death in June, 1893.

XVII

Tchaikovsky's life moved in spiral convolutions. At every turn his way seemed to lie through the same spiritual phases. The alternations of light and shade succeeded each other with a corresponding regularity. When speaking of the depression which darkened his last years, I emphasised the fact that he had gone through a similar condition of mind before every decisive change in his existence. The acute moral tension which preceded his retirement from the Ministry of Justice was followed by the calm and happy summer of 1862. To his glad and hopeful mood at the beginning of 1877 succeeded the crisis which compelled him to go abroad for rest and change. So, too, this year, 1893, opened with a period of serene content, for which the creation of his Sixth, or so-called " Pathetic," Symphony was mainly accountable. The composition of this work seems to have been an act of exorcism, whereby he cast out all the dark spirits which had possessed him in the preceding years.

The first mention of this Symphony occurs in a letter to his brother Anatol, dated February 10th (22nd), 1893, in which he speaks of being completely absorbed in his new project. The following day, writing to Vladimir Davidov, he enters into fuller particulars :—

" I must tell you how happy I am about my work. As you know, I destroyed a Symphony which I had partly composed and orchestrated in the autumn. I did wisely, for it contained little that was really fine—an empty pattern of sounds without any inspiration. Just as I was starting on my journey (the visit to Paris in December, 1892) the idea came to me for a new Symphony. This time with a programme; but a programme of a kind which remains an enigma to all—let them guess it who can. The work will be entitled " A Programme Symphony " (No. 6). This programme is penetrated by subjective sentiment. During my journey, while composing it in my mind, I frequently shed tears. Now I am home again I have settled down to sketch out the work, and it goes with such ardour that in less than four days I have completed the first movement, while the rest of the Symphony is clearly outlined in my head. There will be much that is novel as regards form in this work. For instance, the Finale will not be a great Allegro, but an Adagio of considerable dimensions. You cannot imagine what joy I feel at the conviction that my day is not yet over, and that I may still accomplish much. Perhaps I may be mistaken, but it does not seem likely. Do not speak of this to anyone but Modeste."

After an interval of three years Tchaikovsky once more conducted a concert of the Moscow Musical Society on February 14th (26th). This was in response to a letter from Safonov begging him to make up their former personal differences and to take part again in the work of Nicholas Rubinstein, of imperishable memory. The Overture-Fantasia *Hamlet* was played at this concert for the first time in Moscow.

About the end of February Tchaikovsky again returned to Moscow to hear a new Suite *From Childhood's Days*, by George Konius, which pleased him very much. Through the influence of the Grand Duke Constantine, Tchaikovsky succeeded in getting an annual pension of 1,200 roubles (£120) for the struggling young composer.

At this time he suffered from a terrible attack of headache, which never left him, and threatened to become a chronic ailment. It departed, however, with extraordinary suddenness on the fourteenth day after the first paroxysm.

On March 11th (23rd) he visited Kharkov, where he remained till the 16th (28th), and enjoyed a series of triumphs similar to those he had experienced in Odessa earlier in the year.

By March 18th (30th) Tchaikovsky was back in Klin. Here he received news that Ippolitov-Ivanov was leaving

Tiflis to join the Moscow Conservatoire. In his answer, which is hardly a letter of congratulation, Tchaikovsky refers to his last Symphony, which he does not *intend to tear up*, to the sketch of a new Pianoforte Concerto, and to several pieces for piano which he hopes to compose in the near future.

He spent the Easter holidays in the society of his relatives and intimate friends in Petersburg, and, but for the hopeless illness of his oldest friend, the poet Apukhtin, this visit would have been a very quiet and cheerful interlude in his life.

To Vladimir Davidov.

"KLIN, *April 15th (27th)*, 1893.

"I am engaged in making musical pancakes.[1] To-day I have tossed the tenth. It is remarkable ; the more I do, the easier and pleasanter the occupation grows. At first it was uphill work, and the first two pieces are the outcome of a great effort of will; but now I can scarcely fix the ideas in my mind, they succeed each other with such rapidity. If I could spend a whole year in the country, and my publisher was prepared to take all I composed, I might—if I chose to work *à la* Leikin—make about 36,000 roubles a year!"

To Modeste Tchaikovsky.

"MOSCOW, *April 22nd (May 4th)*, 1893.

"Ah, dear Modi, I do not believe I shall get the thirty pieces written! I have finished eighteen in fifteen days and brought them with me to Moscow. But now I must stay here four days (the performance at the Conservatoire, one morning with the Synodal singers, and my birthday with old friends), then go on to Nijny and return here in time for the first performance of Rakhmaninov's *Aleko*. I

---

[1] Jurgenson had commissioned Tchaikovsky to send him as many songs and pianoforte pieces as he liked, and while awaiting at Klin the day of his departure for London, the composer determined to write one number every day.

shall not be home before the 30th (May 12th), and I start on the 10th (22nd) of May, . . . but perhaps I may knock off a few songs very quickly."

To P. Jurgenson.

"KLIN, *May 2nd,* 1893.

" I intended to ask my old fee—100 roubles for each number. Now, in consequence of the number of paying propositions made to me (I swear it is true), I must put up my prices a little. But I will not forget that you have also published my greater works, from which you will not derive any profit for a long time to come. So let it stand at the old fee. . . . It is a pity I had not more time for writing.

" Should anything happen to Karl,[1] and the family be in need, do not hesitate to help them out of my present, or future, funds. . . ."

To P. Jurgenson.

"PETERSBURG, *May 6th* (18*th*), 1893.

". . . . As regards my fee, I must tell you that Gutheil has never made me any proposals, because all Russian publishers know that I am not to be caught by any bait they may offer. But abroad my relations with you are not understood, therefore I often receive advances from other countries. Many of them (André of Offenbach) have offered me far higher fees than I get from you (of course, I am only speaking of short compositions). . . . I cannot lose sight of the fact that many of my symphonies and operas have cost you more than they bring in. Of course, they will sell better some day, but at present I do not like to bleed you. You are not as rich as an Abraham, a Schott, or a Simrock. . . . If (on your honour) you do not consider it too much to give me another fifty, I will agree to it. Naturally I shall be very glad, for this has been a heavy year.

" I want nothing for the Mozart,[2] because I have not put much of myself into it."

---

[1] Karl Albrecht, who was on his death-bed
[2] The Quartet *Night.*

To Vladimir Davidov.

"BERLIN, *May* 15*th* (27*th*), 1893.

". . . . This time I wept and suffered more than ever, perhaps because I let my thoughts dwell too much on our last year's journey. It is purely a psychophysical pheno- menon! And how I loathe trains, the atmosphere of railway carriages, and fellow-travellers! . . . I travel too much, that is why I dislike it more and more. It is quite green here, and flowers blooming everywhere—but it does not give me any pleasure, and I am only conscious of an incredible and overwhelming home-sickness."

To Modeste Tchaikovsky.

"LONDON, *May* 17*th* (29*th*), 1893.

" I arrived here early this morning. I had some difficulty to find a room—all the hotels are packed. The concert takes place on May 20th (June 1st), after which I must rush around for about a week, for the Cambridge ceremony does not come off until the 11th or 12th, and on the 13th —our 1st of June—I begin my homeward journey. I am continually thinking of you all. I never realise all my affection for you so much as when away from home, and oppressed with loneliness and nostalgia."

To Vladimir Davidov.

"LONDON, *May* 17*th* (29*th*), 1893.

" Is it not strange that of my own free will I have elected to undergo this torture? What fiend can have suggested it to me? Several times during my journey yesterday I resolved to throw up the whole thing and turn tail. But what a disgrace to turn back for no good reason! Yesterday I suffered so much that I could neither sleep nor eat, which is very unusual for me. I suffer not only from torments which cannot be put into words (there is one place in my new Symphony—the Sixth—where they seem to me adequately expressed), but from a dislike to strangers, and an indefinable terror— though of what the devil only knows. This state makes itself felt by internal pains and loss of power in my legs. However, it is for the last time in my life. Only for a heap of money will I ever go anywhere again, and never for more than three days at a time. And to think I must kick my heels here for another fortnight!! It seems like eternity. I arrived early this morning, *via* Cologne and Ostend. The crossing took three hours, but it was not rough. . . . On the steps of my hotel I met the French pianist Diemer, and to my great astonishment found myself delighted to see him. He is an old acquaintance, and very well disposed towards me. In consequence of our meeting I had to go to his 'Recital.' Saint-Saëns also takes part in the concert at which I am conducting."

Profiting by the presence in England of the composers who were about to receive the honorary degree at Cambridge, the Philharmonic Society gave two concerts in which they took part. At the first of these Tchaikovsky conducted his Fourth Symphony with brilliant success. According to the Press notices, none of his works previously performed had pleased so well, or added so much to his reputation in England.

To Modeste Tchaikovsky.

"LONDON, *May 22nd (June 3rd),* 1893.

" . . . The concert was brilliant. It was unanimously agreed that I had a real triumph, so that Saint-Saëns, who followed me, suffered somewhat from my unusual success. Of course, this is pleasant enough, but what an infliction London life is during the 'season'! Luncheons and dinners which last an interminable time. Yesterday the directors of the Philharmonic gave a dinner at the Westminster Club in honour of Saint-Saëns and myself. It was very smart and luxurious; we sat down to table at seven and rose at 11.30 p.m. (I am not exaggerating). Besides this I am invited to concerts daily and cannot refuse to go. To-day, for instance, I went to Sarasate's concert. He is most kind and amiable to me. Last time I was here in the winter and in bad weather, so that I got no idea of what the town is really like. The devil knows Paris is a mere village compared to London! Walking in Regent Street and Hyde Park, one sees so many carriages, so much splendid and luxurious equipment, that the eye is fairly dazzled. I have been to afternoon tea at the Embassy. Our secretary at the Embassy here, Sazonov, is a charming man. What a number of people I see, and how tired I get! In the morning I suffer a great deal from depression, and later I feel in a kind of daze. I have but one thought: to get it all over. . . . At Cambridge I will keep a full diary. It seems to me it will be a very droll business. Grieg is ill. All the other recipients will come. . . ."

To Modeste Tchaikovsky.

"LONDON, *May* 29*th* (*June* 10*th*), 1893.

" This letter will not be in time to reach you in ' Peter.' . . . I have not had a chance of writing. This is an infernal life. Not a moment's peace: perpetual agitation, dread, home-sickness, fatigue. However, the hour of escape is at hand. Besides which, I must say I find many excellent folks here, who show me every kind of attention. All the doctors designate have now arrived except Grieg, who is too ill. Next to Saint-Saëns, Boïto appeals most to me. Bruch is an unsympathetic, inflated sort of personage. I go to Cambridge the day after to-morrow, and do not stay at an hotel, but in the house of Dr. Maitland, who has written me a very kind letter of invitation. I shall only be there one night. On the day of our arrival there will be a concert and dinner, and on the following day—the ceremony. By four o'clock it will be all over."

In 1893, in consequence of the fiftieth anniversary of the Cambridge University Musical Society, the list of those who received the Doctor's degree, *honoris causa*, was distinguished by an unusual number of musicians: Tchaikovsky, Saint-Saëns, Boïto, Max Bruch and Edvard Grieg.

The festivities at Cambridge began on June 12th (new

TCHAIKOVSKY IN 1893
(From a photograph taken in London)

style) with a concert, the programme of which included a work by each of the five recipients of the musical degree, and one by Dr. Stanford,[1] the director of the society.

The programme was as follows : (1) Fragment from *Odysseus* for soli, chorus, and orchestra (Max Bruch); (2) Fantasia for pianoforte and orchestra, *Africa*, the composer at the piano (Saint-Saëns); (3) Prologue from *Mefistofele* for solo, chorus, and orchestra (Boïto); (4) Symphonic poem, *Francesca da Rimini* (op. 32), (Tchaikovsky); (5) *Peer Gynt* Suite (op. 46) (Grieg); (6) Ode, *The East to the West*, for chorus and orchestra (op. 52) (Stanford).

The various numbers were conducted by the respective composers, with the exception of Grieg's Suite and the Fantasia *Africa*, which were given under the bâton of Dr. Stanford.

The singers were Mr. and Mrs. Henschel, Mme. Marie Brema, and Plunket Green.

In his *Portraits et Souvenirs* Saint-Saëns has given the following description of this concert, and I cannot refrain from interrupting my narrative in order to quote what the French composer says of my brother's *Francesca*.

" Piquant charms and dazzling fireworks abound in Tchaikovsky's *Francesca da Rimini*, which bristles with difficulties, and shrinks from no violence of effect. The gentlest and kindest of men has let loose a whirlwind in this work, and shows as little pity for his interpreters and hearers as Satan for sinners. But the composer's talent and astounding technique are so great that the critic can only feel pleasure in the work. A long melodic phrase, the love-song of Paola and Francesca, soars above this tempest, this *bufera infernale*, which attracted Liszt before Tchaikovky, and engendered his Dante Symphony. Liszt's Francesca is more touching and more Italian in character than that of the great Slavonic composer ; the whole work is so typical that we seem to see the profile of Dante

---

[1] This was before Sir Charles Villiers Stanford was knighted.

projected in it. Tchaikovsky's art is more subtle, the out-lines clearer, the material more attractive; from a purely musical point of view the work is better. Liszt's version is perhaps more to the taste of the poet or painter. On the whole, they can fitly stand side by side; either of them is worthy of Dante, and as regards noise, both leave nothing to be desired." [1]

The concert was followed by a banquet in the hall of King's College, at which a hundred guests sat down to table. As it was purely a musical festivity, only those who were to receive the honorary musical degree were invited to this banquet. The place of honour, next to the chairman, was given to Saint-Saëns, the eldest of the guests. Never had Tchaikovsky greater reason to con-gratulate himself upon his comparative youth, for, together with the honour, the difficult task of replying to a toast on behalf of his colleagues fell to the lot of Saint-Saëns.

After the dinner came a brilliant reception to the com-posers in the hall of the Museum.

Besides the musicians, there were several other recipients of the honorary degree, including the Maharajah of Bohon-ager, Lord Herschel, Lord Roberts, Dr. Julius Stupitza, Professor of English Philology in the University of Berlin, and the Irish scholar, Standish O'Grady.

On the morning of June 13th all the future doctors assembled in the Arts School and attired themselves in their splendid doctors' robes of red and white; after which they took up their positions, and the procession started. Saint-Saëns, in the volume already quoted, says:

" We were attired in ample robes of silk, parti-coloured scarlet and white, with full sleeves, and on our heads college-caps of black velvet with gold tassels. Thus decked out, we walked in procession through the town, under a tropical sun. At the head of the group of doctors went the King of Bohonager in a turban of cloth of gold,

---

[1] *Portraits et Souvenirs*, Saint-Saëns, p. 141.

sparkling with fabulous jewels and a diamond necklace. Dare I confess that, as the enemy of the commonplace, and of the neuter tints of our modern garb, I was enchanted with the adventure?

" The people stood on each side of the railings, and cheered us with some enthusiasm, especially Lord Roberts."

" Meanwhile the Senate House, in which the degrees were conferred, had become crowded with undergraduates and guests. The former were not merely spectators, but —as we afterwards discovered—participated in the event. When the Vice-Chancellor and other members of the Senate had taken their places, the ceremony began. Each recipient rises in turn from his seat, while the public orator recounts his claims to recognition in a Latin oration. Here the undergraduates begin to play their part. According to ancient tradition, they are allowed to hiss, cheer, and make jokes at the expense of the new doctors. At every joke the orator waits until the noise and laughter has subsided, then continues to read aloud. When this is done, the recipient is led up to the Vice-Chancellor, who greets him as doctor *in nomine Patri, Filii et Spiritus Sancti.* This formula was not used in the case of the Maharajah."

The oration delivered in honour of Tchaikovsky ran as follows :—

" Russorum ex imperio immenso hodie ad nos delatus est viri illustris, Rubinsteinii, discipulus insignis, qui neque Italiam neque Helvetiam inexploratam reliquit, sed patriae carmina popularia ante omnia dilexit. Ingenii Slavonici et ardorem fervidum et languorem subtristem quam feliciter interpretatur! Musicorum modorum in argumentis animo concipiendis quam amplus est! in numeris modulandis quam distinctus! in flexionibus variandis quam subtilis! in orchestrae (ut aiunt) partibus inter se diversis una componendis quam splendidus! Talium virorum animo grato admiramur ingenium illud facile et promptum, quod, velut ipsa rerum natura, nulla, necessitate coactum sed quasi sua sponte pulcherrimum quidque in luminis oras quotannis submittit.

"Audiamus Propertium :

> "'aspice quot submittit humus formosa colores ;
> et veniunt hederae sponte sua melius.'

"Etiam nosmet ipsi hodie fronti tam felici hederae nostrae corollam sponte imponimus.

"Duco ad vos Petrum Tchaikovsky."

After the ceremony there was a breakfast given by the Vice-Chancellor, at which all attended in their robes. At the end of the meal, in obedience to the tradition of centuries, a loving-cup was passed round.

The breakfast was followed by a garden-party, the hostess being the wife of the Vice-Chancellor.

By evening Tchaikovsky was back in London, where he gave a farewell dinner to some of his new friends. Among these I must mention the fine baritone, Eugene Oudin. Tchaikovsky was soon very sincerely attached to him, both as a man and an artist. Upon his initiative Oudin was invited to sing at the Symphony Concerts in Moscow and Petersburg.

The following day Tchaikovsky left for Paris.

To P. Jurgenson.

"Paris, *June 3rd* (15*th*), 1893.

"Cambridge, with its peculiar customs which retain much that is medieval, with its colleges that resemble monasteries, and its buildings recalling a remote past, made a very agreeable impression upon me."

To N. Konradi.

"Paris, *June 3rd* (15*th*), 1893.

"At Cambridge I stayed with Professor Maitland. This would have been dreadfully embarrassing for me, if he and his wife had not proved to be some of the most charming people I ever met; and Russophiles into the bargain, which is the greatest rarity in England. Now all is over, it is pleasant to look back upon my visit to England, and to remember the extraordinary cordiality shown to me everywhere, although, in consequence of my peculiar temperament, while there, I tormented and worried myself to fiddle-strings."

XVIII

Tchaikovsky's home-coming was by no means joyful. The shadow of death was all around him. Hardly had he heard of the death of his old friend Karl Albrecht than a letter from the Countess Vassiliev-Shilovsky informed him that her husband had passed away. Besides this, Apukhtin lay dying in Petersburg, and in Moscow another valued friend, Zvierev, was in an equally hopeless condition.

A few years earlier one such grief would have affected Tchaikovsky more keenly than all of them taken together seemed to do at this juncture. Now death appeared to him less enigmatical and fearful. Whether his feelings were less acute, or whether the mental sufferings of later years had taught him that death was often a deliverance, I cannot say. I merely lay emphasis on the fact that, in spite of the discomforting news which met him in all directions, from the time of his return from England to the end of his life, Tchaikovsky was as serene and cheerful as at any period in his existence.

He looked forward with joy to meeting his nephew Vladimir Davidov at Grankino, in the government of Poltava. He always felt well in the glorious air of the steppes.

From Grankino he went to stay with his brother Nicholas at Oukolovo.

To Vladimir Davidov.

"*July* 19*th* (31*st*), 1893.

" I spent two very pleasant days in Moscow. Tell Modi I was very ill the day after he left. They said it was from drinking too much cold water at dinner and supper. . . . The day after to-morrow I start upon the Symphony again. I must write letters for the next two days."

To Modeste Tchaikovsky.

"*July* 22*nd* (*August* 3*rd*), 1893.

" I am up to my eyes in the Symphony. The further I go, the more difficult the orchestration becomes. Twenty years ago I should have rushed it through without a second thought, and it would have turned out all right. Now I am turning coward, and have lost my self-confidence. I have been sitting all day over two pages, yet they will not come out as I wish. In spite of this, the work makes progress, and I should not have done so much anywhere else but at home.

" Thanks to Alexis' exertions, my house has a very coquettish appearance. All is in order ; a mass of flowers in the garden, good paths, and a new fence with gates. I am well cared for. And yet I get terribly bored unless I am working. . . ."

To Vladimir Davidov.

"*August* 3*rd* (15*th*), 1893.

" The Symphony which I intended to dedicate to you— although I have now changed my mind[1]—is progressing. I am very well pleased with its contents, but not quite so satis-fied with the orchestration. It does not realise my dreams. To me, it will seem quite natural, and not in the least astonishing, if this Symphony meets with abuse, or scant appreciation at first. I certainly regard it as quite the best—and especially the ' most sincere '—of all my works. I love it as I never loved any one of my musical offspring before."

[1] This was merely a playful threat because his nephew had neglected to answer his letters.

To P. Jurgenson.

"KLIN, *August 12th* (*24th*), 1893.

"DEAR FRIEND,—I have finished the orchestration of the new Symphony. . . . I have made the arrangement for four hands myself, and must play it through, so I have asked the youngest Konius to come here, that we may try it together. As regards the score and parts, I cannot put them in order before the first performance, which takes place in Petersburg on October 16th (28th). . . . On my word of honour, I have never felt such self-satisfaction, such pride, such happiness, as in the consciousness that I am really the creator of this beautiful work."

To the same.

"KLIN, *August 20th* (*September 1st*), 1893.

"I shall take the Symphony with me to Petersburg to-day. I promise not to give away the score. The arrangement for four hands needs a thorough revision. I have entrusted this to Leo Konius. I wished him to receive a fee of at least 100 roubles, but he refused. . . ."

Tchaikovsky spent two days with Laroche in Petersburg. Even the prospect of his journey to Hamburg did not suffice to damp his cheerful frame of mind. He does not appear to have written any letters during his absence from Russia, which was of very brief duration.

"On his return from Hamburg he met me in St. Petersburg," says Modeste, "and stayed with me a day or two. I had not seen him so bright for a long time past. He was keenly interested in the forthcoming season of the Musical Society, and was preparing the programme of the fourth concert, which he was to conduct.

"At this time there was a change in the circumstances of my own life. Having finished the education of N. Konradi, I decided to set up housekeeping with my nephew Vladimir Davidov, who had completed his course at the School of Jurisprudence and was now an independent man. My brother was naturally very much interested in all the arrangements of our new home.

"At this time we discussed subjects for a new opera. Peter Ilich's favourite author in later life was George Eliot. Once during his travels abroad he had come across her finest book, *The Mill on the Floss*, and from that time he considered she had no rival but Tolstoi as a writer of fiction. *Adam Bede, Silas Marner*, and *Middlemarch* stirred him to the greatest enthusiasm, and he read them over and over again. He cared less for *Romola*, but was particularly fond of *Scenes from Clerical Life*. For a time he seriously contemplated founding the libretto of his next opera upon *The Sad Fortunes of the Rev. Amos Barton*. He wished me to read the tale and give him my opinion : I must confess that, from his own account of it, I persuaded him to give up the idea.

"I do not know if I actually convinced him, or whether he lost interest in it himself, but he never referred to this tale again when he spoke of other subjects for a libretto.

"We separated early in September, and he went to our brother Anatol, who was spending the summer and autumn with his family at Mikhailovskoe."

Here he enjoyed a very happy visit. "It is indescribably beautiful," he wrote to Modeste. "It is altogether pleasant and successful. The weather is wonderful. All day long I wander in the forest and bring home quantities of mushrooms."

His high opinion of the new Symphony was still unchanged, for he wrote to the Grand Duke Constantine Constantinovich on September 21st (October 3rd), "Without exaggeration I have put my whole soul into this work." Yet in spite of his cheerful attitude, a momentary cloud of depression passed over him at this time. Writing to Modeste from Moscow, a few days later, he says : "Just lately I have been dreadfully bored and misanthropical. I do not know why. I sit in my room and see no one but the waiter. I long for home, work, and my normal existence."

On September 25th he returned to Klin for the last time.

To Anna Merkling.

"*September 29th (October 11th),* 1893.

"I am now very busy with the orchestration of the Pianoforte Concerto. I shall soon appear on the banks of the Neva. You will see me about the 10th."

On October 7th (19th) Tchaikovsky left Klin never to return. The following day he intended to be present at the memorial service for his friend Zvierev and then to go on to Petersburg. As the train passed the village of Frolovskoe, he pointed to the churchyard, remarking to his fellow-travellers: "I shall be buried there, and people will point out my grave as they go by." He repeated this wish to be buried at Frolovskoe while talking to Taneiev at the memorial service for Zvierev. Beyond these two references to his death, prompted no doubt by the sad ceremony with which he was preoccupied, Tchaikovsky does not appear to have shown any symptoms of depression or foreboding.

Kashkin has given the following account of his friend's last visit to Moscow :—

"We met at the memorial service in the church, and afterwards Peter Ilich went to Zvierev's grave. On October 9th (21st) he had promised to go to the Conservatoire to hear the vocal quartet ('Night') which he had arranged from Mozart's pianoforte Fantasia. The master's music had not been altered, Tchaikovsky had only written words to it. . . . Madame Lavrovsky had promised that her pupils should learn the work. We assembled in the concert hall of the Conservatoire, and I sat with Tchaikovsky. The quartet was beautifully sung . . . Tchaikovsky afterwards told me this music had the most indescribable charm for him, but he could not explain, even to himself, why this simple melody gave him such pleasure. . . .

"At that time Pollini, the Director of the Hamburg Opera, was staying in Moscow. He was an ardent admirer of Tchaikovsky, and had given some of his operas in Hamburg. When—as invited—I went to supper with Tchaikovsky at the Moscow Restaurant, I met Pollini, Safonov, and two foreign guests. We talked over Pollini's idea of making a great concert tour through Russia, with a German orchestra under a Russian conductor . . . Tchaikovsky was to conduct his own works and Safonov the rest of the programme. . . . After the others had gone, and Peter Ilich and I were left to ourselves, he told me all about Cambridge, and spoke very warmly of the Professor in whose house he had stayed, and of one of the other recipients of the honorary degree—Arrigo Boïto, who had charmed him with his intellect and culture. . . . Unconsciously the talk turned to our recent losses : to the death of Albrecht and Zvierev. We thought of the gaps time had made in our circle of old friends and how few now remained. Involuntarily the question arose : Who will be the next to take the road from which there is no return? With complete assurance of its truth, I declared that Tchaikovsky would outlive us all. He disputed the probability, but ended by saying he had never felt better or happier in his life. He had to catch the night mail to Petersburg, where he was going to conduct his Sixth Symphony, which was still unknown to me. He said he had no doubt as to the first three movements, but the last was still a problem, and perhaps after the performance in Petersburg he should destroy the Finale and replace it by another. The concert of the Musical Society in Moscow was fixed for October 23rd (November 4th). We arranged, if we should not see each other there, to meet at the Moscow Restaurant, for Tchaikovsky was anxious to introduce the singer Eugene Oudin to the musical circle in Moscow. Here our conversation ended. Tchaikovsky went to the station. It never occurred to me to see him off, for neither of us cared for that kind of thing; besides, we should meet again in a fortnight. We parted without the least presentiment that it was for the last time."

XIX

Tchaikovsky arrived in Petersburg on October 10th (22nd). He was met by his brother Modeste and his favourite nephew. He was delighted with their new abode and his spirits were excellent—so long as his arrival remained unknown and he was master of his time.

One thing only depressed him : at the rehearsals the Sixth Symphony made no impression upon the orchestra. He always set store by the opinion of the musicians. Moreover, he feared lest the interpretation of the Symphony might suffer from their coldness. Tchaikovsky only conducted his works well when he knew they appealed to the players. To obtain delicate *nuances* and a good balance of tone he needed his surroundings to be sympathetic and appreciative. A look of indifference, a coolness on the part of any of the band, seemed to paralyse him ; he lost his head, went through the work perfunctorily, and cut the rehearsal as short as possible, so as to release the musicians from a wearisome task. Whenever he conducted a work of his own for the first time, a kind of uncertainty—almost carelessness—in the execution of details was apparent, and the whole interpretation lacked force and definite expression. The Fifth Symphony and *Hamlet* were so long making their way merely because the composer had failed to make them effective. The same reason accounts for the failure of the orchestral ballade, *The Voyevode*.

Tchaikovsky was easily disenchanted with his work by the adverse opinion of others. But on this occasion his judgment remained unshaken, and even the indifference of the orchestra did not alter his opinion that this Symphony was " the best thing I ever composed or ever shall compose." He did not, however, succeed in convincing the public or the performers. At the concert on the 16th (28th) the work fell rather flat. It was applauded and the composer was recalled; but the enthusiasm did not surpass what was usually shown for one of Tchaikovsky's new works. The Symphony produced nothing approaching to that powerful and thrilling impression it made shortly afterwards (November 6th (18th), 1893) under Napravnik, which has since been repeated in so many other cities.

The Press did not speak of the new Symphony with as much admiration as Tchaikovsky had expected, but on the whole the notices were appreciative. The *St. Petersburg Viedomosti* thought "the thematic material of the work was not very original, the leading subjects were neither new nor significant. The last movement, Adagio Lamentoso, was the best." The *Syn Otechestva* discovered a phrase in the first movement which recalled Gounod's *Romeo and Juliet*, while Grieg was reflected in the Finale. The *Novoe Vremya* said: "The new Symphony is evidently the outcome of a journey abroad; it contains much that is clever and resourceful as regards orchestral colour, besides grace and delicacy (in the two middle movements), but *as far as inspiration is concerned it stands far below Tchaikovsky's other Symphonies.* Only one newspaper, *The Birjevya Viedomosti*, spoke of the work in terms of unqualified praise, while finding fault with the composer's conducting of the work.

The morning after the concert I found my brother sitting at the breakfast-table with the score of the Symphony before him. He had agreed to send it to Jurgenson in Moscow that very day, and could not decide upon a title. He did not wish to designate it merely by a number, and had abandoned his original intention of calling it "a programme Symphony." "Why programme," he said, "since I do not intend to expound any meaning?" I suggested "tragic Symphony" as an appropriate title. But this did not please him either. I left the room while Peter Ilich was still in a state of indecision. Suddenly the word "pathetic" occurred to me, and I returned to suggest it. I remember, as though it were yesterday, how my brother exclaimed: "Bravo, Modeste, splendid! *Pathetic!*" Then and there, in my presence, he added to the score the title by which the Symphony has always been known.[1]

I do not relate this incident in order to connect my name with this work. Probably I should never have mentioned it but for the fact that it serves to illustrate in a simple way how far the conjectures of the most enlightened commentators may wander from the truth.

Hugo Riemann, in his thematic analysis of the Sixth Symphony, sees the solution of this title in "the striking resemblance between the fundamental idea of this work and the chief subject of Beethoven's *Sonata Pathétique*," of which Tchaikovsky never dreamed:

After having despatched the score to Moscow with this title, Tchaikovsky changed his mind, as may be seen from the following letter to Jurgenson :—

"*October 18th*, 1893.

"Be so kind as to put on the title page what stands below.

To Vladimir Lvovich Davidov

(No. 6)

Composed by P. T.

"I hope it is not too late.

---

[1] There was no other witness of this incident but myself. But it is clear from the programme of the concert of October 16th (28th) that this title had not then been given to the work. Moreover, anyone can see by a glance at the title-page that this name was written later than the rest.

3 A

" It is very strange about this Symphony. It was not exactly a failure, but was received with some hesitation. As far as I am concerned, I am prouder of it than of any of my previous works. However, we can soon talk it over together, for I shall be in Moscow on Saturday."

At this time he talked a great deal about the re-modelling of *The Oprichnik* and *The Maid of Orleans*, which he had in view for the immediate future. He did not confide to me his intentions as to the former opera; but as regards *The Maid of Orleans*, we discussed the alteration of the last scene, and I made a point of his arranging this, like so many other parts of the opera, from Schiller's poem. The idea seemed to interest him, but it was not permitted to him to come to a definite conclusion on the subject.

During these last days he was neither very cheerful, nor yet depressed. In the circle of his intimate friends he was contented and jovial; among strangers he was, as usual, nervous and excited and, as time went on, tired out and dull. But nothing gave the smallest hint of his approaching end.

On Tuesday, October 19th (31st), he went to a private performance of Rubinstein's *The Maccabees*. On the 20th (November 1st) he was still in good health and dined with his old friend Vera Boutakov (*née* Davidov). Afterwards he went to see Ostrovsky's play, *A Warm Heart*, at the Alexander Theatre. During the interval he went with me to see the actor Varlamov in his dressing-room. The conversation turned upon spiritualism. Varlamov de-scribed in his own humorous style—which cannot be transferred to paper—his loathing for "all those abomi-nations" which reminded one of death. Peter Ilich laughed at Varlamov's quaint way of expressing himself.

" There is plenty of time," said Tchaikovsky, " before we need reckon with this snub-nosed horror; it will not come to snatch us off just yet! I feel I shall live a long time."

From the theatre, Tchaikovsky went with his nephews, Count Litke and Baron Buxhövden, to the Restaurant Leiner. I joined them an hour later, and found one or two other visitors—of whom Glazounov was one. They had already had their supper; and I was afterwards told my brother had eaten macaroni and drunk, as usual, white wine and soda water. We went home about two a.m. Peter Ilich was perfectly well and serene.

On the morning of Thursday, October 21st (November 2nd), Tchaikovsky did not appear as usual at the early breakfast-table. His brother went to his room and found him slightly indisposed. He complained of his digestion being upset and of a bad night. About eleven a.m. he dressed and went out to see Napravnik. Half an hour later he returned, still feeling unwell. He absolutely declined to send for a doctor. His condition gave no anxiety to Modeste, who had often seen him suffer from similar derangements.

He joined his brother and nephew at lunch, although he ate nothing. But this was probably the fatal moment in his indisposition for, while talking, he poured out a glass of water and drank a long draught. The water had not been boiled, and they were dismayed at his imprudence. But he was not in the least alarmed, and tried to calm their fears. He dreaded cholera less than any other illness. After this his condition grew worse; but he attributed all his discomfort to a copious dose of Hunyadi which he had taken earlier in the day, and still declined to send for his favourite doctor, Bertenson. Towards evening Modeste grew so anxious that he sent for the doctor on his own account. Meanwhile Tchaikovsky was tended by his brother's servant Nazar, who had once travelled with him to Italy.

About eight p.m. Bertenson arrived. He saw at once that the illness was serious, and sent for his brother in consultation. The sufferer had grown very weak, and complained of terrible oppression on his chest. More than once he said, " I believe this is death."

After a short consultation the brothers Bertenson, the two leading physicians in Petersburg, pronounced it to be a case of cholera.

All night long those who nursed him in turn fought against the cramps ; towards morning with some hope of success. His courage was wonderful, and in the intervals between the paroxysms of pain he made little jokes with those around him. He constantly begged his nurses to take some rest, and was grateful for the smallest service.

On Friday his condition seemed more hopeful, and he himself believed he had been " snatched from the jaws of death." But on the following day his mental depression returned. " Leave me," he said to his doctors, " you can do no good. I shall never recover."

Gradually he passed into the second stage of the cholera, with its most dangerous symptom—complete inactivity of the kidneys. He slept more, but his sleep was restless, and sometimes he wandered in his mind. At these times he continually repeated the name of Nadejda Filaretovna von Meck in an indignant, or reproachful, tone. Conscious-ness returned at longer intervals, and when his servant Alexis arrived from Klin he was no longer able to recog-nise him. A warm bath was tried as a last resource, but without avail, and soon afterwards his pulse grew so weak that the end seemed imminent. At the desire of his brother Nicholas, a priest was sent for from the Isaac Cathedral. He did not administer the sacrament, as Tchaikovsky was now quite unconscious, but prayed in clear and distinct tones, which, however, did not seem to reach the ears of the dying man.

At three o'clock on the morning of October 25th (November 6th) Tchaikovsky passed away in the presence of his brothers Nicholas and Modeste, his nephews Litke, Buxhövden, and Vladimir Davidov, the three doctors, and his faithful servant Alexis Safronov.   At the last moment an indescribable look of clear recognition lit up his face— a gleam which only died away with his last breath.

My work is finished. With this account of Tchaikovsky's last moments my task, which was to express the man, is accomplished.

To characterise the artist in every phase of his development, and to determine his position in the history of music, is beyond my powers.   If all the documental and authentic evidence I have collected in this book should serve as fundamental material for another writer capable of fulfilling such a task, the most cherished aim of all my efforts will have been attained.

MODESTE TCHAIKOVSKY

ROME, 1902

APPENDIX A

CHRONOLOGICAL LIST OF TCHAIKOVSKY'S COMPOSITIONS FROM 1866–1893

First Season, 1866–1867

1. Op. 15. Festival Overture upon the Danish National Hymn; completed October, 1866. Published by Jurgenson.

2. Op. 13. Symphony in G minor, No. 1, "Winter Dreams." Begun in March, completed in November, 1866. Jurgenson.

3. Op. 1. Russian Scherzo and Impromptu. Composed early in 1867. The first of these compositions was originally entitled "Capriccio." It is based on the first theme of the Andante in the quartet in B major, which Tchaikovsky composed while still at the Conservatoire in 1865. The theme itself is a Malo-Russian folksong, heard at Kamenka. The Impromptu—a still earlier work—was never intended for publication. It chanced to be in the same manuscript-book as the Capriccio, which was given to Jurgenson by Rubinstein, without any intimation that the Impromptu was not to be published. The Russian Scherzo was performed at Rubinstein's concert in 1867. Both these works—like the *First Symphony*—were dedicated to Nicholas Rubinstein, and published by Jurgenson.

4. Op. 2. *Souvenir de Hapsal*—three pianoforte pieces: (*a*) "The Ruin," (*b*) "Scherzo," (*c*) "Chant sans Paroles." June and July, 1867. Hapsal. Only the first and third of these pieces were composed at Hapsal; the second dates back to the days of the Conservatoire. This *opus* number is dedicated to Vera Davidov. Jurgenson. Besides these works, Tchaikovsky was engaged from the beginning of 1867 upon his opera, *The Voyevode*.

1867–1868

The Voyevode was the sole work of this season.

In a letter dated November 25th (December 7th) Tchaikovsky speaks of having completed the third act, which is as good as saying that he had finished the whole opera, because he rarely broke through his custom of working straight through a composition. The instrumentation remained, and this was finished in Paris during the summer.

The Voyevode, or *A Dream on the Volga,* is a play in five acts, with a prologue, by A. N. Ostrovsky. The opera libretto is condensed into three acts, the prologue being omitted.

The chief beauty of the play, the scenes from national life, so charmingly depicted by Ostrovsky, had been ruthlessly cut out of the libretto, and only an insipid and uninteresting story left. The charm of national colour, the characteristic details of the secondary *dramatis personæ,* such as Nedviga, the apparition of the Domovoi, or "house spirit," the gloomy figure of Mizgir—of all these things the libretto had been completely denuded.

But it was not so much Ostrovsky as Tchaikovsky who was to blame, for it is evident from the manuscript which the latter used while composing the music that he eliminated every episode which did not bear directly upon the tale. A few years later Tchaikovsky would not have missed so many good opportunities of effective musical illustration.

Ostrovsky's collaboration was practically limited to Act I., which is also the best, and to a portion of Act II. The remainder is almost entirely of Tchaikovsky's own writing.

Of this opera only the "Dances of the Serving Maids" and the "Entr'acte" were published as Op. 3. Jurgenson. The rest of the score was destroyed by the composer during the seventies. The orchestral and choral parts and some of the solos—unfortunately not the principal ones—are still preserved in the library of the Imperial Opera House in Moscow.

1868–1869

1. Op. 77. Symphonic Poem, *Fatum.* Begun about the middle of September, 1868. Sketch completed on October 21st

(November 2nd). Orchestrated in November and December. Produced for the first time by the Musical Society in Moscow, February 25th (March 9th), 1869, conducted by N. Rubinstein. This work is dedicated to M. A. Balakirev. During the seventies Tchaikovsky destroyed the score, but the orchestral parts remained intact, and the work was reconstructed from these, and published in 1896, by Belaiev, in Leipzig.

2. Op. 4. Valse Caprice for pianoforte. Composed in October, 1868. Dedicated to Anton Door. Jurgenson.

3. Op. 5. Romance for pianoforte. November, 1868. Dedicated to Désirée Artôt. Jurgenson.

4. Twenty-five Russian folksongs, arranged for pianoforte, four hands. These were probably finished during the autumn months, and printed in November, 1868.

5. Recitatives and choruses for *Le Domino Noir*, by Auber. This work has entirely disappeared; it cannot be found in the library of the Petersburg or Moscow Opera.

6. *Undine*, an opera in three acts, begun in January and completed in July, 1869. The text by Count Sollogoub.

The libretto of *Undine* contained scenes more interesting and grateful for musical treatment than *The Voyevode*, but was so unskilfully put together and so lacking in logical sequence that it is even inferior to the dry, uninteresting, but literary verse of the latter. The music—judging from the fragments that have been preserved—seems to have possessed a certain vitality.

The composer destroyed the score of *Undine* in 1873. All that remains of the music is Undine's aria, " The spring is my brother," which was afterwards utilised in *Sniegourochka*, and the Wedding March in the last act, which Tchaikovsky employed in the Andantino Marziale of his Second Symphony. Besides these two fragments, Kashkin says an Adagio in the ballet, " The Swan Lake," was originally the love-duet between Gulbrand and Undine.

Part of this opera was produced at a concert given by the Capellmeister Merten, March 16th (28th), 1870. Laroche wrote :—

" Unfortunately, I was not able to attend the concert itself, but I had heard these fragments from *Undine* at the rehearsals, and observed not only the careful and delicate orchestration for which Tchaikovsky's music is remarkable, but picturesque suggestions of the fantastic realms of the water sprites. Other parts—notably the finale—appeared to me lacking in spontaneity. On the whole, however, the new score is worthy of attention."

1869–1870

1. Twenty-five Russian folksongs, arranged for pianoforte, four hands. Completed September 25th, 1869. Published, together with the twenty-five of the previous year, by Jurgenson, Moscow.

2. *Romeo and Juliet.* Overture-Fantasia for orchestra, founded on Shakespeare's tragedy. Begun September 25th (October 7th); sketch completed by October 7th (19th), and orchestrated by November 15th (27th), 1869. During the summer of 1870 the work was completely revised. According to Kashkin, the Introduction was entirely new; the funeral march at the close of the work was omitted and a fresh ending substituted for it, while many alterations were made in the orchestration as a whole. The overture is dedicated to Mily Alexandrovich Balakirev, and was performed for the first time at Moscow, under the bâton of N. Rubinstein, March 4th (16th), 1870. Published by Bote and Bock, Berlin, 1871.

3. Pianoforte arrangement for four hands of the overture *Ivan the Terrible*, by Anton Rubinstein. Bessel, St. Petersburg.

4. Op. 6. Six songs.[1] Written between November 15th (27th) and December 19th (31st), 1869. (1) "Glaub' nicht mein Freund," words by Count A. Tolstoi, dedicated to A. G. Menshikov. (2) "Nicht Worte," words by Plestcheiev, dedicated to N. Kashkin. (3) "Wie wehe, wie süss," words by Countess Rostopchin, dedicated to A. D. Kochetov. (4) "Die Thräne bebt," words by Count A. Tolstoi, dedicated to P. Jurgenson. (5) "Warum," words by Mey, dedicated to I. Klimenko. (6) "Nur wer die Sehnsucht kennt," words by Mey (from Goethe), dedicated to Madame Khvostova. P. Jurgenson, Moscow.

5. "Chorus of Insects," from the unfinished opera *Mandragora*,

---

[1] As several English versions exist of many of Tchaikovsky's songs, and some of these so-called translations have not even titles in common with the original texts, it is less misleading to keep to the German titles.—R. N.

January 13th (25th), 1870. The score of this work has been entirely lost. The pianoforte arrangement is preserved by Jurgenson. In 1898 Glazounov orchestrated it.

6. Op. 7. Valse Scherzo (A major) for pianoforte, dedicated to Alexandra Ilinichna Davidov. P. Jurgenson.

7. Op. 8. Capriccio (G flat) for piano, dedicated to K. Klindworth. P. Jurgenson. Both these pieces were completed about February 3rd (15th), 1870.

Besides the above, Tchaikovsky began his opera, *The Oprichnik*, about the end of January, 1870.

1870–1871

1. Op. 9. Three pianoforte pieces. (1) "Rêverie," dedicated to N. Murometz. (2) "Polka de Salon," dedicated to A. Zograf. (3) "Mazurka de Salon," dedicated to A. L. Dubuque.

2. Song, "So schnell vergessen," words by Apukhtin. This and the above works were composed before October 26th (November 7th), 1870, and published by Jurgenson, Moscow.

3. "Nature and Love." Trio for two sopranos and one contralto, with chorus and pianoforte accompaniment; dedicated to Madame Valzek. It was composed in December expressly for this lady's pupils, and performed for the first time at Tchaikovsky's concert on March 16th (28th), 1871. It was published by Jurgenson after the composer's death.

4. Op. 11. Quartet No. 1 (D major), for two violins, viola, and violoncello. Dedicated to Serge Rachinsky. Composed during February, 1871, and first performed at the composer's concert, March 16th (28th), 1871. The Andante of this quartet is based on a Russian folksong which Tchaikovsky wrote down at Kamenka in the summer of 1869. It was sung in Great Russian by a man who was working outside the room in which he was engaged in orchestrating his *Undine*.

5. A Course of Harmony, completed during the summer at Nizy. Jurgenson.

Besides the above, Tchaikovsky was working during the whole of this period on his opera, *The Oprichnik*.

1871–1872

1. Op. 10. Two pianoforte pieces : " Nocturne " and " Humoresque." Probably composed in December, 1871, during his stay at Nice. Part of the second piece consists of a French popular song. These pieces are both dedicated to Vladimir Shilovsky.

2. Cantata for chorus, orchestra, and tenor solo. Text by Polonsky. Composed during February and March, 1872. Performed May 31st (June 12th), 1872, under the conductorship of K. Davidov. The manuscript of the score is in the library of the Imperial Opera House, Moscow.

3. *The Oprichnik*, an opera in four acts. Begun at the end of January, 1870, completed in April, 1872. Dedicated to His Imperial Highness the Grand Duke Constantine Nicholaevich. Published by Bessel, St. Petersburg.

Without entering into a detailed criticism of Lajetnikov's tragedy, I must call attention to some of its features which are calculated to make it an easy subject for the librettist to handle ; these special features lie in its admirable plot. The interest of the love-intrigue, which is well sustained, a whole series of effective situations, the dark yet poetic colouring of its sinister period (Ivan the Terrible), the variety of episodes well suited to musical illustration (such as the love-duet in the first act, the scenes with the populace, the picturesque figures of the Oprichniks, the pathos of the oath scene, "The Terrible" himself, and the death of Andrew), all contribute to make an effective and moving opera.

But it did not fulfil these expectations. The most serious hindrance came from the Censor. The striking figure of Ivan the Terrible, which seemed so well adapted to musical representation, was not permitted to appear. For an outline of the plot of this opera, see Appendix B.

1872–1873

1. Op. 17. Symphony No. 2 (C minor), composed during June, July, and August, 1872. Orchestrated in September and October of the same year, and completed early in November.

Dedicated to the Moscow section of the Imperial Russian Musical Society. First performed, under N. Rubinstein, in Moscow, January 26th (February 7th), 1873. Published by V. Bessel, St. Petersburg. The second movement, Andantino Marziale, is taken from the opera *Undine*. Speaking of this work, Kashkin says, "It may be called 'The Little Russian' Symphony, because its chief themes are Little Russian folksongs."[1] Later on the composer made considerable alterations, and entirely rewrote the first movement.

2. Op. 16. Six songs. (1) "Wiegenlied," words by Maikov, dedicated to Frau N. N. Rimsky-Korsakov. (2) "Warte noch," words by Grekov, dedicated to N. A. Rimsky-Korsakov. (3) "Erfass nur einmal," words by Maikov, dedicated to G. A. Laroche. (4) "Oh, möchtest du einmal noch singen," words by Plestcheiev, dedicated to N. A. Hubert. (5) "Was nun?" Words by the composer, dedicated to N. Rubinstein. (6) "Neugriechisches Lied," words by Maikov, dedicated to K. Albrecht. The precise date of these songs is not known. Probably they were written in December, 1872. Published by V. Bessel, St. Petersburg.

3. Op. 12. Music to *Sniegourochka, a Legend of Springtide*, by A. N. Ostrovsky. Composed during March and April, 1873. First performed at the Opera, Moscow, May 11th (23rd), 1873. Jurgenson, Moscow. One or two numbers of this work are transferred from *Undine*.

4. "Perpetuum mobile," from a sonata by Weber, arranged for the left hand only. Dedicated to Madame Zograf. Published 1873, by Jurgenson.

Besides the above, Tchaikovsky worked at the symphonic fantasia, *The Tempest*, between August 7th–17th (19th–29th), 1873.

His literary work comprised seventeen articles, in which he reviewed the chief musical events of the season in Moscow.

---

[1] The Introduction is the Malo-Russian variant of "Down by Mother Volga," the Finale is based upon a popular tune called "The Crane."—R.N.

1873-1874

1. Op. 18. *The Tempest*, symphonic fantasia for full orchestra upon a Shakespearean programme. Composed between 7th (19th) and 17th (29th) August, 1873; orchestrated by October 10th (22nd). Dedicated to Vladimir Vassilievich Stassov. First performed December 7th (19th), 1873, under N. Rubinstein. Jurgenson.

2. Op. 21. Six pianoforte pieces upon a theme. (1) Prelude, (2) Fugue, (3) Impromptu, (4) Funeral March, (5) Mazurka, (6) Scherzo. Dedicated to Anton Rubinstein. Composed before October 30th (November 11th), 1873. Bessel.

3. Op. 22. Quartet No. 2 (F major), for two violins, viola, and violoncello. Dedicated to the Grand Duke Constantine. Commenced at the end of December, 1873, or early in January, 1874, and finished by the 26th of that month. Shortly afterwards it was played at a musical evening at N. Rubinstein's, and probably Tchaikovsky afterwards made some changes in it, as he was still engaged upon the work in the middle of February. First public performance March 10th (22nd), 1874. Jurgenson.

4. Op. 14. *Vakoula the Smith* (Kouznetz Vakoula, known also as *Cherevichek* and *Les Caprices d'Oxane*), opera in three acts and seven scenes. The libretto is taken from a tale by Gogol and set to verse by J. Polonsky. Dedicated to the memory of the Grand Duchess Helena. Composed and orchestrated during the summer of 1874. Partially remodelled about 1885. Published by Jurgenson.

1874-1875

1. Op. 25. Six songs: (1) "Herz, o lass dich von Schlummer umfangen," words by Scherbin, dedicated to A. P. Kroutikov. (2) "Wie hier die Schrift in Aschengluth," words by Tioutchev, dedicated to D. Orlov. (3) "Mignon's Lied," words by Goethe, dedicated to M. Kamenskaya. (4) "Der Kanarienvogel," words by Mey, dedicated to V. Raab. (5) "Mit ihr ein Wort gesprochen hab' ich nie," words by Mey, dedicated to I. Melnikov. (6) "Einst zum Narren Jemand spricht," words by Mey. These

songs were probably composed in September, 1874. Published by V. Bessel.

2. Op. 19. Six pianoforte pieces : (1) " Rêverie," dedicated to N. D. Kondratiev. (2) "Scherzo-humoristique," dedicated to Vera Timanov. (3) " Feuillet d'album," dedicated to A. Abramov. (4) " Nocturne," dedicated to Frau Terminsky. (5) Capriccio, dedicated to E. Langer. (6) " Thème avec Variations," dedicated to H. Laroche. The manuscript is dated October 27th (November 8th), 1873. Jurgenson.

3. Op. 23. Concerto for pianoforte and orchestra (in B♭ minor). Composed in November and December, 1874. The orchestration was completed, according to a note on the score, February 9th (21st), 1875. Dedicated to Hans von Bülow. Published by Jurgenson. In a letter to Frau von Meck, Tchaikovsky says he took as the principal subject of the first movement a phrase sung by Malo-Russian blind beggars at a village fair at Kamenka.

Besides the example just quoted, he also borrowed another air, the chansonette, " Il faut s'amuser, danser, et rire," which the twins used to hum early in the seventies, in remembrance of a certain charming singer.

4. Op. 26. Serenade for violin, with orchestral accompaniment (B minor). Composed January, 1875. Dedicated to L. Auer. Jurgenson.

5. Op. 27. Six songs : (1) "An den Schlaf," words by Ogariev. (2) "Ob sich die Wolke dort," words by Grekov. (3) "Geh' nicht von mir," words by Fet. (4) " Abend," words by Chevchenko. (5) " Klage," words by Mickiewicz. (6) "Dem Vöglein gleich," words by Mickiewicz. All six dedicated to Madame Lavrovskaya. The date of composition not precisely known. Jurgenson.

6. Op. 28. Six songs : (1) "Nein, wen ich liebe," words from de Musset, dedicated to A. Nikholaev. (2) " Die rothe Perlenschnur," words by Syrokomli, dedicated to D. Dodonov. (3)

"Warum im Traume," words by Mey, dedicated to Frau Ilina. (4) "Er liebte mich so sehr," words by Apukhtin, dedicated to E. Marsini. (5) "Kein Wort von Dir," words by Alexis Tolstoi, dedicated to B. Korsov. (6) "Ein einzig Wörtchen," text by P. Tchaikovsky, dedicated to Frau E. Kadmina. The date of completion is given on the manuscript as April 11th (23rd), 1875, in Moscow. Jurgenson.

7. Op. 29. Symphony No. 3 (in D major) in five movements. The score bears the following note in the composer's own writing: "Commenced June 5th (17th) at Ussovo, completed August 1st (13th), 1875, at Verbovka." Published by Jurgenson. Played for the first time in Moscow, November 7th (19th), 1875.

Besides the above works, Tchaikovsky was engaged during part of August, 1875, upon the Ballet, *The Swan Lake.*

His literary activity was very considerable. Between September, 1874, and April, 1875, he wrote not less than fifteen articles.

1875–1876

1. Op. 30. Quartet No. 3 in E flat minor, for two violins, viola, and 'cello, dedicated to the memory of F. Laub. The first sketch dates from the beginning of January, 1876, in Paris. Finished, according to date upon the manuscript, February 18th (March 1st), 1876. Performed for the first time March 18th (30th) of the same year at Grijimaly's concert. Published by Jurgenson.

2. Op. 20. *The Swan Lake.* Ballet in four acts. Begun August, 1875, finished at the end of March, 1876. Published by Jurgenson. First performance at the Opera House, Moscow, February 20th (March 4th), 1877.

3. Op. 37. *The Seasons,* twelve pieces for piano. These were written in the course of the year, one piece each month, and were commissioned by the publisher of a St. Petersburg musical journal. Kashkin tells us that Tchaikovsky did not consider this a very important work, but in order not to miss sending each number at the right time, he ordered his servant to remind him

when a certain date came round in each month. The man carried out his master's order, coming at the right day with the reminder: "Peter Ilich, is it not time to send to St. Petersburg?" upon which Tchaikovsky would sit down at once and write the required piece without a pause. Later the pieces were collected and republished by Jurgenson.

4. The translation of the libretto and arrangement of the recitatives of Mozart's *Figaro*, which Tchaikovsky undertook (at the desire of N. Rubinstein) for a performance of this opera by the students of the Conservatoire.

This season Peter Ilich brought his literary work to an end. His last criticisms dealt with Wagner's Trilogy, and remained unfinished.

1876–1877

1. Op. 31. Slavonic March for full orchestra. First performance in November, 1877, under N. Rubinstein's bâton, at a symphony concert in Moscow. Jurgenson.

2. Op. 32. *Francesca da Rimini* (after Dante), symphonic fantasia for full orchestra. Dedicated to S. I. Taneiev. Tchaikovsky sketched the plan of this work during his visit to Paris in the summer of 1876. He did not actually work at the composition until the end of September. The sketch was finished October 14th (26th), the orchestration November 5th (17th). First performance, under N. Rubinstein, at a symphony concert, Moscow, February 26th (March 10th), 1877. Jurgenson.

3. Op. 33. *Variations on a Rococo Theme*, for violoncello and orchestra. Dedicated to G. Fitzenhagen. Composed December, 1876. Jurgenson.

4. Op. 34. Valse Scherzo, for violin and orchestra. Dedicated to Joseph Kotek. Composed early in January, 1877. Jurgenson.

During this season Tchaikovsky sketched out his Fourth Symphony and two-thirds of his opera, *Eugene Oniegin*.

1877–1878

1. Op. 36, Symphony No. 4 (F minor), in four movements. Dedicated to "My best friend." The first sketch was finished in

May, 1877. On August 11th (23rd) Tchaikovsky began the instrumentation of the work, and completed the first movement on September 12th (24th). After an interval of two months he returned to the Symphony, about the end of November. The Andante was finished on December 15th (27th), the Scherzo on the 20th (January 1st) 1878, and the Finale on the 26th (January 7th, 1878). The first performance of the Symphony took place February 10th (22nd), 1878, at a concert of the Russian Musical Society, conducted by N. Rubinstein.

2. Op. 24, *Eugene Oniegin*, lyric scenes, in three acts and seven scenes. The libretto is freely arranged from Poushkin by the composer himself and K. S. Shilovsky. The idea of this opera originated with the celebrated singer, Madame E. A. Lavrovsky.

On May 18th (30th), 1877, Tchaikovsky sketched the plan for a libretto.

On June 6th (18th) the second scene of the first act (the Letter Scene) was finished, and by June 15th (27th) the entire act was complete. By June 23rd (July 5th), two-thirds of the opera were ready. After a month's respite, Tchaikovsky returned to the work at Kamenka, in August, and completed the opera. Here he also began the instrumentation. During September and the first half of October he did not work upon it at all; afterwards he continued the instrumentation, finishing the whole of the first act and despatching it to Moscow by the 23rd (November 4th). In November Tchaikovsky orchestrated the first scene of the second act. The whole of December was devoted to the Fourth Symphony. On January 2nd (14th) he took up the opera once more, at San Remo, and, completed it by the 20th (February 1st) of this month. In the summer of 1880, at the request of the Director of the Imperial Opera, Tchaikovsky added an *écossaise* to the first scene of Act II. and made some slight changes in the Finale.

The first performance of the opera took place on March 17th (29th), 1879, by the students of the Moscow Conservatoire, in the Small Theatre. For an account of the plot, see Appendix B.

3. Op. 38. Six songs, dedicated to A. Tchaikovsky. (1) " Don Juan's Serenade," words by Count A. Tolstoi ; (2) " Das war im

3 B

ersten Lenzesstrahl" (A. Tolstoi); (3) "Im erregenden Tanze" (A. Tolstoi); (4) "Ach wenn du könntest" (A. Tolstoi); (5) "Aus dem Jenseits" (Lermontov); (6) "Pimpinella" (Florentine song). Published by P. I. Jurgenson, Moscow.

4. Op. 40. Twelve pieces for pianoforte (medium difficulty), dedicated to M. Tchaikovsky. (1) "Etude," (2) "Chanson triste," (3) "Marche funèbre," (4) "Mazurka in C major," (5) "Mazurka in D major," (6) "Chant sans paroles," (7) "Au village," (8) "Valse in A major," (9) "Valse in A major," (10) "Danse russe," (11) "Scherzo in F major," (12) "Rêverie interrompue." Of these pieces, No. 12 was composed first. The middle section of this piece is a Venetian song, which was sung almost every evening under his window in Venice. The other pieces date from various times, the "Danse russe" from 1876, having been originally intended as a number for the Ballet, *The Swan Lake*. Jurgenson, Moscow.

5. Op. 37. Sonata for pianoforte (G major), in four movements. Dedicated to Carl Klindworth. Commenced early in March, 1878, at Clarens, and completed on April 30th (May 12th). First performed in public by Nicholas Rubinstein, in Moscow, October 21st (November 2nd), 1879.

6. Op. 35. Concerto for violin and orchestra. Originally dedicated to L. Auer. Tchaikovsky afterwards substituted the name of A. Brodsky. Begun early in March, 1878, at Clarens, and the sketch finished by the 16th (28th) of the same month. The original Andante did not satisfy the composer, who wrote a new one. The instrumentation was completed by the end of April. First performance by A. Brodsky, in Vienna (1879). Jurgenson.

7. Op. 42. "Souvenir d'un lieu cher," three pieces for violin and pianoforte accompaniment. No. 1 is the original Andante of the Violin Concerto. The other two pieces were composed at Brailov about the end of May. Jurgenson.

8. Op. 41. The Liturgy of St. John Chrysostom, for four-part mixed chorus. Commenced May, 1878, at Kamenka, and finished on the 27th (June 8th) at Brailov. Jurgenson.

9. Op. 39. Kinderalbum, twenty-four easy pieces for pianoforte (*à la* Schumann). Dedicated to Volodya Davidov. P. I. Jurgenson.

10. "Skobeliev March," composed by "Sinopov." Tchaikovsky concealed the authorship of this piece, because he considered it of no value. It was commissioned by Jurgenson at the end of April, and composed at Kamenka.

Besides these works, Tchaikovsky translated in December, 1877, the Italian words of six songs by Glinka, and wrote the text of a vocal quartet, also by Glinka.

The greater part of his First Suite was also completed during August, 1878.

1878–1879

1. Op. 43. First Suite, for full orchestra, in six movements.

The first sketches were made at Verbovka between August 15th and 25th, 1878. Originally the Suite was intended to have five movements only: Introduction and Fugue, Scherzo, Andante, Intermezzo ("Echo du bal"), and Rondo. Of these, three movements were completed, the fourth sketched out, and the fifth projected, when Tchaikovsky laid it aside, only to return to it in November while in Florence. On the 13th (25th) of this month it was finished. The last two movements, however, received different titles, "March Miniature" (4th) and "Giants' Dance" (5th). In August, 1879, the composer added a sixth movement, Divertimento. The work was first performed in Moscow, under Nicholas Rubinstein. Published by Jurgenson.

2. *The Maid of Orleans*, an opera in four acts and six scenes, dedicated to E. Napravnik.

The libretto of this work was written by Tchaikovsky himself. It is chiefly based upon Joukovsky's translation of Schiller's *Maid of Orleans*, but some ideas were also derived from Wallon, Barbier's play, and the libretto of Mermet's opera on the same subject. It is a pity the composer did nor confine himself to Schiller's work, and more especially as regards the uninteresting and gloomy ending. Shortly before his death Tchaikovsky frequently spoke of altering the last scene and substituting Schiller's close. With this intention, he purchased the works of the German poet, but unfortunately he was not destined to read the tragedy again. For the plot of *The Maid of Orleans*, see Appendix B.

1879–1880

1. Op. 44. Second Concerto, for pianoforte and orchestra, in three movements. Dedicated to N. Rubinstein. Played for the first time in public on May 22nd (June 3rd), 1882, by S. I. Taneiev. Jurgenson.

2. The revised edition of the Second Symphony. Published by Bessel.

3. The " Italian Capriccio," for full orchestra. Dedicated to K. Davidov. The opening fanfare in this work is a bugle call of the Italian cavalry, which Tchaikovsky heard every evening while living in the Hôtel Constanzi, next to the barracks of the Royal Cuirassiers. Jurgenson.

4. Music for a *tableau vivant :* " Montenegro at the moment of receiving the news of war between Russia and Turkey. A village elder reading out the manifesto." This music was never performed, as the projected entertainment fell through. The manuscript has entirely disappeared.

5. Six vocal duets, with pianoforte accompaniment. Dedicated to Tatiana Davidov : (*a*) " Der Abend," (*b*) " Ballade," (*c*) " Thränen," (*d*) " Im Garten," (*e*) " Leidenschaft," (*f*) " Dämmerung." Jurgenson.

6. Op. 47. Seven songs, with pianoforte accompaniment. Dedicated to A. V. Panaiev : (*a*) " Wenn ich das gewusst," (*b*) " Durch die Gefilde des Himmels," (*c*) " Der Dämmerung Schleier sank," (*d*) " Schlaf ein, betrübtes Lieb," (*e*) " Gesegnet sei mir Wald und Au," (*f*) " Ob Heller Tag," (*g*) " War ich nicht ein Halm." Jurgenson.

Besides the above, Tchaikovsky revised the overture, *Romeo and Juliet.*

1880–1881

1. Serenade for string orchestra, in four movements. Dedicated to Carl Albrecht. First performance January 16th (28th), under the direction of Erdmannsdörfer. Published by Jurgenson.

2. Op. 49. *The Year 1812*, festival overture for full orchestra. Composed for the consecration of the Cathedral of the Saviour, Moscow. Jurgenson.

Besides the above, an attempt to harmonise the Vesper Service and the first sketch of the opera, *Mazeppa*.

1881–1882

1. Op. 50. Trio for pianoforte, violin, and violoncello. Dedicated to the memory of a great artist (N. G. Rubinstein). The variation theme of the second movement is a reminiscence of an excursion made in company with Nicholas Rubinstein, and other colleagues from the Moscow Conservatoire, shortly after the first performance of *Sniegourochka* (*The Snow Maiden*), in the spring of 1873. The Trio was played for the first time in public on October 18th (30th), 1882, by Taneiev, Grijimaly, and Fitzenhagen. Published by Jurgenson.

2. An attempt to harmonise Divine Service. Setting for mixed chorus. Seventeen numbers. Jurgenson.

From June to October Tchaikovsky was occupied in editing the works of Bortniansky.

During this year he began the sketch of the opera, *Mazeppa*. By the middle of July two acts were completed.

1882–1883

1. Op. 51. Six pieces for pianoforte: (1) "Valse de Salon," (2) "Polka peu dansante," (3) "Menuetto scherzoso," (4) "Natha —Valse," (5) "Romance," (6) "Valse sentimentale."

These pieces were commissioned by the brothers Jurgenson and composed at Kamenka about the end of August.

2. Verses upon the theme of the "Slavsia," from Glinka's *A Life for the Tsar*, winding up with the Russian National Anthem, for chorus and orchestra.

This chorus was sung by 7,500 students in Moscow, May 10th (22nd), 1883, at the moment when the Emperor Alexander III. appeared at the Red Staircase upon his solemn entry to the Kremlin. (Manuscript only.)

3. Festal Coronation March for orchestra. Commissioned by the city of Moscow, first performed at Sokolinky, on May 23rd (June 4th), at a fête in honour of the Coronation. Jurgenson.

4. *Mazeppa*, an opera, in three acts and six scenes. The

subject is taken from Poushkin's poem, *Poltava*, arranged by Bourenin and the composer himself.

The opera was first performed at the Imperial Opera, Moscow, February 3rd (15th), 1884. Jurgenson. For the plot, see Appendix B.

Besides the above, Tchaikovsky began his Second Suite for orchestra during the summer of 1883.

1883 TO JANUARY, 1885

1. Op. 53. Suite No. 2, in four movements, for full orchestra. Dedicated to Madame P. W. Tchaikovsky. First performed at an extra concert of the Russian Musical Society, February 4th (16th), 1884, in Moscow, under the direction of Max Erdmannsdörfer. Published by Jurgenson.

2. Op. 54. Sixteen Children's Songs, with pianoforte accompaniment. Published by Jurgenson.

3. Op. 55. Suite No. 3, in four movements, for full orchestra. Dedicated to M. Erdmannsdörfer. First performance in Petersburg, in January, 1885, under the direction of Hans von Bülow. Published by Jurgenson.

4. Op. 56. Fantasia Concerto, in two movements, for pianoforte, with orchestral accompaniment. Originally dedicated to Madame A. Essipoff; afterwards to Madame Sophie Menter. Played for the first time by S. Taneiev, February 22nd (March 6th), 1885, in Moscow. Published by Jurgenson.

5. Impromptu Capriccio for pianoforte. Dedicated to Madame S. Jurgenson. Originally published in the "Subscribers' Album" of Paris *Gaulois*. Was taken over later by Jurgenson.

6. Elegy for string orchestra. Composed in memory of the actor, I. Samarin. Published by Jurgenson.

7. Three church anthems. Published by Jurgenson.

8. Op. 57. Six songs, with pianoforte accompaniment. (1) "O, sprich, wovon die Nachtigall," (2) "Auf's bleiche Herbstgefild," (3) "O, frage nicht," (4) "Schlaf' ein," (5) "Der Tod," (6) "Nur du allein." Published by Jurgenson. Besides the above, Tchaikovsky had been working, in November, 1884, at the reconstruction of his opera, *Vakoula the Smith*.

FROM JANUARY 1ST TO SEPTEMBER 12TH, 1885

1. Remodelling the opera *Vakoula the Smith* as *Les Caprices d'Oxane*. Besides simplifying the orchestration and harmony and cutting down the work, as he first proposed, Tchaikovsky also introduced some entirely new numbers: (1) the duet between Vakoula and Oxane and the Finale of the second scene in first act, (2) the Schoolmaster's song, (3) the quintet in the first scene of the second act, (4) the couplets in third act. Published by Jurgenson.

2. Hymn in honour of Saints Cyril and Methodius. This hymn is an old Slavonic melody arranged for a choir :—

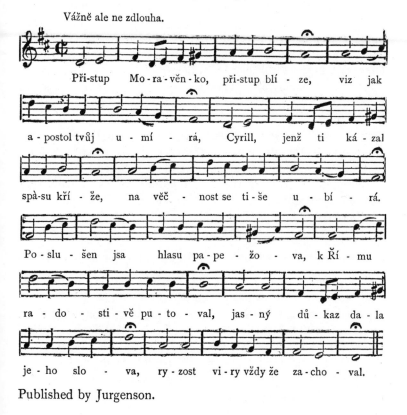

Vážně ale ne zdlouha.

Při-stup Mo-ra-věn-ko, při-stup blí - ze, viz jak
a - postol tvůj u - mí - rá, Cyrill, jenž ti ká - zal
spà-su kří - že, na věč - nost se ti-še u - bí - rá.
Po-slu - šen jsa hlasu pa-pe - žo - va, k Ří - mu
ra - do - sti - vě pu - to - val, jas-ný dů - kaz da - la
je - ho slo - va, ry - zost vi - ry vždy že za - cho - val.

Published by Jurgenson.

3. Five church hymns. Published by Jurgenson.

4 "Ecossaise," for the sixth scene in the opera *Eugene Oniegin*. Tchaikovsky composed and orchestrated this piece in Maidanovo and sent it to St. Petersburg all in one day.

5. Op. 58. *Manfred*. A Symphony in four scenes for full orchestra, from a dramatic poem by Lord Byron. Dedicated to Mily Balakirev. The first sketches for this work were made in April, 1885. According to the note on the score, it was finished December 12th (24th), 1885, and played for the first time March 11th (23rd), 1886, under the direction of Erdmanns-dörfer, in Moscow. Published by Jurgenson.

1885–1886

1. Text and music of a chorus for the fiftieth anniversary of the foundation of the Imperial School of Jurisprudence. Composed at Maidanovo, September, 1885. Manuscript.

2. "Jurists' March," for full orchestra. Composed at Kamenka, October, 1885. Published by Jurgenson.

3. The "Domovoi" ("House Spirit"), from a scene in Ostrovsky's play, *The Voyevode*. Composed January, 1886. Manuscript.

4. Op. 59. "Dumka." Russian village scene for the pianoforte. Dedicated to the Principal of the Paris Conservatoire, A. Marmontel. Composed at Maidanovo end of February. Published by Jurgenson. Besides these unimportant works, Tchaikovsky was engaged during the whole season upon his opera, *The Enchantress*.

1886–1887

(FROM SEPTEMBER 1ST, 1886, TO JANUARY 1ST, 1888)

1. Op. 60. Twelve songs, with pianoforte accompaniment. Dedicated to Her Majesty the Empress Maria Feodorovna. (1) "Die gestrige Nacht," (2) "Verschwiegenheit," (3) "O, wüsstest Du," (4) "Die Nachtigall," (5) "Schlichte Worte," (6) "Die Schlaflose Nächte," (7) "Lied der Zigeunerin," (8) "Lebewohl," (9) "Die Nacht," (10) "Lockung," (11) "Heldenmut," (12) "Sternennacht." Published by Jurgenson.

2. *The Enchantress*, opera in four acts. The libretto by

I. V. Shpajinsky, author of the drama of the same name. First performed on October 20th (November 1st), 1887, at the Maryinsky Theatre, St. Petersburg, and conducted by the composer. Jurgenson. For plot, see Appendix B.

3. Op. 61. *Mozartiana*. Suite No. 4, in four movements, arranged from various works of Mozart and orchestrated for full orchestra. In his short preface to the score Tchaikovsky gives the following reasons which prompted this work : " A large number of the most beautiful of Mozart's smaller works are, for some reason, little known, not only to the public, but to musicians. The composer's object in arranging this Suite was to bring more frequently before the public works which, however modest in form, are gems of musical literature." First performed at Moscow, November 14th (26th), 1887, under the direction of the composer. Jurgenson.

4. Op. 62. "Pezzo Capriccioso," for violoncello, with orchestral accompaniment. Dedicated to A. Brandoukov. Played by him for the first time, November 25th (December 7th), 1889. Jurgenson.

5. Op. 63. Six songs. Dedicated to the Grand Duke Constantine Constantinovich. (1) " Nicht sogleich," (2) " Am offenen Fenster," (3) " Fahrt hin, ihr Träume," (4) Wiedersehen," (5) " Kein Lichtlein glänzt," (6) "Serenade." Jurgenson.

6. A chorus for men's voices *a capella*. Dedicated to the Students' Choir of the Moscow University. Published by Jurgenson.

1888 (FROM JANUARY 1ST TO SEPTEMBER 1ST)

1. Op. 64. Symphony No. 5 (E minor), in four movements, for full orchestra Dedicated to Herr Theodor Ave-Lallemant of Hamburg. First performance in Petersburg, November, 1888, conducted by the composer. Published by Jurgenson.

2. Op. 65. Six songs to French words, with pianoforte accompaniment. Dedicated to Désirée Artôt. (1) "Où vas-tu souffle d'aurore?" (2) " Déception," (3) " Sérénade," (4) " Qu'importe que l'hiver," (5) "Les larmes," (6) " Rondel." Composed in the course of the summer. Jurgenson.

3. "Die Nachtigall," chorus *a capella*. Dedicated to the

mixed choir of the Petersburg Imperial Opera House.   Exact date of composition unknown.   Jurgenson.

Besides the above, Tchaikovsky completed the sketches for the overture-fantasia, *Hamlet.*

1888–1889

1. Orchestration of an overture by Laroche.   Manuscript.

2. Op. 67.   *Hamlet,* overture-fantasia for full orchestra. Dedicated to Edvard Grieg.   Jurgenson.

3. Valse Scherzo, for pianoforte.   Jurgenson.

4. Op. 66.   *Dornröschen* (Sleeping Beauty).   Ballet in three acts, with a prologue.   Dedicated to I. A. Vsievolojsky.   The subject is taken from Perrault's fairy tale of the same name.

The first performance of the Ballet took place January 3rd (15th), 1890, in the Maryinsky Theatre, Petersburg.   Jurgenson.

1889–1890

1. Impromptu for pianoforte.   Dedicated to A. Rubinstein. Jurgenson.

2. "Greeting to A. G. Rubinstein," chorus *a capella.* Jurgenson.

3. *Pique Dame.*   Opera in three acts and seven scenes. Libretto by Modeste Tchaikovsky.   The subject is taken from Poushkin's novel of the same name.   The first performance took place in the Maryinsky Theatre, in Petersburg, December 7th (19th), 1890.   Published by Jurgenson.   For plot, see Appendix B.

Besides the above, on June 13th Tchaikovsky began to compose a Sextet for Strings, of which the sketches were finished by June 30th.

1890–1891

1. Op. 67a.   Music to Shakespeare's *Hamlet.*   Overture, melodramas, fanfares, marches, and entr'actes for small orchestra. Seventeen numbers in all, of which, however, some are transferred from earlier works.   Jurgenson.

2. Three choruses *a capella.*   Composed at Frolovskoe, and

dedicated to I. A. Melnikov's "Gratuitous Choral Class." Published in Melnikov's *Collection of Russian Choruses.*

Besides the above, Tchaikovsky finished the sketches of the *Nut-cracker* Ballet and of the opera of *Iolanthe.*

1891–1892

1. Op. 78. *The Voyevode,* symphonic ballad, for full orchestra (after Poushkin). First performance under the direction of the composer, at a concert given by Siloti, November 6th (18th), 1891. The following day Tchaikovsky himself destroyed the score of this work, the band parts remaining in Siloti's keeping. After the composer's death the score was restored from the parts and published by Belaiev.

2. Op. 69. *Iolanthe.* Lyrical opera in one act. The subject founded on the drama, *King René's Daughter,* by the Danish poet, Henrik Herz. The libretto by Modeste Tchaikovsky. First performed in Petersburg in the Maryinsky Theatre, December 6th (18th), 1892. Published by Jurgenson. See Appendix B.

3. Op. 70. "Souvenir de Florence." Sextet for two violins, two violas, and two violoncellos, in four movements. Dedicated to the Petersburg Chamber Music Society. First performance by this society November 25th (December 7th), 1892. Published by Jurgenson.

4. Op. 71. *The Nut-cracker.* Fairy Ballet in two acts and three scenes. The subject is borrowed from A. Dumas' version of Hoffman's fairy tale. The following programme was suggested to Tchaikovsky by the gifted ballet-master, Petipa :—

No. 1. Soft music. Sixty-four bars.

No. 2. The tree is lit up. Sparkling music. Eight bars.

No. 3. Enter the children. Animated and joyous music. Twenty-four bars.

No. 4. A moment of surprise and admiration. A few bars of tremolo.

No. 5. A march. Sixty-four bars.

No. 6. Entrée des Incroyables. Sixteen bars, rococo (tempo menuet).

No. 7. Galop.

No. 8. Enter Drosselmeyer. Awe-inspiring but comic music. A broad movement, sixteen to twenty-four bars.

The music gradually changes character—twenty-four bars. It becomes less serious, lighter, and finally gay in tone.

Grave music for eight bars, then pause.

Repeat the eight bars—pause.

Four bars which express astonishment.

No. 9. Eight bars in mazurka rhythm. Eight more. Sixteen still in mazurka rhythm.

No. 10. A piquant, spicy valse, strongly rhythmic. Forty-eight bars.

1892–1893

1. Military march. Dedicated to the 98th Infantry Regiment. Tchaikovsky's cousin, Andrew Petrovich Tchaikovsky, colonel of this regiment, asked him in February, 1893, to compose this march.

2. Op. 72. Eighteen pieces for pianoforte. (1) "Impromptu," (2) "Berceuse," (3) "Tendres reproches," (4) "Danse caractéristique," (5) "Méditation," (6) "Mazurque pour danser," (7) "Polacca de Concert," (8) "Dialogue," (9) "Un poco di Schumann," (10) "Scherzo-Fantaisie," (11) "Valse-Bluette," (12) "L'Espiègle," (13) "Echo rustique," (14) "Chant élégiaque," (15) "Un poco di Chopin," (16) "Valse à cinq temps," (17) "Passé lointain," (18) "Scène dansante. Invitation au trépak." Published by Jurgenson.

3. Op. 73. Six songs, with pianoforte accompaniment. Words by D. Rathaus. Dedicated to N. Figner. (1) "An den schlummernden Strom," (2) "Nachts," (3) "O, du mondhelle Nacht," (4) "Sonne ging zur Ruhe," (5) "In Trüber Stunde," (6) "Weil ich wie einstmals." Published by Jurgenson.

4. "Night." Quartet for soprano, alto, tenor, and bass, with pianoforte accompaniment. Words by P. Tchaikovsky. The music is founded on Mozart's Pianoforte Fantasia No. 4.

In 1892 Vladimir Napravnik, who was staying with Tchaikovsky at Maidanovo, played to him very frequently. This pleased his host, and on one occasion Napravnik's clever rendering of Mozart's fantasia roused him to so much enthusiasm that he resolved to make a quartet from the middle movement. He carried out this intention in May, 1893. Jurgenson.

5. Op. 74. Symphony No. 6, in four movements, for full orchestra. Dedicated to V. Davidov. Performed for the first time in Petersburg, October, 16th (28th), 1893. Conducted by the composer. Jurgenson.

6. Op. 75. Concerto No. 3, for pianoforte and orchestra. Dedicated to Louis Diemer. This Concerto was taken from a Symphony which Tcháikovsky began in May, 1892, and all but completed. He afterwards destroyed the Symphony. The Concerto was first played in Petersburg by Taneiev. Published by Jurgenson.

Besides the above, the following works were found at Klin after Tchaikovsky's death :—

1. *Momento lirico.* A piece, nearly completed, for the pianoforte. Taneiev only pieced together the separate sketches. Published by Jurgenson.

2. Duet, " Romeo and Juliet." In this work Taneiev had more to amplify, as he had to supply the entire accompaniments of the solo parts. He borrowed these from Tchaikovsky's orchestral fantasia on the same subject.

3. Andante and Finale, for pianoforte and orchestra. Both movements were arranged by Tchaikovsky himself from sketches for the Symphony planned in 1892. The orchestration is by Taneiev, who was the first to play the work in public at Belaiev's first Russian Symphony Concert, February 8th (20th), 1896. Thus Taneiev accomplished his rôle as the original interpreter of all Tchaikovsky's pianoforte works (excepting the Concerto in B flat minor, which was played for the first time by Kross). Published by Belaiev.

APPENDIX B

THE PLOTS OF TCHAIKOVSKY'S CHIEF OPERAS

1. *The Oprichnik.* The Oprichniks were a band of dissolute young noblemen, the chosen body-guard of Ivan the Terrible, who swore by fearful and unnatural oaths to carry out every command of the despot they served. Sometimes they masqueraded as monks and celebrated "black mass." In reality they were robbers and murderers, hated and feared by the people whom they oppressed. Andrew Morozov, the descendant of a noble, but impoverished, house, and the only son of the widowed Lady Morozova, is in love with the beautiful Natalia, daughter of Prince Jemchoujny. His poverty disqualifies him as a suitor. Natalia's father promises her hand to the elderly boyard Mitkov. While desperately in need of money, Andrew falls in with Basmanov, a young Oprichnik, who persuades him to join their community, telling him that an Oprichnik can always fill his own pockets. Andrew consents, believing it to be his only chance of revenging himself upon Prince Jemchoujny. The Lady Morozova is a high-minded, religious woman. Andrew, anxious to relieve her poverty, takes her money which he has borrowed from Basmanov. His mother refuses to touch what she knows to be the fruit of robbery and murder, and implores her son not to associate with the hated Oprichniks. Andrew, who is devoted to his mother, promises to respect her wishes. Afterwards the desire for power and vengeance prevails, and he consents to take the oath of the Oprichnik band. The first sacrifice demanded of him is the complete renunciation of his mother and Natalia. Lady Morozova is now heart-broken, deserted by her son and hated by the populace, who insult her in the public square as the "mother of an Oprichnik." She is about to take refuge in the

church, when Natalia flies to her for protection. She has escaped from her father and her middle-aged suitor Mitkov. Prince Jemchoujny appears on the scene and .orders his rebellious daughter to return to her home. His chidings are interrupted by the arrival of the Oprichniks, awakening terror and hatred among the people. Andrew catches sight of his mother, whom he has not seen for many days, and rushes to embrace her, when the sinister theme of the Oprichniks is heard in the orchestra, reminding him of his vows. Lady Morozova turns from her son, disowns him, and solemnly curses him as an Oprichnik. In the last act Andrew, unable to abandon Natalia to her fate, resolves to marry her in spite of his vows. But Prince Viazminsky, the leader of the Oprichniks, cherishes an old grudge against the family of Morozov, and works for Andrew's downfall. He breaks in upon the wedding-feast with a message from the Tsar. Ivan the Terrible has heard of the bride's beauty, and desires her attendance at the royal apartments. Andrew, with gloomy forebodings in his heart, prepares to escort his bride, when Viazminsky, with a meaning smile, explains that the invitation is for the bride *alone*. Andrew refuses to let his wife go into the royal presence without his protection. Viazminsky proclaims him a traitor to his vows. Natalia is carried off by force, and the Oprichniks lead Andrew into the market-place to suffer the death penalty at their hands. Meanwhile Lady Morozova, who has relented, comes to bless her son on his wedding-day. She enters the deserted hall, where Viazminsky, alone, is gloating over the success of his intrigue. She inquires unsuspectingly for Andrew, and he leads her to the window. Horror-stricken, she witnesses the execution of her son, and falls dead at the feet of her triumphant enemy.

2. *Vakoula the Smith*, afterwards known as *Cherevichek* ("The Little Shoes"), and finally republished as *Les Caprices d'Oxane*. Christmas Eve. A moonlight night, in the village of Dikanka. Solokha, the witch, comes out of one of the huts, and is joined by the devil. They decide to fly off together. The witch goes to fetch a broomstick, and the devil in his monologue sings of his hatred of Vakoula the Smith, because the latter has drawn a caricature of him upon the church wall. He invokes a snowstorm. Solokha reappears, and they elope together, stealing the moon and

stars as they go, and leaving the village plunged in darkness. Vakoula is making love to the beautiful daughter of Choub the Cossack. To-night Choub is going to supper with the sacristan, and Vakoula will take the opportunity of visiting his sweetheart, who, however, remains deaf to all his entreaties. Meanwhile Choub loses his way in the darkness, and after wandering round in a circle finds himself at his own hut. Vakoula mistakes him for a rival lover, and drives him away from his own threshold.

The second act shows the interior of the witch's hut, where Solokha is making herself smart after her ride through space on a broomstick. The devil comes out of the stove and makes love to her. They dance the *Gopak*, while little imps emerge from every nook and cranny in the form of crickets and beetles. A knock is heard, and the devil hides himself in an empty sack. Enter the Headman of the village. Another knock, and the Headman, who does not want to be caught with Solokha, disposes of himself in another sack. This time the sacristan comes in, and the same ruse is enacted; and, finally, Choub appears on the scene and, at a fourth knock, he too takes refuge in a sack. The last comer is the witch's son Vakoula. He is so wrapped up in his love troubles, that he picks up the sacks in an absent-minded way and carries them off to the smithy. In the scene that follows the villagers are singing Christmas carols in the village street. The moon has returned to its place. Oxana, who is among the singers, catches sight of Vakoula and cannot refrain from teazing him a little more. She tells him she will marry him if he will bring her the Tsaritsa's own shoes. Vakoula goes off in a temper, taking the sack containing the devil and leaving the others in the road. The children peep inside and discover the Headman, the sacristan, and Choub.

In the third act Vakoula goes to drown himself in the forest pool. He puts the sack containing the devil at the edge of the water. The evil spirit offers to give Oxana to the smith in exchange for his soul. Vakoula consents, and will sign the contract in his blood. The devil lets him go for a moment, and Vakoula overpowers him in turn. He makes the devil promise to take him to the Tsaritsa, and they take flight for St. Petersburg. A room in the Palace: the herald announces a victory of the Russian army. The Zaparogue Cossacks are summoned before the Tsar. The Cossacks dance a *Gopak*. Vakoula takes the opportunity of begging for the Tsaritsa's shoes, which are granted to him. The devil takes him back to his native village. Christmas morning: Vakoula finds Oxana bewailing his supposed loss. He consoles her with the shoes, and she consents to become his wife.

3. *Eugene Oniegin.* Madame Lerin and the old nurse are making preserves in the garden of a Russian country house. From indoors a duet is heard. Tatiana and her sister Olga are singing to the accompaniment of a harp. The peasants appear on the scene, carrying the last sheaf from the harvest fields. National songs and dances. The announcement of guests creates a considerable commotion in the quiet country household. They prove to be Lensky, a young neighbour, fresh from a German university, and Oniegin, a dandy from the capital, on a visit to his friend. Madame Lerin and the nurse retire to prepare supper. The young people saunter in the garden, Lensky with Olga, Tatiana with Oniegin. Tatiana is shy at first, then falls in love with the stranger. In the second scene Tatiana is sitting in her room by moonlight. The old nurse comes to scold her for not being asleep. There follows a long, confidential talk between them (recitative with soft accompaniment based on Tatiana's theme). When her nurse has gone, Tatiana sits dreaming of her love for Oniegin. How will he guess her secret, unless she reveals it herself? In her innocence of the world she resolves to write him a love letter. She begs the nurse to convey it to Oniegin. The old woman hesitates, but cannot refuse anything to the child of her heart. Reluctantly she departs on her errand. The third scene takes us back to the garden. Oniegin meets Tatiana. He cannot appreciate the directness and sweetness of the girl's nature. Jaded and world-worn, Tatiana seems to him insipid and provincial, while at the same time he finds her forward. He thanks her coldly for her letter, assures her he is not a marrying man, and gives her some cynical advice as to the wisdom of acting with more maidenly reserve in future. Then he leaves her, crushed with shame and disappointment.

3 C

The second act opens upon a ballroom scene. It is Tatiana's birthday. Oniegin, whom Lensky has dragged to the dance against his will, amuses himself by flirting with Olga. The complimentary couplets sung to Tatiana by the elderly Frenchman Triquet are a favourite number in this scene. As the ball progresses Lensky, mad with jealousy, loses his self-control and insults Oniegin. The latter now feels some qualms of conscience, but the hot-headed youth forces a challenge upon him, and he consents to fight. The party breaks up in consternation. The second scene is devoted to the duel in which Oniegin kills Vladimir Lensky.

Some years are supposed to elapse between the second and third acts. A reception at a fashionable house in Petersburg. Oniegin is seen standing apart from the guests, in gloomy reflection. He has returned home after a self-imposed exile. Remorse for Lensky's death haunts him, and he can find no satisfaction in love or folly. All the guests are impatient for the arrival of the acknowledged belle of society, Princess Gremin. When she comes on the scene, Oniegin recognises Tatiana, transformed into a stately, gracious woman of the world. Her husband is elderly, but distinguished, handsome, and devoted to his beautiful young wife. Oniegin's chilly egotism is thawed, and he falls passionately in love with the woman he once despised. The last scene takes place in the boudoir of the Princess Gremin. She is reading a letter from Oniegin, in which he declares his love. This communication throws her into a state of agitation, and, before she can recover herself, Oniegin breaks in upon her in person. In a long, impassioned duet he implores her to have pity and to fly with him. With some of the rake's vanity still left in his nature, he cannot at first realise that she can resist him. Tatiana respects and honours her husband. At first she tries to punish Oniegin for the past. Then she struggles between duty and reawakened love. Finally, with a supreme effort, she breaks away from him at the very moment when she has confessed her true feelings. When the curtain falls, Oniegin, baffled and despairing, is left alone on the stage.

4. *The Maid of Orleans.* A village festival at Domrémy. Thibaut, Joan's father, and Raimond, her lover, appear upon the scene.

Thibaut says it is no time for dancing and singing; a maid needs a man to protect her, and therefore he wishes Joan to marry Raimond. She is silent, but finally confesses that she has chosen another destiny. Her father is angry and reproachful. A fire is seen on the horizon, and the tocsin is heard. Old Bertrand comes in. He speaks of the desperate state of the country and the approach of the English army. Suddenly Joan rises up and speaks with prophetic inspiration. She feels the hour for action has come, and bids farewell to her birthplace. The angels appear to Joan and incite her to heroic deeds.

Third act. A field near Rheims. The meeting of Joan and Lionel. They fight. Joan overcomes him, and stands above him with her drawn sword. At this moment she catches sight of his face, and falls in love with him. He returns her passion. Dunois comes upon the scene, and Lionel tells him that he wishes to join the French army. Dunois is delighted that such a great leader should come over to France. He leads him away in the King's name. Joan collapses, and discovers she is wounded. Second scene. The coronation of Charles VII. The King announces to the people that Joan has saved the country. Her father declares that she has been supported by the powers of hell, rather than the angels of heaven. No one believes him. Lionel and Dunois are ready to do combat on her behalf. The Archbishop of Rheims asks her if she is "pure." She believes herself a sinner in intention, and will not reply. All leave her. Lionel comes to console her in her abandonment. She turns from him in indignation, as from "her worst enemy."

Fourth act. The forest. Lionel pursues Joan. At first she flees from him, then suddenly yields to their mutual passion. They hear the English trumpets in the distance. Joan refuses to escape. She is taken prisoner, and Lionel is slain. Second scene. Rouen. Joan is led to the stake. For a moment she loses courage, but is sustained by a chorus of angels. She is bound to the stake. A priest offers her a wooden crucifix. The faggots are lighted.

5. *Mazeppa.*—First act. First scene. Kochoubey's garden, where his daughter Maria, after parting with her girl friends, sings of her love for her father's guest, Mazeppa. Enter Andrew,

a young Cossack, who has loved Maria from childhood. He knows her secret passion for Mazeppa. Kochoubey and his wife come into the garden with their guests, including Mazeppa and Iskra. The former asks Kochoubey's consent to his marriage with Maria. Songs and dances take place during the discussion. Mazeppa insinuates that Maria cannot marry any one but himself, and her father indignantly orders him to leave the house. He does so, but first wrings from Maria the confession that she cares for him more than for her parents. Second scene. Kochoubey's house. Maria has fled with Mazeppa. His wife bemoans the loss of her child, and instigates her husband to vengeance. He promises to denounce Mazeppa to the Tsar. Andrew undertakes to lay his complaint at the foot of the throne.

Second act. A dungeon in the castle of Bielotserkovsky. Kochoubey is imprisoned there, because Mazeppa has treacherously impeached him at Court before he had time to lay his own grievances before the Tsar. This scene contains a dramatic moment, in which Kochoubey is confronted with Mazeppa's tool —Orlik. In the second scene Mazeppa gives orders to Orlik for the execution of Kochoubey on the following day. Then Maria appears. Love scene with Mazeppa. She does not know the full extent of his cruelty and treachery, and still cares for him, in spite of her vague forebodings. Her mother appears on the scene, and reveals the terrible destiny which awaits Maria's father. Mother and daughter hurry away to try if they can save Kochoubey. Third scene. The place of execution. The populace are waiting to see the death of Kochoubey and Iskra. Dance of a drunken Cossack. Procession to the scaffold. Maria and her mother arrive at the moment when the axe falls, and the former loses consciousness when she realises that it is too late to effect a rescue.

Third act. Symphonic sketch, "The Battle of Poltava." The deserted garden and homestead of the Kochoubeys. Andrew appears. All day in the battle he has striven to meet Mazeppa, and slay him in single combat, but in vain. Now he has come to take a last leave of the spot where he and Maria spent their happy childhood. Enter Mazeppa and Orlik. Andrew reproaches the former for all the misery he has brought upon Maria, and challenges him to fight. Andrew is mortally wounded. Then Maria wanders in. Her misfortunes have upset her reason. Mazeppa tells her to follow him, but she refuses, and he abandons her to her fate. She sees Andrew, but does not fully recognise him. She takes the dying Cossack in her arms, and sings him to his last sleep with a childish lullaby. The peasantry, attracted by the noise of the fight between Mazeppa and Andrew, now arrive upon the scene. Maria starts up suddenly, and, with a mad laugh, throws herself into the stream.

6. *The Enchantress* ("Charodeika"). First act. The banks of the Oka, near Nijny-Novgorod. National customs. Kouma Nastasia appears outside her inn and welcomes her customers. A boat comes down the river. The Prince—son of the Governor of Nijny—is returning from the chase. He drifts by, and Kouma remains pensive at the river's edge. She is in love with the Prince. The Governor and his Counsellor, Prince Mamirov, suddenly appear on the scene. The latter, who is the representative of respectability and decency, detests Kouma. He has compelled the Governor to come and see for himself what a gang of disorderly characters meet in Nastasia's inn. The people are very agitated at this arrival, and wish to remain near Kouma in order to protect her from violence. But she begs them to retire. Then she puts on her best attire and goes out to meet the unexpected guests. The Prince immediately falls a victim to her charms. He accepts a cup of wine from the beautiful innkeeper, and gives her his ring in return. Kouma, not contented with her victory over the two men, is seized with a desire to humiliate Mamirov, and asks him to join in the mummers' dance. He refuses, but the Governor— now completely under the spell of Kouma Nastasia's beauty— orders him to do so. Mamirov dances amid the laughter of the spectators.

Second act. The garden of the Governor's house. His wife is discovered, deep in thought. Her maid Nenila is near at hand. The Governor's wife is jealous, because her husband now spends all his days with Kouma. She vows to revenge herself. Mamirov fans her smouldering wrath. Enter the Prince, who perceives that his mother is in trouble and tries to console her. They enter the house together. The Wanderer comes upon the scene, and Mamirov orders him to report upon everything that takes place in Kouma's inn. Then the Governor himself arrives. He is full of his passion for Kouma Nastasia. There follows a stormy scene between husband and wife. The Governor returns to Kouma. The Wanderer reveals to the Prince the real reason of the quarrel between the Governor and his wife, the son swears to avenge his mother's wrongs and to kill Kouma, whom he has never seen.

Third act. Kouma's house. Evening. The Governor tells Kouma he loves her, but she does not respond. He threatens her, but she declares she would sooner lose her life than yield to him. He goes away in anger. Kouma's uncle warns her that the young Prince has sworn to avenge his mother, and is coming to kill her that very night. She sends all her friends away and remains alone. She would rather die by the Prince's hand than accept the Governor as her lover. She puts out the light, lies down on her bed, and awaits the end. The Prince comes, creeps to the bedside, draws the curtain aside, and drops his dagger, spell-bound by the beauty of the woman. A lengthy duet. The Prince becomes wholly entranced by Kouma's charms.

Fourth act. A dark forest on the banks of the Oka. The cave of Koudma the Wizard. The Prince comes on the scene, attired as for hunting. He inquires of Koudma whether all is now ready for his flight with Kouma. He departs with his huntsmen. Enter the Wanderer, bringing the Governor's wife, disguised as a beggar-woman. She has come to ask the wizard for some fatal spell to destroy Kouma. The Wanderer flees in terror, and the Governor's wife enters the cave alone. A boat arrives containing Kouma and her friends. They land, leaving her alone to wait for the Prince. The revengeful wife approaches Kouma and offers her a refreshing drink, into which she drops the fatal poison. Kouma drinks. The Prince returns and rushes to embrace her. All is ready for their flight, but the poison has already done its work—Kouma dies in her lover's arms. The Governor's wife confesses her guilt, and the Prince in despair repulses her. Enter the Governor in search of the fugitives. He cannot see Kouma, and believes she is being hidden from him.

Maddened with jealousy, he hurls himself upon his son and kills him. His wife curses him as a murderer. The body of the Prince is borne away and the Governor remains alone. A terrible storms breaks over his head. Overcome with remorse and terror, he falls down in a mortal swoon.

7. *Pique Dame.* First act. First scene. The Summer Garden in Petersburg. Spring. Chorus of nurses and governesses. Some of the "golden youth" of the capital appear on the scene. They speak of Hermann's extraordinary passion for gambling. Enter Hermann and Tomsky. The former talks of his love for a distinguished girl with whose name he is not acquainted, although he often meets her in the street, accompanied by an old lady of forbidding appearance. Enter Prince Yeletsky, who announces his engagement to the very girl in whom Hermann is interested. Hermann is depressed because his poverty is a hindrance to his suit. While the sight of Liza always awakens his best feelings, that of her grandmother fills him with a vague horror. Tomsky tells him a tale to the effect that the old Countess possesses the secret combination of three cards, which accounts for her extraordinary luck at the gaming tables. Hermann, in his morbid mental condition, believes himself destined to acquire this secret at any price. A terrible thunderstorm still further upsets his mind, and he begins to realise with horror that he is capable of committing a murder. He resolves to put an end to himself, but not until he has declared his love to Liza.

Second scene. Liza and her young friends are amusing themselves with singing and dancing. The governess appears on the scene, and the merry party is broken up. Liza is left alone. She is not in love with her fiancé, for her imagination is entirely occupied with the mysterious young man whom she so often meets out of doors. Suddenly Hermann appears before her. He threatens to kill himself on the spot if she will not listen to him. Just as she has gathered courage to drive him away, the old Countess comes in, alarmed by the commotion in her granddaughter's apartment. Liza conceals Hermann. The sight of the old Countess brings back his *idée fixe* of the three cards. When Liza has succeeded in calming her grandmother, and has induced her to return to her room, she goes back to Hermann with the intention of dismissing him; but in the end his passion prevails over her scruples.

Second act. Third scene. A fancy-dress ball. Prince Yeletsky pays his addresses to Liza, who does not respond. Hermann is among the guests. At the sight of the Countess the insane longing to possess the secret of her luck comes over him again. In a *tête-à-tête* with Liza he implores her to let him visit her that night. She tells him how he may gain access to her room unperceived.

Fourth scene. The Countess's bedroom. Hermann appears through the secret door. He hears steps, and hides himself again. The old Countess returns from the ball. She goes into her boudoir, and presently reappears in her night attire. She is tired and cross, and complains that in her youth parties were more amusing than they are now. She dismisses her maid, and falls asleep humming to herself an air from an old-fashioned opera. Hermann awakes her. She is so terrified that she dies suddenly, without having revealed her secret. Liza appears, and can no longer conceal from herself that Hermann only made love to her in order to carry out his mad scheme.

Third act. Fifth scene. Evening. The barracks. Hermann alone in his quarters is haunted by remorse. In his terror he rushes from the room, but is met on the threshold by the apparition of the Countess showing him the three cards. Sixth scene. Liza is waiting for Hermann near the Winter Canal. Midnight strikes, and Liza in despair is about to do away with herself when he appears on the scene. At the sight of her his madness subsides, and he thinks only of his love for her. But he soon begins to rave about the three cards, and no longer recognises Liza. In despair she throws herself into the Neva. Seventh scene. Hermann at the gambling tables. He wins on the first two cards shown him by the ghost of the Countess. When it comes to the third card no one will venture to stake against him except Prince Yeletsky. Instead of the expected ace, Hermann turns up the queen of spades, and loses all his winnings. The apparition of the Countess appears to him once more, and he stabs himself in a fit of madness.

8. *Iolanthe.* The blind daughter of King René of Provence

lives among the Vosges Mountains under the care of her nurse Martha and her husband Bertrand. In order that she may not realise her blindness, the King has forbidden the word "light" to be used in her presence. The girl is sad without knowing why. Her friends bring her flowers and try to amuse her, but in vain. She falls asleep in the garden, and is carried into the castle by her nurse. The King arrives, accompanied by the famous Moorish physician, Ebn-Khakya. The latter says he must see Iolanthe, even in her sleep, before he can pronounce an opinion as to her sight. After a time he informs the King that she can only be cured by a great desire to see; therefore she must be made conscious of her condition. The King refuses to follow this advice. Robert, Duke of Burgundy, and the Knight, de Vaudemont, come by accident to the castle. The former has been betrothed from childhood to Iolanthe, and is now on his way to King René's court in order to woo his future bride. He has never seen her, and is in no hurry to wed. They see the notice which warns them that it is death to enter the castle grounds. But Vaudemont catches a glimpse of the maiden asleep on the terrace, and is spell-bound. Robert tries to make him leave these haunts of witchcraft, but he refuses, and the Duke goes to summon his men in order that he may carry off his friend by force. A duet between Vaudemont and Iolanthe. He does not realise her blindness until she asks him, "What is light?" He breaks through the atmosphere of secrecy in which she lives. She knows she is blind and longs for light. King René is horror-stricken, but Ebn-Khakya reminds him that now her sight may be restored. To stimulate her desire, René declares Vaudemont must be put to death unless her blindness is cured. Iolanthe is prepared to undergo any pain to save Vaudemont, whom she loves. The physician leads her away. Robert of Burgundy returns with his men. He recognises King René, and begs to be freed from his obligation to marry his daughter. The King consents, and promises Iolanthe's hand to Vaudemont. Her girl friends arrive on the scene and announce that the cure is successful. Iolanthe appears with bandaged eyes. Ebn-Khakya takes off the handkerchief, and her sight is restored. The opera concludes with a hymn of thanksgiving.

APPENDIX C

EXTRACTS FROM GERMAN PRESS NOTICES DURING TCHAIKOVSKY'S TOURS ABROAD IN 1888 AND 1889

LEIPZIG "SIGNALE"

"*January*, 1888.

"So far we have only become acquainted with three or four works by Peter Tchaikovsky, a follower of the Neo, or young, Russian school of 'storm and stress' composers, and these works, to speak frankly, have not won our sympathies; not because the composer is lacking in talent and skill, but because the manner in which he employs his gifts is repellent to us. Equally frankly we are ready to confess that we went to hear the Suite (op. 43) included in this programme, somewhat in fear and trembling, being prepared for all kinds of monstrosities, distortions, and repulsiveness. But it turned out otherwise. . . . The Fugue and Introduction at the beginning of the Suite bore honourable witness to the composer's contrapuntal science; of the other movements—the Divertimento, Intermezzo, Marche miniature, and Gavotte—the march seems least worthy of praise, for it merely recalls the tea-caddy-decoration style of art applied to music, and rather spoils than enhances the work.

"The composer, who conducted his Suite, must have been equally pleased with the way in which it was played and the reception accorded by the public. For the Gewandhaus audience, in recalling him *twice*, paid Herr Tchaikovsky a compliment rarely bestowed on any but a few of the most prominent composers of the day. He will carry away the impression that there is no question of Russophobia among *musical* people in Leipzig.

"E. BERNSDORF."

"MUSIKALISCHES WOCHENBLATT," NO. 3, JAHRGANG XIX

"*January* 12*th*, 1888.

" *Leipzig.* The first week of the New Year was really rich in interesting musical events. At the twelfth Subscription Concert Herr Tchaikovsky conducted his orchestral Suite (op. 43). . . . Undoubtedly the choice of this work was not calculated to display the composer to the Gewandhaus audience in his full creative strength. The Suite opens with a very promising Fugue, cleverly and effectively worked out, and continues very passably well with a Divertimento and an Intermezzo, two movements which are not profound, but possess much charm of sonority. The last two movements—Marche miniature and Gavotte—deteriorate so distinctly into a mere pattern of sounds, that it is impossible to derive from them any real artistic enjoyment. The sister work, of which Siloti gave several movements last season, is far stronger and more original. Still less can op. 43 be compared with the two chamber works played at the concert of the Liszt-Verein : the deeply reflective Trio dedicated to the memory of Nicholas Rubinstein, and the Quartet, delightful in every movement, but wonderful as regards the Andante. . . . The Liszt-Verein presented Herr Tchaikovsky with a splendid laurel-wreath."

" NEUE ZEITSCRIFT FUR MUSIK," NO. 2

" LEIPZIG, *January* 11*th*, 1888.

" Besides the exhaustively developed Fugue, which displays great contrapuntal skill and sureness, all the rest is of second-rate musical interest. We feel this the more strongly because the composer has been impolitic enough to pad out his fleeting ideas into pretentious movements of a quarter of an hour's duration. What is the use of a monotonous *fugato* which comes into the Introduction *before* the Fugue itself ? In the remaining movements we are conscious that the music has a ' society tone,' which finds expression in a pleasant conversational style : it has an aroma of Bizet, Délibes, and Co., and is sometimes reminiscent of the heroes of French Grand Opera and sometimes of Wagner. Naturally such methods only produce a frivolous eclecticism that can lead to no lasting results. Besides its aimless length—forty-five minutes—this Suite impresses us most by its evidences of submission to the shallow tastes of the hour. Here Tchaikovsky is posing too much in the part of Proteus; consequently he is not all that he *can be*.

"A far happier and more sympathetic view of Tchaikovsky is presented by his great Trio in A minor (op. 50)—also of extra-ordinary length—and the String Quartet (op. 11). . . . These works are of far superior quality and finer material; they have intellect, temperament, and imagination; here the composer never descends to the commonplace. The Trio—especially the *Pezzo elegiaco*—bears the imprint of a profound seriousness, impregnated with sorrow and lamentation. The Quartet, which was composed much earlier, shows chiefly a pleasing *naïveté*. The Andante is our favourite movement; we might compare it to a slumbering lily of the valley.   "BERNHARD VOGEL."

"LEIPZIGER TAGEBLATT"

"LEIPZIG, *January 6th*, 1888.

"We give decided preference to the first movement of the Suite (op. 43), especially as regards the Fugue, the subject of which, being full of energy and easily grasped, offers material for sustained and interesting development, in which, one after another, all the instruments take part, until the movement is steadily worked up to a brilliant and effective close. The Intro-duction pleased us less, partly on account of its being spun out, but also because its contents are only of mediocre quality. The Divertimento treats a folk melody, which is interesting in itself, and is also very effective, thanks to variety of instrumentation. The same may be said of the Intermezzo, in which the 'cellos have a pleasing, but in no way remarkable, melody. This move-ment suffers equally from its prolixity. The little March, given to the wood wind and violins, is in the national style, and owes its effect chiefly to the orchestration. Here the flageolet tones of the violins produce a most original effect. The Gavotte, which forms the last movement, cannot lay claim to great appre-ciation; its effect is rather superficial. The hearty applause after each movement was intended rather for the composer than for his work."

"HAMBURG CORRESPONDENT"
"SIXTH PHILHARMONIC CONCERT

"HAMBURG, *January 20th*, 1888.

"We cannot deny to Tchaikovsky originality, temperament, or a bold flight of fancy, although when he is possessed by the spirit of his race he overthrows every limitation. All logic is then thrown to the winds, and there begins a Witches' Sabbath of sound which offends our sight and hearing, especially the latter. Flashes of genius mingle with musical banalities; delicate and intellectual touches with effects which are often ugly. There is something uncompromising, restless, and jerky about his work. In spite of all his originality, and the unrestrained passion of his emotions, Tchaikovsky is too eclectic in his tendencies ever to attain to independence in the highest meaning of the word. An artist's originality does not lie in the fact that he brings us what is strange and unusual. What deludes the senses is far from sufficient to satisfy the intellect. Tchaikovsky is a gifted, highly cultured, interesting artist. An artist who knows how to excite us by his ideas, but whom we should not venture to describe as a creative force in the highest sense. His music is too deeply rooted in a one-sided national tendency; but when he passes these limits the eclectic becomes prominent, who uses all the influences he has assimilated, although in his own original way. It is not what Tchaikovsky says that is new, but his manner of saying it. He likes to take wild and sudden leaps, allows himself to be carried away by the mood of the moment, and spins these moods out as much as possible, padding them largely with pathos and concealing the lack of really great thoughts by means of dazzling colour, unusual harmonic combinations, and lively, exotic rhythms.   "SITTARD."

"FREMDENBLATT"

"SIXTH PHILHARMONIC CONCERT

"HAMBURG, *January* 20*th*, 1888.

"The Serenade was given to the public about 1883. The first and third movements are the most important, yet, even at its weightiest, it is not worthy to be placed beside the works of our latest German composers. This movement shows some similarity in form to the old French overture, as appears from its division into three parts and the Introduction in slow time. The second movement, a Valse Tempo in the dominant, is as out of keeping with the leading emotion of the opening movement as is the Finale—which is not always very lofty in conception. Undoubtedly the highest recognition would be accorded to the Elégie (third movement) if it, too, had more in common with the first movement. This sense of unity is lacking, in spite of the admirable development of the parts, while the key of D major, and the second sequence of dominants leading to C, is not calculated to give coherence to the whole. From the point of view of instrumentation the Serenade is admirably worked out, and the means selected are so well handled that it is worthy to rank with numerous other serenades for strings which have been turned out by skilled artists in recent years. If in the Serenade many fundamental principles of form have been violated, this method of procedure, which might be attributed to an effort after novelty, stands in no approximate relationship to the music of the Pianoforte Concerto (op. 23), a work which will hardly please German musicians in its entirety. This music bears so essentially the Russian stamp that we must be able to view it entirely from a national standpoint in order to find it interesting. The Concerto, in three extended movements, consists of an endless chain of phrases, and offers only a superficial development of the themes. Each phrase stands by itself, and has no connection with the next. It is not lacking in noisy passages, which cost the pianist enormous efforts, but none of these are the outcome of logical necessity. It is true that the work is not lacking in cleverness, but how regrettable that such an eminent talent should go so far astray ! . . . The Theme and Variations from the Third Suite for orchestra brought the Tchaikovsky performance to a close. Here the composer gives us something clever and skilful, at least as regards the first half of the work ; but our pleasure in these welcome, solid tone-structures only lasts until the violin solo in B minor. After this number the work runs a superficial course, culminating in a very commonplace *Tempo di Polacca.* If this is really Russian, and justified as such, Tchaikovsky's music may have its special qualities for Russian artists. German composers, however, are not likely to derive from it any satisfactory results which could forward the development of their art. . . . " EMIL KRAUSE."

" HAMBURGER NACHRICHTEN "

" *January 20th,* 1888.

" Yesterday Tchaikovsky's Serenade (op. 48), his Pianoforte Concerto op. 23, and Theme and Variations from op. 55 were given at the Philharmonic Concert. In all these works we observed the same half-popular (*volkstümlich*), half-trivial element as regards the melodic invention. We need not, however, lay stress upon this in referring to the individual movements, since the absence of what seems indispensable to a German audience is not a fault in the composer. The Concerto is least calculated to convince the hearer of Tchaikovsky's power of logical development and perfection of form. The first movement conceals its very primitive formal structure under an overpowering rush of harmonic effects, of dazzling kaleidoscopic passages, of intricate treatment of the subjects and of orchestral colour. . . . The Serenade is more lucid in design and far clearer in expression. Its sonority is full and satisfying, and it displays much variety of colouring. By the divisions of the violins, the skilful employment of violas and 'cellos, and the judicious combination and alternation of bowed and pizzicato passages, the composer succeeds in producing many picturesque effects. Interrupted cadences and frequent changes of rhythm break the flow of the work as a whole, but it leaves a general impression of freshness, animation, and attractiveness. The subjects of the fluently handled first Allegro have a piquant quality. The second movement is a slow Valse. Far more distinctive is the first subject of the third movement—with its old-world colouring—which resembles the introduction to the Finale, and is treated, moreover, in the genuine Russian folk-style, being heard first in C major and E flat major. In the Variations from the Third Suite the composer gives us a convincing proof of his musical science and fruitful imagination. The theme itself is only of mediocre quality, musically speaking, but, as the movement proceeds, it increases in importance, in depth, and complexity of the parts, until in the Finale it is worked up to a somewhat obtrusive apotheosis of elemental strength, the outcome of the mere rhythm. This was regarded as a signal for departure by a large section of the audience, who were too much concerned in safeguarding their own tympanums to feel compunction for the disturbance they caused to the more strong-minded, who sat it out to the end."

"VOSSICHE ZEITUNG," NO. 68

"BERLIN, *February 9th*, 1888.

"Not only among the new school of his compatriots, but among all contemporary composers Tchaikovsky is now reckoned as one of the most gifted. He possesses intellect, originality, and invention, and is master alike of the old and the more modern forms. Compared with his fellow-countryman Rubinstein, through whose nature runs a vein of greater amplitude and warmth—Tchaikovsky has more charm and judgment. Both have in common—what we find in every Russian composer with whom we are acquainted—a tendency to exaggeration of form and expression ; but here again, Tchaikovsky seems to possess the most artistic refinement. The songs which Frl. Friede sang yesterday, and the String Quartet, are remarkable for delicacy of invention and beauty of form. The overture to *Romeo and Juliet*, and the Pianoforte Concerto, played by Herr Siloti, are full of characteristic animation and originality of rhythm, harmony, and instrumentation. But here also the defects to which we have alluded are clearly perceptible. The overture becomes wearisome by the spinning out of the same idea; while, according to our conception of the play which inspired this work, the use of the big drum seems rather a coarse effect.

"In the first movement of the Concerto we cannot reconcile ourselves to the noisy, somewhat common-place, principal subject, nor to the frequent and violent interruptions of the musical flow of the work. On the other hand, the Andante, which is a delightful combination of poetry and humour, and the ebullient Finale, in the national style, offer only fresh and undisturbed enjoyment. A clever and animated Fugue from one of the Suites bore witness, by its admirable technical treatment, to the composer's mastery of polyphonic forms."

"BERLINER BÖRSEN-COURIER," NO. 5

"February 9th, 1888.

"The concert—long awaited with great excitement—at which Tchaikovsky, the leading representative of the modern Russian school, was to conduct a series of his own works, took place yesterday. . . . Among the orchestral works the Solemn Overture, *"1812,"* was given for the first time. The *Romeo and Juliet* overture is already known here; it is a symphonic poem which describes more or less the tragic fate of the two lovers. The Introduction shows deep emotion, while the Fugue displays great contrapuntal skill (of which the modern Russian composers give astonishing evidence) and force of ideas. The Andante from op. 11, a charming cabinet picture, most tenderly elaborated, appeals directly to the heart, and is beautiful in its sonority. . . . The overture *"1812"* is a characteristic tone-picture of strife and victory, more ideally than realistically depicted, especially the former. But by far the most weighty and lasting impression was made by the Pianoforte Concerto, which Alexander Siloti played with taste and brilliant virtuosity upon a fine full-toned Blüthner. It is one of Tchaikovsky's best works, fresh in invention, glowing with passion, beautiful as regards its themes and admirable in its development. . . ." "O. E."

"KÖLNISCHE ZEITUNG," NO. 45

"THE EIGHTH GÜRZENICH CONCERT.

"*February* 14*th*, 1889.

"Tchaikovsky's Third Suite made a striking impression upon all who heard it. Although the German public do not possess the key to many incidents in this work—because we know so little of Russia and its people, and what we know is not founded upon accurate observation—yet the music is so inspired, masterly and original, that it cannot fail to make a lasting impression upon any educated and progressive audience. . . .

"It is a question whether Tchaikovsky would not have done well to further elucidate the titles of the various movements—Elégie, Valse mélancolique, Scherzo, etc.—by the addition of a programme. But however desirable this may sometimes seem to listeners who are not Russians, it is doubtful whether the pleasant and stirring character of this work, which we may best define as a play of moods, would not have suffered in being tied down by any precise definition. . . .

"This music is of the kind which is pre-eminently calculated to stir our feelings by its richness of colour, its peculiarities of tonality—in one variation the Phrygian mode is successfully employed—and by its clever workmanship, which betokens an unusual skill in the working out of the parts. If an ingenious development of a theme, or an unusual effect of orchestration, occasionally predominates over the rest, on the whole it is the voice of the heart which is heard throughout the work, lending even an undertone to the glitter and hum of the Scherzo. The composer attains to this highest of all qualities by means of the wealth and charm of his melodic inspiration, the simplicity of his musical idiom, and the freshness of his invention. . . . Tchaikovsky not only possesses the gift of melodic invention, he pays due honour to Melody itself, and makes all the other elements of music hold their breath when Melody is speaking. . . . Simplicity is still the sign of profound truth, and of the promptings of inspiration. Tchaikovsky's creative power prevents this quality from degenerating into superficiality."

3 D

"GENERAL-ANZEIGER"

"FRANKFORT, *February* 16*th*, 1889.

"A novelty headed the programme: the Third Suite, op. 55, by Peter Tchaikovsky, who is generally spoken of as the head of the young Russian school of musicians. . . . As the last notes of the Suite died away, there followed a burst of applause so hearty and so continuous, that nothing equal to it has been accorded to any novelty during recent years, except perhaps when Richard Strauss conducted his First Symphony. . . . The impression made by Tchaikovsky's work was dazzling rather than profound; strictly speaking, it was not so much the Suite as a whole that won this recognition, as the bright, fresh, brilliantly orchestrated Polonaise with which it comes to an end. The second and third movements, Valse mélancolique and Scherzo, only evoked moderate applause: both numbers are in the minor, and seem to be stamped with a peculiar, national, Sarmatian character, they are so strange and gloomy. After the Valse mélancolique, which is quite in keeping with its title, a real Scherzo would have followed better; a Scherzo in the sense of the classical symphonists, rather than a number of this kind, which is rich in rhythmic devices, but poor in that true gaiety which we expect to find in a piece entitled Scherzo. In this number the combination of 6/8 and 2/4 has an unfortunate effect, for the wind instruments always seem to come in a little too late. The variations are most of them very interesting, and one or two appeal direct to the heart. The Fugue is strong, effective, and most skilfully worked out."

"DRESDNER NACHRICHTEN"

"*February* 22*nd*, 1889.

". . . The first number on the programme—Tchaikovsky's Fourth Symphony in F minor—acted like some magic spell upon the audience, somewhat disappointed at the non-appearance of the singer Frl. Leisinger. The Russian master—now undoubtedly the first composer of his nation—not only impressed us as a personality, but proved himself to be such in his Symphony, then given for the first time in Dresden. The work is planned upon large and bold lines and carried out in the same spirit. The ideas are clear-cut and concise; the melody and harmony distinctive and strikingly characteristic. Occasionally, as in the first and last movements, the composer

indulges in an orgy of sound, for which he evokes all the resources of the modern orchestra. At these moments he produces
with true orchestral virtuosity the most piquant and unusual
effects, while always remaining master of the situation; saying
precisely what he has to say, and avoiding all empty phrases and
rambling statements. What he expresses, however, is spirited,
and full of elemental strength and weight. With all this, Tchaikovsky knows how to strike a note of tenderness. The third
movement of his Symphony—the Scherzo 'pizzicato ostinato'—
is a masterly invention, which stands alone in musical literature.
The vein of national feeling which runs throughout the work
accords admirably with its style and beauty. Here and there
it echoes the melancholy and sadness of some solemn, wailing
folksong, but so inspired and perfect is the treatment that both
heart and intellect are completely satisfied.

"An equally fine impression was made by his Pianoforte Concerto (op. 23). This impression would have been still more
profound if the Symphony had not come first; it was a case in
which *le mieux est l'ennemi du bien*. The Concerto is symphonic
in structure, and the piano part is indissolubly welded with the
orchestration. Nor for a moment can we fail to recognise great
mastery of form, inspiration, and emotion; but these qualities do
not impress the hearer so strongly as in the Fourth Symphony. . . .

" DRESDNER-ANZEIGER "

"*February 22nd*, 1889.

"Tchaikovsky may congratulate himself upon the complete
success of his Fourth Symphony (F minor), which opened the
programme of the Fifth Philharmonic Concert. This Symphony
proved to be irreproachable as regards form: a virtue not to be
underrated in a modern production. This original work is not
lacking in vital and stirring material which corresponds to its
nobility of form, although it is so saturated with national colour
that it affects us strangely at first. These melodies, harmonies,
and rhythms, derived from the spirit of the Russian folksongs
and dances, unlike other attempts of the kind, possess sufficient
weight and character to be used as symphonic material. . . .
Equally good and artistic is his Pianoforte Concerto in B♭ minor,
which is more of the new German school. This Concerto is
a gigantic work of its kind, which demands for its execution the
most perfect technique and extraordinary physical strength. . . .

" FERDINAND GLEICH."

"VOSSICHE ZEITUNG"

"February 27th, 1889.

"The interest of yesterday's Popular Concert given by the Philharmonic Orchestra was enhanced by the presence of Herr Tchaikovsky, who conducted two of his own works: a Serenade for strings and the symphonic poem, *Francesca da Rimini.* The Serenade is a cheerful composition, fluent, pleasing, and not without a touch of humour. It is not remarkable for originality, so much as for a skilful and artistic treatment of the thematic material, particularly noticeable in the last movement of the work. The valse section, which is especially full of charm and graceful in the elaboration of the melodies, had to be repeated. We had already heard the symphonic poem at Bilse's concerts. This time the work did not impress us more favourably, Sometimes it repels by its violence; sometimes it wearies by the constant repetition of an insignificant subject. A few clever episodes and occasional moments in which it keeps within the limits of the beautiful make the general effect of this work not too intolerable. . . ."

"BERLINER TAGEBLATT"

"February 27, 1889.

". . . . Tchaikovsky's Serenade for strings consists of a series of charming little pieces, in the subjects of which we seem to recognise now and again a well-known face from some operetta. But these reminiscences are so delightfully decked out that we are very pleased to meet them again. . . . Musically speaking, the last movement is the most important. Here the composer has evolved a number of clever variations from a Russian theme. The symphonic poem, *Francesca da Rimini,* displays much interesting, but glaring, tone-colour. What Dante has described in ten lines is reproduced with effort in innumerable bars of music; we are endlessly wallowing in the harshest discords, until the attentive hearer undergoes a martyrdom scarcely less painful than the poor souls who are blown hither and thither in Dante's Whirlwind. Tchaikovsky is a gifted tone-poet, whom we have often recognised as such; but this symphonic poem exceeds all limits of what is acceptable. . . ."

ALPHABETICAL INDEX OF NAMES

ALPHABETICAL INDEX OF TCHAIKOVSKY'S WORKS

779